Dealing with
Depression Naturally

Dealing with Depression Naturally:

Complementary and Alternative Therapies for Restoring Emotional Health

Second Edition

Syd Baumel

KEATS PUBLISHING

LOS ANGELES

NTC/Contemporary Publishing Group

The purpose of this book is to educate. It is sold with the understanding that the publisher and author shall have neither liability nor responsibility for any injury caused or alleged to be caused directly or indirectly by the information contained in this book. While every effort has been made to ensure its accuracy, the book's contents should not be construed as medical advice. Each person's health needs are unique. To obtain recommendations appropriate to your particular situation, please consult a qualified health-care provider.

Library of Congress Cataloging-in-Publication Data

Baumel, Syd.
   Dealing with depression naturally : alternative and complementary therapies for Restoring emotional health / Syd Baumel.—2nd ed.
      p. cm.
      Includes bibliographical references and index.
      ISBN 0-658-00291-0
      1. Depression, Mental—Popular works. 2. Depression, Mental—Alternative treatment. 3. Depression, Mental—Treatment. I. Title.
   RC537 .B346 2000
   616.85'27—dc21

                                                                    00-029587

Design by Mary Ballachino/Merrimac Design

Published by Keats Publishing
A division of NTC/Contemporary Publishing Group, Inc.
4255 West Touhy Avenue, Lincolnwood, Illinois 60646-1975 U.S.A.

Printed in the United States of America

International Standard Book Number: 0-658-00291-0
   5 6 7 8 9 10 DOC/DOC 0 9 8 7 6 5 4

For Rhianna, my mother, and my father,
together again, happy and whole.

Contents

PART 3
Other Substances, Other Energies 171

PART 4
Saved by the Body:
From Bodywork to Working Out 221

PART 5
Saved by the Psyche:
Psychotherapies and Medicines of the Mind 253

PART 6
"Unnatural" Antidepressants:
Antidepressant Drugs and Electroconvulsive Therapy   323

Preface to the Second Edition

Depression is a natural human response—a retreat from the front when we despair of having things the way they "must" be. The circumstances that can bring us to this impasse are innumerable. But the array of treatments that can get us past it is almost as diverse.

I'm not just talking about antidepressant drugs, of which there currently are about two dozen. The purpose of this second expanded and revised edition of *Dealing with Depression Naturally* is to provide a reader-friendly treasury of the even larger variety of *natural treatments* available for depression. Whether these treatments are used as alternatives to drugs or as adjuncts, few depressives can afford not to know about them.

Drugs do bring marked relief to a majority of depressives. But they bring full recovery to far fewer—less than half, research suggests—and often at the expense of very unpleasant side effects, especially when high dosages or drug combinations must be used. Nor do these gains usually endure. Relapse or recurrence within months or years is common, even among people who faithfully stick to a full-dosage prescription.

It's also true that few, if any, natural antidepressants can boast of a decisively better record than drugs. But unlike drugs, most natural antidepressants can safely and synergistically be combined in large numbers, like loading up your plate at a fifty-foot buffet. And usually they can be added safely to drugs too. These natural antidepressant "entrees" and "side dishes" are almost always blessed more with "side benefits" than side effects. The more widely they become known, the more people can hope for a safe, pleasant, complete, and enduring recovery from depression.

As you might expect, I believe that natural antidepressants should be the bread and butter of antidepressant therapy, with drugs (salt) used only sparingly when needed. It's encouraging that since the eighties and early nineties when I worked on the first edition of this book, more and more depressives—and even doctors—have come around to this richer, more inclusive model of treating depression. Scientifically well-established natural antidepressants such as the amino acid 5-HTP and the biochemical SAMe, which for decades were ignored by all but a few mainstream academics and progressive practitioners, have finally been "discovered" by depressives and psychiatrists alike. Studies supporting natural antidepressants, which used to die slow, quiet deaths on the pages of medical journals, are now in some cases trumpeted by Ivy League investigators and the mainstream media with the same hoopla reserved for billion-dollar drug breakthroughs. Witness the excitement generated in 1999 by the successful Harvard Medical School trial of fish oil for patients with bipolar disorder (chap. 8).

The "paradigm shift" of the late eighties and nineties that has seen mainstream medicine cozy up to natural and alternative approaches to healing is finally infiltrating the field of psychiatry. Not only are the National Institutes of Health sponsoring expensive clinical trials of complementary and alternative medicine (CAM) treatments for illnesses like heart disease and cancer, they are spending top dollar on trials of St. John's wort and acupuncture for depression, among other CAM psychiatric treatments. I'm hopeful that soon, the public will finally get what it so sensibly wants: a health-care system that integrates the best of all medical worlds—pharmaceutical, surgical, nutritional, botanical, psychosocial, behavioral, non-Western traditional, and more.

In a way, this book is a blueprint of what that system has to offer right now for people who suffer from depression and other mood disorders. In my 1995 effort, I had already written about SAMe, 5-HTP, and fish oil, as well as many other worthy natural antidepressants that still remain obscure. My purpose this time is to continue to try to empower my fellow depressives and manic-depressives with more knowledge and options, to better ensure we all find the solutions we need.

Acknowledgments

My thanks to the people who have helped make this book—in both its editions—a reality.

For responding to my queries, granting me interviews, providing me with resource materials, reviewing my drafts, or assisting in other ways, thanks to Jambur Ananth, M.D., John Bain, Morris Baumel, Laure Branchey, M.D., MaryLynn Bryce, Coleen Dodt, Rhian Edwards, M.Sc., Todd Estroff, M.D., Alan Gelenberg, M.D., Abram Hoffer, M.D., Leo Hollister, M.D., David Horrobin, M.B., Daniel Kripke, M.D., Joseph F. Lipinski, M.D., S. C. Man, M.D., Rudy Nowak, Anna Olson, Butch Owen, Sherman Paskov, Donald Rudin, M.D., Ray Sahelian, M.D., Jonathan W. Stewart, M.D., John Varsamis, M.D., Lowana Veal, Bernard Weiss, M.D., Janna Weiss, Ph.D., José A. Yaryura-Tobias, M.D., Veronica Walsh, Richard Zloty, M.D, and my dear mother, Manya Baumel.

To all my friends, family, acquaintances, and readers who shared their experiences and opinions with me on the subject of depression, thank you for talking, writing, and listening.

For taking on this project ten years ago in its first incarnation, I am indebted to the late Nathan Keats, then president of Keats Publishing, and to the late Don Bensen, then senior editor, to Jean Barilla for her role in editing the first edition, and to those who helped the book reach its audience, in particular Peter Hirsch. To my former partner and eternal friend, Anna Olson, thanks once more for supporting me, especially during the last grueling months.

For his enthusiastic offer in 1999 that I write this second edition, I am deeply grateful to Keats Senior Editor Peter Hoffman. And to Claudia McCowan, who edited this edition, my deep appreciation for her kindness and patience while I struggled night and day through more than one deadline to do just that—and for her gentle way with the gorilla that finally arrived in her e-mail inbox.

May everyone who reads this book be rewarded for our efforts.

How to Use This Book

In the following pages we'll be discussing dozens and dozens of different antidepressant strategies. By the time you get to the end of this book, much of what seemed vivid and meaningful when you first read it will likely be hazy or forgotten, even if (as I hereby give you permission) you skip or skim much of your way through it.

So I encourage you to take notes, mark important passages, scribble marginal comments—do whatever you like to simplify your encounter with this information overload.

It doesn't have to be elaborate. Even a simple "thumbs up," "thumbs down," or "not sure" rating of each antidepressant strategy will make it easier for you to narrow your options later.

Better yet, you can rate each option—or at least the ones you think are worth rating—twice on a scale of –5 to +5: once for how likely you think it is that the approach could work for you; second for how inclined you would be to try it.

Pencils ready?

Then we're off.

Introduction
The Nature of Depression

The Common Cold of Mental Illness

"The common cold of mental illness" is how depression, the most prevalent of all mental disorders, is often described. At any time, some 15 to 20 percent of us at least have a subsyndromal touch of it—we feel a bit "scratchy in the psyche." More seriously, roughly 2 to 4 percent of us are fully in the grips of an episode of what psychiatrists call *major depressive disorder* or *major depression*. So depressed are we, it's as if we have been cruelly uprooted from the comfort of our everyday selves—and, with that, from our connectedness to the rest of humanity, which cannot fathom our unique pain and desolation. Suddenly, we have become ragged beggars at the banquet of life.

Another 2 to 4 percent of us are not so severely depressed. But our chronic, mild depression—our "dysthymia" or *dysthymic disorder*, as psychiatrists who follow the American Psychiatric Association's influential *Diagnostic and Statistical Manual* (DSM-IV) now call it—has hung like a pall over our lives for many, many months or years, eroding our confidence, smothering our initiative, diluting our joys and pleasures.

Still other people with depression are suffering from relatively brief and mild reactions to depressing circumstances (DSM-IV: *adjustment disorder with depressed mood* or *adjustment disorder with mixed anxiety and depressed mood*). Many more are weaving in and out of recurrent brief depressions, which may come and go with no apparent cause and last no longer than a week or two.

Still others are in the depressive phase of a bipolar or cyclothymic disorder. Approximately 1 percent of the population suffers from *bipolar disorder* (long known as manic depression), which is characterized by recurrent episodes of major depression and its polar opposite, mania—a state as hyperactive and often euphoric as it is reckless, impulsive, irritable, or grandiose.

Bipolar disorder is subdivided into *bipolar I* and *bipolar II disorder*. People with bipolar I disorder suffer from manic or *mixed* (manic and depressive) episodes and, usually, major depressive episodes too. People with bipolar II disorder also suffer major depressive episodes, but they have never been more than mildly manic (*hypomanic*). People with *cyclothymia* have moods that swing in the narrowest arc, from brief nonmajor depressions to spells of hypomania. They may be rapid swingers, but they're not *rapid cyclers* (are you getting a headache yet?). Rapid cyclers are people with bipolar disorder who suffer at least four full-blown episodes of depression and/or mania per year.

Some depressive or manic episodes have obvious physical or biological precipitants: for example, *premenstrual, postnatal,* or *postpartum,* and *menopausal* or *perimenopausal* ("before the menopause") depressions; and *seasonal affective disorders,* like winter depression and summer mania. (Here, as everywhere, the DSM names are forever in flux: in DSM-IV, premenstrual syndrome is redubbed *premenstrual dysphoric disorder.*) Similarly, when depression or mania is the direct result of a recognized physical cause like hypothyroidism or chemical intoxication, the DSM-IV diagnostic mouthful is *mood disorder due to a general medical condition* or *substance-induced mood disorder.* More commonly, however, physical conditions promote or aggravate depression or mania, rather than cause it.

In fact, depressives commonly suffer "comorbidly" from other physical or psychiatric conditions in a vicious cycle. A depressive can have a chronic, depressing medical condition like arthritis or multiple sclerosis, an anxiety disorder like social phobia or panic disorder, a substance abuse disorder like alcoholism, or (more rarely) a personality disorder like borderline personality disorder. Purebreed depression is an endangered species.

Given the scientific precision with which DSM disorders are defined, some people suffer from mood disorders that don't meet the criteria for any of the current crop. Their afflictions are diagnosed as *otherwise not specified* mood disorders.

Even young children get clinically depressed. Among adults, depression currently picks most on the young and middle-aged and the very old. A major study in 1989 by Gerald Klerman and Myrna Weissman found that the lifetime prevalence of depression for people born after 1945 was five to twenty times higher than for people born before 1934.

Women are about two to three times as depression-prone as men. If you're female, the odds are about 20 to 25 percent that you'll be laid low at least once by an episode of major depression. If you're a man, the odds are just 8 to 12 percent. Only bipolar disorder is an equal-opportunity mood disorder.

Being Depressed: Signs and Symptoms

Passive negativity—being stuck in a rut—is the hallmark of depression. If there were a motto for depression it might be: "My whole rotten life and I are just one big, hopeless problem—and there's nothing I can do about it."

Being in this fix smothers a depressed person's enthusiasms, suppresses his appetite for life, and reduces him to a dysfunctional shadow of his usual self. Suicidal thoughts or impulses may beckon with the promise of oblivion, or revenge against an uncaring world or God. In the most severe depressions, we can become so drained of all positive feelings—so deadened, so dehumanized—that we believe we've lost our soul itself. In *psychotic* depression (DSM-IV: *major depressive disorder, severe with psychotic features*), this negative worldview becomes delusional. A tycoon may believe he's bankrupt; a healthy young girl that she's literally dead and rotting inside; a "Dudley Do-right" that he's guilty of heinous sins and crimes or even that he's the devil himself.

Physically, the head-to-toe negativity of depression often manifests in chronic tiredness and fatigue, in an increased sensitivity to bodily aches and pains, and in a dulling of the mind's edges—some elderly depressives are misdiagnosed as having Alzheimer's disease. The severely or psychotically depressed person may think, say, and do everything in extreme slow motion—even to the point of catatonia (nervous paralysis). Paradoxically, some depressives are a ball of nervous, agitated energy.

Depression is commonly marked by "vegetative" disturbances: insomnia or hypersomnia (oversleeping), appetite loss or compulsive overeating (sometimes with major weight loss or gain), gastrointestinal dysfunctions (dry mouth, indigestion, constipation), and loss of sex drive.

The more scientists study depressed persons, the clearer it is that the subjective state of being depressed is intertwined with objective disturbances throughout the body, particularly the brain (no surprise there) and the endocrine and immune systems. When we're depressed, this research tells us, we're depressed through and through, from "soul to sole."

Often, depression falls into a recognizable pattern. Perhaps the most common one goes by many names: typical, classic, endogenous, or endogenomorphic. Sleeplessness in the middle of the night or early in the morning, loss of appetite and weight, and being fiendishly down on oneself are its key features. People with an especially severe form of typical major depression that psychiatrists call *melancholia* are locked behind a wall of gloom that virtually no smiling face or sunny circumstance can penetrate. And yet their black mood, which characteristically is worst in the morning, tends to pick up spontaneously at night. These surreally hellish depressions, like the one novelist William Styron endured in his autobiographical *Darkness Visible*, seem to strike the old much more than the young.

In contrast, "atypical" depression, which is more characteristic of dysthymic or bipolar depressions, is characterized by a tendency toward insomnia at bedtime, oversleeping, overeating, leaden paralysis, feeling worst in the evening, being more down on or hostile toward others than yourself, and having a mood that is easily swayed by people and circumstances.

The Natural History of Depression

Perhaps the best thing one can say about major depression is that it usually passes after several months to a year or two, even without treatment. But it sometimes takes a chronic course or leaves behind a dysthymic aftertaste; and those who experience a major depression once are quite likely to experience one again—sometimes, again and again and again.

Bipolar depressives are between poles most of the time, neither manic nor depressed, and may suffer only a few episodes in their lifetime. But rapid cyclers swing high or low several times a year, and cyclothymics can truly be on a roller coaster. As for dysthymic disorder, by definition it persists for years, sometimes for all or most of a person's life.

The good news is that all forms of depression are highly amenable to treatment and prevention, even with conventional care alone. A holistic approach, as advocated in this book, promises a much better prognosis still.

A Multitude of Causes

Until quite recently, the conventional wisdom was that depression is nothing but an exaggerated reaction to life's problems. Today, the pendulum has swung to an equally simpleminded extreme: Depression is nothing but a chemical imbalance—a disease of the brain, as diabetes is of the pancreas.

Neither of these stereotypes does depression justice. Depression is psychosocial and biophysical. It's a quintessentially *biopsychosocial* disorder of the whole person—mind, body, and spirit.

In an ambitious long-term study of thousands of male and female identical and nonidentical twins, Kenneth Kendler and his associates at the Medical College of Virginia have probed the relationship between genetic vulnerabilities, stressful life events, personality, behavior, and major depression. In a 1993 paper, they identified nine factors that accounted for 50 percent of a subgroup of female twins' vulnerability to depression. Stress and genes—the two poles of the pendulum—vied for first and second place.

The evidence is plain that depression—like heart disease and cancer—is born of multiple intimate and interactive causes: from chromosomes to broken homes, from hormonal discord to dark nights of the soul. As Kendler and his associates concluded in 1993, major depression "is a multifactorial disorder, and understanding its etiology will require the rigorous integration of genetic, temperamental, and environmental risk factors."

Research has established that loss, conflict, trauma, and other adverse life events most certainly put us at risk for depression—even for the mood swings of that most "chemical" of mood disorders, bipolar disorder. But the evidence from hundreds of studies of physical causes—medical illnesses, nutritional deficiencies, drugs and chemicals—is just as clear. Any physical insult that saps our energy, impairs our mental abilities, dulls our sensitivity to pleasure, or lowers our tolerance for pain can also lay us low. Furthermore, just as certain ingrained attitudes such as "learned helplessness," low self-esteem, and lack of spiritual or religious faith can set us up for depressive falls, so too can congenital biological defects that hamper our ability to weather the storms that others pass through unscathed. (See, for example, Anisman and Zacharko, 1992.)

In 1999, Kendler and his associate Carol Prescott reported that the identical twins in a sample of nearly four thousand pairs of male and female twins were roughly twice as likely as the nonidenticals to share a history of major depression. This suggested that 39 percent of the genesis of major depression is genetic.

Impressive, right? But so is the remaining 61 percent. Without it, people with the wrong genes would always be depressed. That 61 percent is a window of opportunity. It is more than half a glass full.

Treating Depression

Depression is very treatable—far more so than we think it is when we're under its spell.

There are two major approaches. One is to try to identify and treat specific causes. It isn't necessary to eliminate every one of them. Nature has wired us to rise like a cork above the stagnancy of depression. Disposing of even one significant cause—a bad job, a bad diet—can be enough weight off for us to rise again.

The other approach is to use antidepressant therapies, such as drugs, supplements, or psychotherapy. These address fundamental causes of depression, such as negative thoughts and neurochemical imbalances. Again, because we're homeostatically hardwired for self-healing, antidepressants can work even if we keep our dreary jobs or cleave to our junk-food diets.

Just don't count on it.

The best chance we have for a satisfactory, long-term solution to depression is to seize the best of both therapeutic worlds: Go after the causes and go toe to toe with depression itself.

A Model of Depression

Over the years, I've developed a model of how we become depressed and, by inference, how we recover. The model is essentially my own, but it draws on some of the insights of theorists like Albert Ellis and Martin Seligman.

As I see it, depression is a dysphoric (emotionally unpleasant) retreat from enthusiastic engagement in life that happens whenever three psychological conditions are met:

The first condition is *discontent,* the perception that something is wrong. We cannot become depressed unless there is something in our lives we wish were otherwise—a problem, as we see it. There are, I believe, three kinds of problems that can depress us.

The first are problems involving what we (or other people with whom we closely identify) have or don't have. These are problems of pain, loss, and lack. Here is where we throw up our hands and cry, "I can't bear this [pain, loneliness, unrequited love, abuse, injustice] any more!" This is the land of "when bad things happen to good people."

The second kind of problem involves not our experiences, but our deeds. Here is where feelings of guilt and perceptions of failure or sins of omission or commission come in. "I'm failing to live up to expectations" is the problem here.

Finally, we have problems of identity—not how we feel, not what we do or don't do, but who we are or think we are. This is where shame, low self-esteem, poor self-image, or feelings of inferiority come in: "I'm not good enough." "I'm not worthy."

I doubt there is a single being who is ever free of problems for more than a few minutes or hours. It's our nature to be discontent-meters, problem definers. But this is why merely having a problem, even a dire one, is not enough to make us depressed. For that we need to meet two other conditions.

The first condition is *loss of hope* that our problem can be solved. To become depressed, we have to feel a problem is a lost cause, that there's nothing we can do about it. We have to stop believing the person we love will love us back; to abandon hope that we will be able to do what we feel we must do (or stop doing what we must not); to give up on attaining that personal quality we so wish we possessed.

As tough as this predicament may be, it's still not enough to carry us into the land of depression—that altered state where we are more than just sad, unhappy, discouraged, or pained.

We have a safety valve. It's called *living with things we can't change* (or think we can't change). It's called *taking things philosophically*. It's called *having the serenity to accept the things we can't change*.

If we can accept that what we so want to be will not be, and move on, we won't become depressed. If not, we have fulfilled the third and final condition for depression, and we will be.

That condition is *irreconciliation*: the inability (at least for the time being) either to live with the problem and accept it (which redefines it as a fact of life and no longer a problem to solve), or to walk away from the problem, to cut our losses, detach, put it on the back burner—and get on with the rest of our lives. Irreconciliation means we reject all of life because the persistence of our problem and our abiding love of life are incompatible. "This town ain't big enough for the two of us. If the problem won't go, then I will."

So there is the portrait of a depressed person. She has at least one major self-identified problem. But she has become convinced that the problem is not going to go away no matter what she or anyone else does. Yet she can neither live with it nor forget about it. Instead, she is locked into the notion that the problem must be solved, or all of life is without meaning, value, or purpose.

Now that we have a model of how we get depressed, we have a map to help us get undepressed. The first landmark on the way is that each of the above three conditions is a necessary condition for depression, an ingredient in a recipe without which the cake can't be baked. Take away any one, and we will no longer be depressed. Every depression treatment addresses and, if successful, eliminates one or more of these "ingredients."

This may come as a surprise if you think I've just presented a purely psychological model of depression. On the surface, it is psychological, because I believe depression's center of gravity is the psyche. But psyche, body, and environment are all of a piece. We cannot have a depressed psyche in a nondepressed body—not for long—any more than an ice cube can stay frozen in a bucket of water. Sooner or later, the energy state of the one diffuses to the other. Sooner or later, the states of connected bodies or beings (and nothing is more intimately connected than psyche and soma, mind and body) become equalized. This is true whether it's a pain-wracked body draining the cheer from a serene mind or a troubled soul sapping the vitality from a fit body. It's also the case when a physically toxic or spiritually demoralizing environment rubs up against a vulnerable body or personality. We do have defenses, but they're not made of steel.

There is a positive side to this "Biopsychosocial First Law of Thermodynamics." Just as depressing influences tend to spread from one part of the mind-body-environment continuum to the others, so too do uplifting, antidepressive influences. If, as hundreds of studies indicate, physical inactivity makes for a bodily state that is conducive to mental depression, it's also true that a physically active body is an inhospitable medium for depression. For every vicious mind-body-environment cycle that can spiral us down into the blues, there is a corresponding benign cycle that can help us rise up.

What does this have to do with my model of depression? Those problems that depress us can originate anywhere in the mind-body-environment continuum. We could be failing at school or at work because our thyroid gland is failing to keep our brain perked up, or because we can't get enough sleep because we live near a busy airport, or because we're working or studying in a chemically sick building. We could be depressingly shy and lonely because we weren't loved enough in childhood, or because we're short of a brain chemical that facilitates social ease and comfort, or because we feel hopelessly inferior to a cultural ideal of attractiveness.

Our depressing problems might not even be problems, were it not for something else that's eating us: a chronic pain disorder that makes everything seem sour and wrong; a chip on the shoulder that makes us see hostile or mocking faces behind every bush.

Not just our problems themselves, but how we cope with them can be influenced by factors along the mind-body-environment continuum. Whether we take a problem in stride or are crushed by it can depend on something as elemental as elements in our diet. Not enough magnesium can make us too weak, listless, and achy to cope. A drug we're taking or a chemical we're sniffing in the workshop can make us shadows of our usual problem-solving selves. A heavy load of problems we're just barely handling can make one new problem the straw that breaks the camel's back. A seemingly minor problem that reminds us too much of a big one that shattered us in the past can overwhelm us with echoes of unresolved trauma.

Finally, there is our inability to be reconciled with problems we can't solve. Deeply held cultural or religious values can prevent us from accepting that we are successful enough, thin enough, normal enough, or pure enough to be happy. Perfectionism can make it hard for us to tolerate problems that others shrug off or don't even notice. Even a physical condition that upsets our equilibrium—menopause, "andropause," a severe chronic illness—can make it harder for us to not sweat the small stuff, let alone the big.

In one way or another, every antidepressant strategy—including the many dozens discussed in this book—helps us to overcome or be reconciled with our problems. And when we can live with those problems, we can live again.

Part 1

Betrayed by the Body: Physical Causes of Depression and Their Treatment

Being depressed can be like being in a fog, without the foggiest idea of how to escape. For many of us, our first impulse may be to look for psychosocial explanations and solutions. Yet surprisingly often—perhaps even more often than not—something purely physical is causing or contributing to our depressed state. It could be a pill we're taking for our blood pressure, a medical illness we don't know we have, or any of hundreds of other "somatopsychic" (the opposite of psychosomatic) conditions. Identifying these often elusive causes can save us a lot of unnecessary psychological struggle.

In the next four chapters, we'll examine some of the most common of these physical causes of depression, how we can tell if we have them, and how we can treat them. We'll also take a close look at several others—nutritional deficiencies and bright light deprivation, for example—in later parts of the book.

CHAPTER 1

Emotionally Depressed, or Medically Ill? Revelations of a Complete Medical Examination

Some twenty years ago, researchers at Texas University Medical Center decided to see if a novel medical approach could be of help to 100 psychiatric patients who needed all the help they could get. Delivered under warrant to a Houston psychiatric center, for most the next stop would have been a state mental hospital.

The novel medical approach was really a very old-fashioned one: *a complete medical examination and workup*. It was only for the average psychiatric patient that it was a novelty. But not, as it turned out, an extravagance.

Examined from head to toe, all but 20 of the 100 patients proved to have a previously unrecognized physical illness. And for nearly half of them—including 13 of the 30 depressed patients—the illness was deemed largely or entirely responsible for their psychiatric condition.

"Twenty-eight of these 46 patients," psychiatrist Richard C. W. Hall and his associates reported in the *American Journal of Psychiatry*, "evidenced dramatic and complete clearing of their psychiatric symptoms when medical treatment for the underlying physical disorder was instituted." The rest "were substantially improved."

This was not the first, nor would it be the last time studies would reveal how frequently people who "present" psychiatrically suffer from *etiologic* (causative) physical illnesses. As Todd Estroff and Mark Gold, two psychiatrists expert in the field, point out, more than a hundred physical conditions—often in their mildest, subclinical stages, when telltale physical symptoms are easily confused with the bodily upsets of depression—can cause or promote depression or other psychiatric syndromes. As reviewed in 1980 by psychiatrist Erwin Koranyi, since early in the twentieth century more than a dozen investigations involving thousands of psychiatric patients have consistently demonstrated the scope of the problem—yet have just as consistently been ignored by most physicians. Only in the last few years, as psychiatry has become increasingly "medical," has the physcial examination of psychiatric patients become a more routine and diligent practice.

It's not just severely disturbed psychiatric patients like those examined in Texas whose physical illnesses have been overlooked. A few years earlier, Hall and associates applied their fine-toothed diagnostic comb to 658 new admissions to a suburban psychiatric outpatient clinic. Nearly 10 percent of these garden-variety psychiatric patients proved to have "a medical condition that was thought to be definitely or probably causal of their psychiatric symptoms," the researchers wrote. Interestingly, the sickest group was the "neurotic" depressives, those most likely to have their symptoms shrugged off as "all in their heads."

On the basis of such research, experts like Mark S. Gold and associates (1984) and Roger Kathol estimate that as many as one-third to one-half of depressed patients have a physical disorder that is either the primary cause of their depression or a major contributor. Treating it, they estimate, will relieve the depression about 50 percent of the time. If only all the patients knew they had a disease to treat.

Unfortunately, despite this body of evidence—despite textbook warnings that every psychiatric patient deserves a careful medical examination—as recently as the late 1980s, studies showed that many doctors still pay short shrift to the physical condition of their psychologically disturbed patients. A 1988 study by Chandler and Gerndt revealed that even hospitalized psychiatric patients don't always get this consideration. And when examinations are done, too often they're cursory once-overs, which often yield a spuriously clean bill of health—a false sense of security, that Hall's group charged in 1981 borders on medical malpractice.

What a Complete Medical Examination for Depression Should Entail

The complete medical examination that every depressed person needs (certainly if initial attempts at treatment have been unsatisfactory) has three elements: the history, the physical examination, and laboratory tests.

The History

"For every diagnosis based on physical examination and tests, ten are made first by a careful history-taking," stresses Isadore Rosenfeld, M.D. Your doctor should take at least ten or twenty minutes querying you in detail about your symptoms, medical history, occupation, lifestyle, and anything else that might illuminate the cause(s) of your depression.

The Physical Examination

When the history turns up nothing suspicious, many doctors skip the physical examination. This is a false expedient. When William Summers and his associates at the University of Southern California examined seventy-five psychiatric inpatients, abnormal physical findings not suggested by their histories led Summers et al. to diagnose etiologic physical illnesses in 19 percent of the patients.

Cursory physicals present problems of their own. In the Texas study of the mental hospital–bound patients, cursory examinations uncovered less than 20 percent of the illnesses detected by complete medical exams. An adequate physical, Summers and associates suggest, should take at least fifteen to twenty minutes.

Lab Tests

Lab tests can confirm suspicions raised by the history or physical, but they also can catch subtle disorders, such as hyperparathyroidism and subclinical hypothyroidism, that otherwise would completely elude detection.

Studies have put a percentage value on how useful different lab tests can be. At the top of the list are the *automated blood chemistry panels*, which measure blood levels of a dozen to several dozen important substances—minerals, hormones, antibodies, and so on. In Hall's group's 1980 study, the SMA-34 blood chemistry analysis alone detected more than half of the illnesses that caused or contributed to the patients' psychiatric disorders—more than four times the yield of the slightly cheaper, but much leaner SMA-12 test. With the addition of the complete blood cell count (CBC), the yield rose to 77 percent. Smaller but worthwhile yields also came from urinalysis, the electrocardiogram (ECG), and the electroencephalogram (EEG) performed on patients deprived of sleep to enhance the test's sensitivity.

Hall and his associates recommended that these tests be used routinely on all psychiatric patients. Other experts, like Estroff and Gold and Sternberg, later agreed, but suggested that additional tests—particularly for mild or subclinical hypothyroidism (chap. 2) and nutritional deficiencies (chap. 5)—would add considerably to the yield. Though expensive, brain scans could detect rare, slow-growing tumors that have been known to produce nothing but psychiatric symptoms for years. Other tests that can be ordered, if indicated, include blood, urine, or hair tests for toxic chemicals and blood levels of copper and ceruloplasmin to screen for Wilson's disease in depressives younger than thirty.

How much does it cost? In Hall's group's 1980 report, more than 90 percent of the illnesses were picked up by a protocol that cost about $400—perhaps $1,500 to $2,000 in today's currency. But the most productive of these tests—the SMA-34 and the CBC—cost a small fraction of the total. Very expensive tests, like the EEG, could be reserved (unless obviously indicated) for treatment-resistant depression.

What a Complete Medical Examination Can Reveal

I can only scratch the surface of what a complete medical examination by a qualified, motivated doctor can reveal about the causes of your depression. For a more thorough account by a leader in the field, see *The Good News About Depression* by biopsychiatrist Mark Gold.

Let's begin with age. Increasing years make us more vulnerable to disease, including the depressing kind. "Onset of psychiatric symptoms in a person over forty," David Sternberg, M.D., goes so far as to suggest, "should be considered organic in origin until proven otherwise."

How about your medical history? If you've recently had a stroke to the right side of your brain, you probably have an organic depression because of it. Even a bad bump on the head, especially if it knocked you out, can precipitate a depressive syndrome weeks or months later, if a coagulated blood mass (a subdural hematoma) now presses against your brain.

Have you had any of your gastrointestinal tract removed? If so, malabsorption could be giving you depressing nutritional deficiencies.

Do any illnesses run in your family? Your depression could be an early symptom of such heritable diseases as non-insulin-dependent diabetes mellitus (NIDDM), hypothyroidism, pernicious anemia, lupus, Huntington's disease, celiac disease, or porphyria, among others. Native Americans who have NIDDM have a threefold risk of being depressed.

What about your symptoms? Feeling weak? Much more so than fatigue, weakness is highly suggestive of physical illness. Even chronic fatigue syndrome (CFS)—a painful, depressing disorder—is accompanied by severe muscle weakness, which helps distinguish it from depressive or psychosomatic fatigue. CFS is commonly attributed to chronic, low-grade viral infection, especially by the Epstein-Barr virus (EBV). But indistinguishable syndromes can also occur before or after the full-blown phase of any systemic infectious illness, including mononucleosis, brucellosis (contractable from unpasteurized milk), tuberculosis, infectious hepatitis and encephalitis, syphilis, and AIDS. Chronic fatigue syndromes can also result from chemical intoxications (as in multiple chemical sensitivity syndrome), nutritional deficiencies, multiple allergies, endocrine disorders, or other conditions.

Do you have ED (erectile dysfunction)? It could be because you're depressed—or because of the drug you're taking for your depression. It could also be why you're depressed, if you have a depressing physical disorder that causes impotence, like multiple sclerosis, anemia, adverse reactions to certain drugs or dialysis, and (especially) diabetes.

Excessive thirst or a high level of calcium in your blood may be the only sign that you have an uncommon endocrine disorder called hyperparathyroidism, which can severely depress and derange you for years before it's diagnosed.

Spontaneous tanning without benefit of sunlight or tanning parlors is a telltale sign of Addison's disease, an ennervating, depressing failure of the adrenal glands. The tanning usually occurs in the creases of the palms, around the nipples, or wherever there is pressure from clothing or jewelry. Hiccups are another peculiar symptom of the disease.

A blimpy moon face, facial-hair growth in a woman, an unusual fattening of the trunk, and a "buffalo hump" on the back all signal the presence of a steroid-producing tumor—Cushing's syndrome. At first, Cushing's syndrome makes many people cocky, aggressive, even manic; but eventually up to a third of those with the disease crash down into a deep, sometimes suicidal depression.

A butterfly-shaped rash across the nose and cheeks is a signature of systemic lupus erythematosis, or lupus, a rare autoimmune disease that mostly strikes young women. It causes achy joints and psychiatric symptoms of every description.

Pain in the upper abdomen that feels as if it's boring its way through to your back could be caused by a rare, highly malignant tumor of the pancreas. Sufferers are usually fifty- to seventy-year-old men who just seem very severely depressed. Other symptoms are substantial weight loss, intractable insomnia, a history of alcoholism or diabetes, and, eerily, according to Todd Estroff and Mark Gold, a gut fear that one has a life-threatening disease.

Numbness, tingling, or other queer sensations in your extremities suggest serious vitamin deficiencies or nerve damage from chemical toxins.

Hearing things may really be "all in your head," but if you're seeing, feeling, or smelling things, the problem is almost certainly all in your brain, according to Hall et al. (1978) and Sternberg. A subtle form of epilepsy called *partial complex seizures* (PCS) is one cause. PCS, which includes temporal lobe epilepsy, is a remarkable condition, vividly described by Estroff and Gold. Instead of fits of movement, there are spells of sensations, emotions, thoughts, or impulses: smells that aren't there, feelings or impulses that come out of nowhere, even déjà vu or jamais vu (i.e., feeling that you haven't been here before when you really have).

Many people with PCS are driven in mystical, religious, or philosophical directions or fit the profile of multiple personality disorder.

Extraordinarily suicidal, they often are misdiagnosed as having primary depression. In the 1981 Texas study by Hall's group, fully three of the thirty depressed patients they examined had PCS. The best diagnostic test for PCS, Estroff and Gold advise, is an EEG with nasopharyngeal (up the nose) leads after a night without sleep.

Tremors and loss of coordination are not commonly seen in young people. When they are, they can be an early sign of Wilson's disease, a genetic condition that causes copper to collect in the brain and other organs. Unfortunately, even these symptoms may be misdiagnosed as psychiatric, because the patient is so young and healthy, and plainly depressed. If only more doctors would look these patients in the eye: A rusty-brown ring around the cornea would tell all.

A depressed elderly person who shuffles as if he were "stuck to the floor" could have an easily operable brain disease called normal pressure hydrocephalus.

If the sclerae—the whites—of your eyes have acquired a blueish cast, you could very likely have a depressing iron deficiency.

Panic attacks—thumping heart, shakiness, sweatiness—afflict many depressives. They can be psychiatric, but they also can have a physical basis in such disorders as reactive hypoglycemia (chap. 4), allergy (chap. 4), and pheochromocytoma. Pheochromocytomas are tumors that flood the blood with adrenaline and other fight or flight hormones, often at the oddest moments, like after you've sneezed, shaved, gargled, laughed, or made love. They can also cause severe depression.

Where to Turn

Not all doctors can be counted on to provide you with a careful and complete medical examination when you're depressed. Those best equipped (and most inclined) sometimes call themselves biologically or medically oriented psychiatrists, biopsychiatrists, or biobehavioral medical specialists. You're also likely to get a decent workup in the psychiatric ward of a teaching hospital or from a psychiatrically oriented internist. When you book your appointment, ask for a long one. It could be time and money very well spent.

CHAPTER 2

———— ✦ ————

Sad Glands:
Exploring the Endocrine
Connection

One of the saddest faces I've ever seen was on the pages of a textbook of endocrinology. A case study in *myxedema* (advanced hypothyroidism), her abject look testified to the emotional devastation a shortage of just one hormone can wreak. (Or perhaps the sullen mood that came from posing as a "textbook case.")

Mental disease is a symptom of almost every disease of the endocrine glands: the testicles and ovaries, the adrenal glands, the pancreas, the thyroid, the parathyroids, the pituitary, the pineal.

It's no wonder. The hormones that are dispatched like drugs into the bloodstream by the endocrine glands are probably second only to the chemicals of the brain in shaping how we feel and behave. When an endocrine gland malfunctions, secreting either too few of its hormones or too many, depression is very often a symptom. And as studies like those in chapter 1 have shown, in any crowd of depressed people, a large group with endocrine disorders can invariably be found—that is, by any doctor who cares to look.

Probably the most common of those disorders is *hypothyroidism*.

Hypothyroidism: Sparkless Depression

The thyroid's principal hormones—triiodothyronine (T_3) and its precursor thyroxine (T_4)—are mobile spark plugs, circulating through the bloodstream to fire the metabolism of every organ in the body, including the brain, where they sensitize neurons (the brain's nerve cells) both to the brain's natural stimulants and to the pacifying neurotransmitter serotonin.

Deprived of thyroid hormones, we grow cold, dry, dull, and depressed. If the thyroid deficiency is mild, we may only seem emotionally depressed or burned out. Only sensitive blood tests will tell the true story.

In 1981, psychiatrist Mark Gold and his associates at Fair Oaks Hospital in New Jersey were the first to show how revealing those blood tests can be. Their subjects were 250 patients referred to their specialized clinic for treatment-resistant depression or fatigue. Although standard blood tests of thyroid hormone levels uncovered just two cases of full-blown, clinical, Grade I hypothyroidism, the more sensitive blood tests revealed that eighteen more patients suffered from mild, Grade II hypothyroidism or from subclinical, Grade III hypothyroidism.

These patients, Gold and colleague J. S. Carman later wrote, "had suffered for years, and many had gone from internist to psychiatrist to psychiatrist being tried on psychotherapy, multiple psychopharmacological therapies, and even ECT for lack of response to traditional psychopharmacological treatments." Until they came to Fair Oaks Hospital. Thyroid hormone replacement therapy, sometimes with antidepressants on the side, was all it took to put an end to their long nightmare.

In most subsequent studies involving more than a thousand patients, Gold's group and others have confirmed that mild or subclinical hypothyroidism afflicts some 10 to 15 percent of clinically depressed persons—mostly women—and fully 20 to 50 percent of depressives who aren't responding to antidepressant drugs.

Are You Hypothyroid?

Crude screening for hypothyroidism involves measuring blood levels of thyroid hormones and recognizing physical signs and symptoms of clinical hypothyroidism, such as cold intolerance; thinning hair and eyebrows; drying, thickening, and roughening of the skin; high cholesterol; and irregular menstruation. As Gold et al.'s research suggests, for every case of hypothyroidism that can be spotted this way, three or four more are betrayed by high blood levels of *thyroid-stimulating hormone* (TSH). Yet another five or ten subclinical cases can only be uncovered by the costly (and seldom ordered) *TRH stimulation test* (TRH stands for *thyrotropin-releasing hormone*), and/or by detecting antibodies to the thyroid gland in the blood (also pricey), a sign of the most common form of hypothyroidism today: *autoimmune thyroiditis.*

There is much controversy about the most effective and economical way to adequately screen for hypothyroidism. According to Hendrick et al., some experts believe the newer ultrasensitive radioimmunoassay for TSH renders the TRH stimulation test all but obsolete. The FT_4I (free thyroxine index) also gets high marks. John Dommisse, M.D., thoughtfully argues that measuring absolute and relative blood levels of free-T_3 and its biologically nearly inert precursor, free-T_4, may be a more telling and essential test than any other. On her website (www.onthewayup.com), orthomolecular psychiatrist Priscilla Slagle explains that she also looks for a telltale pattern of high T_4 and low T_3, which suggests a functional state of hypothyroidism, despite a healthy thyroid gland. Studies have shown that depressives tend to have this pattern.

While TSH screening is becoming routine, the far more sensitive (but expensive) TRH stimulation test remains a dark horse. A study by R. P. Kraus et al. suggests a possible compromise. Twenty-three (38 percent) of sixty depressed patients whose TSH levels were in the high normal range (3.00 to 5.50 mIU/L) subsequently tested positive in the TRH test. High-normal TSH results could therefore be considered an indication either for thyroid therapy or the TRH stimulation test.

Some doctors believe the most sensitive test for hypothyroidism can be done cheaply at home with a thermometer. Snuggle one into your armpit for ten minutes before you get up in the morning, and if your temperature is lower than 97.8 degrees Fahrenheit—repeatedly, on at least two or three days—your thyroid may be under par. The inventor of this unorthodox test, Broda Barnes, M.D., advises menstruating women to do it on the second and third days of their period.

Although being depressed should make you wonder if you're hypothyroid, a few things should make you wonder very seriously:

✦ As noted by psychiatrist David Sternberg, lithium produces some degree of hypothyroidism in as many as 40 percent of users. This may account for much of the fatigue, dullness, depressiveness, and rapid cycling that many people on lithium experience. Rapid cyclers, who usually have some degree of hypothyroidism to begin with, are by far the most vulnerable to lithium's antithyroid effect. This would help explain why about one or two in every three rapid cyclers benefit dramatically from very large doses of thyroxine. However, since the 1940s even rapid cyclers with no signs of hypo-thyroidism have responded to this seemingly paradoxical therapy. (A related caution from Hendrick et al.: People who are subclini-cally hypothyroid are especially vulnerable to becoming rapid cy-clers if they're prescribed a tricyclic antidepressant drug.)

⚐ Women have a tendency to develop mild or subclinical hypo-thyroidism after giving birth. Hendrick et al. cite several studies that implicate this hormonal disturbance as a cause of postpartum depression. In one study, 8 out of 303 healthy pregnant women de-veloped postpartum depression and hypothyroidism. They all re-sponded to treatment with thyroid hormone.

⚐ You're also more likely to have hypothyroid depression if you're fe-male; if your depression hasn't responded well to treatment (this doubles or triples your chance of being hypothyroid); if you have any symptoms of hypothyroidism (including subtle ones like mem-ory impairment); if you have premenstrual depression (in several studies, 20 to 95 percent of women so afflicted have had mild or subclinical hypothyroidism); if you're suffering from "mixed state" bipolar disorder (in a study cited by Hendrick et al., 33 percent of these people, who can be depressed one minute and manic the next, had mild hypothyroidism); if you use an intrauterine device and have increased menstrual bleeding; if you're getting old; if you have a family history of hypothyroidism; or if you've ever been aggres-sively treated for *hyper*thyroidism.

Treating Hypothyroidism

Most hypothyroid depressives recover on thyroid hormone alone, but some—usually the subclinical cases—also require antidepressants. Hendrick and her associates recommend that depressives with high TSH (mild hypothyroidism), should try thyroid replacement therapy alone for six weeks before adding drugs, if necessary.

Triiodothyronine (T_3), the most bioactive thyroid hormone, or thyroxine (T_4), T_3's precursor, is the usual prescription. But Mark Gold and his associates prefer whole, dessicated thyroid gland. Closer to nature, and probably more body-friendly than T_4 or T_3 alone, the whole gland contains T_3, T_4, and the little-understood T_1 and T_2 hormones. It may be more user-friendly and clinically reliable than either T_3 or T_4. Indeed, in a study by R. G. Cooke and associates, some depressives treated with T_4 alone only recovered when T_3 was added. Perhaps, as all depressives tend to do, hypothyroid depressives don't readily convert T_4 to T_3. Or perhaps, as a study by Gregory Sullivan and associates suggests, the problem is that *transthyretin*, which carries T_4 across the blood-brain barrier, tends to be scarce in depression.

People on lithium may also need T_3, because lithium impedes the conversion of T_4 to T_3 in the brain, according to Hendrick et al. This could explain why rapid cyclers, who typically are taking lithium, usually require ultra-high doses of T_4. Perhaps a much lower dose of T_3—or whole thyroid—would serve them just as well.

Orthomolecular physicians like Herbert Newbold and naturopaths like Michael Murray also prefer whole thyroid preparations, such as Armour Dessicated Thyroid Hormone, Nathroid, and Westhroid. So does Barnes, who recommends a dosage just high enough to raise a patient's underarm temperature back to normal (97.8 to 98.2 degrees Fahrenheit).

Although unlikely, it may be possible to perk up some slack thyroid glands with supplemental kelp (a rich source of the iodine found in thyroid hormones), tyrosine (the backbone of thyroid hormones), a generous intake of riboflavin (a key catalyst for the hormones' synthesis), and selenium (essential for converting T_4 to T_3). Kelp could be key to treating some cases of lithium-induced hypothyroidism, because, as Hendrick et al. note, lithium interferes with the thyroid gland's uptake of iodine. Over-the-counter thyroid supplements are required by law to have extremely low thyroid hormone levels, but they might at least flesh out a pure T_4 or T_3 prescription.

Most cases of hypothyroidism today are autoimmune. Research (described in chap. 8) suggests that rebalancing the body's fat intake can dampen autoimmunity. For example, several people treated with linseed oil by Donald Rudin completely outgrew their need for thyroid medication.

Thyroid Hormone as an Antidepressant

Since the early 1970s, the depression/thyroid connection has been explored from an entirely different angle. In a large number of clinical trials, depressed patients who did not respond to antidepressant drugs have had a small dose of thyroid hormone (usually T_3) added to their regime. In a 1996 meta-analysis by R. Aronson et al. of eight such controlled trials involving nearly 300 patients, T_3 proved twice as effective as placebo. In practice, the response rate has varied widely from study to study. But, on average, about 50 percent of depressives improve or recover on T_3 augmentation within weeks. Men seem relatively unlikely to respond, and one study suggests that neither do people with severe melancholic or psychotic major depression. In fact, these depressives tend to show laboratory signs suggestive of subclinical *hyper*thyroidism. They would probably be better candidates for thyroid hormone's main competitor in the drug-augmentation business: lithium.

There is a clinical impression that T_3 is a superior augmentor to T_4, but it hasn't been confirmed in all studies. In a remarkable trial by M. Bauer et al., ten out of seventeen people with severe and chronically treatment-resistant depression (twelve of them bipolar) recovered fully within eight to twelve weeks on extremely high doses of T_4 (nearly 500 micrograms per day, on average). Seven of them continued to respond fully for an average two-year follow-up. Yet the "side effects were surprisingly mild," Bauer et al. wrote.

As you might suspect, studies tend to suggest that most responders to T_3 augmentation are actually mildly or subclinically hypothyroid. Similarly, complementary studies suggest that depressives who are mildly hypothyroid, but don't know it, are likely to be highly unresponsive to antidepressant drugs alone.

Very small doses of T_3 are used to augment antidepressants—usually just 25 micrograms per day (range: 5–50 micrograms). These dosages generally produce only mild and transient side effects, such as fine tremor, upset stomach, weakness, or dizziness. There have been cases of mania, especially in bipolar depressed patients unprotected by lithium. But overall there actually seem to be fewer side effects with T_3 than without.

Natural antidepressants that have druglike effects on neurotransmitters (e.g., amino acid precursors [chap. 10], St. John's wort [chap. 13]) can likely be augmented by T_3 or T_4 too. In one patient treated by S. E. Southmayd, the antidepressant effect of sleep deprivation—a normally very short-lived effect, as we'll see in chapter 18—was sustained by T_4.

From Thyroid to Steroid:
Other Endocrine Antidepressants

For every person who owes her depression to hypothyroidism, studies suggest another can probably thank some other endocrine disorder for his sorrow. Even hyperthyroidism, which typically produces symptoms "opposite" to hypothyroidism (nervousness, restlessness, sweatiness), sometimes provokes a paradoxical depressive syndrome, especially in the elderly.

A very thorough medical examination can reveal if you have hyperthyroidism or any other depressing endocrine disorder: hyperparathyroidism, Cushing's syndrome, Addison's disease, diabetes, hypoglycemia, ovarian failure, testicular failure, hypopituitarism, or hyperpituitarism. However, as with hypothyroidism, very mild or subclinical cases may slip through the cracks of cursory examination. Furthermore, just as thyroid hormones can be effective adjuncts for depressives who may not even be hypothyroid, research suggests the same can be true for other hormones.

'Roid Relief: The Good Mood Side of Steroids

Mrs. L was forty-nine years old and one year into early menopause when she developed major depression, with paranoid thoughts and impaired memory. She was briefly hospitalized and prescribed a series of psychotropic drugs until a successful combination was found. But she still felt anxious and depressed every morning. Over the next ten years, whenever Mrs. L tried to cut down on her drugs, her symptoms would return full force.

When Mrs. L was in her early sixties and had been fully menopausal since the age of fifty-two, a psychiatrist recommended she try the estrogen patch for her morning dysphoria. "Within one week," the Finnish psychiatrist S. Korhonen and an associate, S. Saarijarvi, later wrote, "the psychological symptoms had completely disappeared." So buoyed was

Mrs. L, in fact, that she stopped taking her other drugs. This time her symptoms didn't return until six months later. Her gynecologist, it turned out, had switched her to oral estrogen and progesterone, but this had given Mrs. L abdominal pains. So the gynecologist recommended she stop the HRT (hormone replacement therapy) altogether.

When the psychiatrist put Mrs. L back on the patch, "she was totally free of affective symptoms" within two weeks. Two months later, when the doctors wrote their report, Mrs. L was still well. "This case," they commented, "shows that even severe depression in the menopause can be effectively treated with HRT alone."

Mrs. L is emblematic of women—and men—who may be suffering from depression or other symptoms because their bodies lack a steroid hormone, like estrogen or testosterone.

"'Roid rage" among steroid-popping athletes occurs because one of the major target organs of the steroid hormones produced by the sex organs and the adrenal glands is the brain. 'Roid rage is "your brain on steroids." Depression can be your brain *not* on steroids. For Mrs. L, a lack of estrogen was the problem. For other depressives, the problem may be a shortage (or, less often, excess) of progesterone, testosterone, DHEA, pregnenolone, cortisol, or any other steroid hormone.

Estrogen and Progesterone

Estrogen and progesterone play complementary—even antagonistic—roles in women's bodies, including their brains. Estrogen seems to be "yang" to progesterone's "yin," more of a stimulant compared to progesterone's pacifying, even downer, effect.

According to psychiatrist Stephen Stahl of the University of California at San Diego, most of estrogen's numerous effects on major neurotransmitter systems resemble or complement those of antidepressant drugs. Indeed, women seem to need estrogen just to be able to respond to these drugs. In a large multicenter trial cited by Stahl, Prozac worked for just 32 percent of the sixty-year-and-older women. Although this was almost double the response to the placebo, it was about half the response usually seen in young women. But among the elderly women on estrogen, Stahl writes, "the difference between drug and placebo was three times greater."

Such research makes Stahl and others believe that for many treatment-resistant depressed women, the missing link is estrogen. But predicting which women will benefit from estrogen—and progesterone—and who might actually be made worse is a challenge. There are Mrs. Ls, but there also are women who "crash" on these hormones. And many times it seems to be a question of which estrogen or progesterone: oral or transdermal, synthetic or natural?

There are clues. For instance, psychiatrist David Rubinow of the National Institute of Mental Health notes that premenopausal women are more likely than postmenopausal women to have a negative reaction to estrogen. So too, he says, are women with a history of PMS—a little surprising, because estrogen can be an effective treatment for PMS itself.

So, forewarned of the confusing road that lies ahead, let us try to answer that perennial question: "What hormones *do* women want?"

Premenstrual Syndrome

One thing seems sure: The times of life when a woman's hormones are most unsettled are the times when she is most vulnerable to mental disease and most likely to benefit from hormone therapy. The premenstrual period is one such time. Unfortunately, experts can't seem to make up their minds whether PMS is a matter of too much estrogen or progesterone or too little. The smart money is that it depends on the woman.

So far, according to British gynecologist John Studd, the evidence most consistently suggests that when it comes to premenstrual depression, estrogen is the likeliest antidote. In fact, too much progesterone has been implicated by many researchers as a cause of premenstrual depression, not a cure, though sometimes synthetic *progestins* may be giving progesterone a bad name.

It may also be that premenstrual syndrome is not a single condition. In the early 1980s, G. E. Abraham, a doctor who had devoted years of study to PMS, classified the condition into several subtypes. Abraham claimed that women with the most common type, marked by tension, anxiety, irritability, and "detrimental" behavior, typically have high estrogen and low progesterone, and a compulsive fondness for sugar and dairy products. They respond to vitamin B_6 (which lowers estrogen and raises progesterone) and/or to natural progesterone itself. In contrast, the least common form of PMS, according to Abraham, is characterized by severe, often suicidal depression, social withdrawal, mental confusion, and, usually, low estrogen and high progesterone premenstrually.

In keeping with Abraham's observations, studies by Studd and others have usually found estrogen to be beneficial for premenstrual depression. In an eight-month trial by Studd's group, women with severe PMS were prescribed either a 100-milligram or a 200-milligram estraderm patch, twice weekly, with cyclical progestins on the side. The researchers, led by R. N. Smith, reported a satisfaction rate of 45 to 57 percent. The lower dose was much better tolerated and just as effective.

In clinical practice, progesterone has been the more popular prescription for PMS. Yet the research hasn't always been supportive, even for natural progesterone, as advocated by the treatment's pioneer, Katharina Dalton. In a double-blind trial by Ellen Freeman et al., for example, natural micronized progesterone (the most recommended form) was no more effective for severe PMS than placebo. But then the average dosage was extremely high: 1,760 milligrams per day. With hormones, getting the dosage "in the zone" is critical. Natural progesterone advocates like Joseph Martorano, M.D., of the PMS Medical Center in New York, and Marla Ahlgrimm, R.Ph., of Madison Pharmacy Associates, recommend an oral dosage of just 100 to 200 milligrams two to four times a day, or a single slow-release tablet of 300 milligrams.

For suppositories, they recommend 200 to 400 milligrams twice a day—not unlike the dosages of 400 milligrams twice a day employed in a large, well-controlled, multicenter trial by P. J. Magill. This time, the hormone proved decisively superior to placebo for each woman's most severe PMS symptom and for her condition overall. In another double-blind study by E. R. Baker and associates, Abraham's observations about progesterone and the tense, "behaviorally detrimental" form of PMS were validated. In the small seven-month study, vaginal suppositories of progesterone, 200 milligrams twice a day, were significantly superior to placebo in one specific area: "symptoms relating to tension, mood swings, irritability, anxiety, and lack of control." Unfortunately, in another appropriately dosed, large, well-controlled trial of progesterone suppositories, Ellen Freeman and her associates again found progesterone no better than placebo. Similarly, while 300 milligrams orally and 200 milligrams vaginally were effective in a small study by W. Vanselow et al., so were the matching placebos.

Postpartum Depression

Studies suggest that estrogen may also have something to offer for post-partum depression. In a six-month trial by A. J. Gregoire et al., the estrogen patch (estradiol), with oral cyclical progesterone on the side, brought relief or remission to thirty-four women with severe, chronic postpartum major depression much more rapidly (usually within a month) and a little more often than placebos. In a preventive study, D. A. Sichel and associates at Massachusets General Hospital chose seven subjects with a history of postpartum depression (four women) or psychosis (three). After delivery, they were immediately put on a high dosage of oral estrogen. Over the next year, only one woman developed a mood disorder, though statistically three or four should have.

Menopausal and Postmenopausal Depression

When it comes to the menopause, it seems that coming to it is more hormonally traumatic than having passed it. "It appears that it is the change in gonadal hormone levels that influences mood rather than absolute low levels of oestrogen," writes Studd. With that in mind, experts like T. Pearlstein et al. of Brown University School of Medicine recommend that women who become menopausally depressed or disturbed and experience vasomotor symptoms, like hot flashes, be given a trial of hormone replacement therapy (HRT) rather than psychotropic drugs, unless their depression is severe. But for postmenopausally depressed women, estrogen is more likely to work as an augmenting agent than a sole therapy, Studd observes.

What about progesterone?

In order to prevent serious health risks, a prescription for estrogen is often balanced, or "opposed," by progesterone. This may strike the right balance for mental health too. According to psychiatrist Guy Chouinard and his associates at McGill University, progesterone has antidepressantlike effects on neurotransmitters complementary to those of estrogen. Whereas estrogen primarily boosts the activating neurotransmitters norepinephrine and dopamine, progesterone focuses on soothing serotonin. Chouinard and his associates describe the trials and tribulations of two severely depressed and treatment-resistant bipolar women. One, fifty-six years old, had been surgically sterilized years before; the other, forty-nine years old, was of unspecified menopausal status. Neither woman recovered from her long, rocky session with bipolar disorder until a balanced combination of estrogen and progesterone was added to her mood-stabilizing regimen. Adding estrogen alone or with minimal doses of progesterone didn't cut it.

Other Depressions

Can estrogen help other depressed women? Studies have been contradictory: sometimes yes; sometimes no; sometimes no way (their depression worsened).

But, as we've seen, estrogen is an unbalanced ovarian supplement—the ovaries also produce progesterone. And they even pump out a dash of testosterone. A little extra of that last feisty hormone has galvanized some of psychiatrist Herbert Newbold's meekest female patients. In clinical studies by McGill's Barbara Sherwin and others, surgically menopausal women on estrogen or estrogen and testosterone combined were found to be significantly less depressed, "more composed, elated, and energetic," than those on placebo or nothing at all. Significantly, the higher their blood levels of estrogen and testosterone, the better they felt.

Conceivably, depressed women of any age whose levels of estrogen, progesterone, or testosterone are relatively low could benefit from topping them up.

Testosterone

Male menopause has come of age, no longer just the subject of corny jokes about men aging ungracefully. Some endocrinologists now regard andropause as a real syndrome, marked, according to psychiatrist Harvey Sternbach of the UCLA-Neuropsychiatric Institute, by symptoms not unlike those of menopause: loss of muscle and bone mass, waning libido or impotence, fatigue, irritability, failing memory, anxiety, depression—even hot flashes!

Men have been lamenting their change of life since antiquity. And one of the remedies they've reached for time and again are the testicles of goats, wolves, and other animals.

In the last few generations, these gross extracts have given way to replacement therapy with the chief male hormone itself. In the 1930s and '40s, medical journals began publishing reports of how the newly discovered hormone testosterone could alleviate not just the "male climacteric" (andropause) in general, but "involutional melancholia" (clinical depression in andropausal men) in particular. By 1996, according to Sternbach, the ratio of positive studies to negative ones was a stout four to one.

But low testosterone depression is not just an old guy thing. Men of any age can be affected. A recent study by Stuart Seidman and Judith Rabkin of the New York State Psychiatric Institute sought to find young depressed men who might be resistant to antidepressant drugs for this very reason. Their ads attracted sixteen men who had been on antidepressants for several months, but still were grappling with moderate to severe major depression that had persisted for up to two years. Five (31 percent) of the men—only one of whom was over forty—had testosterone levels in the low-normal range (200–350 nanograms per deciliter). They all had been foundering in their social and occupational lives too.

After two weeks of biweekly injections of testosterone enanthate, every single man was markedly or dramatically better. Six weeks later, all were fully recovered—with no side effects. When the researchers switched four of the men to placebo injections, all but one quickly began to relapse.

One group of depressed, hypogonadal men who appear highly responsive to the testosterone solution are those with HIV or AIDS. In another study from the New York State Psychiatric Institute reported by G. J. Wagner et al. in 1996, testosterone worked in two to six weeks for 81 percent of depressed HIV-positive men.

Pushing the envelope, Wagner and Rabkin studied the effect of testosterone in twenty-three AIDS patients with normal blood levels of testosterone who had symptoms of hypogonadism: diminished libido, low mood or energy, and loss of appetite or weight. All of these symptoms improved in a majority of the men after a twelve-week trial of testosterone shots.

The depressed men in a double-blind study by William Vogel and associates also had average testosterone levels. But their diagnosis was chronic, treatment-resistant depression. Some were as old as sixty-two, but others were as young as twenty-seven. After nine weeks, those prescribed an oral, synthetic testosterone substitute had improved as much as those prescribed ample doses of an antidepressant drug, but with far fewer side effects.

An intriguing recent study suggests that testosterone, like other hormones, makes men feel and function best not when it's low, not when it's high, but when it's "in the zone." Alan Booth and associates analyzed data on more than 4,000 U.S. Army veterans whose testosterone levels ranged all the way from 53 to 1,500 nanograms per deciliter of blood. The "zone," it seemed, was around 590 nanograms per deciliter. The more the veterans' testosterone levels deviated from that zone, up or down, the more likely they were depressed. But there was a most interesting wrinkle. Among the high-testosterone men, depression tended to occur only in those who exhibited "signs and symptoms" of high testosterone, known to be fodder for depression in their own right: "antisocial and risk behaviors and the absence of protective factors such as marriage and steady employment."

One over the counter alternative to testosterone, made popular by batter Mark McGwire, is the testosterone precursor androstenedione. Research suggests it has little effect on men with normal testosterone levels (a good thing), but that it can raise estrogen levels (not so good) and lower good cholesterol (not good at all). According to Ward Dean, M.D., a less accessible product called androstenediol is less estrogenic, and one called indole-3-carbinol can block estrogen altogether.

With its occasional over-the-top side effects like sleeplessness, euphoria, and mania, it's hard to doubt that testosterone can be a stimulating antidepressant. But given the possible long-term health hazards of too much testosterone, such as promoting latent prostate cancer and heart disease (by lowering good cholesterol), take this prescription only under careful medical supervision.

DHEA: Fountain of Mirth

For years, DHEA (*dehydroepiandrosterone*) has been sold over the counter as a kind of hormonal fountain of youth for midde-aged people who, as ordained by nature, are running low on this adrenal steroid. (By the time we're eightysomething, we're down to just 5 to 10 percent of our youthful peak output.)

It turns out that DHEA, like other neuroactive steroid hormones that wane with age, really can bring back some of the vim and vigor of youth, according to Owen Wolkowitz and his associates at the University of California Medical Center in San Francisco. And it can treat depression too.

In a small, uncontrolled pilot study by Wolkowitz et al., DHEA relieved major depression in six middle-aged and elderly depressives in direct proportion to the extent that it restored their low DHEA levels to a youthful peak. In 1999, the researchers followed up with a double-blind trial involving twenty-two men and women, aged thirty-three to fifty-three, whose DHEA levels weren't even measured. After six weeks, five of the eleven randomly assigned to DHEA (30 milligrams was gradually increased to 90 milligrams per day) were in remission or very mildly depressed, compared to none of the eleven in the placebo group. The few patients on DHEA alone seemed to respond as well as those on antidepressants (who, until then, had not responded to the drugs).

Most recently, in another double-blind trial, NIMH researchers extended DHEA's victory streak to midlife dysthymia. "The symptoms that improved most significantly," M. Bloch et al. reported, "were anhedonia [loss of pleasure response], loss of energy, lack of motivation, emotional 'numbness,' sadness, inability to cope, and worry." The NIMH is now conducting another randomized controlled trial of DHEA for menopausal and andropausal depression.

There is good reason to expect that older depressives will prove to be DHEA's primary beneficiaries. DHEA not only has direct antidepressantlike effects on the brain, it's a precursor to estrogen and testosterone (which wane with age) and a protective buffer against the one steroid hormone that actually rises with age: cortisol. Drugs that lower cortisol show promise as treatments for severe, high-cortisol depression, but unlike DHEA, they're all poorly tolerated.

DHEA's anticortisol effect may benefit another unlikely group of patients: depressed children. In early research, DHEA was reportedly of great benefit to youngsters with an "inadequate personality" or "emotional and constitutional immaturity." It gave them more confidence, energy, and joie de vivre. Fast forward to 1998. In a study by I. M. Goodyer and associates, low blood levels of DHEA relative to cortisol were a strong predictor that a child's depression would prove chronic and treatment-resistant.

Preliminary clinical studies also suggest DHEA can exert its feel-good effect on people with multiple sclerosis and lupus, and on elderly people with any chronic illness.

Like all hormones, DHEA can be a nuisance. Although it's usually well tolerated in therapeutic doses under 100 milligrams per day, side effects do occur, including androgenic effects in women (male-pattern hair loss or growth, voice deepening, acne, irregular menses), acne, body odor, oily skin, extreme weight loss, palpitations, cardiac arrythmia, and aggravation of prostatitis. In true 'roid fashion, there have been colorful psychiatric reactions too: moodiness, confusion, disinhibition, hyperactivity, hypomania, mania, mixed states of depression and agitation or mania, aggression, psychosis, and severe depression. Doses of DHEA as low as 25 to 50 milligrams per day can significantly increase *insulinlike growth factor* (IGF-I). Because high IGF-I can promote prostate cancer, especially in elderly men, M. Goldberg, M.D., cautions: "For men receiving DHEA supplements, serum levels of DHEA, prostate-specific antigen, and IGF-I should be periodically measured and the minimally effective dose prescribed."

For reasons like this, DHEA is best taken in doses that do no more than elevate blood levels into the young buck or belle range, that is, 25 to 50 milligrams per day, although research suggests higher doses may be required to acutely treat depression. Or one could try DHEA's less provocative precursor: pregnenolone.

Pregnenolone

Perhaps you're thinking: "Which of these scary steroids *dare* I take?" Well, there is a brainy, yet sort-of-no-brainer alternative: pregnenolone.

Pregnenolone is pregnant with steroid possibilities. Every single adrenal and gonadal steroid hormone can trace its lineage to this matriarch of the steroid clan. When you take pregnenolone, you are giving your body a precursor it can use, in its wisdom (we hope), to make just as much estrogen, progesterone, testosterone, DHEA, and yes, even cortisol, as it may need. Pregnenolone is itself a neuroactive hormone—perhaps the body's best homemade smart drug, in the opinion of hormone connoisseur Ray Sahelian, M.D.

It sounds so good on paper. But sadly, there has been precious little clinical research. In the 1940s, when pregnenolone was discovered, it exhibited the same energizing, uplifting effects as DHEA. For example, in one study described by Sahelian, 50 milligrams a day appeared to boost energy, well-being, and productivity in harried piece workers.

But that was about it for pregnenolone and mood/performance research, apart from some animal studies and one contemporary people study from NIMH. Researchers, led by Mark George, found that depressed patients had less than half as much pregnenolone in their cerebrospinal fluid as normals.

Although Sahelian wrote a bestseller on DHEA, he's at least as keen on pregnenolone, which he dubs "nature's feel good hormone" in the title of another book. The California physician reports that pregnenolone has just that effect on many of his patients, and it sharpens their minds and senses too.

In studies, hundreds of people have taken hundreds of milligrams of pregnenolone daily for months with few reported side effects. Sahelian favors a cautious dosage of no more than 30 milligrams per day (twice as much as the average person produces naturally)—with "hormone holidays" for a week or so every month. As the mother of all steroids, pregnenolone theoretically can beget all the risky behavior of her children. But then maybe mother knows better how to practice control.

Filling the Hormone Rx

Most of the hormones discussed in this chapter are available over the counter in the United States, but not in Canada. Even natural estrogen and progesterone can be purchased in the United States without a prescription. Only thyroid hormones and potent whole thyroid products, as well as testosterone, are available only by prescription. Canadians can order hormonal products from the United States, but Canada Customs may send some of them back.

Orthomolecular psychiatrist Priscilla Slagle's The Way Up center sells a select range of hormonal and other supplements (1-800-289-8487; www.thewayup.com). Madison Pharmacy Associates (1-800-558-7046; www.womenshealth.com) specializes in customizing and compounding natural hormone prescriptions for women.

Hormonal Help, Hormonal Hell: A Two-Edged Sword

In its heyday, cortisone was hailed as one of the great wonder drugs of the twentieth century. No small part of the wonder was the euphoria this synthetic version of the adrenal steroid cortisol induced in many of its users when all they had sought was relief from arthritis.

But cortisone soon revealed a dark side. In some users, euphoria turned to mania, and mania collapsed into severe depression.

It would be nice if we could blame it all on the fact that cortisone is a cortisol-like drug. But the same extreme mood swings occur when the real thing is pumped out in excess from a tumor. In people with severe major depression—especially the endogenous or melancholic type—perhaps the most widely replicated biological finding is chronically elevated blood levels of this immunosuppressive stress hormone. Not only does this excess cortisol appear to contribute to the symptoms of depression, but it slowly erodes the body's organs, including the brain.

Yet people with morbidly low cortisol—for instance, those with Addison's disease—also suffer from depression, albeit a sucked-out, as opposed to a stressed-out, kind.

The lesson here is that hormones are essential, like vitamins, but only in the right dose. Too little or too much can cause depression, mania, or other symptoms. Although restoring low levels of a hormone like T_3 or T_4 to normal is quite safe and straightforward, using hormones or their precursors pharmacologically in sizable doses as natural antidepressants or mood stabilizers is a trickier affair. Even if there are no symptoms, there are potential hazards.

People with cardiac arrhythmia, hyperthyroidism, high blood pressure, diabetes, liver disease, or cancer, among other conditions, should consult their doctors before experimenting with over-the-counter steroids. Estrogen and testosterone (and therefore their precursors, DHEA and even pregnenolone) can potentially feed the growth of tumors of the breast, cervix, uterus, and prostate—and malignant melanoma. Steroids are also suspected of promoting the depressing *Candida* syndrome (chap. 4). Men with prostate cancer or severe benign prostatic hypertrophy are advised to steer clear of steroids. A generous intake of antioxidants, of saw palmetto extract or stinging nettles (to protect the prostate), and possibly of nighttime melatonin and phytoestrogen-rich foods like soy and flax, are natural measures that may minimize the cancer-promoting effects of supplemental steroids. But you never know. Nor do we know if nature doesn't "turn down the tap" on hormones when we age because our bodies wouldn't be able to handle them otherwise.

That progesterone protects against estrogen is a clue to the strategy that may minimize the hazards of hormone therapy in general: balance and holism. Pregnenolone is potentially the most balanced and holistic steroid there is for men and women, though ironically it's the one hormone we know least about clinically. The use of whole "glandulars"—dried portions or extracts of the thyroid, adrenals, ovaries, testes, or other endocrine glands—is the most natural and holistic of hormonal therapies. But most doctors think it's old-fashioned and creepy, and there is virtually no modern research to support the practice.

Whatever you take, the safest course is to depart as little as possible from achieving the natural hormonal balance of a healthy body—perhaps even a healthy old body, if that's what you're driving.

CHAPTER 3

·❦·

Mood Poisoning:
Toxic Causes of Depression

It's not unusual when you're depressed to feel as if you've been
drugged or poisoned, and that's why you're such a droopy, foot-
dragging version of your usual self. You could be right. Some depressed people are being drugged or poisoned by the pills in their
medicine cabinets, the chemicals in their workplaces, or other toxic
invaders.

It's become a platitude to observe that our planet is so polluted that
we are all chronically poisoned. But while we fret about the most vivid
hazards—the cancers, the birth defects—some toxicologists warn of
subtler dangers.

"In the earliest form of chronic toxicity," E. L. Baker and his associates at the National Institute for Occupational Safety and Health point
out, "mild mood disorders predominate as the patient's chief complaint." These symptoms "may appear . . . at exposure levels *about one-
tenth to one-hundredth* of those which produce overt symptoms of
clinical poisoning, and in subjects who appear perfectly healthy by
conventional medical criteria" (italics mine), D. Bryce-Smith and
R. Stephens add. And yet "of tens of thousands of potentially neurotoxic air pollutants, only a few have been well studied," laments Ante
Lundberg, M.D. And because safety limits are commonly set with nothing but gross bodily symptoms in mind, acceptable exposure levels can
still pose a threat to that most delicate flower: mental health. This is an
especial concern for the most hypersensitive among us—the "canaries
in a coal mine," or the "outliers," as toxicologists like University of
Rochester's Bernard Weiss (1985) call them.

Toxic depressants can be as close as your medicine cabinet.

Drugs

"Approximately 200 drugs have been reported to cause depression, and others are believed to contribute to depressive reactions," University of California psychiatrists James Dietch and Mark Zetin wrote—*in 1983*.

In a study by D. A. Katerndahl, nearly half of the depressed patients in a family practice were on such drugs. In another study, eight out of thirty-five elderly, heavily medicated depressed patients referred to psychiatrist Robert Hoffman's specialized medical-psychiatric unit at a San Francisco hospital proved to be suffering from a depressive drug reaction.

Doctors have an unfortunate blind spot for the mental mayhem drugs can cause. In Hoffman's study, thirteen of the patients had become clinically delirious on "drugs of well-recognized psychotoxic potential." Yet their doctors caught on in only three cases. Were it not for Hoffman's clinic, the other ten probably would have been treated with yet more drugs.

The prescription, over-the-counter, and "recreational" drugs listed on page 33 have all been implicated as possible, probable, or definite promoters of depression—and in some cases mania too.

That said, there is controversy over whether many of these drugs are guilty as charged. As Drs. Teresa Long and Roger Kathol point out in a critical review, sometimes what is reported as depression really is just extreme fatigue, lethargy, or mental dullness (as if that weren't depressing enough). And much evidence suggests people with a personal or family history of affective disease may account for most of the adverse reactions. Still, even Long and Kathol recommend: "even if there are no data to suggest that a causal relationship between a drug and affective symptoms exists, if a person is placed on a drug and depression occurs . . . good clinical judgment dictates that the medication should be stopped or changed."

If you're taking a drug that isn't listed here, check it out in a good drug reference book or consult your pharmacist. I've listed most drugs by their generic names (brand names are capitalized) and, in some cases, simply by drug class (for example, "narcotics"). If that leaves you in the dark, again consult a reference book or your doctor or pharmacist. Don't discontinue a prescribed drug without consulting your doctor first.

Drugs That Can or May Cause Depression or Mania

- acetazolamide
- actinomycin D
- acyclovir
- alcohol*
- amantadine
- antihistamines (if used long-term)
- anticonvulsants (especially phenobarbital)
- most antipsychotic drugs (i.e., phenothiazines, like Thorazine and Stelazine, and butyrophenones, like Haldol; newer generation dibenzazepine antipsychotics like clozapine are more likely to relieve depression than cause it)
- L-asparaginase
- birth control pills
- calcium channel blockers
- central nervous system stimulants (e.g. amphetamine, caffeine, cocaine, methylphenidate, theophylline)*
- chloroquine
- most cholesterol-lowering drugs (including the popular statins)
- ciproflaxacin
- clonidine
- corticosteroids (e.g., cortisone, prednisone, ACTH, anabolic steroids)*
- co-trimoxazole
- cycloserine
- dapsone
- o,p-DDD
- decongestants and diet pills (if used long-term)
- digoxin
- disulfiram
- DTIC
- ethambutol
- ethchlovynol
- Ftorafur
- glutethimide
- guanethidine
- H2-receptor antagonists (e.g., cimetidine, ranitidine—only
- people with liver or kidney disease may be vulnerable)
- hexamethylenamine
- hydralazine
- hydroxychloroquine
- ibuprofen
- indomethacin
- interferon (may also provoke suicide, during therapy and after discontinuation)
- isonazid
- levodopa (L-dopa)
- marijuana
- mefloquine
- methyldopa
- methyprylon
- metoclopramide
- naproxen
- narcotics (e.g., heroin, morphine, codeine, methadone)*
- nitrogen mustard
- nonsteroidal anti-inflammatory drugs (NSAIDs)
- PCP
- phenylbutazone
- cis-platinum
- procainamide (mania only)
- procarbazine
- propranolol (other beta-blocker drugs whose generic names end in "-olol" are also suspect)
- reserpine
- retinoids (e.g., vitamin A, accutane, isotretinoin)
- sulfonamides ("sulfa drugs")
- tamoxifen
- tobacco*
- toluene (in glue used for "sniffing")
- tranquilizers and sedatives (i.e., benzodiazepines, like Valium and lorazepam; Miltown or Equanil; barbiturates, like phenobarbital)*
- vincristine
- vinblastine
- zompirac sodium

* Depression may also occur upon withdrawal.

Depression can also be promoted by very high doses of some nutritional supplements: niacinamide, vitamin A, vitamin D, calcium (also found in antacids), magnesium (in antacids and cathartics), zinc, iron, copper, choline, and lecithin.

Metals and Minerals

Few people are unaware of how destructive minute doses of lead are to the brains of infants and children. But lead is poison to adults' brains too.

"A high prevalence of nonspecific symptoms such as fatigue, irritability, insomnia, nervousness, headache, and weaknesses has been documented consistently in workers with moderate lead absorption," write Yale University psychiatrists R. S. Schottenfeld and M. R. Cullen. Even low occupational exposure usually translates into a slight increase in such symptoms, according to a study from the University of California by N. A. Maizlish and associates. When Schottenfeld and Cullen examined thirty-one hospital patients with mildly elevated blood levels of lead, nine were depressed—four severely so.

As with lead, so it is with other metals and minerals, including nutritionally essential ones in excess. Thus, lead, mercury, aluminum, organic tin compounds, arsenic, bismuth, boron, vanadium, selenium, calcium, magnesium, zinc, copper, iron, and manganese can all promote depression. The following appear to be the worst culprits.

Lead

Roughly one million Americans are occupationally exposed to high levels of lead, usually as fine dust or fumes from solder, ammunition, bearings, lead shielding, storage batteries, cables, leaded pigments, pottery glazes, leaded gasoline, bootleg whiskey, insecticides, or processed metals.

We're vulnerable to lead poisoning from other sources too:

Lead-soldered food cans. A rough, smeared seam is the giveaway. According to a 1989 study by CBC television's "Marketplace," food in these cans typically contains ten to sixty times as much lead as food in non-lead-soldered cans (i.e., with a smooth seam or round bottom). Lead levels soar even higher when food is stored in open cans.

Eating utensils. Underfired glazed earthenware (beware of amateur and imported products), crystalware (50 percent lead), and possibly pewter cups and novelty glasses with lead enamel decals all can seriously "enrich" your food and drink with lead.

Asian herbal remedies. Lead and other potentially neurotoxic chemicals like mercury and arsenic have traditionally been used as medicinal ingredients in certain Asian compound remedies. However, these are traditionally regarded as safe when used as directed.

Bone-meal and oyster-shell calcium supplements. Many brands contain questionably high lead levels, according to a study by Bourgoin et al.

Lead-soldered water pipes. Always run your tap for a few minutes before using water that has been standing for hours in these old pipes.

Lead water mains. Don't just run your tap—filter the water too.

Paint. Interior paint older than 1978—or worse, from the 1950s or earlier—can contain extremely high levels of lead. This includes the lead-based glaze on old bathtubs. Removing lead paint by sanding or scraping creates a fine, leaden dust that can contaminate your household unless elaborate precautions are taken. Because exterior paints still are allowed to contain lead, loose paint on playground equipment can be a hazard for children.

Soft vinyl (polyvinyl chloride, or PVC). The cheap vinyl miniblinds recalled in 1996 because of their high lead content (a PVC stabilizer) were the tip of the iceberg. Watchdogs like Greenpeace have exposed the high lead content of many other soft vinyl products, including children's clothes and toys. One children's rainsuit contained 2 percent lead, nearly 100 times the level permitted for miniblinds. With 10 to 20 percent of children already "overleaded," soft vinyl should be regarded as a "dumb drug" that has no place in the playroom until manufacturers eliminate its toxic additives.

Candles. The American Lung Association warns that many candles with metal wicks release dangerous amounts of lead, mercury, and other toxins.

Aluminum

Aluminum is a depressing and possibly dementing mineral. To avoid it, bear these facts in mind:

❧ Chronic dialysis increases aluminum in bones nine- to fiftyfold.
❧ Many antacids are laden with aluminum. A postmortem study of peptic ulcer patients (heavy antacid users) found aluminum deposits in their bones to be midway between those of normal subjects and dialysis patients.

Other significant aluminum sources: aluminum cookware (acidic liquids, like tomato sauce, and fluoridated water avidly leach the aluminum); tap water (in some cities); aluminum salts in foods and spices (e.g., baking powder, processed cheese); baby formulas and intravenous fluids; some drugs and pharmaceuticals (e.g., aluminum hydroxide gels, antiperspirants, deodorants); clay dust; the air from corroded air conditioners; and water heaters with aluminum cores.

Copper

Some doctors believe mild copper poisoning is a commonly overlooked cause of a multitude of ills, from hypertension and tinnitus to schizophrenia and depression. Copper-induced depression tends to be of the irritable, sleepless variety. At the orthomolecular (nutritionally oriented) psychiatric clinic of Carl Pfeiffer and R. Mailloux, about two-thirds of the female patients and one-third of the males were found in one year to have an overload of this essential nutrient. Mainstream psychiatrists like R. L. Narang and associates have also found high copper levels in depressives and other psychiatric patients.

Water from copper pipes—especially soft water that has stood for hours—or from reservoirs treated with copper sulfate may be "the most common route of copper intoxication," according to Pfeiffer and Mailloux. Other culprits are vitamin-mineral supplements with 2 milligrams or more of copper, cigarettes, copper cookware, and fungicides containing copper sulphate. High estrogen levels, naturally occurring or due to oral contraceptives or hormone replacement therapy, can also raise copper levels beyond the body's comfort zone.

Orthomolecular psychiatrists claim copper overload can be gradually relieved by copper-lowering supplements: manganese, molybdenum, calcium, magnesium, vitamin C, bioflavonoids, and, most of all, copper's natural antagonist, zinc.

Mercury

Toxic even in the tiniest amounts, mercury readily invades our bodies when we swallow, inhale, or touch it. It not only promotes depression, but sometimes it produces a unique syndrome of extreme shyness, timidity, and blushing self-consciousness.

Minimize exposure to the following mercury sources:

✧ Mercury amalgam dental fillings.
✧ Drugs and pharmaceuticals that contain *thimerosal* or *sodium ethyl mercur*, such as various antiseptics, ointments, cosmetics, laxatives, eye drops, contraceptive gels, douches, and vaccines.
✧ Broken fluorescent lights, thermometers, and scientific instruments that contain mercury.

Mercury can also be found in some fabric softeners, floor polishes, wood preservatives, adhesives, fungicides, paints and dyes (including tattoos), and textiles.

A diet high in fish and seafood could also pose a mercury hazard, especially if lots of tuna, swordfish, shellfish, kelp, and other seaweeds are on the menu. Sadly, these are otherwise healthy foods.

Occupational exposure to mercury can be significant for dentists and dental personnel (or anyone in a poorly ventilated building with a dental office); electroplaters; embalmers; farmers; gold and silver extractors; painters; photographers; taxidermists; and manufacturers of barometers, batteries, pressure gauges, switches, fireworks, explosive caps, fluorescent or neon light bulbs, fur, felt, ink, paint, paper, or jewelry.

Dental Depression: Mercury Poisoning in the Mouth

A hundred and fifty years ago, dentists who dared to fill their patients' cavities with a newfangled alloy of mercury, silver, and tin called *amalgam* risked excommunication by the American Society of Dental Surgeons. Today, it's dentists who have a passion for getting the amalgam *out* of their patients' mouths who are in hot water with their professional association.

The anti-amalgam dentists are convinced the mercury in these cheap, popular dental fillings is a toxic waste site in people's mouths, the cause of many perplexing health problems, chronic fatigue and depression among them. Replace the amalgams with safer substitutes, and the symptoms usually fade or disappear, anti-amalgam dentists like Hal Huggins claim. Indeed, according to dentist Gary Strong, by 1992 five-hundred adverse reaction reports filed with the FDA had attested to that.

There is some good scientific evidence for the anti-amalgam position. Peer-reviewed studies have established that people with amalgam fillings typically have enough mercury vapor on their breath to exceed EPA residential air standards. Chewing releases more mercury and usually puts them in violation of more permissive workplace standards. If their mouths were dental offices, they'd be raided and closed down! (Of course, fresh inhaled air significantly dilutes the mercury concentration.)

Most of this oral mercury vapor goes straight into the bloodstream, boosting not only blood and urine levels, but (autopsy studies show) brain levels too. Indeed, the average person is burdened more by dental mercury than dietary mercury, the World Health Organization concluded in a 1991 report cited by Strong. "A mouth with many fillings could release up to 560 milligrams of mercury over several years . . . a very toxic dose," observes physiologist Robert Siblerud in the *American Journal of Psychotherapy*.

Some, but not all, research suggests this extra mercury is taking a toll. There are conflicting reports, for instance, that amalgams disturb or don't disturb the immune and cardiovascular systems.

Strong cites a study of nearly four hundred people by the Swedish Health Insurance Bureau, which found that replacing amalgams led, after two years, to a 33 percent reduction in sick leave. People surveyed by Siblerud for his 1989 and 1992 reports who have had their amalgams replaced typically report major health improvements. A German survey by Melchart et al. of nearly five thousand dental patients yielded a mixed verdict. There were significantly more symptoms in people prior to amalgam removal than after removal or compared to people who had no amalgams. But people with lots of amalgams didn't seem worse off than those with few. In Sweden, large-scale studies have found no positive association between the number of amalgams in women and ill health, heart disease, cancer, diabetes, or early death.

On the psychological front, the research is also conflicting. One study by D. Echeverria and associates found that even dental personnel with urinary levels of mercury as low as those found in the general population were suffering subtle adverse effects on mood, mental ability, and motor function. In a 1989 study by Siblerud, people with lots of amalgams had twice as many mental symptoms as people with none. Their most conspicuous complaints were typical of mild mercury poisoning: angry outbursts, depression, easy fatigability, and morning tiredness. When Siblerud sent a questionnaire to nearly three hundred people who had had their fillings removed, most of the eighty-six responders said their psychological symptoms had receded or remitted. Depression had improved in thirty-two out of thirty-eight, and "all ten subjects who reported suicidal tendencies said that the condition was improved or eliminated," Siblerud wrote in 1989. (As with all surveys, the large number of nonresponders may have had a different story to tell.) In a later survey by Siblerud, similar benefits were reported by people with multiple sclerosis who had scrapped their amalgams.

Not all research has supported the amalgam fillings/mental illness connection. In a study by John Bratel and associates from Goteborg University in Sweden, fifty patients who believed their ills were caused by their amalgam fillings were more than five times as disturbed psychiatrically as a matched control group. Yet there was no significant difference between the groups in blood, urine, or hair levels of mercury, and higher mercury levels did not make for more severe symptoms. In another study from "the amalgam unit" of Huddinge University Hospital in Sweden, 379 patients who believed their physical and psychological symptoms came from their amalgams were told they were mistaken and were treated medically (many had previously undiagnosed illnesses) and psychosocially instead. According to the investigator, S. Langworth, 90 percent were satisfied with the result.

The American Dental Association steadfastly defends amalgams. It insists they release so little mercury that only people who are allergic could be affected—less than 1 percent of the population, the ADA estimates. But studies cited by Strong put the figure between 5 and 44 percent, while an investigation commissioned by Health Canada in 1996 estimated up to 15 percent of the population was potentially susceptible. Health Canada subsequently advised dentists not to place amalgams in children, pregnant women, or people with impaired kidney function. The German government has also advises dentists to keep amalgams out of the mouths of babes and pregnant women. And in Sweden, where the Social Welfare and Health Administration has concluded (as quoted by Strong) that "amalgam is an unsuitable and toxic dental filling material," amalgam has been banned for all children under nineteen—and for everyone in some counties. By the time you read this, Austria may be completely amalgam-free. Ironically, these measures have largely been motivated by a desire to protect the environment from mercury waste. As to whether the internal environment of most healthy adults is also threatened, the debate continues.

Are your fillings getting you down? Anti-amalgamists claim that almost any ill can be caused by amalgam fillings. Mercury is toxic to most organs and tissues. However, "the most consistent sign of mercury intoxication", writes dentist Joyal Taylor, is low body temperature; the most typical is chronic fatigue (oversleeping, morning tiredness); and the most unique or specific is a metallic taste in the mouth. Allegedly, another symptom is surprisingly common: a passive, "go with the flow" impulse to commit suicide. Hal Huggins, a controversial dentist at the forefront of the anti-amalgam movement, claims suicidal patients are "the second largest section of our practice."

Anti-amalgam dentists commonly use a variety of tests—none of them conclusive, some of questionable validity—to help determine if, and to what extent, a patient has an amalgam problem. These include skin patch tests for mercury allergy, white blood cell counts, and mercury levels in the blood, urine, and hair. Many anti-amalgam dentists also measure the minute electrical current generated by their patients' fillings. "The more fillings with negative current you have," claims Huggins, "the greater the probability that your symptoms are caused—at least in part—by mercury toxicity."

Treatment. Treating amalgam toxicity is not as straightforward as you might expect. Surprisingly, "just removing fillings with no other therapy is probably not going to help very many people with mercury toxicity," says Joyal Taylor. Anti-amalgam therapy, as detailed in self-help books by Taylor, Huggins, and others, is more complex. In a nutshell:

✣ While amalgam fillings are being drilled out, stringent precautions must be taken to prevent exposure to the abraded mercury.

✣ Amalgams with the strongest negative electrical current must be removed first, Huggins warns. When those with a positive current are removed first, the improvement rate plummets from 80 percent to 10 percent, he claims. Some anti-amalgamists are skeptical. Alfred Zamm, M.D., reports that for more than fifty patients whose amalgams were removed in no particular order the results were just fine.

✣ Huggins also insists that if patients don't follow his high-fat detoxificational diet and use his special line of nutritional supplements, their symptoms can flare up during and after amalgam removal, and their "chances for improvement are slight." Again, some colleagues are skeptical. Others recommend a diet high in fiber and sulfur (garlic, onions) and sulfur-rich supplements (methionine, cysteine, MSM) to detoxify the mercury released from tissues when the oral mercury source has been removed.

✣ Replacement materials for amalgams must not be toxic themselves. Gold (if relatively pure), real porcelain, and (less assuredly) white composite resin are considered the safest by dentists like Huggins and Taylor. As for cements, bases, and other adjunctive materials, they recommend dropsin and glass ionomer.

Petrochemicals

We live in an age of petrochemicals. They are everywhere: in plastics, polymers, and other synthetic products of civilization; in paints, fuels, and preservatives. Some toxicologists and physicians regard petrochemicals as the dominant nerve-wreckers of our time. Studies reviewed by Ante Lundberg have shown that when smog levels rise (the result, mostly, of petrochemical combustion), so do psychiatric emergency calls and hospitalizations. "Chronic air pollution leads to feelings of hopelessness," Lundberg comments, citing a study which found that as sulfur dioxide levels rose, well-being sank.

Volatile Organic Solvents and Fuels

Mainstream toxicologists and alternative allergists called *clinical ecologists* (who specialize in subtle food and chemical intolerances) concur that perhaps the worst petrochemical offenders are *volatile* (smellable) *organic solvents and fuels* (VOSF).

Most fuels, including natural gas and oil, are *volatile organic fuels* (VOF). *Volatile organic solvents* (VOS) are commonly found in paints, paint thinners, varnishes, fresh newsprint and photocopies, oil-based correction fluids, permanent-ink pens and markers, glues, cleaning products, cheap perfumes and scented products, fumigants, disinfectants, pesticides, refrigerants, electrical insulators, and furnace or air-conditioner filters sprayed with motor oil.

Whether inhaled, absorbed through the skin, or accidentally swallowed, VOSF very easily cross the blood-brain barrier and may provoke neurobehavioral symptoms. At the Centers for Disease Control and elsewhere, researchers have repeatedly found an abnormal degree of depression, irritability, mental impairment, and other symptoms of so-called "painters' syndrome" in persons chronically exposed to acceptable occupational levels of VOS. Weiss (1983) notes that rayon workers who chronically inhale "safe" levels of the VOS carbon disulfide are unusually prone to suicide.

VOSF with confirmed depressant effects include carbon disulfide, cresol, toluene, methyl chloride, and methyl n-butyl ketone.

Of particular concern to clinical ecologists, such as the late Theron Randolph, and other experts on nontoxic living, such as Carol Venolia, are natural gas and oil. Their fumes, these experts claim, dull or depress many sensitive people. Even the kitchen stove, one doctor quoted by Venolia claims, saddles some homemakers with an intractable depression that "often disappears when their gas range is replaced with an electric one."

Formaldehyde

The ubiquitous preservative formaldehyde is commonly charged with provoking dozens of symptoms, including lethargy and depression.

You'll find it in a host of products, particularly urea formaldehyde foam insulation, "processed woods" (plywood, particleboard, etc.) and the houses and furniture made from them, permanent press fabrics, and some cosmetics.

Plastics

Plastics, particularly the soft kind, leak into air, food, or water, especially when heated. Even hot plastic lampshades "give off odors and fumes that can have a marked effect on mental and physical well-being," claimed Theron Randolph, the father of clinical ecology.

Pesticides

Most pesticides are nerve poisons, with a well-documented ability to induce depression and other neurologic symptoms in overexposed farm workers. Clinical ecologists maintain that even the pesticide residues in sprayed apartments and on supermarket produce can depress sensitive people. In a letter to the *American Journal of Psychiatry*, Norman Rosenthal, a prominent psychiatrist at the National Institute of Mental Health, and Christine Cameron agree. They describe a patient whose mental and physical health became chronically unglued after his house was sprayed for termites. Psychiatrists, they note, "may be in the best position to detect and validate symptoms of intoxication from 'safe' chemicals that do not appear to affect most people. . . . These patients should be encouraged to avoid the harmful chemicals."

Chemicalized Carpets and Other Space-Age Materials

Have you ever wondered how modern broadloom became so miraculously resistant to dirt, spills, mites, mildew, fire, and everything else wicked known to man? *Chemicals.* As many as 150 volatile ones that we may not be so impregnable to, say clinical ecologists and some mainstream toxicologists.

"I've seen people change every single thing but their carpeting, and then find that the carpet was really the cause of it all," says Debra Lynn

Dadd, an expert on nontoxic living (The Editors of *East West*, 1989). "Broadloomitis" has even struck the Environmental Protection Agency. When the agency recarpeted its poorly ventilated Washington head-quarters, more than 5 percent of the employees were soon complaining of fatigue, headaches, mental confusion, and other ills. At least one employee, writes journalist Peter Radetsky, developed multiple chemical sensitivity syndrome. Eventually, that employee and some seventy-five others were granted "work at home" status on medical grounds.

Stainproof upholstery, sunproof drapery, treated woods, and other chemicalized space age marvels also make the blacklist for environmentally sensitive people.

Cosmetics and Other Personal Care Products

Cosmetics, perfumes, soaps, lotions, and other personal care products are also on the list. Not only are products with annoying scents a problem, but so are those whose odors you can't get enough of, according to clinical ecologists. Addictive allergy (chap. 4) may be afoot. Products least likely to offend contain only natural, hypoallergenic ingredients.

Electropollution and Depression

In 1981, when F. S. Perry and associates reported that suicide victims were unusually likely to have lived near a high power transmission line, it was easy to scoff. It's not so easy today. The evidence may be conflicting, but few independent experts scoff now at the idea that "electromagnetic smog" or "electropollution" may promote cancer, birth defects, miscarriages, and other health disasters. (See, for example, the National Institute of Health's 1998 report by Portier and Wolfe.) It now seems reasonable that there may be subtler, neurobehavioral prices to pay too.

Two forms of electromagnetic smog are causing the most concern: the *nonionizing electromagnetic radiation* (NEMR) emitted primarily by broadcast towers, radar installations, and microwave appliances, and the *magnetic fields* surrounding electrical appliances and power lines.

Even at low exposure levels, NEMR and magnetic fields can interfere with subtle electrobiochemical processes. Weak power-line-frequency magnetic fields have been shown to induce depressionlike abnormalities in neurotransmitter and endorphin levels and body rhythms, and to impair sleep quality. Chronic overexposure even seems to promote brain cancer.

In several studies, the association between magnetic fields, suicide, and depression has been further explored. A 1990 study cited by Charles Poole and associates found a normal suicide rate among electric utility workers. But soon after, a study by David Savitz et al. of the University of North Carolina found significantly more signs of depression among electrical workers than controls. In a survey by Poole's group, people living very near a transmission line right-of-way were nearly three times as likely to be depressed as people living far away. In contrast, a study by S. McMahan et al. compared women who lived right next to a power line to ones who lived only a block away. There were no significant differences in depression. But then, in a 1989 study by Stephen Perry et al., depressed patients had stronger power-line magnetic fields outside their homes than healthy controls. Earlier, Perry and a colleague similarly found that people hospitalized for depression were significantly more likely than their healthy apartment-block neighbors to have lived near the main electrical supply cable. Even geomagnetic storms were implicated as a trigger of depression in a study by R. W. Kay.

Cutting Through the Electromagnetic Smog

It's impossible to escape the electronic smog that surrounds us, but we can keep our distance.

- ✧ Try not to live, work, or play within a few hundred yards of high-voltage towers, transmission lines, radio or TV broadcasting towers, or radar installations. Indoors, spend as little time as possible near the main power line.
- ✧ Minimize prolonged exposure at close range to working electrical appliances, particularly those that use motors or heating elements (e.g., space heaters, electric clocks, arc welding equipment, power tools, and possibly fluorescent lights). Motors and elements give off

the strongest magnetic fields, by far. Only use electric blankets and heated water beds that have been wired to neutralize their powerful magnetic fields.

❧ Avoid liberal use of personal radio transmitters (e.g., CBs, cell phones, cordless phones). They expose the brain to worrisomely high levels of NEMR and magnetic fields.

❧ Avoid rooms heated by electric cables. These rooms are permeated by magnetic fields strong enough, some research suggests, to promote miscarriage.

❧ Don't linger within an arm's length of the front, back, or sides of a computer monitor, even if there's a wall between you. Keep your distance from the computer itself, because its chassis also produces a magnetic field.

❧ Keep at least 3 or 4 feet away from the front, back, or sides of small-screen TVs and up to 8 to 10 feet away from very large ones, again even if there's a wall between you.

❧ Avoid lingering near working microwave ovens, especially powerful commercial models. Have the oven inspected for microwave leakage any time there's damage to the door frame or gaskets. Beware of microwave heat-sealers. They're extremely "leaky."

Ill Winds and the Ion Effect

There are places on this planet where "ill winds" blow, bringing sickness and malaise, mishaps and mayhem. At least that's what the locals believe, and they have the records to prove it.

According to *The Ion Effect*, a classic on the subject by Fred Soyka and Alan Edmunds, when the *föhn* blows in Europe or the *sharav* in Israel, significant increases in the suicide, homicide, and accident rates have been documented.

Doctors and biometeorologists, like Israeli authority Felix Sulman, M.D., and Ohio State psychiatrist A. James Giannini, who have studied the phenomenon tell us that these and other ill winds (such as the *mistral* in France, the Santa Ana in California, the summer winds of the Arizona/Mexico desert, and the Chinook of the Rockies) can be a major irritant for weather-sensitive people. The winds can agitate or enervate them, triggering insomnia, panic attacks, lethargic depression, suicide attempts, or other disturbances. They also can aggravate chronic conditions like asthma, arthritis, and depression.

In 1901, scientists discovered the secret of these "witches' winds": They are laden with positively charged air particles. Whenever we breathe, we inhale thousands, sometimes millions, of positively and negatively charged air particles, or *air ions*. These microscopic particles are essential to our health; but only in the right balance. Scientists have found that if they pump up the volume of positive air ions, animals and people typically behave as if they've been caught in a witch's wind. But when they pump up the negative air-ion count, people either feel nothing or, more often, they feel, think, and perform better or find relief from symptoms of positive air-ion excess.

According to Sulman, who is one of the fathers of biometeorology, some 50 percent of people with mood disorders are susceptible to the ion effect, or "weather-sensitive." Depressives who wilt in the summer heat, for example, are especially likely to benefit from negative ion antidote.

So, it seems, are winter depressives. In 1995, in an elegant double-blind trial from Columbia University by Michael and Jiuan Terman, winter depressives who spent thirty minutes every morning near a high-output negative ionizer recovered at a significantly greater rate (58 versus 15 percent) than those who sat near a low-output lookalike. In a subsequent study by the Terman group, high- but not low-output ion-izers relieved winter depression just as effectively as bright light therapy in just ten to fourteen days.

The Termans' results are not surprising. Most effective treatments for winter depression—bright light, Prozac, and other selective serotonin reuptake inhibitors (SSRIs)—are thought to work primarily by boosting the mood-stabilizing neurotransmitter serotonin. Studies suggest negative ions also boost brain levels of serotonin by decreasing its synthesis outside the brain, where serotonin is an irritant.

The effect of negative ions on serotonin could be the key to their benefits. In a study from the Russian Academy of Sciences by I. G. Stavrovskaia et al., negative ions made animals hopped up on adrenaline mellow out or even fall asleep. Clinically, in a controlled trial by J. Misiaszek et al., they speedily tranquilized manic humans.

Positive air-ion excesses don't just come from witches' winds. According to Sulman, weather fronts (especially warm ones), thunderstorms, and sunspots all "are notorious for producing positive ioniza-tion." (Interestingly, because the ionization occurs before these atmos-pheric events, weather-sensitive depressives can "feel" the changes coming.) Positive air-ion excesses and negative air-ion deficiencies also develop where the air is thick with combustion by-products from auto-mobile exhaust, central heating systems, cigarettes, and the like; in well-sealed buildings, where the air passes through hundreds of feet of metal ductwork (the negative ions stick to the metal); in the electro-magnetic fields near power lines and electrical appliances; and in close contact with synthetic clothing, carpets, or other textiles under friction.

Relief can be found in unpolluted country air, where negative air-ion counts typically are high, or near splashing or falling water, where they're sky-high. Electronic negative air-ionizers are routinely used in clinical studies and prescribed by some doctors. The Termans' research suggests the most reliable ionizers are high-output (high-density) ones, such as those manufactured and sold by the IonAir Company (1-800-478-7324; www.breathe.com).

Sulman advises people to keep at least two meters away from an ionizer, while avoiding close contact with synthetic fabrics that will suck up the ions meant for you. Ionizers typically work quickly, in min-utes, hours, or days at most. If they do not, most are refundable.

Treating and Preventing Toxic Depression

There have been no systematic attempts to identify the toxic depress-sants in our environment. For every known culprit, many more await discovery. Ideally, we would purge all these threatening chemicals from our midst. But realistically, we can at least strive to lead a rela-tively nontoxic life—a hypotoxic life, if you will. There are three main strategies:

1. Avoid as many toxic materials as we can.
2. Clean, ventilate, filtrate, and so on, to keep toxins at bay.
3. Use nutritional or other means to enhance our bodies' detoxifica-tional defenses or reduce our sensitivities.

Avoiding Toxic Materials

ᡔ Minimize exposure to smelly synthetic products (if you can smell it, you're ingesting it): paints, solvents, strong cleaning products, or "off-gassing" construction materials. Experts in nontoxic living, like Debra Lynn Dadd and Carol Venolia, recommend inoffensive alternatives like vinegar, salt, baking soda, borax, natural herbal scents and pesticides, chemically untreated rugs, untreated wood, plaster, ceramic, terra cotta, terazzo, brick, marble, cement, heat pumps, wood stoves (if they're airtight and meet other stringent specifications), and passive solar heating systems.

ᡔ Eliminate toxins from your body. Detoxificational regimes are commonly prescribed by naturopaths, herbalists, and other alternative healers. Special diets or fasts, certain nutritional or herbal supplements, massage, exercise, baths, enemas, and other measures are commonly employed to help the body purify and restore itself.

Keeping Toxins at Bay

ᡔ When you work with toxic materials, wear the best quality gloves, face masks, and other protective gear you can afford.

ᡔ Work and live in well-ventilated surroundings. Hermetically sealed and insulated buildings can easily become "sick buildings."

ᡔ Consider using an air purifier. One with activated charcoal and alumina in its filter, or with a HEPA filter, can dispatch most common pollutants. Even houseplants help clean the air.

ᡔ Consider using bottled or distilled water, or filtering your tap water. Even an inexpensive, pitcher-type model with an activated charcoal filter will greatly diminish the organic solvent residues, pesticides, and other contaminants that can promote depression. A filter with an ion-exchange resin will remove most heavy metals too.

ᡔ Clean your foods thoroughly. Nutritionist Ann Louise Gittleman recommends a very dilute Clorox bath ($1/2$ teaspoon Clorox per gallon of water) to eliminate microorganisms and chemical residues. Soak produce in it for fifteen to thirty minutes (short soaks for delicate foods); rinse in clear water for ten minutes, and dry. No amount of cleaning can remove some residues, like the organochlorines on apples and cucumbers. So peeling sometimes is the only alternative.

Improving Our Defenses

Anything that strengthens us tends to strengthen our defenses against toxic materials.

⤴ Take good nutrition (please!). A generous intake of nutritive minerals like calcium, magnesium, zinc, selenium, and manganese competitively inhibits the absorption and utilization of toxic metals like lead, mercury, and aluminum. Vitamin C's antipathy for heavy metals, drugs, alcohol, tobacco, PCBs, and pesticides is especially well documented. In ample doses, other nutrients like vitamins A (or beta-carotene) and E also fight toxins. Moderate doses of methionine, SAMe, choline, and inositol help the liver detoxify chemicals. Many of these nutrients also have mood-normalizing effects.

Some foods are particularly well endowed with detoxificational agents: garlic, onions, broccoli, brussels sprouts, cabbage, legumes, apples, bananas, and oats, among others. Buy organic if you can afford it, to minimize recontamination with pesticides.

⤴ Allergic hypersensitivities to extremely minute levels of chemicals may be amenable to neutralization therapy, therapeutic suggestion, or other system-strengthening strategies. The connection between the medically controversial syndrome of multiple chemical sensitivity, or environmental illness, and psychological malaise is a strong and possibly two-way one. Evidence presented by Peter Radetsky in his excellent account, *Allergic to the Twentieth Century*, suggests relief can come by addressing the problem from either end—chemical or psychological.

CHAPTER 4

Alternative Diagnoses: Reactive Hypoglycemia and Other Controversial Conditions That May Promote Depression

On the fringes of medicine there exists a controversial category of syndromes believed in by only a few doctors. You've probably heard of some of these "fad diagnoses" and claims that they're commonly to blame for a myriad of ills, depression among them.

In this chapter we'll take a look at three of these conditions: the *Candida* or yeast syndrome, reactive hypoglycemia, and brain allergies.

The *Candida* Syndrome

Candida albicans is a strain of yeast that grows on the skin and mucous membranes of most every healthy person. If it grows too much, there can be a local infection, like oral thrush, diaper rash, or vaginal candidiasis. But in people with very weak immune systems, *Candida* infections can invade the internal organs, with life-threatening consequences.

Many holistically inclined clinicians believe in another form of *Candida* syndrome (CS). Following the lead of a Birmingham, Alabama physician named C. Orian Truss, they claim that in as many as one in every three of us the intestinal *Candida* population explodes. Sometimes it spreads throughout our bodies. Even when it doesn't, *Candida*'s by-products and other ill effects remotely upset our health in innumerable ways, with fatigue and depression at the top of the list. By fighting back with a rigorous anti-*Candida* program, the "*Candida* doctors" (as we'll call them) maintain, most victims of CS (also known as the yeast syndrome or *chronic candidiasis*) can regain their health.

Orthomolecular psychiatry pioneer Abram Hoffer, M.D., Ph.D., describes how he too became a believer in CS. A patient of his had been depressed for years, unresponsive both to conventional and orthomolecular (nutritional) treatments. Because she had many signs and symptoms suggestive of CS, Hoffer decided to give Dr. Truss's anti-CS approach a try.

"One month later she was mentally and emotionally normal," Hoffer reports in the foreword to *The Yeast Syndrome*, a popular book on CS by John Parks Trowbridge and Morton Walker. When the woman quit her anti-*Candida* medication a year later, she quickly relapsed. Back on the drug, she recovered and remained well for years.

Richard Podell, a mainstream internist with a healthy interest in alternative therapies, also decided to investigate CS "with selected patients after carefully explaining my skepticism." "Four years later," he reports in his book *Doctor, Why Am I So Tired?*, "my experience is that about 50 percent of patients who score high on Dr. Crook's quiz [a questionnaire to identify CS sufferers, published in *The Yeast Connection*, by William Crook, a leading *Candida* doctor] and who adopt the *Candida* treatment program improve substantially . . . a better result than I would expect from a placebo."

Not everybody is convinced. "Some people have had excellent results with this treatment, though I've found that most people who try it are disappointed," naturopathically inclined MD Jonathan Zuess writes.

In one of apparently just two formal reports on the anti-CS regime to be published in medical journals, Zwerling et al. reported that seventy out of seventy-nine patients who fit the CS picture improved. But in the other, a double-blind study by William Dismukes and associates in which only one important component of the regime—the antifungal drug nystatin—was tested, the drug proved moderately effective, but no more so than a placebo. There was weak evidence, though, that nystatin was superior in the long run.

The issue is confused by an entirely separate line of research. In several small studies, an anti-candidal drug named ketoconazole, often prescribed by anti-*Candida* doctors, has performed well as an antidepressant. The researchers have prescribed it not to fight *Candida*, but to lower blood levels of the adrenal stress hormone cortisol, which is problematically high in most severely depressed persons.

Has ketoconazole actually been effective in these studies because of its anti-*Candida* effect, confirming that depressives are a secret society of yeast syndromites? Or are *Candida* doctors who prescribe ketoconazole relieving stress-related symptoms, like depression, by countering cortisol, not *Candida*?

Predictably, the medical establishment has found the case for CS wanting. But as David Edwards, M.D., argues in a dissenting letter to *JAMA*, CS "may well be without scientific 'proof,' but it certainly is not without scientific support."

Thus mainstream medicine and research (1) agree with the *Candida* doctors that certain commonly prescribed drugs promote recurrent vaginal yeast infections and *Candida* overgrowth in the gut; (2) recognize that the *Candida* doctors' claim that refined carbohydrates encourage *Candida* growth is (as critic Edward Blonz concedes) "not without some logic"; (3) suggest *Candida* produces toxic by-products, including *canditoxin*—a substance, according to Edwards, "reported to produce clear behavioral changes in experimental animals"; (4) note that intestinal infections can create a "leaky gut" that welcomes allergenic food molecules into the bloodstream, paving the way for depressing "brain allergies"; (5) find that women with recurrent vaginal candidiasis are much more likely than other women to be overstressed and to suffer from clinical depression and other psychological symptoms (Irving et al., 1998); and (6) confirm that most of the measures prescribed by *Candida* doctors are indeed effective yeast-busters.

Do You Have Candida Syndrome?

There is no definitive way to diagnose CS. Even blood tests for *Candida* antibodies are merely suggestive, because so many well people have them too. The diagnosis is therefore made "on spec" if a person has more than a few CS symptoms and risk factors.

Common symptoms. Depression; chronic fatigue, weakness, or feeling "sick all over"; extreme mental dullness or fogginess; anxiety, irritability; feelings of unreality; headaches; multiple allergies; strong cravings for sweet or starchy foods (which may give you a temporary lift) and/or for moldy, yeasty, fermented, pickled, smoked, or dried foods, including alcohol; feeling lousy or drained in moldy air (in mildewy basements, for instance); hyperactivity; premenstrual and menstrual disorders; postpartum depression; frequent urogenital inflammations/infections; constipation or diarrhea; abdominal pain, gas, or bloating; chronic skin problems; and loss of sexual interest.

Common risk factors. Yeast or fungal infections; heavy or long-term use of broad-spectrum antibiotics, steroid drugs, or hormones; many pregnancies; diabetes; immunosuppression (e.g., from AIDS or cancer chemotherapy); and ulcers or gastrointestinal surgery.

Treating Candida Syndrome

The proof of the CS pudding is in the eating—in benefiting from the anti-CS regime of a special diet, supplements, and (often) antifungal medication. *Candida* doctors like William Crook claim that while people on this austere program sometimes improve in days, more often it takes weeks, months, or even years. To remain well, they must continue on this regime, albeit usually less restrictively.

The anti-CS regime, briefly, goes like this:

❧ Eliminate or lower your intake of foods, beverages, and drugs that stimulate *Candida* growth: carbohydrate-rich foods, particularly sweets and other refined carbohydrates; yeasty/moldy, fermented, pickled, and dried foods and beverages, including fruit juices (which tend to be yeasty); broad-spectrum antibiotics, steroids, and immunosuppressant drugs.

❧ Take foods, natural supplements, and/or drugs that suppress *Candida*. Foods: garlic, yogurt, onions, kale, turnips, cabbage, horseradish, broccoli. Natural supplements: garlic, caprylic acid, sorbic acid, olive oil, taheebo and mathake herbal tea, tea tree oil, certain homeopathic remedies. Drugs: nystatin, ketoconazole.

❧ Take large doses of "friendly bacteria" to crowd out and suppress *Candida* in the GI tract. This usually means swallowing many capsules of *Lactobacillus* bacteria (available in health food stores) several times a day for a few weeks or more.

✸ *Candida* doctors also prescribe nutritional supplements to correct CS-related deficiencies, to compensate for damage caused by *Candida*, and/or to stimulate the immune system. Favorites are vitamin B$_6$, magnesium, biotin, linseed oil, fish oil, and evening primrose oil. Some doctors also prescribe very dilute, "desensitizing" doses of *Candida* or other molds, and some recommend enemas or colon cleanses.

Reactive Hypoglycemia: Emotional Havoc from the Wrong Kinds of Sweets and Starches

In the 1960s and '70s, if you were into alternative medicine, you were almost certainly into reactive hypoglycemia. Self-help books by the dozen proclaimed that this disorder of blood sugar regulation lurked behind just about every mental disease and malaise, from clinical depression to criminal aggression. The cure was simple, but tough: Just say no to refined carbohydrates (sugar, white flour, etc.), caffeine, and booze.

Medical authorities balked. Reactive hypoglycemia is rare, they protested, and rarely if ever does it cause such a multitude of ills.

The debate over reactive hypoglycemia has died down; the diagnosis is no longer trendy. Yet it is still a diagnosis every depressive would do well to consider.

Will the Real Hypoglycemia Please Stand Up?

On some things, orthodox physicians and proponents of the liberal, alternative view of reactive hypoglycemia—we'll call the latter *hypoglycemia doctors*—agree.

Hypoglycemia means pathologically low (*hypo*) blood (*emia*) sugar (*glyc*). Blood sugar is our major fuel source. It consists entirely of glucose, the most basic carbohydrate in most of the sugars and starches (complex carbohydrates) we eat. Reactive hypoglycemia typically happens like this: After eating or drinking something that sharply raises blood sugar—refined sugar or starch, alcohol, or caffeine (these pull stored sugar from the liver)—the body overreacts. The pancreas secretes so much insulin (the hormone that lowers high blood sugar by helping it get into the cells) that, within a few hours, the blood sugar is too low for comfort.

The brain, especially, feels the pinch, for it depends exclusively on a steady supply of blood sugar for its extraordinary energy needs. Mental confusion, faintness, fatigue, dizziness, headache, spasms, yawning, blurred vision, cold spells, and other symptoms can occur. To compensate, the adrenal glands may pour sugar-mobilizing stress hormones into the blood to release more glucose from the liver. But that can mean trouble of its own, for these hormones can trigger nervousness, trembling, palpitations, and other symptoms—especially hunger. Ironically, that hunger can drive the sufferer right back to the cookie jar.

Traditionally, reactive hypoglycemia has been diagnosed with the help of the *oral glucose tolerance test* (OGTT). On an empty stomach, a patient downs a few ounces of glucose dissolved in water. Over the next four, five, or six hours, her blood sugar is periodically measured. If it drops abnormally low (below 50 or 60 milligrams per deciliter), and if her symptoms flare up at that time, reactive hypoglycemia may be diagnosed. Increasingly, however, experts are refusing to make the diagnosis unless they can measure low blood sugar levels during a real-life symptomatic flare-up—and if a stiff dose of sugar brings prompt relief.

Hypoglycemia doctors (among whom are numbered most orthomolecular psychiatrists) use and interpret the OGTT much more flexibly. Even if the glucose nadir (the lowest blood sugar reading) is in the normal range, doctors like Harvey Ross and Herbert Newbold will still diagnose reactive hypoglycemia if any of several other conditions are met:

❧ The blood sugar fails to rise substantially above the fasting level during the test.

❧ It falls sharply (i.e., by 50 milligrams per deciliter or more per hour) at any time during the test.

❧ The nadir is appreciably lower than the fasting blood sugar level was.

❧ The patient has symptoms at any time during the test.

Predictably, studies in which the OGTT has been strictly interpreted usually have found reactive hypoglycemia in only a small proportion of people so diagnosed by hypoglycemia doctors (e.g., Palardy et al.). But there have been significant exceptions. In studies from NIMH, the

University of Helsinki, and elsewhere, by Kirk Denicoff et al., Thomas Uhde et al., and Markku Linnoila and Matti Virkkunen, among others, an exceptionally high rate of OGTT-defined reactive hypoglycemia has been documented in women with premenstrual syndrome (PMS), phobias, and panic disorder; and among impulsive, violent, suicidal, or self-mutilating acoholic male criminals.

Other research has supported some of the hypoglycemia doctors' liberal quirks of interpreting the OGTT. Careful investigations have led endocrinologists like Fred Hofeldt to concede that "normal" blood sugar nadirs—as high as 75 milligrams per deciliter—do provoke symptoms in some sensitive hypoglycemics.

The hypoglycemic index (HI) is a measure of how sharply blood sugar falls during the ninety minutes preceding the nadir. Several research groups have shown that the HI is high in most people with symptoms of reactive hypoglycemia, whether or not their glucose nadirs are low, and that it's low in most people without symptoms. In a study by psychologists Lori Taylor and S. J. Rachman, subjects with high HIs experienced up to five times the psychological symptomatology before, during, and after their nadir as subjects with low HIs.

Other research supports, albeit in a left-handed way, the hypoglycemia doctors' willingness to diagnose reactive hypoglycemia no matter when symptoms occur during the OGTT. Researchers at MIT and other centers have shown that people—especially women—tend to become lethargic and drowsy thirty minutes to two or three hours after eating a very sweet or starchy, low-protein meal (Spring et al.). Ironically, these reactions have occurred while blood sugar is still *rising*. So the culprit must be something other than reactive hypoglycemia. The researchers believe it's soporifically high brain levels of serotonin, because insulin, which rises sharply after a carbohydrate meal, indirectly promotes the passage of serotonin's precursor, tryptophan, into the brain. Whatever the explanation, these findings confirm that *hyper*-glycemic foods—sweets and starches that rapidly raise blood sugar—are a problem for some people. Even a typically skeptical authority like Jonathan B. Jaspan of the Pritzker School of Medicine in Chicago maintains that people who think they have reactive hypoglycemia, but don't ("reactive nonhypoglycemia"), do have some kind of problem handling refined carbohydrates and are better off without them.

Yet depressives are more likely to see refined carbohydrates as a solution. Research from MIT, NIMH, and many other centers has established that many depressives—particularly winter, premenstrual, atypical, and alcoholic depressives—compulsively snack on hyperglycemic foods to feel *better*, less fatigued, less tense, less confused—and less depressed. G. E. Abraham found that women with PMS ate nearly three times as much sugar as healthy controls. To MIT's Richard and Judith Wurtman, these carbohydrate fixes are benign "self-medication"—an instinctive attempt to raise depressingly low brain levels of serotonin. But to the hypoglycemia doctors, the sweet fix's rewards are fleeting. It perpetuates in the long run what it medicates for the moment.

The bottom line is that carbohydrate-craving depressives remain depressed. And their habit promotes obesity, tooth decay, heart disease, malnutrition, and other health problems. But if they give up their drug of choice, hypoglycemia doctors claim, their symptoms gradually fade. "My research," writes Larry Christensen, chair of the psychology department at the University of South Alabama, "has revealed that eliminating added sugar and caffeine from your diet will not only help you control your depression in the short term, but also that these beneficial effects will last over time."

One of those effects could be a normalization of serotonin metabolism. High in unrefined, complex carbohydrates, the most popular diet for reactive hypoglycemia is conducive to a steady, stable supply of tryptophan (serotonin's precursor) to the brain. In contrast, the typical high-protein, refined-carbohydrate-rich diet of modern Westerners may provoke an unstable, feast-and-famine serotonin situation above the neck.

In recent years, more and more academic, mainstream psychiatrists and behavioral scientists have joined the hypoglycemia doctors' club. Internist Richard Podell reports: "About 40 percent of my patients whose history suggests a sugar-related problem improve after adopting an antihypoglycemia diet. Most continue to benefit for months or years. Thus I don't believe they are fooling themselves with a placebo effect."

Columbia University psychiatrist Richard Brown and Baylor University neuropharmacologist Teodoro Bottiglieri write: "Although it's never been studied [actually it has—see below], we believe that a high-sugar diet may contribute to depression by creating sugar 'highs and lows' that can result in sagging spirits. Sticking to complex carbohydrates—and avoiding junk food—can help keep you off the sugar roller coaster."

Those studies? The leader in the field is Larry Christensen. Impressed by the passionate literature of the hypoglycemia doctors, Christensen decided to investigate.

In a study published in the *Journal of Abnormal Psychology* in 1985, Christensen and his associates prescribed a *euglycemic* (good for your blood sugar) diet to four psychologically distressed people with symptoms suggestive of reactive hypoglycemia and/or caffeine intolerance. All improved markedly. When they returned to their previous junky diets two weeks later, they all relapsed. Back on the euglycemic diet they improved again. At least three had suffered from depression, including one fairly severe case that was turned off and on by each dietary switch. Later, three of the subjects were deliberately deceived: Sugar and caffeine, they were told, weren't their problem after all. Greatly relieved, they returned to their old diets—and relapsed again.

This was the first of several such studies Christensen's group would publish. All have demonstrated, as the researchers wrote in 1991 in *Biological Psychiatry*, that "a refined sucrose- and caffeine-free diet ameliorates depression and other symptoms such as anxiety and fatigue in selected individuals."

Do You Have Reactive Hypoglycemia?

An OGTT, especially if interpreted by a hypoglycemia doctor, can help clarify if you have reactive hypoglycemia. Influential naturopath Michael Murray believes "the glucose-insulin tolerance test (G-ITT) [which also detects abnormal rises in insulin] . . . is a much more sensitive indicator of hypoglycemia." The larger issue, however, is if refined carbohydrates are a problem for you, for whatever reason—even, as sympathetic skeptic Dr. Jaspan puts it, "reactive nonhypoglycemia." If the timing of your symptoms or carbohydrate craving leads you to suspect they are, there is no harm in trying a euglycemic diet on for size. Refined carbohydrates aren't good for you anyway; and coffee is no health food either. (Green and even black tea are; but their caffeine content may be poorly tolerated by some depressives.)

According to Christensen, the following symptoms predict that a person is likely to respond to his euglycemic (no sugar, no caffeine) diet: depressive downswings that come without apparent cause; moodiness—not just depression, but anger, irritability, or tearfulness; feeling drained (even after a night's sleep); and frequent headaches.

Treating Reactive Hypoglycemia

Two very different kinds of diets are recommended by hypoglycemia doctors (and conventional doctors too) for reactive hypoglycemia. Both diets are in accord that sugar and sweets (including sucrose, glucose, dextrose, maltose, corn syrup, and honey, but not necessarilly fructose), caffeine, alcohol, and tobacco should be eliminated; that refined complex carbohydrates (e.g., white bread) must be used very sparingly, if at all; and that nonstarchy vegetables may be eaten freely. But the traditional Seale-Harris euglycemic diet severely restricts *all* carbohydrate-rich foods, including fresh fruits, whole grains, and legumes, and heartily recommends large servings of fatty animal foods. This, of course, clashes with what most health authorities recommend today.

The other, more popular euglycemic diet poses no such problems. Popularized by the late naturopath Paavo Airola, it prescribes a low intake of meat and dairy foods and a high intake of whole, complex-carbohydrate (high-fiber) foods: whole grains, legumes, nuts, seeds, vegetables, and fresh fruits (provided they're not too sweet).

Still, some people reportedly fare better on the Seale-Harris diet. If you're one of them, you certainly can fashion a healthy version of it by selecting your fat and protein mainly from fish and seafood, wild game, fowl, low-fat dairy foods, nuts, seeds, and beans.

Whichever diet you choose, expect mild to severe cravings and withdrawal symptoms for the first few days or even weeks. Then you may be in for a pleasant surprise: "Most individuals can expect relief from their depression and moodiness within four to seven days," writes Christensen, "although some individuals have to be on the diet for two weeks to experience relief."

Orthomolecular psychiatrist Harvey Ross finds his patients follow a longer and subtler course of response to the stricter, high-protein, very-low-carbohydrate (no sugar or starchy vegetables, very little fruit), and no caffeine, alcohol, or artificial sweeteners diet he prescribes, along with megadoses of vitamins like niacin and C. Typically, the response follows three distinct phases, each lasting five to seven weeks. For people for whom the diet is a major stretch, the first phase is often so unpleasant they have to be continually encouraged to keep it up. But finally the day comes when "energy abounds, depression lifts, no anxieties are to be found, pains have disappeared and, in general, there is . . . a feeling of being cured," Ross writes. But it is a rocky honeymoon. Good days are followed by days back in the dumper. Gradually, though, the ups and downs merge into the third stage.

This stage is a bit of a shakedown, for while Ross's patients are distinctly better by now, some of them aren't better enough and require additional treatment.

"At this point," Ross writes, "I usually recommend psychotherapy." As we'll see, other doctors might also look for "brain allergies" to common foods, like milk or wheat. And there are many dozens of other antidepressants to try besides psychotherapy.

Some hypoglycemia doctors claim carbohydrate craving and reactive hypoglycemia can be mitigated by foods and supplements like flax or linseed oil, buckwheat, brewer's yeast, chromium, lipoic acid, *Gymnema sylvestre*, garlic, and herbal "bitters." Bright light, which reduces depression and carbohydrate cravings in people with winter depression, might also help. I find that eating most of my protein during the day and opting for a high-complex carbohydrate supper significantly tempers my evening sweet tooth. At night, a high-protein meal lowers the brain's tryptophan supply precisely when it needs it, not only to make serotonin but to manufacture the darkness hormone melatonin, too. This deficit could be what drives many people to crave carbohydrates at night.

If a strict euglycemic regime works for you, experts like Christensen and Ross say you can eventually loosen up on it to see how tough on yourself you really need to be.

Finally, sensitivity to refined carbohydrates or caffeine could be due to other treatable conditions, such as allergies, CS, digestive disorders, nutritional deficiencies, endocrine disorders, and even emotional distress, or depression itself. These conditions can feed each other in a vicious circle. Treat one, and you treat the others. A study by Fuad Lechin et al., for example, suggests that many depressed reactive hypoglycemics can be relieved of both conditions with serotonin-boosting antidepressants like Prozac. Natural serotonin boosters, like tryptophan, 5-HTP, and St. John's wort, can likely have the same effect, judging by evidence of their effectiveness for winter depression—carbohydrate craving and all. So while a healthy diet is a must, a strict euglycemic diet may be only optional if other antidepressant strategies are on the menu.

Allergic Depression

Allergies just ain't what they used to be.

For many doctors and their patients, allergies mean something much more than just sneezing, wheezing, or itching whenever the immune system fires off its rockets at a peanut or cat dander. The allergies these people are talking about needn't have anything to do with the immune system. And instead of making you scratchy, they can make you weepy. Indeed, they can make you almost anything at all: achy, arthritic, depressed, psychotic, schizophrenic, even suicidal.

Ironically, these newfangled allergies are just what doctors meant more than a century ago when they coined the term *allergy* to signify any altered or abnormal (*allos*) physiological reaction (*ergon*) to any material. Allergy simply meant *x* doesn't agree with person *y*. Today, allergists who subscribe to this view call themselves clinical ecologists or specialists in environmental medicine. They and like-minded practitioners, including most orthomolecular psychiatrists, naturopaths, and herbalists, reject the narrow, orthodox definition of allergy as a necessarily immunologic reaction, almost always triggered by a protein and confined to the skin, the respiratory system, or the digestive tract.

Clinical ecologists maintain that almost any kind of chemical can trigger an allergy anywhere in the body, including the brain, with or without the immune system. Orthodox allergists and toxicologists also recognize nonimmunologic allergies. But they call them adverse food reactions, intolerances, or idiosyncratic toxic or pharmacologic reactions, and unlike clinical ecologists, they consider such reactions, especially the psychobehavioral ones, to be rare. So they rarely look for them.

Clinical ecologists have a special name for the allergies they consider a common cause of mental or neurologic symptoms: *cerebral allergies*, or *brain allergies*.

Brain Allergies

For nearly a hundred years, medical journals have attested to the existence of what most doctors still regard as myth: brain allergies.

"Allergies of the nervous system," wrote Kay Hall in a lengthy 1976 review in *Annals of Allergy*, the journal of the American College of Allergists, "cause diverse behavioral disturbances, including headaches, convulsions, learning disabilities, schizophrenia, and depression."

The case for brain allergies has been strengthened in the past twenty years by a growing number of double-blind, placebo-controlled trials. These have been published in major peer-reviewed medical journals by mainstream investigators from the University of Texas El Paso, the University of Chicago Medical Center, the University of Munchen in Germany, and the Royal Children's Hospital in Victoria, Australia, among other centers.

Judging by these studies, hidden food allergies seem to be a common cause of attention deficit hyperactivity disorder (ADHD) and other behavioral disorders in children and of migraine headaches in people of all ages. They may also be an occasional or frequent causative factor in epilepsy, schizophrenia, and depression.

Yet most authorities have ignored or minimized these studies, dismissing brain allergies as "an epidemic of nonsense," as Stanford's Abba Terr put it in 1987. But other academics, including Iris Bell of the University of Arizona, Norman Rosenthal of NIMH, and Paul S. Marshall of the Hennepin County Medical Center in Minneapolis, have been mildly to markedly impressed.

Jonathan Brostoff, a textbook authority on allergy and immunology from Middlesex Hospital Medical School, has little doubt that food intolerances "can *sometimes* be at the root of serious mental illness." He cites an elderly woman with a long history of depression and gastrointestinal symptoms. An elimination diet revealed that milk was her nemesis. Two years later, she was still symptom-free on a milk-free diet. The casebooks of clinical ecologists like the late Theron Randolph and orthomolecular psychiatrists like William Philpott and Abram Hoffer are filled with such examples.

Some authoritries have been more than just impressed. When James C. Breneman, then chairman of the Food Allergy Committee of the American College of Allergists, revised his textbook on food allergy in 1984, he declared brain allergy to be a common cause of everything from poor concentration and neurosis to epilepsy and schizophrenia.

The Depression Link

Depression is one of the most commonly noted symptoms of brain allergy. "When one is relieved, so is the other," observes Abram Hoffer. "Treatment of the allergy will, in most cases, 'cure' the depression. I have seen this in several hundred patients over the past six years and can no longer doubt this conclusion."

At the Deaconess Hospital in St. Louis, psychiatrist George Ulett reports that severe, suicidal depression is one of "the myriad symptoms" he has found in food-allergic patients. "Such patients as these," he observes, "have improved markedly on diets eliminating those foods to which they reacted positively."

Controlled research has tended to support these observations.

⊁ As noted independently by Iris Bell and Paul Marshall, studies have consistently found an abnormally high rate of atopic (conventional immunologic) allergy among depressives. In a study by A. Arthur Sugerman et al., depressed patients had four and a half times as many antibody reactions to thirty-three foods and inhalants as normal subjects. "Perhaps removing egg white, milk, and cereal grains from their diets [the most common allergens] would prove to be an inexpensive way to initiate treatment for depressives," the researchers concluded.

⊁ In a double-blind study, C. Keith Conners, a leading authority on ADHD, provoked mental and behavioral symptoms in nine out of ten adults with capsules of foods to which they had tested allergic. Placebo capsules had no effect.

⊁ In a similar study, David S. King of the University of California gave thirty psychiatric patients sublingual (under the tongue) extracts of foods to which they had been diagnosed allergic at a clinical ecology clinic. The patients had significantly more adverse psychological reactions, including severe depression, after the foods than after placebos. Later, those who followed the clinical ecology prescription fared better than those who didn't. The "blindness" of King's study, however, has been questioned.

There have been very few negative studies. In one by Don L. Jewett and associates, eighteen patients, some of them depressed, reacted no more to injections of their supposed allergens than to placebo shots. The shots were even administered double-blind by their own clinical ecologists. However, as reported by Peter Radetsky, David King has questioned the study's methodology.

Why do depression and allergy seem so often to go together? In a lengthy paper on the subject, Paul Marshall cites evidence that the two conditions share a common neurotransmitter imbalance: too much acetylcholine, not enough norepinephrine. Acetylcholine is a downer in excess, while norepinephrine is a major feel-good neurotransmitter. Lowering acetylcholine and boosting norepinephrine are two of the major effects of many antidepressant drugs. Depression and allergy each independently stimulates this neurotransmitter imbalance, Marshall hypothesizes, thereby feeding each other in a vicious cycle.

How Food Can Depress: Some Clues

About twenty years ago, scientists made a startling discovery. Milk, wheat, and probably other commonly eaten foods contain proteins which, when broken down in the gut, yield small amino acid chains, or polypeptides, that are more or less identical to the body's own morphinelike *endorphins*. They labeled these compounds *exorphins*.

It was as if people could get a shot of morphine from a glass of milk or a bagel—with one important qualification: There was little evidence that, in people with normally functioning digestive systems, these large molecules wouldn't simply be broken down into their component amino acids before they could be absorbed.

But scientists had also found that some people have a "leaky gut." Their intestines are damaged in such a way (by alcohol, aspirin, celiac disease, among other causes) that they become abnormally permeable to large molecules, like exorphins. In a paper published in the *British Journal of Psychiatry* in 1987, fully eleven out of thirty-two chronic psychiatric inpatients proved to have such a gut.

"The findings of this study," N. C. Wood and his associates wrote, "are consistent with the hypothesis that a proportion of patients with chronic psychiatric illness, including schizophrenia, have abnormal small intestinal mucosal permeability, resulting in an increased absorption of endorphinlike molecules from the intestine, which induce behavioural abnormalities . . ."

Does this mean that a leaky gut allows some depressives to "self-medicate" with the exorphins in milk or wheat? Do they become addicted, suffering withdrawal symptoms when deprived of these comfort foods? Would some exorphins bind with endorphin receptors in the brain *without activating them*, thereby acting as mood-lowering endorphin antagonists? Could a leaky gut make some people depressed by admitting other large, psychotoxic molecules?

All we can say is that for people with leaky guts, some foods may be like mood-altering drugs that make them feel worse, not better, if not sooner, then later.

The most conspicuous sufferers of leaky gut are people with celiac disease. For the small number of victims of this inborn error of metabolism, the delicate absorptive lining of their small intestine is attacked by a polypeptide called *alpha-gliadin*, found in the type of gluten (a protein) that occurs in wheat and most other cereal grains. Not only does this give celiacs an extraordinarily leaky gut; but adding insult to injury, it grossly impairs their ability to absorb desirable nutrients.

Gastrointestinal symptoms like diarrhea, constipation, and flatulence assail celiac patients who don't avoid the offending grains. So do psychiatric symptoms, particularly depression.

Celiac disease often goes undiagnosed until well into adulthood. For example, L. Corvaglia and associates from the University of Bologna discovered three undiagnosed cases of celiac disease among the parents of their pediatric celiac patients. None of these adults had any notable GI symptoms, but all were persistently depressed. "In all three patients," Corvaglia et al. wrote, "the depressive symptoms improved quickly with a gluten-free diet."

In celiacs diagnosed years after the damage has begun, gluten avoidance alone is not always enough to restore their health. The depressed adult celiacs in a study by C. Hallert et al. only perked up when a daily megadose of vitamin B_6 (80 milligrams) was added to their regime. They may well have become B_6-dependent. Indeed, according to Lloyd Rosenvold, M.D., for some celiacs the damage is so bad they require routine injections of some nutrients.

Rosenvold is one of a number of experts who believe that for every person with celiac disease, there are many walking wounded with milder forms of the illness or with gluten intolerance. Similarly, M. Goggins and D. Kelleher of Trinity College in Dublin note, "recent data suggest that there is an extended spectrum of gluten sensitivity that includes first-degree relatives [of people with celiac disease] and patients with latent celiac disease." Rosenvold believes all depressives should wonder if gluten is bringing them down.

It would be a very simple world if there were only one food chemical that people couldn't tolerate. Recently, M. Ledochowski and associates from the University of Innsbruck in Austria identified two more potentially depressing culprits. They had already observed that women with lactose intolerance—a bloaty, indigestive reaction to milk sugar— also tend to suffer from PMS or depression. When they tested thirty normal women, they found that those who had lactose intolerance (20 percent) suffered significantly more symptoms of depression than those who didn't. All that undigested lactose, Ledochowski et al. speculated, might be promoting depression by interfering with tryptophan absorption—and therefore the synthesis of serene serotonin in the brain.

In another study, Ledochowski et al. found much the same problem with fructose (fruit sugar). Men and (especially) women whose chronic gastrointestinal symptoms were found, by lab testing, to be caused by fructose malabsorption were significantly more depressed than those who tested negative. Though their findings were preliminary, Ledochowski et al. suggest that lactose or fructose malabsorption should be investigated as a posssible cause in anyone who suffers both from gastrointestinal symptoms and depression or PMS.

Clinical ecologists cast a much wider net. Foods contain thousands of chemicals, natural and synthetic, that most people have no trouble absorbing. And therein lies the problem. For some people, some of these chemicals may be depressing news.

Food Additives and Pesticide Residues

Not just foods, but food chemicals—additives, pesticide residues—can cause brain allergies in sensitive people.

The allergist Benjamin Feingold first brought this to public attention in the 1970s. His additive-free diet for hyperactive children was roundly condemned by medical authorities and gave the food industry severe heartburn. But careful research has gradually led many independent experts to concede that some children with ADHD or other behavioral disorders do react to additives in their foods. Most recently, in October 1999, Michael Jacobson and David Schardt of the Center for Science in the Public Interest published a major review of the literature on diet and behavior disorders in children. They reported that seventeen out of twenty-three controlled studies "found evidence that some children's behavior significantly worsens after they consume artificial colors or certain foods, such as milk or wheat." Some of the studies suggested a majority of ADHD children are affected. The report was endorsed by several academic experts on ADHD who joined CSPI in writing to Donna Shalala, Secretary of the U.S. Department of Health and Human Services, to urge her to encourage parents of children with behavior disorders—and health-care professionals—to look for dietary causes before resorting to drugs.

Benjamin Feingold claimed that adults can react psychologically to food colorings too. Clinical ecologists concur, also implicating pesticide residues. A patient of Theron Randolph's "became depressed for days whenever she ate commercially available oranges." No such problem with organic ones.

In his book *Diet for a Poisoned Planet*, David Steinman lists the pesticide residues in hundreds of foods and suggests ways to devise a low-pesticide diet. "Once you follow these instructions," advises EPA senior science advisor William Marcus in the foreword, "feelings of tiredness and lack of clarity of thought will diminish and feelings of general well-being will return once again."

Do You Have Allergic Depression?

Clinical ecologists believe most people suffer from food or chemical allergies, with depressives particularly hard-hit. (Theron Randolph was convinced that most cases of bipolar disorder are also allergy-driven.) Some things, they say, should make you very suspicious.

➴ A history of old-fashioned atopic allergy (e.g., hayfever, allergic asthma, or eczema).

➴ Symptoms highly suggestive of allergy: dark circles under the eyes ("allergic shiners"); large daily weight fluctuations from water retention; fluctuating visual acuity. Also suggestive: fatigue and mental fogginess, especially in the morning; tension or irritability, possibly alternating with fatigue and depression (you may have outgrown this "tension-fatigue syndrome" in childhood and graduated to bipolar disorder); extreme sensitivity to noise, light, heat, or cold; multiple aches and pains; spells of hyperarousal (e.g., palpitations, sweating, trembling).

➴ Addiction to foods or other substances. Clinical ecologists and some mainstream researchers, like John Crayton and E. C. Hughes et al., find that addictive eating suggests allergy is afoot. The craved foods or drugs (tobacco, coffee, alcohol) relieve the very symptoms they later provoke. Addictive allergies to commonly eaten foods like wheat, milk, and chocolate seem to account for most brain allergies.

Diagnosing Allergy

Clinical ecologists employ a variety of techniques to diagnose allergy. These include sublingual or intradermal (under the skin) provocation with suspected allergens, muscle testing, pulse testing, and lab tests (RAST, DIMSOFT, cytotoxic testing). (Traditional skin-patch testing is considered too insensitive.) Most of these techniques are controversial and unproven.

Naturopath Michael Murray prefers blood tests that measure the antibodies IgE and IgG. He uses a food allergy panel from Meridian Valley Clinical Laboratory ([206] 859-8700), which tests for more than a hundred foods. However, IgE and IgG are strictly indicative of immunological allergies, which account for many, but not all, allergies.

At least one diagnostic technique is regarded highly by clinical ecologists and conventional allergists alike: *avoidance and provocation*.

Avoidance and provocation. The principle is simple: If you avoid a food (or any other suspected allergen) for a few days or weeks and your symptoms improve, only to return when you eat the food again, you're probably allergic to it.

Because most allergic people are intolerant of many foods, avoidance testing usually involves going on an elimination diet (no common food allergens allowed), a hypoallergenic liquid diet such as Vivonex, or a complete fast. Common environmental allergens like natural gas and perfumes may also be avoided.

At first, people with allergies typically go through withdrawal, marked by cravings and symptomatic flare-ups. Some depressives even become suicidal. But after four to seven days (seldom longer), most feel better, and some feel better than ever.

Avoided foods are now reintroduced, one per meal or one per day. Because avoidance has "cleared the person's system," her sensitivity to avoided allergens is now dramatically heightened. A person who says he "never felt better" after a week off milk or eggs may find, when he eats them again, that he "never felt worse." (A stiff dose of baking soda or vitamin C or B_6, clinical ecologists say, can relieve these overreactions.)

Treatment

Avoiding the enemy. The simplest treatment is to avoid the enemy. Unfortunately, most people with brain allergies are at odds with a whole cupboardful of foods, most of them staples or cherished favorites like wheat, milk, eggs, sugar, chocolate, tea, coffee, and common food additives. Familiarity breeds allergy. Fortunately, prolonged avoidance can breed renewed tolerance.

After a few months, clinical ecologists report, people can usually reintroduce allergenic foods into their diets without ill effect—provided they don't get too familiar again. Enter the *rotary diversified diet*. A staple of clinical ecology, it prohibits eating any food more than once every four days or eating members of the same food family (like potatoes and tomatoes) more than once every two days.

Avoiding the enemy isn't the only strategy. You also can fight it.

Neutralization therapy. Clinical ecologists report that just as they can turn allergic reactions on with sublingual drops or shots, they usually can turn them off with highly dilute—almost homeopathic—doses of the very same allergens. When their patients take these diluted allergens regularly, clinical ecologists claim, their tolerance for the foods is usually vastly improved. A few studies, like the one by Jewett et al., cast serious doubt on these claims. But in a 1992 double-blind, placebo-controlled study by Egger et al., bimonthly injections of diluted allergens (mixed with a digestive enzyme) did enable sixteen out of twenty hyperactive children to tolerate their food allergens without relapse.

Allergy-busting supplements. In megadoses, certain nutrients can help prevent or relieve allergic reactions, claim clinical ecologists and like-minded doctors. The major ones are niacin, vitamin B_6, omega-3 fatty acids, and (especially) vitamin C. Others include vitamin B_5, methionine, calcium, free-form amino acids, and lithium. Interestingly, most of these nutrients can be antidepressants too.

Treating underlying disorders. Allergic reactivity is promoted by a variety of factors, many of them treatable. We've already met "leaky gut." It's promoted by emotional distress, certain drugs (like alcohol and aspirin), celiac disease, and intestinal overgrowth of gut-damaging microbes, like *Candida* and *Giardia*.

Other promoters of allergy include a trigger-happy immune system; indigestion and malabsorption; nutritional deficiency; genetic flaws, such as those responsible for lactose intolerance and celiac disease; alcohol abuse; diabetes; hypothyroidism; liver disease; febrile illnesses; emotional distress; and possibly mercury-amalgam dental fillings, menstruation, and too much fluorescent light.

As with reactive hypoglycemia, brain allergy appears to bear a "reciprocausal" (to coin a term) relationship with emotional distress. When emotional distress spreads its shock waves through the body, the digestive and immune systems, which are on the front lines of resistance to potential allergens, are not spared. The flip side of the equation is illustrated by a study from the University of Auckland by T. M. Laidlaw and associates. When seven healthy subjects were repeatedly exposed to skin allergens, the sizes of their weals varied widely. Mood, it turned out, had a lot to do with it. "The more lively the subject felt," the researchers wrote, "the smaller was the allergic response."

So "change your mind and you may change your allergies." In a study by psychiatrist Donna E. Stewart (an outspoken critic of clinical ecology), people who attributed their psychiatric symptoms to multiple allergies responded to psychotherapy instead. Similarly, hypnotherapy has been reported by Emmett Miller and others to help some people decondition their trigger-happy immune systems. It would be callous to automatically "psychologize" the challenge that severely allergic people face, but the power of suggestion should not be underestimated.

Getting Help

The following organizations can help you find a qualified practitioner of clinical ecology:

American Academy of Environmental Medicine
ph: (316) 684-5500
fax: (316) 684-5709
www.healthy.net/aaem/

Human Ecology Action League (HEAL)
ph: (404) 248-1898
fax: (404) 248-0162

Part 2

———— ✿ ————

Food for Good Thoughts: Healing Moods with Diet and Supplements

Health nuts have been proclaiming it for generations, but only recently has the medical mainstream joined the chorus:

When it comes to preventing and even treating disease, diet makes a difference. A really big difference. And as we've already seen in chapter 4, that also goes for mood disorders.

Of all the influences in our lives, nothing affects us so intimately, materially, and continuously as food. Our umbilical cord to Mother Earth, food (and water) supplies us with all the energy and raw materials (except oxygen) we need to continually repair and rebuild ourselves—from nephrons to neurons.

In the next eight chapters we'll see how the good things in food— the vitamins and other nutrients and natural chemicals—can, if we don't get enough of them, make us vulnerable to mood disorders. And we'll see how extra helpings of many of these substances can do just the opposite. We'll also see how too much of certain foods or food constituents, or other questionable eating habits, can upset our moods. Finally, chapter 11 will provide detailed guidance on using nutritional supplements safely and effectively.

Above all, we'll see how returning to a healthy, balanced way of eating is one of the most important foundations we can lay for mental health.

CHAPTER 5

The Orthomolecular Approach to Depression

O rthomolecular psychiatry is the Rodney Dangerfield of modern psychiatry. It gets no respect, even as its fundamentals become more and more a part of the mainstream. Thyroid, estrogen, and other hormones; SAMe, tryptophan, 5-HTP, and omega-3 fatty acids are all commonly prescribed or seriously investigated orthomolecular psychiatric treatments. Yet hardly anyone dares call them "orthomolecular." They're more likely to be classed with all the other "drugs," from Prozac to Paxil.

To orthomolecular psychiatrists and their late, great mentor, the Nobel Laureate chemist Linus Pauling, there is a world of difference. At the heart of orthomolecular psychiatry is a concept Pauling elucidated in 1968 in the prestigious journal *Science*: A promising way to treat mental illness is to ensure that the brain is supplied with an optimal (ortho) concentration of the nutrients or other natural substances (molecular) it needs for its normal functioning. And for some people,"ortho" may be very different from what it is for others.

Orthomolecular theory clashes with the traditional medical view that people with psychiatric conditions have the same nutritional needs as everyone else, needs that can be met by an ordinary diet. At most, the status quo goes, a recommended daily allowance (RDA) multivitamin and mineral supplement on the side should be all they need to get all the nutrients they need.

The orthomolecular view is not so complacent. Even the most nutritious diet, it contends, can fail to meet the extraordinary nutritional needs many psychiatric patients are likely to have. Often, even an RDA supplement won't do.

The evidence for the orthomolecular approach is more scientific than most doctors would suppose. Formerly known as *megavitamin therapy* until Pauling reconceptualized it in 1968, orthomolecular psychiatry evolved in the 1950s and '60s in a skeptical and hostile medical climate. A withering task-force report from the American Psychiatric Association in 1973 all but relegated the movement to leper status.

In the lingering chill, the cornerstone of orthomolecular therapy—megadoses of vitamin B_3—continue, to this day, to be ostracized by mainstream psychiatry. But other nutrients and biochemicals have proven less untouchable. Little by little, an independent body of scientific research supporting orthomolecular psychiatry—by any other name—has grown. That research, and the studies and clinical experience of orthomolecular psychiatrists themselves, is the stuff of which the next seven chapters are made.

But first (and you have my permission to skip the rest of this chapter if you're not in the mood for dry stuff), I'd like to enumerate some of the key reasons, as currently understood, why we stand to gain so much from nutritional supplements when we're depressed.

Many—perhaps most—depressed persons have subclinical nutritional deficiencies.

When a person has low blood levels of a nutrient or other laboratory signs of deficiency, but no specific "clinical" (physical) signs or symptoms, he is said to have a subclinical deficiency. Researchers have consistently found subclinical deficiencies of nutrients required for maintaining normal mood in an abnormally high percentage of depressed patients. A growing number of mainstream authorities, such as Richard Brown and Teodoro Bottiglieri of Columbia University and Baylor University, respectively (authors of *Stop Depression Now*), and Simon Young of McGill University, suspect such deficiencies are a commonly overlooked cause of depression, treatment resistance, or relapse in recovered depressives.

Some depressives may need certain nutrients in quantities much greater than any diet can provide.

It's medically well recognized, but little known to the general public, that some people have genetic defects that grossly exaggerate their need for certain nutrients. Typically, these vitamin dependencies (also known as *vitamin-responsive genetic abnormalities*) announce themselves with a bang in infancy or early childhood through seizures, mental retardation, or other severe symptoms. Megadoses of the needed vitamin are the medically accepted cure.

Orthomolecular psychiatrists suspect that milder vitamin dependencies underlie the mental disorders of many adults. Christopher Reading, who has studied the nutritional status of four thousand patients, reports that some have been unable to maintain normal blood levels of certain vitamins without taking supplements that are hundreds of times the RDA. One of Reading's schizophrenic patients was borderline deficient in vitamin B_3 even while taking 3 grams a day, or about 150 to 200 times the RDA. Many patients need much higher doses still to bring their blood levels well above normal before they feel better.

Mainstream research contains many hints and traces of support for the orthomolecular view of nutritional dependency. For Harvey Mudd of the National Institute of Mental Health, the existence of vitamin-responsive genetic abnormalities is food for orthomolecular thought. It "raise[s] the question of whether there is, properly speaking, a 'normal' requirement for a vitamin or whether the patients [with vitamin-responsive genetic abnormalities] do not represent merely the extremes on a broad distribution curve of the vitamin requirements of individuals within the population," Mudd writes. This is one of the cornerstones of orthomolecular psychiatry.

Some depressed people, despite having adequate diets and negative test results for nutritional deficiencies, may have* hidden *deficiencies.
It's possible to have normal nutrient levels in your food and in your blood, yet still be suffering from a depressing nutritional deficiency if the levels in your brain are low.

Nutrients have to run a gauntlet of hoops and hurdles before they get to the brain:

✕ First they must be absorbed from the digestive tract. Disturbed digestion, parasites, and certain drugs, microorganisms, and genetic diseases can prevent us from absorbing all the nutrients we need. The cholesterol-lowering drug cholestyramine, for instance, interferes with the absorption of the B vitamin folic acid. Folic acid deficiency is very strongly implicated as a cause of depression. Patients on long-term therapy with cholestyramine have an inexplicably high rate of death by suicide and "accident."

❧ Once absorbed into the bloodstream, many nutrients must attach themselves to special molecules that carry them to the tissues. Sometimes, explains Mudd, when these carrier molecules are genetically defective in form or deficient in quantity, therapeutic megadoses of the vitamins they're meant to carry can compensate. This, for example, is the case for people who have a deficiency of *transcobalamin II*, the carrier for vitamin B_{12}. Orthomolecular psychiatrists suspect such defects also account for many of their own patients' responses to megadoses of B_{12} and other vitamins.

❧ Many nutrients are useless until they've been converted in the body into their metabolically active form(s). Inadequate conversion is another cause of vitamin dependency. And again, huge doses of the unconverted vitamin sometimes overcome the limitation. Conversion defects also show up in many psychiatric patients examined by orthomolecular (Abbey) and mainstream researchers (Smithies et al.) alike. In depressives, the conversion of the amino acid methionine into the more bioactive *s-adenosylmethionine*, better known as *SAMe*, has been shown by J. R. Smithies and associates to be sluggish. As we'll see, SAMe is one of the most successful natural antidepressants. Yet large doses of methionine also seem effective, probably compensating for the conversion slowdown.

❧ The brain is very fussy about what it picks up from the bloodstream. Its blood-brain barrier (BBB) ensures that even many nutrients have a hard time getting through en masse without a lift from carrier molecules.

In 1968, in his seminal paper on orthomolecular psychiatry, Linus Pauling hypothesized that faulty transport of nutrients or other biochemicals across the BBB could result in "localized cerebral [brain] deficiencies." Such deficiencies, Pauling wrote, could be a cryptic cause of mental illness. Megadoses of the missing nutrients might overcome the bottleneck.

Mainstream psychiatrists were quick to remind Pauling that he'd won his Nobel Prize in chemistry, not medicine. But subsequent research has added weight to Pauling's case. Low nutrient levels in the cerebrospinal fluid (an indirect measure of brain levels), despite normal levels in the blood, have been reported in people with

Alzheimer's disease, AIDS, postpartum and toxic depression, and other conditions. Large doses of the missing nutrients have, in preliminary reports, been reported beneficial. (See, for example, Frenkel et al., Ikeda et al., and van Tiggelen et al.)

In 1990, Iris Bell and her associates at Harvard Medical School speculated that in elderly psychiatric patients "low normal peripheral blood vitamin levels might . . . coexist with deficient CNS [central nervous system] levels." Recently, studies by Sullivan and others have also implicated a deficiency of thyroid hormone restricted to the brain as a cause of depression and rapid-cycling disorder.

In large or megadoses, some nutrients can be antidotes to depressing chemicals or mitigate depressive allergic reactions.
Vitamin C excels here, helping the liver detoxify a panoply of neurotoxins, "chelating" (grabbing up) many depressing heavy metals and carrying them away in the urine, and attenuating some allergic reactions with its anti-inflammatory effect. A generous intake of essential minerals like calcium, magnesium, and zinc blocks neurotoxic heavy metals at absorption sites in the gut and at enzyme sites throughout the body where the heavy metals are wont to impersonate the essential minerals, with adverse results.

Nutritional supplements can compensate for heavy nutrient losses caused by chronic stress.
In 1986, psychiatrists M. T. Abou-Saleh and Alec Coppen of the Medical Research Council in Britain put forward "a nutritional deficiency model for the psychoses." With a respectful nod to the orthomolecular trailblazers, the two suggested that stressed-out people may be depleting themselves of adaptive neurochemicals and the nutrients they need to make them. Such deficiencies might then "predispose, provoke, promote or aggravate psychiatric illness such as depression."

Nutritional supplements may compensate for the dysfunctions of defective or deficient enzymes.
Every one of our bodily processes is catalyzed by enzymes. We have about fifty thousand of these complex, genetically coded proteins. Increasingly, scientists are discovering that gene-enzyme defects or

deficiencies are a major risk factor for cancer, cardiovascular disease, and many, if not all other human maladies, including mood disorders.

Typically, these dysfunctional genetic variations or mutations are clinically less than obvious—invisible, in fact, to the naked medical eye. As Linus Pauling noted in *How to Live Longer and Feel Better*, "it is harder to recognize a mild genetic disease than a serious one, but the mild genetic diseases may in the aggregate cause more suffering than the serious ones, because so many more people suffer from them."

There's a nutritional connection here. Most enzymes are useless until they've bonded with specific vitamin-derived coenzymes and (often) mineral cofactors. This has enormous clinical potential. As the vitamin dependency diseases have shown, large doses of coenzyme precursors (i.e., vitamins) can make up for the flaws of certain genetically defective enzymes. Orthomolecular theorists also believe that some faulty enzymes can be compensated for by providing them with a surplus of the nutrients they are supposed to metabolize into other biochemicals. Dietary amino acids, for example, are enzymatically metabolized into major mood-regulating neurotransmitters like serotonin and norepinephrine. The enzymes that perform this function are the ones most highly suspected by biological psychiatrists of being genetically defective in people with depression and other mood disorders. Vitamins, minerals, amino acids, essential fatty acids, and other nutrients that can potentially compensate for these gene-enzyme defects are among the most important natural antidepressants.

In megadoses, some nutrients could have druglike *antidepressant effects, above and beyond their normal physiological functions.*
Megadoses of niacinamide (a form of vitamin B_3), for instance, have Valiumlike effects in the brain, according to a study by Möhler et al. published in 1979 in *Nature*. Megadoses of vitamin B_1 may be monoamine oxidase inhibitors, like several major antidepressant drugs.

The relationship between nutrition and mental health is as complex as it is rich with possibilities. It's now time to explore those possibilities.

CHAPTER 6

Vitamin Power

In his book, *The Good News About Depression*, psychiatrist Mark Gold tells about a woman who began to wonder if her depression might be due to a vitamin deficiency. When she asked her psychiatrist, he just paused in that invisible rolling of the eyes kind of way. Finally, he offered an interpretation: She was just looking for an out from the "real work" of her therapy. The woman did indeed have a deficiency of vitamin B_6. "With treatment," writes Gold, "her longtime depression lifted substantially."

Vitamins comprise only a tiny portion of the food we eat. We swallow no more than a few milligrams of most each day. But deprive us of even one of these micronutrients and we would sicken and die a slow and horrible death.

We need these essential nutrients we cannot make ourselves primarily because they help catalyze our myriad bodily processes—including those that keep our brains in gear. Some vitamins seem to contribute to mood stability more than others—even to be natural antidepressants.

Vitamin B_1 (Thiamin): The Energy Vitamin

The brain depends on the energy of blood sugar as no other organ does. Yet without vitamin B_1, that sugar might as well be sawdust.

B_1—"the energy vitamin"—is a key coenzyme for burning (oxidizing) glucose (blood sugar), and fats and amino acids too. People who become deficient in B_1—and studies suggest about a third of depressed persons are at least mildly so—tend to become nervous wrecks: anxious, fearful, irritable, exhausted, depressed—even suicidal.

It's easy to become B_1-deficient if you swallow a lot of empty calories, especially sugar and other refined carbohydrates, or if you drink too much alcohol or caffeine. Refined carbohydrates are broken down into glucose, but they lack the B_1 required to burn it. In a 1980 study by Derrick Lonsdale and Raymond Shamberger, twelve out of twenty mildly B_1-deficient psychiatric patients were guilty of these very food sins. When all twenty were given B_1 supplements and told to follow a diet low in refined carbohydrates, their mild beriberilike symptoms (beriberi is the classic form of B_1-deficiency), such as chronic fatigue, chest and stomach pains, indigestion, difficulty sleeping, and personality problems, gradually faded or disappeared. More recently, B_1 also improved mood and energy in young women with normal B_1 levels, compared to placebo (Benton 1997).

In megadoses, B_1 is regarded by orthomolecular psychiatrists like Abram Hoffer (1987), Herbert Newbold, and Priscilla Slagle as a speed-like stimulant that can, as Newbold puts it, help some people "raise themselves out of the valley of depression."

These responses likely involve more than glucose metabolism. A 1981 study by D. J. Connor suggests moderate inhibition (40 percent) by megadoses of B_1 of the enzyme *monoamine oxidase* (MAO) could be involved. MAO breaks down mood-lifting neurotransmitters, which is why inhibiting it strongly by 80 to 90 percent is the presumed *modus operandi* of some of the most powerful antidepressant drugs, the MAO inhibitors (MAOIs). An observation by Eric Braverman and associates that megadoses of B_1 sometimes raise blood pressure—a side effect of MAOIs when mixed with certain foods or medications—confirms that B_1 may be an MAOI. If so, B_1, like other MAOIs, may be particularly effective for people with atypical depression.

Vitamin B_3 (Niacin, Niacinamide, NAD, NADH): Orthomolecular Psychiatry's Main Course

If orthomolecular psychiatry has a cradle, the baby in the cradle is vitamin B_3.

In the late 1930s and 1940s, a few pioneering psychiatrists began to experiment with B_3 as a treatment for mental illness. They had good reason to. In 1937, one of the world's direst diseases—pellagra—had yielded its secret: It was caused by a simple deficiency of vitamin B_3 or its precursor, tryptophan.

Could it be, these psychiatrists wondered, that people who suffer from pellagralike neuropsychiatric symptoms—depression, psychosis, dementia—might also benefit from B_3, perhaps (as some pellagrins required) in super-high doses? The answer, several of them reported, was yes.

In the 1950s and 1960s, researchers led by Canadian psychiatrists Abram Hoffer and Humphry Osmond picked up the ball. They published several successful placebo-controlled clinical studies of megavitamin therapy with B_3 for acute schizophrenics, laying the groundwork for orthomolecular psychiatry. But by the early 1970s, their research was repudiated by the psychiatric establishment, almost entirely on the basis of several failed trials of B_3 for chronic schizophrenics.

There is a depression connection here. One of the most credible independent clinical trials of niacin for schizophrenia suggested that nonchronic schizophrenics of a particularly retarded depressive bent have the most to gain from the vitamin. In that two-year study, sponsored by the National Institute of Mental Health, a small subgroup of patients who fit the above description fared twice as well on niacin as they did on placebo as an adjunct to antipsychotic drugs. Patients with "a history of a cyclothymic disposition" also fared much better on niacin than placebo, Richard Wittenborn and associates noted in 1974.

This wasn't the first hint that niacin is an antidepressant. In the early fifties, several researchers had tested megadoses of niacin as an antidepressant, with mostly favorable results. In a 1950 study by Annette Washburne, all but one of fifteen highly retarded, lethargic, and withdrawn depressives (including a few schizophrenics) improved within just three to five days on 500 to 2,500 milligrams per day of niacin, with routine psychotherapy. Most enjoyed dramatic relief or complete remission. The patients, Washburne noted, "stressed a lifting or lightening of the depression, improvement in the speed of thinking, increase in and desire for social activity, and a return of work interest." Much later, eleven suffered another episode of depression, and again responded to B_3.

In contrast, a small study three years later by W. L. Tonge found niacin no better than placebo. But Tonge's maximum dosage was

900 milligrams per day, while Washburne's was 2,500 milligrams (the average orthomolecular dosage is 3,000 milligrams). Tonge observed that the older patients in his study accounted for all seven of the niacin nonresponders. Washburne's patients had been young.

Like other orthomolecular psychiatrists, Abram Hoffer is convinced niacin is an antidepressant. He says it has a special synergy with another, chemically related natural antidepressant: tryptophan. "I find that the combination of niacin and tryptophan works really well," Hoffer told me in 1999, "especially for cases who cannot tolerate [antidepressant] drugs. This combination also increases serotonin levels, but it does much more."

"Vitamin B_3," writes Herbert Newbold, "has proved to be a most useful weapon in the fight against severe emotional disorders and it can be of great benefit to many other people who are nervous, tired, depressed, or mildly overwrought."

Among niacin's greatest beneficiaries, orthomolecular psychiatrists claim, are:

➺ *Alcoholics.* The most famous case was Bill W., the founder of Alcoholics Anonymous and a friend of Hoffer's. According to Hoffer, Bill W. shed his lifelong nervous tension within weeks of beginning niacin therapy in 1960.

John Cleary, M.D., believes niacin "is an effective, inexpensive, and rapid correction of the metabolic disorder which we label alcoholism," and, along with its coenzyme derivative, NAD (see sidebar on page 85), helpful for other forms of drug abuse too.

➺ *Post-traumatic stress sufferers.* Hoffer believes that survivors of severe, chronic malnutrition can acquire a B_3 dependency—an exaggerated need for the vitamin—that only megadoses can cure. In *Common Questions on Schizophrenia and Their Answers*, he reports outstanding results treating in this way the residual symptoms of concentration camp survivors and World War II veterans of brutal Hong Kong prison camps, including a former lieutenant governor of Saskatchewan.

➺ *The senile.* Niacin seems to have a special affinity for the aging and elderly (notwithstanding Tonge's study). "Megadoses of niacin most often give a lift and a feeling of buoyancy to older people," writes Newbold. Niacin and some of its derivatives have performed like

NADH: A Better Kind of Niacin?

Like other vitamins, niacin is the precursor to a biologically more active compound, a coenzyme called *nicotinamide adenine dinucleotide*, or NAD. Over the years, Hoffer and others have reported powerful psychiatric benefits from NAD, but others have reported no effects at all. Likely, these inconsistencies occur because NAD is an extremely unstable compound, easily destroyed in the stomach. But NADH—a recently patented form of NAD (proprietary name: ENADA)— isn't.

"I suspect that in many cases it [NADH] will be better than niacin," says Hoffer. "I'm convinced it will become par for the course in alleviating depression, fatigue, and even minor mental sluggishness," adds Robert Atkins, M.D. "The vast majority of my patients have enjoyed a significant boost in vigor," Atkins comments—as long as they take a high enough dosage of this expensive supplement.

Over the last decade or so, several clinical trials have suggested that NADH can be beneficial for several neurological and psychiatric conditions, notably Parkinson's and Alzheimer's disease. Most recently, in a well-controlled pilot study from Georgetown University School of Medicine by Linda Forsyth and associates, a month on NADH (ENADA, 10 milligrams per day) helped four times as many patients with chronic fatigue syndrome as placebo. When the double-blind was broken and all twenty-six patients were put on NADH for a full year, improvement jumped from 31 percent in the original NADH group to 72 percent in all twenty-six—a remarkably high response rate for CFS. Although CFS and depression go together, in this study depressed patients were specifically excluded.

Hard evidence that NADH, which is widely touted as a mood-lifter, is an antidepressant is still lacking. In theory, NADH should at least be an antidepressant adjunct. Together with the B vitamin folic acid, NADH is needed for the synthesis of *tetrahydrobiopterin* (BH_4), which in turn is a key coenzyme for building the brain's major antidepressant neurotransmitters: norepinephrine, serotonin, and dopamine. BH_4 seems to be an antidepressant itself.

Studies showing that NADH excels at boosting dynamic dopamine suggest it holds the most promise for fatigued, retarded, apathetic, or unmotivated depressives.

"smart drugs" in controlled studies, even lessening the symptoms of senile dementia. Anecdotally, in *Nutrients to Age Without Senility*, Hoffer contends that niacin can even stop dementia in its early stages. His own mother was one of his proudest cases.

Vitamin B₆ (Pyridoxine): Healer and More

B$_6$ is yet another vitamin which, in its coenzyme form *(pyridoxal-5-phosphate)*, is absolutely essential for the synthesis of good-mood neurotransmitters, like serotonin, norepinephrine, and GABA. In study after study, low levels of B$_6$ have been found in 10 to 100 percent of clinically depressed persons. In a recent study from the University of Miami School of Medicine, levels of fatigue, depression, and confusion in recently bereaved homosexual men were as high as their B$_6$ levels were low. "Adequate pyridoxine [B$_6$] status," T. Baldewicz et al. concluded, "may be necessary to avert psychological distress in the setting of bereavement." Likely this applies to all stressed-out people.

Few researchers have tested B$_6$ as an antidepressant. Psychiatrist Jonathan Stewart, whose group found low B$_6$ levels in 21 out of 101 depressed patients in 1984, told me he later treated two such patients with B$_6$ for three weeks with no apparent benefit. No luck either for a few depressives made B$_6$-deficient by their MAOI antidepressants. In contrast, M. J. Hoes reported in 1982 that megadoses of B$_6$ and zinc significantly lowered depression and anxiety in depressed patients within four weeks. (The antidepressant response was even better when tryptophan—which we'll meet in chap. 10—was included.) And in a small placebo-controlled study by V. Wynn et al., B$_6$ was highly effective for severe depression in women made B$_6$-deficient by oral contraceptives. Finally, as mentioned earlier in a double-blind trial by Iris Bell et al., a very modest dose of B$_6$, B$_1$, and B$_2$ enhanced the response of elderly depressives to antidepressant drugs.

B$_6$'s greatest claim to fame as an antidepressant comes from roughly two dozen studies of women with premenstrual syndrome (PMS). Recently, nine of the best designed of these trials—all double-blind, randomized, and placebo-controlled, and involving nearly a thousand women—were meta-analyzed by Katrina Wyatt and associates. B$_6$ proved decidedly superior to placebo, both for PMS in general and for premenstrual depression in particular.

Depressives have lots of options besides vitamin B$_6$ to treat their condition. But the choices are not so numerous for people with a depressive type of schizophrenia called *schizoaffective disorder*. According to the late Carl Pfeiffer (an influential pioneer of orthomolecular psychiatry), many schizoaffectives have a metabolic defect that washes their B$_6$ and zinc away in the urine. These so-called "pyrollurics," Pfeiffer wrote in 1975, typically have china doll complexions, white spots on their fingernails, stretch marks, and a hard time remembering their dreams. Though the evidence is purely anecdotal, Pfeiffer and others claim that super-megadoses of B$_6$ (up to thousands of milligrams a day) and zinc often help these usually very helpless people.

Suspect B$_6$ deficiency if you're stressed, depressed, pregnant, or autistic, or if you're using oral contraceptives, estrogen, phenelzine (and perhaps other MAOIs), or theophylline.

Folic Acid (Folate, Folacin): The B Vitamin Depressives Most Often Lack

No nutritional deficiency is as strongly and persuasively linked to depression as folic acid deficiency. In more than a dozen studies, blood or red blood cell levels of this B vitamin have almost always been abnormally low in 15 to 40 percent of depressed persons.

There are good reasons to believe this is neither a coincidence nor an inconsequential side effect of a depressively poor diet:

✦ Folic acid is converted into a coenzyme called *5-methyl-tetrahydrofolate* (5-MTHF, or methylfolate), which helps synthesize the potent natural antidepressant *s-adenosylmethione* (SAMe; see chap. 10) and promotes the synthesis of another good-mood neurochemical called *phosphatidylserine*. 5-MTHF is also needed to synthesize *tetrahydrobiopterin* (BH$_4$), a biochemical that not only helps synthesize the brain's major antidepressant neurotransmitters, but also stimulates their release. BH$_4$ has itself relieved depression in some, but not all, of a few small trials. Combined with the neurotransmitter precursors tyrosine and tryptophan, BH$_4$ brought a "dramatic response" to a man who had been chronically depressed and treatment-resistant for ten years, according to M. T. Abou-Saleh and Alec Coppen.

❧ Studies have repeatedly shown that the lower a depressed person's level of folate, the more depressed she likely is. Melancholic and other endogenous depressives typically tip the bottom of the folate scale. In contrast, depressives endowed with high blood levels of folate (spontaneously or courtesy of supplements) tend to suffer brief depressions and short hospitalizations, and to respond better to antidepressant drugs. In one study, after ninety-nine depressives had been on an antidepressant drug for five weeks, those whose red blood cell levels of folate rose the most enjoyed the most relief from depression. In other studies (e.g., Coppen et al., 1986), recovered depressives and bipolars with high folate levels from their diets or prescribed supplements have usually been much less vulnerable to manic or depressive relapse.

❧ Bipolar disorder also is related to folate status. In a remarkable study by C. I. Hasanah et al., forty-five hospitalized manic patients were found to have red blood cell folate levels that were just 22 percent of those of a matched control group. Yet there was no difference in serum (blood) folate levels between the two groups, suggesting that the blood-cell deficiency resulted from a metabolic failure to transfer the vitamin from blood to tissues. The brain, of course, could be one such tissue.

With such evidence, many distinguished mainstream psychiatrists and neuroscientists have speculated that folic acid could be a key to treating and preventing affective disease. But the clinical evidence so far is scant, though mostly positive. For example:

❧ T. Abou-Saleh and Alec Coppen describe a woman who developed a severe postpartum psychotic depression that responded neither to drugs nor ECT. It turned out she had no measurable levels of folate. Within ten days of treatment with the vitamin she was completely normal.

❧ In the mid-1970s, Canadian researchers led by M. I. Botez identified a subgroup of patients whose antidepressant-resistant chronic fatigue and depression was accompanied by folic acid deficiency. The deficiency, it seemed, was the result of malabsorption due to chronic digestive disorders and abnormal diets. In twenty-four of these patients, folic acid proved more effective than a placebo. In fifty, a large dosage of folate brought overall improvement within a few months, with almost all fifty enjoying a good to very good improvement in their moods.

✧ In three trials, megadoses of methylfolate (not available commercially as of this writing) have proven to be an acute antidepressant. In a double-blind trial by R. Crellin and associates (1992), the coenzyme was as potent as a tricyclic antidepressant drug.

To orthomolecular psychiatrists this is not at all surprising. For decades, they've claimed that megadoses of folate can be a mood-lifting stimulant, albeit with a bit of an edge. "Megadoses of folic acid," Herbert Newbold observed in 1975, "may either stimulate or sedate. Often people simply experience an increased sense of well-being. . . . Still others feel just rotten."

The discovery that low blood levels of folic acid are a major risk factor for cardiovascular disease has heightened medical respect for the vitamin. (This, incidentally, suggests an explanation for the high rate of heart disease among depressives.) Although doctors usually test for folate deficiency in elderly neuropsychiatric patients because it can also cause dementia, any depressive—especially one who skimps on green leafy vegetables and/or legumes or organ meats—is likely to test low, as are anorexics, pregnant women, and rapidly growing children and teenage girls. Folate depleters include anticonvulsant drugs, alcohol, oral contraceptives, certain anticancer drugs, antibiotics, cholestyramine (and perhaps other bile acid sequestrants), and pregnancy.

Vitamin B_{12} (Cobalamin, Hydroxocobalamin, Cyanocobalamin, Methylcobalamin): A Shot in Time Saves Mind

Some of the most florid psychoses in the medical literature, often involving elderly people run amok, testify to the perils of unrecognized vitamin B_{12} deficiency. And that's only during the early stages. When the cause is B_{12} malabsorption (pernicious anemia), as the years pass and B_{12} levels dwindle to nothing, irreversible brain damage and dementia slowly, insidiously ensue.

Less dramatic, but more commonly a symptom of early B_{12} deficiency is depression, typically of the listless, mentally foggy kind. In the 1950s, one such woman had so convincing a case of endogenous depression that shock therapy was administered, in vain. Four years later, her slow-onset B_{12} deficiency was finally diagnosed. A few days and shots of B_{12} later, "she showed a dramatic clinical improvement and came to life again," her doctor T. N. Fraser reported. After another couple of months, "she looked the picture of health."

Because pernicious anemia is a highly age-related disease, most doctors today suspect it in elderly patients with neuropsychiatric symptoms. But studies suggest any depressed person has a 10 to 30 percent chance of being B_{12}-shy, usually without pernicious anemia (malabsorption) as the cause.

Any depressive with low B_{12} should have it replenished in case it might help. In practice, many orthomolecular psychiatrists believe all depressives should try B_{12}, even by injection. For years, B_{12} shots (large oral doses are very poorly absorbed) have been an alternative treatment for fatigued, run-down, or depressed patients. The practice has been the butt of many jokes among skeptics. Yet what research there is has supported it.

In 1973, in a double-blind trial by Ellis and Nasser, B_{12} shots boosted energy and lifted mood in chronically fatigued patients significantly more than shots of water. Later, in a single-blind study, orthomolecular psychiatrist Herbert Newbold reported that his B_{12}-responsive patients "invariably" could tell whether they had received B_{12} or water. Newbold noted that B_{12} is not a stimulant, but a "normalizer" that helps some of his patients sleep better and even makes one less manic. (Mania is also a symptom of B_{12} deficiency.)

There is an intriguing reason why some people with normal blood levels of B_{12} may need megadoses. They may have a B_{12} deficiency that is confined to the brain.

Although most doctors would never consider such a possibility, studies have uncovered cerebral deficiencies of B_{12} (using cerebrospinal fluid levels as a measure) in some people with postnatal depression, Alzheimer's disease, and toxic neuropsychiatric disorders, including toxic depression. Cees van Tiggelen and associates suspect this cryptic condition may also afflict people with histories of nitrous oxide intoxication, alcoholics (including those with alcohol-related dementia), long-term users of dilantin, Agent Orange victims, and people with brain atrophy.

B_{12} has its mainstream advocates too. In 1975, psychiatrists K. Geagea and Jambur Ananth, then at McGill University, remarked that "astonishing results can be obtained in some cases with B_{12} therapy, even if B_{12} levels are within normal range."

In 1999, in their book *Stop Depression Now*, Columbia University psychiatrist Richard Brown and Baylor University neuropharmacologist Teodoro Bottiglieri recommend that all psychiatric patients take a daily megadose of 1 milligram of oral B_{12}. In *The Way Up from Down*, UCLA psychiatrist Priscilla Slagle suggests: "If you are over fifty-five, vegetarian or alcoholic, have extreme fatigue, poor memory, low thyroid or weight loss, I recommend you take 1,000 to 2,000 micrograms of the sublingual form [of B_{12}] every morning."

Vitamin C (Ascorbic Acid, Ascorbate): Mood Stabilizer by the Megadose

Under heavy stress, most animals ramp up their production by tenfold to a hundredfold of a coping molecule named *ascorbic acid*, better known as vitamin C. Animals who don't, simply can't. Like us. We can only boost our vitamin C levels modestly by eating vitamin C–rich foods. If we want heavy artillery, we need to take supplements—the orthomolecular prescription. Herbert Newbold describes a binge-eating patient whose obesity, fatigue, depression, and suicidal tendencies persisted until she stopped eating meat and worked up to a "heroic dosage of 60,000 milligrams of vitamin C daily"—1,000 times the RDA.

Vitamin C does more than handle psychological stress. It also helps the immune system fight infections and cancer, while moderating its allergic and autoimmune tendencies. And C is one of the body's ablest detoxifiers, teaming up with the liver's detoxificational enzymes to neutralize all manner of drugs and pollutants. It also acts as a bouncer for heavy metals, among other purificational deeds.

Vitamin C's detoxificational prowess attracted Scottish psychiatrist Graham Naylor and his associates in the 1980s. They and others found that in acutely manic and depressed persons, blood levels of vanadium, a trace metal, usually soar, only to fall when the patients recover.

Although vanadium is an essential nutrient, in miners who get a toxic megadose, it's a well-documented downer. And megadoses of C are a proven antidote.

Naylor's group at the University of Dundee has conducted several studies of vitamin C as a mood stabilizer. In a double-blind trial in 1981 by Naylor and Anne Smith, a single 3-gram megadose of the vitamin had a significantly more favorable acute effect on eleven manic and twelve depressed patients than a placebo. Vitamin C's effect peaked at four hours, reducing symptom severity in both the depressives and manics by roughly 40 percent. The placebo was virtually inert.

Surprisingly, that's the extent of the research on vitamin C for affective illness. But with chronic stress, toxic depression, and immune system dysregulation (allergy, autoimmune disorders) being so much a part of the scenery of mood disorder, the orthomolecular routine of prescribing megadoses of vitamin C seems like sound medicine.

Other Vitamins

Other vitamins may also help treat depression.

✢ Vitamin B_2 (riboflavin) is often low in depressives, and experimentally induced B_2-deficiency has provoked depression in healthy men (Sterner and Price). In a placebo-controlled study from Harvard Medical School, B_2, together with B_1 and B_6, in doses found in any potent multivitamin supplement, doubled the response to antidepressant drugs (Bell et al., 1992).

✢ Two other B vitamins, biotin and pantothenic acid (vitamin B_5), have also been anecdotally reported to have some antidepressant value.

✢ Long reputed to be a tonic, in a 1995 study by Brusov et al., megadoses of vitamin E converted nearly half of seventeen antidepressant drug-nonresponders to responders. Alas, vitamin E's protective blood-thinning effect seems to increase the risk of bleeding strokes. Perhaps the more natural mixed tocopherol form would avert this hazard.

CHAPTER 7

———————— ❦ ————————

Balancing Minerals
to Balance Emotions

One can only guess how many lives have been saved by a simple element named lithium. Since modern psychiatry's rediscovery of this mineral's mood-stabilizing effects, lithium has proven the single most effective antidote to the astronomical suicide rate among people with bipolar disorder.

When it comes to minerals and mood, lithium is just the tip of the iceberg.

Minerals abound not only in the sea, but in the sea within us and in everything we eat. At least fifteen of these most elementary chemicals are as essential to our health as vitamins—for good reason:

- Like vitamins, essential minerals help catalyze most physiologic reactions.
- Some minerals are key components of important biochemicals, like hemoglobin (iron) and thyroid hormone (iodine).
- Electrically charged minerals (*electrolytes*) help carry the flow of electrochemical impulses from neuron (brain nerve cell) to neuron.

There is still much to learn about minerals and mood, but what we already know can make a big difference.

Level-Headed Lithium

Some day, nutritionists may confirm their suspicion that lithium, a mineral found naturally in food and water, is an essential nutrient. On that day, one of psychiatry's most potent "drugs" will become an ortho-molecular medicine.

Popularly thought of as a magic bullet for bipolar disorder, lithium is actually considerably less—and more. Less, because while it helps many bipolar persons, it's a magic bullet for only a few. More, because lithium allays other conditions too, including plain old "unipolar" depression.

Not only is lithium a mild antidepressant (Souza and Goodwin), it may outperform antidepressant drugs in preventing recurrent episodes. In bipolar persons, lithium does much more than temper mood swings. A recent review by Richard Baldessarini and associates of Harvard Medical School showed it reduces their disastrous suicide rate *sevenfold*.

For unipolar depression, lithium's main claim to fame is as a potent augmentor of antidepressant drugs. Numerous controlled studies have shown it converts about 50 to 70 percent of drug nonresponders into responders in days or weeks (Rouillon and Gorwood, 1998). Research also suggests lithium can accelerate the response to these medications.

In preliminary reports lithium has also augmented the amino acid tryptophan and sleep deprivation therapy. It very likely can augment other natural antidepressants too.

Lithium has traditionally been prescribed in stiff megadoses that would give even an orthomolecular psychiatrist pause. Recently, the trend has been toward lithium lite, for some studies suggest lower doses lessen side effects without compromising efficacy. Abram Hoffer has prescribed low doses for decades. In 1978, he wrote: "I have been using 300 milligrams of lithium per day for a number of patients to improve energy levels, remove fatigue, eliminate depression, and alter mood changes associated with multiple food allergies, and the results have been gratifying." Depressives who are "retarded" and have lost lots of weight may be especially responsive to the lithium touch.

The War Between Sodium and Potassium

If there is an unhealthy mineral imbalance that everyone knows at least half about, it's too much sodium (as in table salt) and not enough potassium (as in fresh food), the essential mineral that balances sodium in the body. By the time a potato has been transformed into a salty chip, the natural sodium/potassium balance has been turned completely on its head. Overindulgence in such processed foods is a well-recognized cause of high blood pressure in salt-sensitive people. Few, however, know it might be a cause of affective disorder.

Researchers like Graham Naylor, P. L. Reddy, and their associates have been monitoring the sodium/potassium balance in people with depression and bipolar disorder for decades. They've found it's usually even worse than the average person's. The cause, it seems, is the *sodium pump*.

Sodium pumps (also known as the Na-K ATPase) are little enzyme stations built into the membranes of every cell. Their job is to ensure cells have enough potassium, but not too much sodium. We evolved on prehistoric diets that made getting sodium the challenge. These diets are estimated to have had an abundant potassium-to-sodium ratio of between ten and fifty to one. Today's diets typically have a ratio of around two to one—*in favor of sodium*. Confronted with a modern diet turned topsy-turvy in its sodium/potassium balance, our sodium pumps have to pump their Stone-Aged bottoms off to keep our cells from getting overloaded with sodium. People with the genetically least-capable sodium pumps are probably the ones who get high blood pressure, and maybe affective disorder too.

Studies by Graham Naylor's group (e.g., Naylor and Smith, 1981), P. L. Reddy et al., and many others have shown that acutely depressed and manic patients tend to have acutely depressed sodium pumps. In the brain, where rapidly pumping sodium out of neurons is the key to efficiently sending electrochemical messages, this is an obvious liability. A neuron stuffed with sodium is also less capable of importing the major mood-stabilizing neurotransmitter, serotonin, and other needed chemicals too.

In a word, the sodium/potassium imbalance that defines so many people's diets could be contributing to a kind of bloating of the brain cells that makes for less efficient, more brittle brain function.

No one has ever attempted to see what would happen if depressives or bipolars were put on a diet low in sodium (we need very little) and high in potassium (we need a lot). But there are hints the results would be rewarding.

❧ In a study by T. C. Beard et al., people with high blood pressure felt happier and less depressed on a low-sodium diet.

❧ Premenstrual hormone changes promote sodium retention. Worse, women with PMS compound the problem by consuming nearly twice as much sodium as others, according to G. E. Abraham. No wonder cutting down on sodium is such a commonly recommended antidote for this often-depressing disorder.

"Other depressive states as well can be aggravated by excessive salt intake," suggests orthomolecular psychiatrist Michael Lesser.

Just don't overdo it. Too little sodium can also be depressing, and even provoke mania. But you're very unlikely to become sodium-deficient unless you follow a drastically sodium-restricted diet or drink water like a fish while on a moderate one. Medical conditions can also make you sodium-deficient, notably edema, kidney failure, and dehydration. So can overmedication with diuretics and normal doses of SSRI antidepressants, like Prozac and Paxil. SSRIs have sometimes caused severe, even dangerous hyponatremia (low blood sodium), mostly in elderly patients.

Mood-Stabilizing Magnesium

Wherever there is an energy-producing chemical reaction in the body, the mineral magnesium is there lending a hand—if we've eaten enough of it. Alas, most people don't even consume the RDA, unless they're committed to beans, greens, and whole grains.

As with other minerals, deficiencies *and excesses* of magnesium can be depressing or deranging. Studies of magnesium status in people with depression are all over the map, from low to high to normal. But there has been a tendency, in line with theoretical expectations, to find low blood and red blood cell levels of magnesium.

Clinically, too, there is more evidence that depressives and bipolars need more magnesium, not less. As George Kirov and Karmen Tsachev point out, not only do most healthy people consume minimal magnesium, but acute psychiatric stress increases magnesium needs and its turnover while deranging the body's magnesium homeostasis. Blood levels represent only a tiny fraction of our magnesium reserves. In

stressed-out depressives, it's conceivable that high blood levels—
perhaps even high red blood cell levels—represent magnesium on its
way *out* of organs like the heart and brain that need it most.

Some studies that have peeked into the brains of depressives support this possibility. In the 1980s, C. M. Banki and associates noted a
trend for magnesium levels to be low in the cerebrospinal fluid (CSF)
of depressed patients. For suicidally depressed patients, it was more
than a trend. Their low CSF magnesium levels were strongly associated
with very low CSF levels of 5-HIAA, the breakdown product of the neurotransmitter serotonin. Low serotonin is biological psychiatry's most
infamous correlate of violent suicide attempts or acts. For Banki's depressives, at least, it seemed that low magnesium and low serotonin
were mutually related to suicidal depression.

By then, supplements of magnesium had already shown clinical
promise. Prior to the Second World War, large doses had been used
successfully to treat mania and prevent bipolar mood swings. Inspired
many decades later by this dusty research, psychiatrist Guy Chouinard
and his colleagues at McGill University conducted an award-winning
trial of magnesium (in the well-absorbed form of magnesium aspartate
tablets) in nine severe and hard-to-treat rapid cyclers.

One patient was removed from the study because her manic episode
didn't let up. But seven others were so improved during the first eight
weeks of the uncontrolled study that six were discharged from the hospital (the seventh, also improved, simply had nowhere to go). By the end
of the six-month follow-up period, magnesium had proven more effective than lithium had ever been for four of the original nine patients.

Given the ability of lithium to augment the effectiveness of antidepressant drugs, one wonders if high doses of magnesium could do
the same.

Your chances of being magnesium-deficient are increased if you're
under heavy stress; have high blood pressure, coronary heart disease,
rapid heartbeat, tremors, spasms, hypersensitivity to sensory stimuli (as
in easy startling), seizures, malabsorption, malnutrition, or chronic
fluid loss; if you drink lots of alcohol or coffee; take oral contraceptives
or diuretics; or if you're pregnant.

With research implicating marginal magnesium intake as a cause of
heart disease, depressives and bipolars have nothing to lose by at least
trying on for size a magnesium-rich diet.

Calcium: Friend or Foe?

If magnesium's relationship to depression is ambiguous, calcium's is downright enigmatic. Deficiencies and excesses of calcium can both cause depression. But on the face of it, excess would seem to be the problem for people with clinical depression. In most studies, their blood and CSF levels tend to be high, and to drop to normal upon recovery (e.g., Pavlinac et al.). Bipolars tend to have particularly calcium-loaded cells when depressed and when manic. In fact, lowering their calcium, whether with lithium, calcium channel blocking drugs, or a calcium-restricted diet, "lowers" their mania, while calcium supplements only make them more agitated (Carman et al.). Alas, these findings, although pregnant with clinical potential, are to doctors as a tree fallen in an abandoned forest.

One thing is for sure: Abnormalities in the body's calcium balance are well established in affective disease. That calcium is a major signaling chemical inside brain cells—a so-called "second messenger," with neurotransmitters like serotonin being the first—probably has a lot to do with it. There is evidence that when neurons are signaled by serotonin, calcium responds more strongly in depressives, especially anxious depressives, and manics than it does in nondepressives. A depresssed magnesium pump, leading to a glut of intracellular calcium, could be the cause. And somehow, this could foster mood destabilization.

Ironically, in two preliminary controlled trials, depression—ordinary (Winters and Winters) and premenstrual (Alvir and Thys-Jacobs)—has been relieved, not worsened, by ample doses of calcium.

So should you take more calcium, or less? Perhaps the following suggestions can help:

⌇ If your calcium intake is low or your meat intake is high (meat leaches the body's calcium) and if you're anxious (calcium may be a natural sedative), increasing it might be worth a try, as long as you keep up your magnesium intake. But be careful if you're bipolar.

⌇ If your calcium intake is high, relief from depression or mania may come from consuming less calcium, and/or from consuming more magnesium, *especially* if you're bipolar.

❧ A recent NIMH study by Michelson et al. found very significantly reduced bone density in women with current or past major depression. This suggests the high calcium levels of depression are at the expense of low bone levels. Exercise, sunshine, vitamin D, and a low- or no-meat diet could rectify this imbalance, perhaps with favorable effects on mood.

A Taste of Zinc

How much does zinc have to do with depression? Consider this: People with a rare genetic disease called *acrodermatitis enteropathica* can barely absorb any of this trace essential mineral. Half have just one symptom: "periodic, typical, disabling depressions" (Edwards).

Among clinically depressed women, zinc deficiency is rampant. In a study by Karley Little and associates of the University of Kentucky, eight of twenty-one depressed women—but just one of nine depressed men—had it. Among the most severely depressed patients (typically endogenous or psychotic), fully two out of three were zinc deficient. Other studies have confirmed that depressed women, but seldom men, tend to be zinc-deficient.

Interestingly, zinc deficiency, which can radically distort the sense of taste, smell, and appetite, also seems prevalent in people with eating disorders, most of whom are female, many of whom are depressed. Zinc deficiency could therefore be a common denominator among depressed bulimics, anorexics, and binge eaters. Anecdotally, zinc supplements have been reported therapeutic.

Formally, only one small, preliminary report by Bryce-Smith and Simpson suggests that zinc can help zinc-deficient depressives. Orthomolecular psychiatrists like Michael Lesser and Priscilla Slagle would concur. They usually see zinc deficiency in relationship to an excess of its natural antagonist copper, with depression, anxiety, agitation, paranoia, and insomnia being typical symptoms. An abnormally low zinc-to-copper ratio in depressives has been confirmed by mainstream research groups, most recently by Maes et al. and also by C. Posaci et al. in PMS. (Though rare, copper deficiency can also cause depression.)

Your chances of being zinc-deficient, copper-loaded, or both are heightened if you avoid zinc-rich foods like organ meats, shellfish, legumes, red meat, and whole grains; if your sense of taste or smell is weak or distorted; if you have "stretch marks," white spots on brittle fingernails, an eating disorder, high estrogen levels, diabetes, lung cancer, hemolytic anemia, cirrhosis of the liver, or a recent history of infection or surgery; if you drink soft water from copper water pipes; or if your intake of calcium, iron, copper, or alcohol is very high. In children, stunted growth or retarded sexual development is suggestive of zinc deficiency.

Iron: The Happiness Mineral

Iron deficiency may be the only medical condition recognized as a cause of unhappiness, at least in babies (Addy, 1986). It's not hard to understand why. What toddler could be happy if iron-poor blood deprived it of enough oxygen to keep up with the other bouncing babies on the block? What little nipper, hobbled by an iron deficiency-induced shortfall of the coping neurotransmitter norepinephrine, could keep its chin up in the face of diaper rash, toilet training, and unstable computer operating-system upgrades?

Iron deficiency can cause weakness, lethargy, mental slowness and dullness, malaise, or depression in babies of all ages. Growing children and menstruating women who shun iron-rich foods (e.g., organ meats, prune juice, shellfish, legumes, dried peaches and apricots, red meat, whole-grain cereals, and dark leafy green vegetables) are at special risk. So is anyone with pallor (especially inside the mouth), bluish whites of the eyes, or a recent history of blood loss (surgery, injury, ulcers, etc.), pregnancy, lactation, heavy use of tea, coffee, or antacids, or pica (compulsive craving for dirt, clay, ice, crunchy or salty foods, or tomatoes).

Maes et al. found significantly poorer iron status in adult depressives compared to controls. It may be no coincidence that low iron impairs the conversion of the inactive form of thyroid hormone, T_4, to its active form, T_3.

Too much iron, however, can be depressing. Such was the case for seven depressed and other psychiatric patients treated by P. Cutler whose symptoms gradually improved with chelation therapy.

Sanguine Selenium

Best known as an antioxidant cancer-fighter, the trace mineral selenium also has a feel-good side.

In a double-blind study from Wales by Benton and Cook, fifty normal subjects received a modest daily supplement of 100 micrograms of selenium or a placebo for five weeks. Only the selenium significantly reduced depression, anxiety, and fatigue, especially in subjects whose diets had been low in the trace mineral to begin with. Orthomolecular psychiatrist Abram Hoffer finds selenium helpful for clinical depression. "I have been giving my depressed patients 200 micrograms twice each day when they do not want to take drugs," he and coauthor Morton Walker wrote in 1996, "and the results have been good."

Rubidium: Lithium's Frisky Brother

Rubidium has a lot in common with its sister element lithium. Also suspected to be an essential nutrient (our diets provide a few milligrams a day), rubidium appears to be a potent, mood-modifying mineral when taken in megadoses. That's not all it has in common with lithium.

Lithium's antimanic effect was first reported by Australian psychiatrist John Cade in 1949. Yet it wasn't until the early seventies that the unpatentable "orphan drug" finally made it into North American pharmacies. Ironically, it was then that American psychiatrists published the first evidence of rubidium's antidepressant effect. That effect, as one of those psychiatrists, Ronald Fieve, writes, has since been confirmed by "half a dozen major university research teams in Italy." But like lithium before it, rubidium chloride is still available only in Europe.

Rubidium, which pumps up the get-up-and-go neurotransmitter dopamine and the good-times neurotransmitter norepinephrine, behaves like mellow lithium's complement: a fast-acting, stimulating antidepressant, ideal for depressives who are very slowed down and apathetic. Indeed (as reviewed by Placidi et al.), just as some bipolars become dull or depressed on lithium, on rubidium some depressives become manic. Likely the fruit of rubidium's dopaminergic effect, this probably also accounts for rubidium's ability to make schizophrenics more delusional (but less withdrawn and retarded) and people with Parkinson's disease less stiff and frozen.

Perhaps like SAMe, 5-HTP, and other natural antidepressant "orphan drugs" from Europe, rubidium will soon cross the Atlantic too. It should be well received, for even in megadoses rubidium has a mild side-effect profile.

Mood-Mineral Cocktail, Anyone?

"The fifth-century physician Aurelianus," R. Papaioannou and Carl Pfeiffer write, "recommended mineral waters for the treatment of manic insanity and melancholia." Typically, those waters were rich in such elements as lithium, rubidium, magnesium, and calcium. Knowing what we know now, it seems reasonable that they could have had a mood-stabilizing effect on people who drank or bathed in them, absorbing the minerals through the skin.

In a modern University of Texas study cited by Papaioannou and Pfeiffer, more lithium in municipal water supplies was associated with fewer admissions to state mental hospitals and lower homicide and suicide rates. Hard-water supplies are also likely to be rich in the other minerals that gave those ancient spas their mood-stabilizing repute.

Perhaps the mineral prescription for affective illness should be less like a magic bullet and more like a mixed beverage, specially blended to contain just the right balance of lithium, rubidium, magnesium, and so forth for each person, based on diagnosis, symptoms, and lab tests.

Placidi's group have taken a step in that direction. They kept a bipolar patient stable for two years (at last count) on a balance of lithium and rubidium. In the decade prior, on lithium alone, the patient had experienced at least one episode of mania and depression each year.

CHAPTER 8

❧❧

Separating the Good Fats
from the Bad

In the early 1980s, Harvard-trained research physician Donald Rudin conducted a pilot study of what, at the time, must have seemed a singularly kooky treatment: *linseed oil*—the stuff, when rancid, that gives oil paint its peculiarly stale odor. For his subjects, Rudin chose forty-four patients whose chronic ills, he wrote in 1996, represented "the common garden variety complaints that take up most of the time of doctors and psychiatrists today."

Rudin's hypothesis was that all or most of these conditions, from irritable bowel syndrome and migraine headache, to depression and bipolar disorder, were at least partially caused by an endemic nutritional imbalance: too much saturated fat and partially hydrogenated oils (as found mostly in factory-farmed meat and commercial baked goods), and not enough of the nutritionally essential fatty acids of the *omega-3* family (as found mostly in fatty cold-water fish and dark leafy greens).

To test his hypothesis, Rudin had each patient take an ample daily dose of linseed oil—the remarkably omega-3-rich oil of flaxseeds—along with a small amount of vitamin E to prevent rancidity and B vitamins to facilitate the omega-3's conversion to other important biochemicals in the body.

For the two- to three-year span of the study, almost every patient stuck with the plan. And most of them, Rudin reported, gradually enjoyed significant and persistent improvements in both physical and mental health.

Twelve patients had suffered primarily from psychiatric conditions. Two dropped out: one for fear of gaining weight on the high-cal supplement; the other, a bipolar patient who developed severe rapid cycling, possibly from the linseed oil. Of the other ten, seven improved substantially.

Most dramatic was a twenty-six-year-old woman diagnosed schizophrenic since the age of sixteen. Despite "brief lucid moments each day," nothing had helped "Debi" for long. But within thirty minutes of her first dose of linseed oil she felt calmer. A week later, her daily hallucinations, intrusive thoughts, and "bizarre, sometimes violent, behavior" subsided. Soon they disappeared entirely.

"I've been free of schizophrenia ever since," Debi wrote to Dr. Rudin years later. While continuing on an omega-3-rich diet, Debi had outgrown her need for both linseed oil and antipsychotic drugs and had become a registered psychiatric nurse.

It wasn't until the late 1990s that the medical establishment began to catch up. In a double-blind, placebo-controlled multicenter trial published in 1999, an extremely high daily dose of fish oil proved so therapeutic for patients with bipolar disorder that the researchers, led by Harvard's Andrew Stoll, felt compelled to end the study early and put everyone on the nautical elixir. By the time the study saw print, virtually all the patients had stuck with the fishy prescription for up to two years "with continued efficacy."

Stoll et al. had chosen a particularly unstable group of bipolar I and II patients. Although well or only mildly symptomatic, all thirty had a history of frequent manic or depressive episodes. Roughly one-third were rapid cyclers. Not unexpectedly, of the sixteen randomly assigned to olive oil (the placebo) as an adjunct to medication-as-usual, only 40 percent were still okay or better by the end of the 120-day study. In contrast, of the fourteen randomly assigned to adjunctive fish oil, nearly 90 percent were. The fish oilers fared significantly better by most other measures too. In particular, their depression scores dropped nearly by half. The control group's rose nearly 25 percent.

Stoll and colleague Loren Marangell attempted to put their study into perspective: "[Omega-3] fatty acids . . . seem to be deficient in 'western diets.' . . . Thus, this study may represent the first demonstration of an effective nutritional therapy for bipolar disorder."

Omega-3 fatty acids are integral components of the brain's cellular membranes, including the crucial synapses where neurons exchange chemical signals. Although the brain can use other essential fatty acids

(EFAs) to build its supple neuronal membranes—notably the arachi-donic acid (AA) that abounds in factory-farmed meat—it prefers the highly polyunsaturated and flexible EFAs that abound in fish oil and other wild animals. These long-chain EFAs are called eicosapentanoic acid (EPA) and docosahexanoic acid (DHA). Most people can make them from the patriarch of the omega-3s, alpha-linolenic acid (ALA), the EFA that abounds in linseed oil, but some people (as we'll see) can't.

When EPA and DHA are incorporated into neuronal membranes, Stoll and associates point out, the neurons become more electrochemi-cally stable, less liable to "fly off the handle." This is the kind of stabil-ity created by lithium, Depakote, and other successful treatments for bipolar disorder. Stoll et al. might therefore have expected fish oil to work best for the manic pole of bipolar disorder. Yet in the brief course of their study, most of fish oil's advantage over olive oil was in prevent-ing depression.

But what about unipolar depression? In 1998, Joseph Hibbeln of the National Institute of Alcohol Abuse and Alcoholism compared the rate of major depression in nine countries to the estimated per-capita fish consumption, and the results were astonishing. At one extreme, a cluster of Western countries including the United States and Canada had an annual prevalence of major depression in the range of 3 to 6 percent and a modest per-capita fish intake of roughly 25 to 70 pounds. At the other extreme, Japan, with a per capita fish intake of nearly 150 pounds, had a paltry major depression rate of 0.12 percent. High fish intake predicted low depression rate to the tune of a whop-ping 84 percent correlation, where 100 percent would have represented a one-to-one correspondence.

As scientists say, "correlation is not causation." But in the case of fish intake and depression, there is good evidence that eating more of the former *will* make you less of the latter.

For one thing, rates of major depressive disorder in industrialized countries have risen dramatically in the past 100 years, while modern farming and food processing have gradually stripped most of the highly perishable omega-3 content from the menu. We have gone from an ancient ancestral diet estimated to have contained equal parts omega-6 and omega-3 to one in which omega-6 predominates by between 10 and 25 to 1, according to Hibbeln and colleague Norman

Salem, Jr. This radical omega shift is already well-implicated as a promoter of coronary heart disease. If it also promotes depression, we would expect to see more CHD among depressives. And we do.

"Depression," Rhian Edwards of the University of Sheffield and her associates note, "is the strongest psychological predictor of coronary heart disease." The correlation gets even hotter than that.

In all but one of about half-a-dozen controlled studies by the Sheffield group and three others, the red blood cell membranes and/or serum cholesterol of depressives have been significantly shy of omega-3s. In a 1998 study by Edwards et al., there was a remarkably strong tendency—a 75 percent correlation—for major depressives with the least omega-3s in their diets and red blood cell membranes to be the most severely depressed. Several of these studies have found that two of the major omega-6 fatty acids, linoleic acid (LA) and AA, are also higher in depressives than in controls. In one study cited by Hibbeln, there was a powerful correlation between the ratio of AA to EPA and severity of depression.

We are getting a very strong hint that too much omega-6 (especially the AA of factory-farmed meat) and too little omega-3 makes Johnny a very depressed boy. Recently Rhian Edwards took the inevitable next step and conducted a placebo-controlled clinical trial of fish oil for patients with unipolar major depression. Her yet-to-be-published results, along with those to come from other researchers, may soon change how psychiatrists treat depression.

Fish Oil and Beyond

The flax and fish oil story is the tip of an iceberg that is telling us there is much more to dietary fat than fish preventing heart attacks or bacon grease clogging arteries. Fat is very much a brain thing. It's about moods and feelings, too.

The integral role fats play in the structure and function of neuronal membranes looms large in explaining this influence. But EFAs are also the precursors to an important class of hormonelike compounds called *prostaglandins.*

Prostaglandins (PGs) come in three complementary varieties or series. The 2-series of PGs tends (among other things) to provoke inflammation and blood clotting; the 1- and 3-series do just the opposite. The 2-series is made from the essential fatty acid AA, which is unnaturally abundant in the cellular membranes of grain-fed animals. Our bodies are happy to produce AA in moderation from the LA in grains and oils. They also use some of this LA to produce the 1-series. And they synthesize the 3-series from plant and animal sources of omega-3s.

Given the proper fat-balanced diet (as outlined on page 113 in "Keys to a Good-Fat Diet"), most of us can produce a healthy balance of PGs. Yet we clearly lack this balance when we're depressed. Studies have repeatedly found soaring levels of 2-series PGs—up to eight to eighteen times normal—in the body fluids of people with clinical depression (e.g., Nishino et al.).

Signs of systemic inflammation also have been repeatedly recorded in people with major depression. In part, inflammation is mediated by 2-series PGs, and one of its consequences, as shown by C. Song and associates, is to reduce the supply of tryptophan to the brain. This itself could be a key to depression, because low blood levels of this precursor to mood-stabilizing serotonin are commonly found in depressed patients. Because most antidepressants largely work by boosting serotonin, lowering 2-series PGs might work too.

Research suggests depression is also associated with a deficiency of 1-series PGs, specifically, prostaglandin E_1 (PGE_1), and that excesses of PGE_1 are associated with euphoria and mania, according to EFA experts David Horrobin and Mehar Manku.

If a glut of 2-series PGs and a deficiency of 1-series PGs really does promote depression, then correcting this imbalance should help. There is lots of evidence it does.

Gamma-Linolenic Acid

The EFA gamma-linolenic acid (GLA) is a very efficient precursor to PGE_1 and other 1-series PGs. We normally produce GLA ourselves from linoleic acid (LA), the omega-6 EFA that abounds in vegetable oils. But in people with certain disorders, including premenstrual syndrome (PMS), chronic viral infections, and perhaps depression, a bottleneck in the conversion of LA to GLA sometimes exists, according to David Horrobin. Evening primrose oil, or other good sources of GLA like borage oil and black currant seed oil, should overcome this block.

In most of at least nine placebo-controlled trials, evening primrose oil has indeed proven highly effective for PMS, particularly premenstrual depression. In a small controlled trial, it has also relieved depression and hyperactivity in children, according to Jonathan Zuess, M.D. Combined with EPA and DHA (the fish oil omega-3s), GLA dramatically outperformed placebo in relieving the fatigue, depression, and other symptoms of thirty-nine patients with postviral chronic fatigue syndrome in a study by P. O. Behan and associates of the University of Glasgow.

There are no trials of evening primrose oil for depression itself, but anecdotally Drs. Ann Nazzaro and Donald Lombard find it useful as an adjunct to antidepressant drugs. In clinical trials, Horrobin has told me, mood elevation has been a consistent "side effect." The oil has also exhibited the classic sign of being an antidepressant: It has, Zuess warns, triggered mania in some people with bipolar disorder.

Linseed Oil

In many cultures, fresh linseed oil—the oil of flaxseeds—is a time-honored health food. Likely it's because no oil seed is as rich in alpha-linolenic acid (ALA), the EFA precursor to the long-chain omega-3s found in fish oil. Linseed oil also contains lots of LA, but for people on a typical modern diet, linseed oil's net effect is to reduce 2-series PGs while increasing the 3-series and possibly the 1-series too.

Which is one reason why orthomolecular psychiatrists so often prescribe it. Donald Rudin reports that linseed oil has remedied some very tough cases of depression and bipolar disorder. It doesn't seem to be a placebo effect. Some patients have become manic on the oil. Others, after quitting prematurely or being switched to a "placebo" like corn or safflower oil, have quickly relapsed.

Recently, Harvard's Andrew Stoll reported that linseed oil (like fish oil) appeared to stabilize the moods of more than fifty bipolar patients. Some were able to cut down on their medications or quit (Nidecker).

People who benefit psychiatrically from linseed oil, Rudin finds, tend to have other omega-3 deficiency symptoms, such as chronic fatigue; dandruff; dry, rough, flaky skin; tinnitus (chronic buzzing or ringing in the ears); cold intolerance; allergies; and inflammatory bowel disorders. Theoretically, any conditions brought on or worsened by cold, including winter depression, might respond to linseed oil or to fish oil.

Fish Oil

The fat of cold-adapted animals, such as cold-water fish, is uniquely rich in EPA and DHA. The direct precursor to the 3-series of PGs, EPA is better positioned metabolically than the ALA found in linseed oil to counter the glut of 2-series PGs in depression, according to Horrobin and colleague Y-S Huang. DHA can be directly incorporated into neuronal membranes—no need to synthesize it from ALA. So fish oil, as even Rudin speculates, may work better for some people than linseed oil. Indeed, some people appear genetically incapable of converting ALA to EPA and DHA.

Fish oil is a promising way to treat and prevent depression and bipolar disorder. A growing body of research suggests it can also relieve a wide range of depression-related disorders, including PMS, schizophrenia, AIDS depression and dementia, dyslexia, attention deficit hyperactivity disorder (ADHD), senile dementia (e.g., Alzheimer's disease), and possibly early-onset alcoholism.

University of Washington psychiatrist Michael Norden reports some striking preliminary results using fish oil. One of his winter depressives achieved "the most complete cure of seasonal depression that I've ever seen from a single treatment—and I specialize in treating the condition," Norden writes. The cure was "a small amount of GLA combined with a larger amount of EPA." It worked within days, wiping the man's depression score down to "0" after a few weeks. Whenever he tried to get along without the fatty acids, he relapsed within weeks.

I cite this case with some pride, because in the first edition of this book, I speculated that omega-3s, which organisms produce more abundantly to adapt to cold weather, might be therapeutic for winter depression and other cold-weather-related conditions. Udo Erasmus would not be surprised. "Traditional Inuit did not get depressed and suicidal during winters of total darkness," he writes in his definitive tome on fatty acids. Their diet was chockablock with omega-3s from northern fish and marine mammals. There may be a message here for anyone of northern ancestry. In Canada, depression, domestic violence, impulsive crime, early-onset alcoholism, and suicide afflict an unusually high percentage of aboriginal people. There undeniably are social causes, yet each one of these ills has also been linked to a deficiency of the neurotransmitter serotonin.

Until recently, I could only muse that overindulgence in "the white man's" white bread and other refined carbohydrates, as well as his liquor, were to blame. In theory, these habits could trigger feast and famine fluctuations of serotonin in the brain, especially in people genetically inexperienced with such fare. But when I read of the research implicating DHA as a kind of serotonin stabilizer, I felt I had a sounder explanation.

Some years ago, a British Columbia doctor named C. E. Bates determined that the Pacific province's coastal Indians, who have subsisted on EPA- and DHA-rich salmon for thousands of years, can barely make any EPA or DHA from the ALA present in small amounts in the modern Western diet. Unlike most Caucasians, they are genetically dependent on a dietary source of these long-chain omega-3s, and on the long-chain omega-6 EFA, AA. They are "obligatory carnivores."

Citing his own and others' research, Bates disclosed that coastal Indians who replace their traditional salmon-based diet with more affordable supermarket fare—including AA-rich, but EPA- and DHA-lacking meat and animal products—suffer profound adverse health effects. Mostly autoimmune and inflammatory in nature, these include strikingly higher rates of diabetes, arthritis, lupus, allergy, obesity, alcoholism, schizophrenia, depression, and suicide.

"The depression we observe," Bates wrote, "is never vegetative, but characterized by agitation, restlessness, irritability, and a hair trigger temper." If there is such a thing as a quintessentially low serotonin depression, this is it. But Bates and other doctors report that when their coastal Indian patients return to a more traditional diet, they enjoy immense improvements in their myriad symptoms.

They're not alone. Thousands of miles away, according to Hibbeln and Salem, coastal Finns who, true to their ancestry, eat lots of fish, suffer significantly fewer violent deaths and suicides than their inland brethren who now shun fish.

The Confusion about Cholesterol

For years, scientists have been squirming over a body of data that just can't be. Low blood cholesterol is supposed to be good for you. It keeps your arteries clear. Yet in most clinical trials it has also meant slightly, but significantly, more depression, suicide, fatal accidents, and deaths by homicide: The patient killed himself, but boy, were his arteries clean!

There is no relief from this discordant data in the epidemiological literature. In study after study, low cholesterol has kept popping up in people with a history of violence, early-onset alcoholism, depression, and other psychobehavioral dysfunctions. These are precisely the aberrations one would expect in people with serotonin deficiency. And this is exactly what scientists believe is happening.

In the brain, cholesterol is an abundant, integral component of neuronal membranes, helping serotonin bind to the synaptic receptors that heed its laid-back call. In a 1994 study by Jay Kaplan et al., raising or lowering the cholesterol content of monkeys' diets correspondingly boosted or lowered the serotonin activity in their brains. It had the same effect—in reverse—on the monkeys' disposition to impulsive behavior and violence. How can we reconcile the cholesterol we love to hate with these dissonant findings?

We can start by remembering that cholesterol is a chemical our livers go out of their way to make. It is the precursor to pregnenolone, the mother of all our steroid hormones, including such mood regulators as estrogen, progesterone, testosterone, and DHEA. It's possible that for some people whose livers aren't up to producing enough cholesterol, something like an RDA of dietary cholesterol might actually be a good thing.

But there could be a somewhat different explanation for "the cholesterol paradox." Only a tiny fraction of cholesterol—the portion that flows in the bloodstream—gives the rest a bad name. And of that portion, it's only the "bad," low-density lipoprotein cholesterol (LDL-C) that plugs our arteries. And that's only if it's been oxidized because our blood is low in antioxidants like vitamins C and E. The "good," high-density lipoprotein cholesterol (HDL-C) in the bloodstream actually lowers the risk of cardiovascular disease. Yet many cholesterol-lowering drugs and diets indiscriminately lower both the good and the bad.

I've noticed a trend: Clinical trials in which HDL-C is raised (as with niacin and the statin drugs) are not plagued by the low serotonin curse. There is other evidence. For example, in a study of suicide attempters by G. Engstrom et al., high blood levels of HDL-C meant high brain serotonin; not so for high LDL-C. In a study by A. S. Wells et al., a low-fat diet put healthy volunteers in a rather angry, hostile, "low serotonin" mood. The only cholesterol it lowered was the good kind. In a study of three hundred healthy Swedish women by M. Horsten et al., whereas very, very low total cholesterol levels were indeed associated with more symptoms of depression, high HDL-C was significantly associated with fewer symptoms.

And then there is niacin and aerobic exercise. Megadoses of niacin are a well-established treatment for high cholesterol. But while niacin lowers LDL-C, it substantially raises HDL-C. And as we've seen, niacin seems to make people less depressed and suicidal, not more.

For its part, moderate aerobic exercise is not only an optimal activity for lowering bad cholesterol and raising good, it's an exceptionally well-documented ward against depression and malaise. So the research tends to suggest it's not low cholesterol per se that's the problem, but low HDL-cholesterol—low good cholesterol.

There is some conflicting evidence: In Jay Kaplan et al.'s monkey study, a heavily cholesterol-supplemented high-fat diet, compared to an identical diet with no added cholesterol, nearly tripled total blood cholesterol and cut HDL-C in half. Yet it nearly doubled the monkeys' brain serotonin and made for a mellower group of monkeys.

Joseph Hibbeln and Norman Salem Jr. believe they have a counter-explanation—if not for Kaplan's carefully controlled study, then at least for many others. They note that, historically, low-cholesterol diets have been of the high–vegetable oil and high-margarine kind, which result in a major increase in the ratio of omega-6 to omega-3 fatty acids. Yet, omega-3s are the only EFAs that raise HDL-C. And they're the best EFAs for building supple, responsive synapses for serotonin.

For the monkeys on Kaplan et al.'s high-fat, low-omega-3 diet, the extra cholesterol may have been a necessary evil. But on a diet with an optimal omega-3/omega-6 balance, perhaps it is safe, after all, to keep watching our cholesterol without worrying that we'll lose sight of our serotonin.

Combining and Balancing Fatty Acid Supplements

Many, if not most, depressives suffer from some combination of too much arachidonic acid (AA) and 2-series PGs, and too little omega-3 EFAs and 1-series PGs. For orthomolecular and nutritionally inclined doctors like Rudin and Norden, the remedy typically involves a combination of omega-3 and GLA supplements. But no prescription for balancing EFAs would be complete without considering the food we eat.

Keys to a Good-Fat Diet

The dietary fat imbalance associated with depression is implicated in many other so-called "diseases of civilization," including cancer, heart disease, arthritis, and multiple sclerosis. Righting that imbalance is a move every organ and tissue of your body will thank you for.

So what exactly is wrong with the fat in our diets? To begin with, there's all the saturated fat. Even our most carnivorous ancestors hunted (and later bred) animals that were much, much leaner than today's factory-farmed captives. And what fat these animals had was mostly unsaturated and full of omega-3s and other EFAs in a balance better suited to our own bodies. In contrast, today's cooped up meat machines are marbled with saturated fat, and their cell membranes are stuffed with AA because they're fed omega-3-deficient grains, not grass. Eating them gives us second-class cellular membranes too and causes our bad cholesterol to rise, our 1- and 3-series PGs to fall, and our 2-series PGs to soar. If this imbalance gets extreme enough, our moods may become unbalanced too.

Then there are all the refined and partially hydrogenated vegetable oils in the modern diet. Clear, odorless, and usually flavorless, extreme processing has rid them of most of the nutrients we need to handle them safely. Instead, they bear traces of toxic solvents and hordes of mutant *trans*-fatty acids. Trans-fatty acids are the evil twins—spawned in the cauldron of ultra-high-heat processing—of the oil's original *cis*-fatty acids. In our bodies, trans- usurp the place of cis-, with metabolically dysfunctional, toxic, atherogenic, and possibly carcinogenic consequences.

So what kind of fat should we eat? Here are some guidelines:

⤳ We need to minimize our consumption of the following: the flesh or whole-fat dairy products of grain-fed, factory-farmed animals; processed vegetable oils, shortenings and hydrogenated (artificially saturated) or partially hydrogenated oils or margarines and any foods made with them (sadly, this means almost all commercially baked or fried fare). We should never traumatize polyunsaturated oils with high-temperature frying or baking. We should try to avoid these modes of cooking altogether; but if we must, it's best to use small amounts of relatively heat-tolerant fats: butter, clarified butter (ghee), lard, or tropical oil. We shouldn't reuse (i.e., redamage) heated oils or fats.

⤳ We should try to eat foods indigenous to our climate. North Americans who live in temperate regions (as most of us do) should eat more whole wheat, soybeans and other beans, walnuts, hazelnuts, chestnuts, flaxseeds, pumpkin seeds, dark green leafy vegetables, and (for nonvegetarians) cold-water fish and seafood, wild regional game, and traditionally reared local farm animals, such as free-range chickens and grazing cattle.

⤳ We should use oils that are unrefined and as fresh and well preserved as possible. The most healthful oils have at least a moderate omega-3 content (linseed, hemp, walnut, soybean, canola, wheat germ), have been mechanically or expeller pressed (not chemically extracted) from organically grown nuts or seeds (this includes first-press oils), are crude or unrefined (no bleaching, deodorizing, etc.), are refrigerated in an opaque container with a "best before" date if they're highly polyunsaturated (which makes them very perishable), and may be preserved with vitamin E or other antioxidants. Though extra-virgin olive oil is healthy, it's too low in EFAs to be "medicinal."

CHAPTER 9

❧

Uplifting Aminos: SAMe, 5-HTP, and Other Brain Boosters

O f all the nutrients in the orthomolecular arsenal, none seem to come as close to being the natural equivalent of antidepressant drugs as amino acids. Amino acids are the building blocks from which all our body's proteins are made. They're also the precursors for most of the body's known antidepressant substances—the hormones, neurotransmitters, endorphins, and other mood-regulating compounds that tend to be lacking in depression. Some aminos are neurotransmitters themselves.

Two of today's most popular natural antidepressants—SAMe and 5-HTP—are amino acids. They keep some pretty impressive company.

Speedy SAMMY
(S-Adenosylmethionine—SAMe, SAM-e, SAM)

Five years ago, in the first edition of this book, I called it "SAM," as most experts did. Today the media (and SAM's handlers in the supplement business) have taken to calling this biochemical of the hour "SAMe" (pronounced *Sammy*) or "SAM-e" (pronounced *Sam Ee*), to create even more confusion.

The fact that the mass media are calling s-adenosylmethionine—a very busy biochemical found everywhere in our bodies—anything at all testifies to how far natural antidepressants have come. When St. John's wort broke the credibility barrier in 1997, 5-HTP soon vaulted across in its wake. And now, at the turn of the millennium, it's SAMe's turn. And it's about time.

In Italy, doctors have been scrawling SAMe's name onto prescription pads since the mid-1970s, not just as a treatment for depression, but for osteoarthritis, liver disease, and other conditions too. SAMe even outsells Prozac on that sun-dappled peninsula.

Well before SAMe hit the limelight on this side of the Atlantic, some of America's psychiatric elite had welcomed it into their research clinics. There was a real buzz about the ebullient newcomer.

"It appears that S-adenosylmethionine is a rapid and effective treatment for major depression and has few side effects," wrote Kim Bell and her associates at the University of California in 1988. Writing in a 1995 psychiatry textbook, Robert Post, chief of biological psychiatry at the National Institute of Mental Health, admiringly cited "the rapid onset of effects of SAM in a high percentage of patients and the relative absence of side effects in a large number of controlled studies."

By then, Columbia University psychiatrist Richard Brown had begun importing SAMe for his treatment-resistant and drug-intolerant patients. In 1999, he turned his enthusiasm for SAMe into the bestseller *Stop Depression Now*, coauthored with Baylor University's recognized SAMe expert, Teodoro Bottiglieri, and health writer, Carol Colman. The book heralds SAMe as a "breakthrough supplement" and "medical marvel."

Why all the excitement? SAMe is extremely well tolerated—people complain of more side effects on placebo, Brown and his coauthors write. In many clinical studies, it has actually worked much faster than drugs, relieving depression in a week or two rather than the usual six to eight. It shows signs of being a team worker too. In a large, double-blind study from Mexico, SAMe made an antidepressant drug work faster.

But it's also true that in every study where SAMe has sprinted to the finish line it has been injected. Although Brown and some users find oral SAMe fast too, studies so far suggest it's not significantly speedier than drugs. That said, even in the mostly brief trials of oral SAMe, as meta-analyzed by Bressa, the amino has proven markedly effective for about half of all depressives, and twice as potent as placebo.

Brown has called SAMe "the best antidepressant I've ever prescribed." Many depressives would agree. A colleague of Brown's is "a highly esteemed psychiatrist" who could never understand why so many of his patients found the user-friendly SSRIs (e.g., Prozac) so un-user-friendly. Then he got depressed. Two SSRIs later, he got the message. "Now he uses SAM-e, his depression is gone, and so are the side effects," gloats Brown.

On the Internet and on the street, SAMe is hot stuff. Perhaps because of its expense (about $2 to $6 a day for most users), reports often come from depressives who have tried everything else. Although some have come up empty-handed, for others SAMe has delivered. And usually fast.

A woman who had grown tired of "Side-Effexor" (her play on the name of a potent antidepressant drug) switched to SAMe, and just four days later she wrote to an Internet newsgroup: "I'm very impressed. . . . I feel great, I need less sleep. . . . I find it very energizing, but without making me nervous. I've also felt very comfortable talking to strangers, etc. . . . I recommend it VERY highly." Six weeks later, she told me it was still working—still "turning up the color" on her experiences, though she was having to get a full night's sleep again.

Like other antidepressants, SAMe can "poop out" (at least a little) for some people.

SAMe got off to a such a good start for Ellen James (not her real name) that after less than two weeks she dumped her prescription for Wellbutrin, which hadn't done much for her major depression anyway. A few days later, Ellen, who had also been dysthymic for years, "suddenly realized I felt good." Five weeks into her trial of SAMe, Ellen declared: "I feel better today than I've felt since I can remember."

Unfortunately, the honeymoon didn't last. A few weeks later, Ellen had "lost a good deal of the initial euphoria." Good days now alternated with days of lethargy and low motivation. Ellen's dysthymia— and the personal issues, such as being overweight, that fueled it—had reared its ugly head again.

Ellen responded by diversifying her antidepressant portfolio. She added 5-HTP, *Ginkgo biloba*, phosphatidylserine, omega-3 fatty acids, "anything I discovered that could possibly be helpful for depression." And she regained some lost ground.

Five months into her SAMe-plus experience, Ellen writes: "I am feeling pretty good. Actually, as of today, I'm feeling *very* good, primarily because of this regimen, I think." Ellen is now planning to branch out into lifestyle antidepressants like good diet, exercise, and meditation. She is, in fact, doing what most people do who adopt a natural approach to depression: following a holistic course.

What is the secret of SAMe's success? *Methylation.* Methylation is the transfer of a biochemical unit called a *methyl group* from a methyl donor, like SAMe, to a methyl-hungry receiver. In the brain, where

SAMe is methyl donor numero uno, methylation can result in anything from the transformation of an amino acid into a neurotransmitter to the rejuvenation of a neuron's membranes. All the major neurotransmitters that tend to be deficient in depression—serotonin, norepinephrine, dopamine—need SAMe for their synthesis. And although they also need SAMe for their breakdown, research suggests SAMe's net effect at therapeutic doses is to boost serotonin, and probably NE and dopamine as well.

Is SAMe for You?

Studies suggests that *retarded depressions*, marked by lethargy, apathy, guilt, and suicidal impulses, may be most responsive to SAMe. "Most patients taking SAM-e report a dramatic increase in energy levels, a report I hear more often for SAM-e than for any other antidepressant," writes Brown. Bipolar depressives, for whom such sluggish depressions are the norm, are often highly responsive to SAMe, to the point of hypomania. The lethargic depressions of winter SAD (seasonal affective disorder) also seem SAMe-responsive, as does postpartum depression, 50 percent of whose sufferers, according to Brown, have a bipolar tendency. Brown also recommends SAMe for menopausal mood swings and sleep disturbances, for PMS, and for subsyndromal depression, also known as the blues.

Consistent with several controlled clinical trials, Brown's patients and some Internet users have found that SAMe can relieve the pain, depression, and disturbed sleep of fibromyalgia. "Many of my [fibromyalgia] patients . . . report that it has helped them more than anything else," writes Brown.

Several other depression-related conditions also seem to benefit from SAMe (and perhaps SAMe's precursor methionine): senile dementia (e.g., Alzheimer's disease), migraine, residual (adult) attention deficit hyperactivity disorder, osteoarthritis and other chronic pain conditions, Sjögren's syndrome, Parkinson's disease, and drug dependency. Because chronic liver disease greatly compromises the body's production of SAMe (more than half of the eight or so grams we produce each day is made by the liver), depressives with liver disease (for which SAMe is therapeutic) may particularly need SAMe.

Methionine: Poor Man's SAMe

With SAMe being so costly, it's nice to know it has a cheap precursor: the essential amino acid methionine. In animal research cited by Eric Braverman, M.D., and associates, methionine has actually crossed the blood-brain barrier and raised levels of SAMe better than SAMe itself. And while depressives tend to convert methionine to SAMe rather sluggishly, researchers like McGill University's Simon Young (1993) still see methionine as a contender. Some people believe another methyl donor, trimethylglycine (TMG), could serve as a cheap substitute for SAMe.

Tryptophan and 5-HTP: The Serotonin Boosters

Tryptophan: The Suppressed Antidepressant

There was a time when tryptophan was to treating depression naturally what St. John's wort and SAMe are today.

Although few people back in the 1980s used supplements to battle the blues, tryptophan was the star. Even some progressive psychiatrists prescribed it. Supportive clinical trials had appeared in medical journals for decades. In the 1960s, the dawning years of the antidepressant drug era, tryptophan's triumphs over depression helped inspire one of the major biochemical theories of depression: *the serotonin hypothesis*. Since then, study after study has implicated a shortage of serotonin, which is made from tryptophan, as a key causative factor in depression.

Consider the evidence:

- Most antidepressant drugs boost the quantity or activity of serotonin in the brain.
- Depressives tend to have low blood levels of tryptophan, in particular relative to other amino acids that compete with it for passage across the blood-brain barrier. Many laboratory studies also suggest that serotonin—or serotonin activity— is low in the brains of most depressed and bipolar persons, especially those who are (or were) violently suicidal.
- A special tryptophan-free amino acid formula induces an acute tryptophan deficiency in people who take it. In depressives who have re-

covered on a serotonergic (serotonin-boosting) antidepressant, or in winter depressives who have reponded to light therapy, the formula usually provokes a temporary relapse.

In the early nineties, the serotonin hypothesis finally found its greatest prophet—Prozac, the first antidepressant to work more or less exclusively by amplifying the activity of serotonin in the brain. Ironically, Prozac and the other SSRIs that followed in its wake cornered the market just as tryptophan lost it. In the fall of 1989, tryptophan turned deadly. In months it was off store shelves, never fully to return.

The cause of tryptophan's fall from grace was a tragic health disaster that continues to affect thousands of victims to this day. More than thirty people died—those hardest hit by a mysterious autoimmune illness called *eosinophilia-myalgia syndrome* (EMS). Within a few years, numerous independent investigations established that the crippling disease had been due to contamination of tryptophan by one major manufacturer, Showa Denko of Japan. Showa Denko had begun using a genetically engineered bacterium to synthesize the amino acid, and they'd streamlined their purification process. New contaminants in the product, scientists concluded, were the likely cause of EMS.

Although millions of people had used tryptophan safely for decades, the FDA and most other countries' health regulators have kept tryptophan off the open market to this day. However, the FDA still allows manufacturers to add the essential amino acid to baby formulas and intravenous meals. And in some countries, like Canada, "Tryptan" is still available by prescription; in the United States, compounding pharmacies sell generic tryptophan by prescription.

Although tryptophan's use has dwindled dramatically, cases of EMS have come to a grinding halt. Even new clinical trials have been published, adding to the case that tryptophan is a safe and effective antidepressant when used in the correct dosage.

It wasn't always that way. A large number of successful early trials of tryptophan had been marred by a few dismal flops, leading to the supplement's textbook acceptance only as an augmentor of antidepressant drugs. Poring over this conflicting research in the early eighties, Herman van Praag, Alan Gelenberg, and other experts observed that, at least for unipolar depressives, there was a strong trend for tryptophan's failures to have occurred when it was prescribed at—or hiked up to—a relatively high dosage. Perhaps, they speculated, tryptophan has a *therapeutic window*, a dose-response curve in which high dosages are as ineffective as low ones.

It wasn't more than 20/20 hindsight. In roughly half a dozen trials since, in which low to moderate dosages of tryptophan have been used, the amino acid has usually come through with flying colors. For example, it has repeatedly proved effective as an alternative or adjunct to bright light for recurrent winter depression.

Tryptophan's waning antidepressant effect at high dosages is a tip-off that tryptophan is not a simple antidepressant, but rather a mood stabilizer—an upper at low doses and a downer at high doses, like lithium, valproic acid, and other medications for bipolar disorder. Not only is tryptophan unlikely to provoke mania or hypomania in bipolar depressives, in very high doses it can do just the opposite. Its potent antimanic effect has been demonstrated in most controlled clinical trials by McGill University psychiatrist Guy Chouinard and other investigators, whether alone or as an adjunct to lithium. In Canada, where psychiatrists like Chouinard have made Tryptan a staple of their mood-stabilizing arsenal, bipolar disorder is one of the prescription tryptophan's labelled indications.

Tryptophan still has a loyal following. When it was pulled from the market, some users suffered depressive relapses that only resolved when their psychiatrists procured more of the amino acid for them. Doctors like Ray Sahelian still have patients for whom nothing can take tryptophan's place—not even tryptophan's more potent heir apparent: 5-hydroxytryptophan.

Turbo-Tryptophan: 5-hydroxytryptophan (5-HTP)

In the late 1990s, a close relative of tryptophan with much sturdier research behind it finally gained passage across the Atlantic from Europe, where it had been prescribed for decades. By the summer of 1999, 5-hydroxytryptophan—better known as 5-HTP—was vying for third place among twenty-six antidepressants (mostly drugs) in the ratings of visitors to the popular website deja.com. The supplement garnered an overall score of 3.3 out of 5, just 0.3 points shy of the highest rated antidepressant, the Prozac rival Zoloft.

5-HTP is the intermediate between tryptophan and serotonin. Being just one easy step away from serotonin, with (unlike tryptophan) nothing to do but take it, 5-HTP is a much more efficient serotonin precursor. It has another surprising ace up its sleeve: 5-HTP is taken up not only by serotonergic neurons, but by neurons that secrete norepinephrine (NE) and dopamine (DA) too. Somehow this triggers an increase in NE and DA neurotransmission, making 5-HTP a psychopharmacologically much more versatile and potentially stimulating antidepressant than tryptophan.

Since the early 1970s, 5-HTP has demonstrated its antidepressive mettle in 12 of 16 clinical trials (including some as brief as one or two weeks), proving itself significantly superior to placebo (and tryptophan) and/or as effective as antidepressant drugs in most of the dozen or so controlled matches. It has usually been pitted against moderate to severe major depression, often of a recurrent or refractory nature. According to W. Poldinger and associates, about two in every three 5-HTP-treated depressives have enjoyed marked improvement or remission. In 5-HTP's most recent trial—a double-blind, randomized study involving 69 mostly moderately to severely depressed patients—5-HTP proved marginally more effective and significantly better tolerated than Luvox, one of the most user-friendly SSRIs.

Are Tryptophan and 5-HTP for You?

Tryptophan and 5-HTP, research suggests, can work for all varieties and severities of depression. They may be particularly well suited for melancholic and treatment-resistant major depressions, for these typically are associated with high levels of the stress hormone cortisol, which lowers blood levels of tryptophan. Tryptophan's value for psychotic (delusional) depression is unclear, though it would be one of the least likely antidepressants to enflame it.

As described in my book *Serotonin* and Michael Norden's excellent *Beyond Prozac*, agents like 5-HTP and tryptophan that boost serotonin cut a remarkably broad therapeutic swath across the spectrum of mental and neurologic disorders. If, in addition to your depression, you have any of the following conditions, tryptophan or 5-HTP could be of special value. (See table 9.1.)

As described on pages 136–138 in chapter 11, certain lab tests may also help predict if tryptophan or 5-HTP is for you.

Table 9.1.
Conditions for Which Tryptophan or 5-HTP May Be Helpful

Condition	Supplement
Obsessive-compulsive disorder	tryptophan*, especially as an adjunct to serotonergic drugs
Panic disorder and other anxiety disorders	5-HTP**
Insomnia	tryptophan,* 5-HTP**
Chronic pain	tryptophan,* 5-HTP**
Migraine and other headaches	5-HTP,* tryptophan**
Fibromyalgia	5-HTP*
Overeating (including bulimia nervosa), especially "carbohydrate craving"	tryptophan,* 5-HTP*
Premenstrual syndrome	tryptophan**
Attention deficit hyperactivity disorder	tryptophan**
Autism	tryptophan,** 5-HTP**
Depression or other psychiatric symptoms in people who have AIDS or are HIV positive	tryptophan**, 5-HTP**
Substance abuse (including alcoholism and smoking)	tryptophan,** 5-HTP**
Uncontrollable rage	tryptophan**
Impulsive behavior disorders, especially involving aggression or violence, including self-harm	tryptophan**
Schizophrenia	tryptophan**
Tourette's syndrome	tryptophan,** 5-HTP**
Parkinson's disease	tryptophan,** 5-HTP**
Dementia, including Alzheimer's disease	tryptophan,** 5-HTP**

Note: In a few of these conditions—migraines, schizophrenia, and Parkinson's disease, for example—tryptophan and/or 5-HTP have worsened some people's symptoms, so use with caution.

* Evidence for the supplement's efficacy is relatively strong.
** Evidence for the supplement's efficacy is conflicting or preliminary.

Tyrosine and Phenylalanine: The Up, Up, and Away Aminos

Animals get depressed too. Indeed, psychologists routinely create "animal models" of depression by subjecting their captives to a capricious schedule of severe, uncontrollable stress until the broken creatures withdraw into a shell of "learned helplessness," a convincing analogue of human depression. (Children, please don't do this at home. Scientists, please don't do this at all.)

Coping with chronic stress, whether you're a mistreated puppy in a psych lab or a panicky yuppie in a bear market, costs chemicals. One of the most important is the neurotransmitter *norepinephrine* (NE). An overload of stress can severely deplete NE, and with it the respective puppy or yuppie's ability to keep on keeping on.

If only they had some extra tyrosine! Tyrosine is the amino acid from which NE is made. In some studies, stressed-out animals *have* had an extra helping of tyrosine. And it's enabled them to keep on ticking almost as smoothly as animals under no stress at all.

Is there a lesson here for depressives?

NE is more than just a stress-adaptive chemical. It also helps stimulate the so-called pleasure centers of the brain, the nerve centers for our moments of pleasure and fulfillment. NE deficiency could help account for the *anhedonia* (lack of pleasure response) that is a hallmark of clinical depression. Although NE is by no means the only chemical our happiness depends upon, NE deficiency has for decades been regarded, with serotonin deficiency, as the chemical imbalance most likely to underlie depression. Boosting NE has continually rivaled or complemented boosting serotonin as the chief antidepressant strategy. Although this has usually been done with drugs, some doctors and researchers have turned to NE's dietary precursors: tyrosine and its precursor, phenylalanine.

Tyrosine: The No-Sweat Antidepressant

Tyrosine is the precursor not only to NE, but to the dynamic neurotransmitter dopamine and to the exciting hormones of the thyroid gland and the adrenal cortex. For doctors like Andrew Weil and Michael Murray, who often treat depression nutritionally, tyrosine is a popular first-line treatment and a valued last resort. Sheldon Hendler of the University of California at San Diego finds it particularly effective for his premenstrual syndrome and chronic fatigue patients. Priscilla Slagle, an associate clinical professor of psychiatry at the UCLA Medical Center, features tyrosine and other amino acids in her orthomolecular regime for depression. Biopsychiatrist Mark S. Gold includes tyrosine among the "triggers" he tries on depressives who aren't responding to drug therapy. Orthomolecular physician Eric Braverman and his associates describe an elderly patient whose thirteen-year ordeal of recurrent winter depression refused to yield to anything—not drugs, not supplements, not Florida—except tyrosine.

For Martin Heller (not his real name), the SSRI Zoloft provided a four-year respite from depression. But then, as SSRIs often do, it "pooped out." Four months of deep depression later, Heller decided to augment with tyrosine. "Within three days I felt much much better," he recalls. Six months later Heller's mood was still reasonably good as he began to explore other natural antidepressants to improve his recovery.

After an inauspicious debut in a small, unsuccessful—and unpublished—trial (Coppen, 1970), tyrosine gathered steam in the 1980s. Harvard Medical School's Alan Gelenberg and his associates tested the amino acid on a chronically depressed patient. The woman recovered completely, only to relapse on placebo, then recover again on tyrosine. Gelenberg and company followed up with two larger double-blind trials. In the first, tyrosine performed as well as drugs normally do. In a larger, but brief (four-week) 1990 study involving sixty-three depressives, those on tyrosine enjoyed a respectable 45 percent decrease in symptoms—just shy of imipramine's 50 percent reduction, but not "significantly" (i.e., statistically) better than placebo's 35 percent. Meanwhile, in placebo-controlled trials by Herman van Praag (1984) and associates, tyrosine hastened and improved depressives' response to 5-HTP and pulled others out of a 5-HTP "poop out." And in France, Jacques Mouret et al. identified tyrosine as a rapid antidote for what they term "dopamine-dependent depressions," sluggishly reminiscent of Parkinson's disease and narcolepsy.

The Phabulous Phenylalanines

There is evidence that tyronsine's precursor, phenylalanine (PA), doesn't convert well to tyrosine in acutely depressed persons. PA, however, has some antidepressant tricks of its own. The "D" form of PA (D-phenylalanine, or DPA) inhibits the breakdown of those warm and fuzzy, feel-good neuropeptides, the endorphins. And PA of any kind is converted into a stimulating neurochemical called *2-phenylethylamine* (PEA). For reasons like these, both the natural "L" form of PA (L-phenylalanine, or LPA) and the synthetic DPA found in DL-phenylalanine (DLPA) supplements have carved a unique niche for themselves in the natural (more or less) antidepressant armamentarium.

Peppy DLPA

In 1983, a prominent biological psychiatrist named Michael Liebowitz popularized the notion that PEA is the brain's natural amphetamine, the ebullient neuromodulator that makes us feel giddy when we fall in love or ecstatic when we win a lottery or get a promotion. Psychiatrists have long hypothesized that a deficiency of this releaser of neuronal NE and dopamine is a major cause of depression. PEA is consistently low in the body fluids of depressives. In all but one of about half a dozen studies, low doses of DPA or DLPA have proven remarkably effective for hundreds of patients suffering from mild to severe depression. In one incredible trial, roughly 90 percent of the 417 mostly endogenous depressives recovered within two months on DPA. Unfortunately, in what seems to be the only completely independent trial, by psychiatrist John Mann, DPA worked for just two out of eleven patients, while two others actually deteriorated. (For an overview of these studies see Beckmann, 1983, or Fox and Fox, 1985.)

Although DLPA has never achieved the superstardom of St. John's wort or SAMe, many nutritionally oriented practitioners have long appreciated its power. (DPA is hard to obtain, and PEA is not available at all.) University of the Pacific internist Arnold Fox devoted an entire book to DLPA for chronic pain and depression. And in 1995, natural health guru Andrew Weil, M.D., recommended DLPA as his antidepressant supplement of choice.

Feel-Good L-Phenylalanine

Like so many natural antidepressants, L-phenylalanine's vocation for mood-lifting was first revealed long, long ago—in 1966, to be precise. But it wasn't until nearly twenty years later that William Birkmayer and his associates returned for another look. A very low dose of LPA (250 milligrams per day) sparked recovery or improvement in more than 80 percent of 155 depressives who had been unresponsive to the weak antidepressant L-deprenyl. Around the same time, psychiatrist Hector Sabelli and his associates administered very large doses of LPA (up to 14 grams per day) to forty depressed patients at Rush-Presbyterian-St. Luke's Medical Center in Chicago. Though most had been chronically treatment-resistant, eleven recovered completely, twenty improved substantially, and two were bouyed to the point of hypomania. Other small reports have continued to suggest that LPA—over a wide dose range, whether alone or as an augmentor—is a potent and usually rapid antidepressant. In a study by Sabelli, for instance, a cocktail of LPA, low-dose L-deprenyl, and vitamin B_6 "terminated" six out of ten severe, intractable depressions in just three days.

I discovered LPA myself in the early 1980s, and it's been my main chemical shield against depression ever since. Nutritionally oriented practitioners like Priscilla Slagle and Andrew Weil also know LPA's value. But for most depressives, this inexpensive supplement remains an undeservedly dark horse.

Are Tyrosine and Phenylalanine for You?

Research suggests any kind of depression may respond to tyrosine or PA, but their stimulating effects make them obvious first choices for the sluggish, apathetic kind. Bipolar depression usually fits this description; but to prevent manic or hypomanic reactions, mood stabilizers like lithium and tryptophan should also be on hand. Depressives with other excitable conditions—anxiety disorders, psychosis, poor impulse control (temper, violence), tics, dyskinesias, seizures—should be on guard too. In theory, depressives with Tourette syndrome may benefit from low doses of DLPA or LPA, but be made worse by tyrosine.

Their condition is associated with high dopamine but low LPA, PEA, and NE.

You may also be a good candidate for tyrosine or PA if:

⤳ Lab tests suggest you have a deficiency (see pages 136–138 in chapter 11). Some research suggests women on oral contraceptives or suffering postpartum depression may be tyrosine-deficient.

⤳ Severe mental or physical stress is draining your brain's NE reserves.

⤳ You have Parkinson's disease. As the precursor to L-dopa (the primary treatment for Parkinson's), some scientists believe tyrosine may be a useful adjunct or alternative. Oddly, phenylalanine appears to aggravate Parkinson's disease.

⤳ You're emotionally hooked on the euphoria of romance, applause, or the sweet smell of victory—rejection or defeat sends you reeling. If Michael Liebowitz is right, it could be PEA that's pressing your reward buttons, and PA could make you less dependent on outside "pressure."

⤳ You crave stimulants like cocaine, amphetamines, chocolate, nicotine, or caffeine. Stimulants tend to work by releasing the brain's own stimulants, like PEA and NE. But eventually they can deplete these chemicals, causing lethargy and depression. PA and/or tyrosine will not only replenish them, they may even reduce the need for stimulants in the first place, as tyrosine did for two of psychiatrist Ivan Goldberg's amphetamine-responsive depressives.

⤳ You have chronic pain. Studies discussed by Arnold Fox, who prescribes DLPA for this purpose, suggest DLPA can relieve it.

⤳ You have winter depression. It worked for one of Braverman et al.'s patients, and a recent study by A. Neumeister and associates suggests a lack of NE is just as involved in the syndrome as a shortage of serotonin.

Other Amino Acids and Mood Disorders

The story of amino acids and depression doesn't stop here.

⤳ There is a steadily growing body of evidence that depression is promoted by a deficiency of the amino-acid neurotransmitter gamma-aminobutyric acid (GABA), and that drugs which stimulate or imitate GABA (including certain benzodiazepine tranquilizers, like alprazolam)—perhaps even GABA itself—can be therapeutic. GABA has antianxiety and anticonvulsant effects; but too much of this natural tranquilizer may cause or worsen depression. Perhaps GABA could help people whose mood disorders are secondary to partial complex seizures.

A very close relative of GABA, gabapentin (Neurontin), is an anticonvulsant that shows signs of being a very well-tolerated mood stabilizer for bipolar disorder. Though not as well absorbed by the brain, GABA may have similar benefits for anxious, irritable, or bipolar depressives at dosages as high as several grams a day, according to Braverman et al. The dosage should be built up slowly to prevent oversedation.

- Orthomolecular practitioners like Sheldon Hendler and Eric Braverman have found low blood levels not just of tryptophan, tyrosine, phenylalanine, and methionine, but also of glutamine, threonine, glycine, taurine, and/or aspartic acid in some of their depressed patients. They report that supplements have often proved therapeutic. Threonine deficiency, in particular, appears common in patients with severe depression. Braverman and his associates have found 1 to 2 grams of threonine per day to be most useful for patients with agitated or psychotic depression or bipolar disorder.

- Some clinical and metabolic studies suggest that low doses of L-dopa combined with a peripheral decarboxylase inhibitor (a prescription drug called Sinemet) may be useful for depressives who, like people with Parkinson's disease, are extremely slowed down ("retarded") and perhaps suicidal.

- For years, there have been anecdotal reports that high doses of the inhibitory neurotransmitter glycine can allay aggression and mania. Eric Braverman and his associates report that in their orthomolecular clinic, single doses of 15 to 30 grams (we usually eat 2 or so grams a day) aborted manic episodes in two out of two patients within an hour. In recent studies from Israel (Heresco-Levy), megadoses of glycine significantly relieved apathy, social withdrawal, and depression in treatment-resistant chronic schizophrenics.

CHAPTER 10

———— ✿ ————

A Few More Good Nutrients

Not every good thing in food is a vitamin, mineral, essential fatty acid, or amino acid. Some of the most exciting nutrients—such as the cancer-fighting pigment lycopene and the heart-friendly bioflavonoids that make red wine a health food—defy traditional categorization. And some of these nutrients can be mood medicine too.

Calm Choline

Choline is the dietary precursor to acetylcholine, the neurotransmitter that fades away with people's memory in Alzheimer's disease. Acetylcholine also bears a striking see-saw relationship with mood (Risch and Janowsky, 1984). Lower it with drugs (including the pre-Prozac antidepressants), and some people become euphoric or manic. Boost it with drugs or large doses of choline or lecithin (a choline-rich foodstuff), and some people become depressed. Or just normal.

Until recently, it looked as if choline might be a therapeutic downer for bipolar disorder, but nothing more. In a 1982 placebo-controlled trial by Bruce Cohen and associates at Harvard, lecithin rapidly grounded five out of six high-flying manic patients. Other researchers reported similar benefits. But recently the Harvard group has produced provocative new evidence that, for rapid-cycling bipolars at least, choline could be a full-fledged mood stabilizer.

The subjects chosen by Andrew Stoll and his associates were six severely ill, chronic rapid cyclers who had failed to respond adequately to lithium or to anything else. Because lithium may potentiate choline's effects, the patients were maintained on lithium in addition to 3 to 8 grams per day of choline.

Comparing the first month on choline to the previous month without, the differences were remarkable. Most enjoyed substantial reductions in both mania and depression. One thirty-six-year-old man had been depressed every day the previous month. "After four days of choline therapy, he had a complete remission of depressive symptoms," the researchers wrote. Sixteen weeks later he was still stable and feeling no side effects.

Not all patients were immune to choline's depressing effect. One woman saw her self-rated mania shrink by over 80 percent on choline. But her depression rose by 50 percent, leading to a trade-in of the choline for an antidepressant drug, which provoked another manic reaction. (As we'll see in a moment, inositol—*yang* to choline's *yin*— might have been a more apt choice.)

Although the study was uncontrolled, the improvements were exceptional. Thanks to magnetic resonance imaging, the researchers determined that choline was ineffective only in the two patients whose brain levels of choline didn't rise. Both, it turned out, were also taking a very high dose of thyroxine, a highly effective treatment for rapid cycling that lowers brain choline. When one of these patients had his thyroxine dose lowered, his brain choline went up, and so did his response to the nutrient.

Although choline has yet to catch on with most psychiatrists, nutritionally oriented practitioners like Sheldon Hendler and Priscilla Slagle have used it—and lecithin—in their mood-stabilizing arsenal for years.

Up with Inositol

Years and years ago, neuroscientists thought of the brain as a massive telephone exchange, its billions of neurons linked together in an awesome network. Then they made a startling discovery: The neurons reach out to each other with spaghettilike fingers (axons), but they don't actually touch. To communicate, they must squirt little chemicals—neurotransmitters—across the tiny gap that separates them: the synaptic cleft. The neurotransmitters then land on the receiving neuron's postsynaptic receptors, and then . . .

Well, it turns out that even that isn't enough to complete the phone call. Inside the receptors there are chemicals called second messengers, which must carry the neurotransmitter's signal right into the body of the receiving neuron. Then, and only then, can it get the message. When it comes to the brain's major mood-regulating neurotransmitters, that second messenger very often is a molecule called *phosphatidyl inositol*.

The last few years have seen a mini-boom of psychiatric research on phosphatidyl inositol and its precursor, the dietary sugar inositol. Studies have shown that inositol and the phosphatidyl inositol second messenger system are altered in key brain areas of depressives, suicide victims, and people with bipolar disorder. The emerging picture is that low activity in the phosphatidyl inositol second messenger system correlates with depression and high activity with mania.

Israeli researchers have pursued the clinical implications, using severe, treatment-resistant depressives as their subjects. In a preliminary trial, Belmaker et al. found that nine out of eleven such patients were markedly improved by megadoses of inositol. Some researchers, however, have also observed several cases of inositol-induced mania or hypomania (Levine et al.).

In placebo-controlled trials, megadoses of inositol have allayed other conditions sometimes associated with depression: agoraphobia, panic attacks, and obsessive-compulsive disorder. But they've aggravated attention deficit disorder.

Some people are benefiting from much lower doses of inositol. Low doses of inositol, according to preliminary research, also can relieve some of the side effects (e.g., excessive thirst, frequent urination) of lithium, which inhibits inositol synthesis.

The Power of Carnitine

L-carnitine is a "conditionally essential amino acid," meaning we can make it ourselves, though perhaps not always as much as we need. Carnitine's main claim to fame is stoking the body's cellular powerhouses, the mitochondria—hence its concentration in the heart and muscles.

In a not-so-surprising study from the Chronic Fatigue Syndrome Center in Chicago, symptoms of CFS were worst in patients with the lowest blood levels of carnitine and carnitine's more active metabolite, acetylcarnitine. In a controlled eight-week trial from the center by A. V. and S. Plioplys, L-carnitine supplements significantly relieved most symptoms in thirty CFS patients. Only one dropped out.

Carnitine has allayed fatigue in people with other conditions too. If you're a weary —and, perhaps, vegetarian—depressive, this supplement could be for you.

For its part, acetylcarnitine appears to be more than an energy tonic. Controlled trials suggest it's a "smart drug" for elderly people, and that it protects the brain from strokes and other insults. It may also be a "happy drug"; in three placebo-controlled trials by R. Bella et al. and others, it has been mildly effective for depression and dysthymia in nondemented elderly patients.

Phosphatidylserine: A Good-Mood Brain Food

Phosphatidylserine (PS) is another orthomolecular smart drug. It's a phospholipid, a type of fat (often laden with omega-3 fatty acids) that is the stuff of cellular membranes. When it comes to neuronal membranes, PS is the phospholipid of choice.

Animal and human clinical trials suggest supplements of PS improve not only cognition, but also depressionlike symptoms of withdrawal and apathy. Indeed, in a preliminary trial from the University of Milan by M. Maggioni et al., PS relieved clinical depression in ten elderly women.

CHAPTER 11

Using Nutritional Supplements

This chapter will provide you with detailed information on using antidepressant supplements as safely and effectively as possible. Unfortunately, not all the details are known. Our collective experience with supplements is mostly anecdotal, with limited long-term data. But the record so far shows that, used as recommended, supplements tend to be very well tolerated and are rarely associated with serious side effects.

If you know what you're doing and are determined, I believe you can safely "do it yourself" with supplements. But there are obvious advantages to seeking expert help, especially if your depression is severe and self-treatment would be too demanding.

One organization that can help you is the International Society for Orthomolecular Medicine ([416] 733-2117; fax: [416] 733-2352; www.orthomed.org/isom/isom.htm). The ISOM's website has lots of information and links to orthomolecular treatment centers around the world.

The American Holistic Medical Association ([703] 556-9245; www.holisticmedicine.org) has a range of licensed professionals (medical doctors, naturopaths, chiropractors, psychologists, etc.) among its members who specialize in nutritional and/or other natural approaches.

The American Association of Naturopathic Physicians ([206] 298-0126; fax: [206] 298-0129; www.naturopathic.org) can help you find a licensed naturopath who specializes in diet, herbs, nutritional supplements, acupuncture, and other natural healing modalities.

Testing for Nutritional Deficiencies

You don't need to know if you're nutritionally deficient to use supplements effectively, but lab tests can help you zero in on the supplements most likely to succeed. Unfortunately, few doctors other than orthomolecular specialists are inclined to accommodate you here, unless you have clinical signs, symptoms, or risk factors. The more of the following nonspecific ones you have (or the specific ones mentioned in previous chapters), the more suspicious you should be:

Signs and symptoms: Depression and any of its symptoms; lesions in and around the mouth (e.g., swollen, inflamed tongue; bleeding gums; cracks around the mouth); skin disorders (oily, dry, rough, or flaky skin; easy bruising; dandruff); hair loss; severe mental impairment; strange sensations, particularly in the extremities (e.g., numbness, tingling, burning); weak legs; dizziness, incoordination.

Risk factors: Poor diet; chronic emotional distress; immoderate use of alcohol or caffeine; smoking; chronic exposure to toxic chemicals and pollutants; pregnancy and nursing; use of certain drugs (e.g., birth control pills, MAOIs, anticonvulsants, cholestyramine); surgery or injury; dialysis; chronic infection; chronic gastrointestinal disorders resulting in malabsorption; rapid growth spurt; old age.

The following tests for nutritional deficiencies are considered the most sensitive. But even they're fallible. They can't, for example, detect a deficiency confined to the brain. This is why some practitioners prescribe supplements even when tests are negative.

Tests for Vitamin Deficiencies

B_1: Erythrocyte transketolase
B_2: Erythrocyte glutathione reductase
B_3: N-methylnicotinamide
B_6: Pyridoxal-5-phosphate, erythrocyte glutamic-pyruvic transaminase, kynurenic acid, and/or xanthurenic acid
Folic acid: FIGLU (forminoglutamic acid), and/or RBC (red blood cell) folate

B$_{12}$: Serum B$_{12}$ (microbiological assay only) or (preferably) serum or
urinary MMA (methylmalonic acid) or homocysteine, and/or the
deoxyuridine suppression test
Vitamin C: White blood cell ascorbate
Carnitine: Serum carnitine or (preferably) muscle or liver carnitine

Tests for Mineral Deficiencies

Magnesium: RBC magnesium or (preferably) muscle magnesium or a
magnesium loading test
Calcium: Ionized calcium
Iron: Serum ferritin
Zinc: Blood and urine tests are standard, but D. Bryce-Smith and
R. I. D. Simpson claim to have found a simple taste test (sold in
some health food stores) more reliable. Five to 10 milliliters of a
zinc solution (1 gram zinc sulphate heptahydrate [sold in drug-
stores] in 1 liter of distilled water) is held in the mouth for ten seconds. People who are not zinc deficient notice a strong, usually
unpleasant, metallic taste. People who are taste little or nothing.

Tests for Fatty Acid Deficiencies or Imbalances

The most revealing tests are measures of the absolute and relative levels
in blood cell membranes or cholesterol esters of important fatty acids,
notably alpha-linolenic acid (ALA), linoleic acid (LA), dihomogamma-
linolenic acid (DGLA), gamma-linolenic acid (GLA), arachidonic acid
(AA), docosahexanoic acid (DHA), and eicosapentanoic acid (EPA).

Tests for Amino Acid Deficiencies

Probably the most revealing test is the ratio in the blood plasma of tyrosine, phenylalanine, tryptophan, and methionine to each other and
to the other large, neutral amino acids that compete with them for passage across the blood-brain barrier. Low ratios of any of these amino
acids suggest the brain is undersupplied with them and supplements
may help. So may poor erythrocyte membrane transport of any of these
amino acids (Azorin et al.).

An indirect gauge is low blood or urinary levels of the major metabolites of the neurotransmitters made from tyrosine (MHPG, HVA), phenylalanine (PAA, MHPG, HVA), or tryptophan (5-HIAA).

Orthomolecular clinicians like Eric Braverman and his associates and Priscilla Slagle have found that testing for and topping up low blood levels of the following amino acids in depressed patients can also be rewarding: GABA, threonine, histamine, glycine, glutamic acid, taurine, and aspartic acid.

Where to Find Natural Antidepressants

As of this writing, all of the supplements discussed in this chapter were available "wherever nutritional supplements are sold," with a few exceptions:

❧ Except for 5-HTP and SAMe, most amino acids are unavailable over the counter (OTC) in Canada. They can, however, be legally ordered or imported for personal use from the United States or other countries (see below). Tryptophan is available in Canada by prescription as the "drug" Tryptan. Recent federal reforms may soon make it easy for Canadians to obtain almost any supplement OTC.

❧ Tryptophan is available in the United States by prescription from certain compounding pharmacies and OTC from at least one U.S. seller (see below).

❧ Carbidopa is available only from some compounding pharmacies.

Here are some current sellers of hard-to-find supplements:

❧ BIOS Biochemicals ([520] 326-7610, www.biochemicals.com) and England's International Antiaging Systems (IAS) (011-44-541-514144, www.smart-drugs.com) sell tryptophan without a prescription.

❧ The Life Extension Foundation (1-800-841-5433; lef.org) and Life-Link (1-888-433-5266; www.lifelinknet.com) are two rare suppliers of the clinically most effective form of vitamin B_{12}: methylcobalamin, a.k.a. Xobaline.

❧ Orthomolecular psychiatrist Priscilla Slagle (1-800-289-8487; www.thewayup.com) sells most antidepressant supplements, including such exotica as D-phenylalanine (Endorpheryl), several

B vitamins in their more bioavailable coenzyme forms, and Norival (300 milligrams of N-acetyl-L-tyrosine—supposedly more bioactive than tyrosine itself—synergistically combined with 25 micrograms of biopterin and 10 milligrams of pyridoxyl-5-phosphate.

✻ Medical Center Compounding Pharmacy (1-800-723-7455; www.mcpharmacy.com/) sells tryptophan and carbidopa by prescription.

✻ Canadians can order amino acids from the companies mentioned above as well as many others, like Vitamin Research Products (1-800-877-2447, www.vrp.com) and MotherNature.com (1-800-517-9020; www.mothernature.com).

Usage: General Considerations

Clinical Response

Some nutritional supplements—vitamin C, thiamine, niacin/NADH, linseed oil, and SAMe, for instance—can bring noticeable relief from depression for some people within days or even hours. But usually supplements take weeks to lift depression. However, other fast-acting antidepressants, like bright light (chap. 15), sleep deprivation (chap. 18), and sleep phase advance or delay (chap. 19), can be combined with the slowpokes to hasten recovery.

After you've recovered from a serious mood disorder on nutritional supplements, it's prudent to wait at least a few months before venturing to taper down slowly to a maintenance dosage or quitting. Early or rapid discontinuation encourage early relapse. Indeed, research with antidepressant drugs suggests it may be advisable not to cut down at all if you have a severe recurrent disorder, unless perhaps you've found other effective maintenance therapies, such as dietary reform, exercise, meditation, and regular sleep habits.

As noted below, the dosage of certain supplements actually needs to be lowered after awhile to maintain clinical response.

Dosage and Administration

The dose ranges below are commonly employed to treat depression or bipolar disorder in research and clinical practice. But as the saying goes, your mileage may vary. To find a dosage that's right for you, it's best to start at the bottom of the dose range (or even lower) and increase gradually, while watching for improvements or adverse reactions. Going slowly is critical if a nutrient has a *therapeutic window* (i.e., it's only effective within a narrow dose range) or if too much can worsen depression or provoke mania.

Most supplements are absorbed and utilized best in capsule or powder form, when taken with food, and—if the dosage is high—divided into two or more doses each day. Exceptions are noted below. Some doctors will inject supplements to bypass possibly poor oral absorption (common in the elderly).

Some people do best on hypoallergenic supplements. Taking a supplement every day for a long time could provoke allergy to the main ingredient or to any fillers. One way around this, if your condition permits, is to take a "holiday" from any supplement every few months, as Ray Sahelian, M.D., often recommends. This is least likely to be necessary for the chemically simple supplements (e.g., minerals), more of a possibility for complex or organic supplements, like herbs (chap. 13) and hormones (chap. 12). Alternating brands also shuffles your exposure to potential allergens.

Combining Supplements with Each Other and with Drugs

More and more people are seeking the best of both worlds from natural antidepressants and antidepressant drugs. Although some are delighted to find they can scrap their prescriptions, others find that supplements allow them to respond better to their drugs or get by on a lower dosage.

Unfortunately, there is much confusion about the safety of these combinations, even among doctors, pharmacists, and writers of self-help books. In the following pages, I will share what I know, but I encourage you to seek other, perhaps more knowledgeable and (by the time you read this) up-to-date sources, including my website, www.escape.ca/~sgb.

Hazardous combinations seem confined to those that strongly boost the same neurotransmitter by different mechanisms. MAOI drugs, for instance, inhibit the breakdown of serotonin, NE, and blood pressure–elevating amines in foods and beverages. Combine MAOIs with drugs or supplements that block the reuptake (reabsorption) of serotonin into the neurons that secrete it, or with serotonin's precursors, or with hypertensive amines, and you have the potential makings of serious and (rarely) deadly reactions called the *serotonin syndrome* and *hypertensive crisis*.

Among natural antidepressants, there are combinations that, in theory, belong to this potent but prickly family. For example, St. John's wort is an inhibitor of serotonin, norepinephrine, and dopamine reuptake (and possibly a mild MAOI, in some products), so it could be hazardous to combine it with tryptophan, 5-HTP, tyrosine, phenylalanine, SAMe, methionine, or maybe even folic acid. But these combinations could also prove that much more therapeutic. Used cautiously, they could be more effective, yet still safe, for many depressions.

In contrast, combining antidepressants that boost *different* neurotransmitters seems to create a synergy that is safe. The MAOIs, most cyclic antidepressants, and the newer antidepressant Effexor (venlafaxine) all simultaneously boost serotonin, NE, and sometimes dopamine and PEA too. A natural equivalent is to combine a serotonin precursor (tryptophan or 5-HTP) with an NE precursor (tyrosine or perhaps phenylalanine) and a PEA precursor (DPA, DLPA, or LPA). Such a combination could be more effective than any of these nutrients alone. Orthomolecular practitioners like Michael Murray and Priscilla Slagle often prescribe combinations, sometimes with a touch of medication, using their patients' symptoms, their response to treatment, and (in some clinics) blood tests to guide them. Controlled research like van Praag's of 5-HTP and tyrosine suggests such combinations can provide a therapeutic edge.

Generally, combinations are actually more conducive to safety, not less. Lopsidedly high doses of a few nutrients can lead to an imbalance among the whole family of nutrients that work together in the body. Too much of one can block others that compete with it for absorption or utilization. It can be a burden if nutrients that help metabolize a supplement aren't taken too. Vitamins need other vitamins to help convert them into their bioactive coenzyme forms. Fatty acids and amino acids are particularly demanding of other nutrients for safe processing. Methionine without folic acid is a strong invitation to heart disease and other illnesses.

The best insurance against supplementing your way into nutritional imbalance is to eat a wholesome, nutrient-rich diet (chap. 12) and to take a medium- to high-potency multivitamin and mineral supplement, while following the recommendations for balancing specific supplements provided below and/or the advice of a knowledgeable practitioner.

Safety and Side Effects

By now you're probably girded enough not to be startled by the following lists of side effects, cautions, and contraindications. Although sometimes numerous, the side effects associated with nutritional supplements (whether actual or coincidental), when used as indicated, typically are mild and infrequent. In fact, most people on supplements don't feel as if they're "taking anything," as they typically do on antidepressant drugs.

Although some supplements, like a modest dose of folic acid, can be good for pregnant women and their fetuses, sadly, not enough is known about the effects of very large doses or megadoses of supplements during pregnancy to ensure their safety. The same must be said for young children.

The Foundation:
A Multivitamin and Mineral Supplement

A wholesome, nutrient-rich diet and a well-endowed medium- to high-potency multivitamin and mineral supplement, or "multi," are the essential backbone of any supplement program. They may even be sufficient to gradually correct many of the nutritional deficiencies that contribute to depression. A multi is also an ounce of prevention. In a large double-blind study by D. Benton and associates from the University of Swansea in Wales, taking a high-potency multivitamin supplement for a year significantly improved the spirits and mental health of healthy young adults.

Look for a multi that includes as many nonessential and obscure nutrients (e.g., manganese, chromium, boron, cobalt, lithium) as possible. You never know what your body may be missing.

Vitamins

Vitamin B₁ *(Thiamine)*

RDI*: 1.5 milligrams

Dosage and administration: 100 milligrams to 6 grams per day. Because B_1 is very poorly absorbed, many small doses raise B_1 levels much better than just one or two large ones.

Cost: Cheap (about 10 to 25 cents per day).

Safety and side effects: Gastric distress; may raise blood pressure. An unconfirmed study by Connor found that a megadose of 500 milligrams per day caused moderate (40 percent) MAO inhibition. If that's so, people who take megadoses of B_1 may need to consider observing the dietary and drug precautions for MAOI drug users and be cautious about taking antidepressant drugs and natural antidepressants that may not mix well with MAOIs. In practice, although Braverman et al. mention elevated blood pressure as a side effect of B_1, there have been no reports of hypertensive crises in orthomolecular patients taking megadoses of B_1, typically with many other supplements and sometimes with antidepressant drugs.

---

*RDI stands for *reference daily intake*. It's replacing the old *recommended daily or dietary allowance* standard, though the numbers are changing very little. The RDIs listed here are for average adults. They vary somewhat for adults with special needs. For example, they're usually higher during pregnancy and lactation.

Vitamin B₃ *(Niacin, NADH, inositol hexaniacinate, etc.)*

RDI: 20 milligrams

Dosage and administration: Niacin: 500 milligrams to 40 grams per day—usually 3 to 6 grams per day. (Slow-release forms are effective at half to one-third the dosage, but the risk of liver damage appears much greater.) NADH: usually 5 to 15 milligrams before breakfast. Inositol hexaniacinate (IHN) and xanthinol nicotinate: probably the same dosage as niacin.

Cost: Niacin: cheap; IHN and xanthinol nicotinate: pricey (about 75 cents to $1.50 per day); NADH (brand name ENADA): expensive ($1.50 to $3.00 per day).

Side effects: Doses of niacin over 100 to 200 milligrams produce dramatic but harmless acute flushing and mild burning. This reaction abates with regular use. It can be diminished by taking niacin with meals or cold liquids or by using slow-release niacin or no-flush niacin (IHN). Michael Lesser finds that enjoying the flush augurs well psychotherapeutically.

Other side effects: Nausea, vomiting, abdominal pain, frontal headaches, overstimulation and restlessness, darkening of the skin, itchiness, impaired vision, swollen ankles, cardiac arrythmia, liver dysfunction, hyperglycemia, and gouty arthritis.

In an online article (www.arxc.com/townsend/nadhreac.htm), NADH's developer, Jorg Birkmayer, M.D., claims that more than three thousand users have experienced no negative side effects and that "toxicology tests have indicated that NADH is safe in levels up to . . . 7,000 times greater than the recommended level of 5 milligrams per day." But too much NADH can make people hyper or sleepless, according to Robert Atkins, M.D.

Cautions and contraindications: Psychiatrists like Herbert Newbold advise against using more than 500 milligrams per day of niacin without medical supervision.

Niacin may be contraindicated (consult your doctor) if you have peptic ulcers, diabetes, high blood pressure, gout, porphyria, gall bladder disease, or liver disease. Because megadoses (especially of the slow-release forms) may cause hepatitis or liver damage, liver function tests should be done regularly, perhaps every six months. According to Abram Hoffer (1987), who has been prescribing megadoses of B_3 since the 1950s, about 1 in 2,000 patients develops a mild liver disease (obstructive jaundice), which soon clears when the B_3 is stopped. (SAMe, which protects the liver, could be an apt adjunct.) Hoffer disputes the existence of some of the above side effects and contraindications. He also argues that concerns that megadoses could cause birth defects are based on spurious animal studies and not supported by extensive clinical experience.

IHN is said by Michael Murray and others to have the same therapeutic effects as niacin, without the hazards. "No adverse effects have been reported from the use of inositol hexaniacinate [IHN] in dosages as high as four grams daily," according to an anonymous 1998 monograph in *Alternative Medicine Review*. But the supplement has seen much less clinical use than niacin, and the monograph conservatively recommends the same kinds of cautions as for niacin.

Vitamin B₆ (Pyridoxine)

RDI: 2 milligrams

Dosage: Usually 50 to 500 milligrams per day. For PMS, Wyatt et al.'s meta-analysis suggests 50 to 100 milligrams per day is as likely to work as higher dosages. The coenzyme form of B_6, *pyridoxal-5-phosphate* (P-5-P), is more bioactive and more effective for some people, according to Priscilla Slagle. Its dosage is about 10 to 120 milligrams per day.

Cost: Pyridoxine: very cheap (less than 10 cents per day); P-5-P: moderate (about 25 to 75 cents per day).

Side effects: Mild memory impairment. Some people—usually on super-megadoses (1 gram or more), but sometimes on dosages as low as 200 to 300 milligrams—have developed neurologic symptoms, such as numbness and staggering, or skin disorders. Clinicians like Slagle, Hoffer, and M. G. Brush and Marta Perry, who don't see these reactions in their patients, attribute them to the use of inappropriately high megadoses of B_6 or to failure to balance B_6 with other B vitamins and magnesium.

Cautions: B_6 supplements can convert the L-dopa used for Parkinson's disease to dopamine before it reaches the brain, unless carbidopa is prescribed too (as it normally is). The same may apply when taking tryptophan, 5-HTP, tyrosine, or phenylalanine (see below).

Folic Acid (Folate, Folacin)

RDI: 400 micrograms

Dosage and administration: Folic acid, methylfolate (not yet commercially available), folinic acid (5-formyltetrahydrofolate; leucovorin, Folacal): about 1 to 100 milligrams per day. Folinic acid is a very close relative of methylfolate (5-methyltetrahydrofolate), the coenzyme form of folic acid. It's therefore more likely to be clinically effective than folic acid. Generically known as leucovorin, folinic acid is available by prescription as Citrovorum or Wellcovorin. It's normally used to treat cancer or AIDS. It's also available as a supplement called Folacal, but only from health professionals who order it for their patients from Thorne Research ([208] 263-1337; www.thorne.com).

Folic acid, methylfolate, and probably folinic acid too, appear to have a therapeutic window. This may be because high enough megadoses can lower serotonin rather than raise it. Perhaps this is why responders sometimes have to lower the dosage after awhile to maintain their improvement.

Cost: Folic acid: cheap/moderate. Folinic acid: expensive.

Side effects: Folic acid: Usually after weeks or months on fairly high doses, some people have become abnormally euphoric or unpleasantly hypomanic—restless, sleepless, rambunctious, aggressive—perhaps because of serotonin depletion. Other side effects include abnormal taste, gastrointestinal disturbances, weight loss, malaise, depression, and an apparent allergic hypersensitivity (pain, flushing, itching, hives, fever). Methylfolate and folinic acid: probably similar. Megadoses of folinic acid have apparently caused stomatitis (inflammation or ulceration of the mouth or throat) and rare cases of leukopenia (low white cell count).

Cautions and contraindications: According to Braverman et al., large doses of folic acid (and probably the other folates) are poorly tolerated by people with allergies, including the "china doll" schizoaffectives described on page 87 in chapter 6. Megadoses also may provoke seizures in some epileptics and promote mild zinc deficiency if zinc intake is low. Even low doses can invalidate crude (and outdated) screening tests for vitamin B_{12} deficiency (simply warn your doctor before testing).

Vitamin B_{12} (Cobalamin, Cyanocobalamin, Methylcobalamin, Hydroxocobalamin)

RDI: 6 micrograms

Dosage: By injection: from 1,000 micrograms every few days up to 10,000 to 25,000 micrograms per day. Oral (including sublingual) and nasal gel: probably 500 to 25,000 micrograms per day. Sublingual and (especially) nasal gel products may rival B_{12} shots in their ability to increase blood levels. Studies like that of Mayer et al. suggest the cyanocobalamin form of B_{12} typically used in supplements isn't as clinically effective as methylcobalamin.

Cost: moderate to pricey.

Side effects, cautions, contraindications: Evidently, none.

Vitamin C (Ascorbic Acid, Ascorbate)

RDI: 60 milligrams

Dosage: From 1 or 2 grams per day up to 200 grams per day, using "bowel tolerance" as a guide (i.e., as much as you can take without getting loose stools). For megadoses (more than a few grams a day), don't use pills; use pure crystalline ascorbic acid or ascorbate.

Cost: Cheap/moderate.

Side effects and hazards: Aside from loose stools, side effects are rare. They include dry nose and nosebleeds, abdominal cramps, nausea, vomiting, heartburn, flushing, headache, fatigue, and insomnia. There is disputed (e.g., by Hoffer) evidence that megadoses can adversely lower blood levels of copper, temporarily lower fertility, and even (paradoxically, in light of other evidence) impede the detoxification of some substances, promote cancer, and shorten lifespan (e.g., Miller and Hayes). This didn't prevent Linus Pauling from megadosing well into his nineties, when (it must be said) he died of cancer.

Cautions and contraindications: Megadoses of more than 20 grams per day of buffered ascorbates might cause excesses or imbalances of the buffering minerals (calcium, magnesium, or sodium). Calcium/magnesium ascorbate is least likely to offend. In fact, prolonged megadosing with unbuffered ascorbic acid may leach these minerals from the body, according to Philpott and Kalita. If you take more than a few grams of C a day, it might be wise to take some of it as calcium/magnesium ascorbate.

High blood or urinary levels of C can interfere with certain lab tests (alert your doctor). Hoffer and others dispute evidence that megadoses may increase iron absorption to a dangerous degree for people at risk for or suffering from hemochromatosis (iron overload), aggravate sickle cell anemia and G-6PD deficiency (conditions not uncommon among blacks), interfere with certain drugs (warfarin, tricyclic antidepressants), and create an exaggerated need (probably temporary) for vitamin C in the newborns of mothers who took megadoses during pregnancy.

Evidence that megadoses can promote the growth of calcium-oxalate kidney stones and even serious kidney damage in vulnerable (though probably rare) individuals is also hotly disputed. If mega-C does promote the development of kidney stones, taking extra vitamin B_6 (probably less than 100 milligrams per day) or using buffered ascorbates can be preventive, Philpott and Kalita claim.

Minerals

A good diet (see chap. 12) with lots of whole plant foods can go a long way—perhaps all the way—toward providing the minerals we need, in the right balance. When mineral supplements are taken, it's important not to take too much of one without getting enough of the others. Except where specified below, a good diet and multi should provide that balance.

Lithium

RDI: None. The average diet provides about 2 milligrams per day.
Dosage: Traditionally 900 to 1,200 milligrams of lithium carbonate per day (lower in the elderly), by prescription only. This provides about 170 to 225 milligram of lithium. Recently, the trend has been toward much lower dosages and blood levels to reduce side effects and hazards. Some studies suggest lithium-lite even enhances clinical response, though others suggest the opposite. As an adjunct or maintenance therapy for unipolar depression, effective dosages can be as low as 150 to 300 milligrams per day of lithium carbonate, especially in the elderly, whose aged kidneys tend to excrete lithium poorly.

Another form of lithium—lithium orotate—is available over the counter in the United States, but not in Canada (nor can Canadians import it). Although a 120-milligram capsule contains just 4.8 milligrams of lithium, some animal research suggests a little lithium orotate goes a very long way. In a long-term uncontrolled study by

H. E. Sartori, just 150 milligrams per day of the orotate—which is favored by many naturopathically oriented clinicians—appeared to help some dry alcoholics stay sober. Enthusiasts claim that lithium orotate is safer than lithium carbonate, but a 1979 animal study by D. F. Smith and M. Schou suggests it may be harder on the kidneys.

Major side effects: Weight gain, tremor, thirst, diarrhea, frequent urination, and possibly kidney damage and hyperparathyroidism. Megadoses of lithium promote autoimmune disorders, especially hypothyroidism, which may affect nearly half of long-term users (usually in mild or subclinical form), provoking lethargy, dullness, depressive relapses, and rapid cycling. Lithium orotate caused mild side effects (weakness, loss of appetite, mild apathy) in eight of forty-two long-term users in Sartori's study. Cutting the dose to four or five times a week relieved these side effects.

Cost: Cheap.

Cautions and contraindications: Contraindicated for hypothyroid depressives. May worsen rapid cycling bipolar disorder. Not recommended if you have a personal or family history of autoimmune disorders. Although lithium is commonly combined with other antidepressants, such combinations have (rarely) triggered severe adverse reactions, including two fatalities documented by E. F. Staufenberg and D. Tantam. The risk is greatest with strongly serotonergic antidepressants, like MAOIs, SSRIs, clomipramine, tryptophan, and 5-HTP.

Magnesium

RDI: 400 milligrams

Dosage: Generally around 400 to 1,200 milligrams of inorganic magnesium (e.g., magnesium oxide) or about half to one-quarter as much chelated magnesium (e.g., aspartate or orotate) per day.

Cost: Inorganic: cheap; chelated: moderate to pricey.

Side effects: Soft stools, diarrhea, dizziness or faintness from lowered blood pressure. Excess may cause sluggishness, mental impairment, worsening depression.

Cautions and contraindications: Weak or failing kidneys can cause toxic magnesium retention. Slagle thinks magnesium may be contraindicated if you have myasthenia gravis or Addison's disease. High doses may induce calcium deficiency if calcium intake is low.

Calcium

RDI: 1,000 milligrams
Dosage: 500 to 2,000 milligrams per day of inorganic calcium (e.g., calcium carbonate or citrate). As recently as 1993, B. P. Bourgoin et al. found that most bone meal and oyster shell calcium supplements had questionably high lead levels.
Cost: Cheap.
Side effects: Large doses may worsen depression or mania.

Zinc

RDI: 15 milligrams
Dosage: 15 to 60 milligrams per day
Cost: Very cheap.
Side effects: Nausea, drowsiness.
Cautions: Dosages above 50 milligrams per day can reduce blood levels of good (HDL) cholesterol, probably by inducing mild copper deficiency. To prevent a potentially depressing manganese (Mn) deficiency, the late Carl Pfeiffer recommended adjunctive manganese gluconate; perhaps 3 to 5 milligrams of Mn per 10 milligrams of zinc.

Iron

RDI: 18 milligrams
Dosage: Iron supplements greater than the 5 to 15 milligrams found in most multivitamin formulas are best taken under medical supervision, especially if you're a man or a postmenopausal woman. Otherwise, iron overload may occur and not only worsen your depression but put you at increased risk of heart disease. Relatively high iron levels are, in fact, associated with a number of diseases, though not necessarily causatively.
Side effects: Constipation.

Selenium

RDI: None. Suggested dietary intake: 50 to 200 micrograms per day.
Dosage: Usually 200 to 400 micrograms per day.

Cost: Cheap.

Side effects: Selenium appears very safe and well tolerated at therapeutic doses. In a large, placebo-controlled trial from the University of Arizona by Clark et al., 200 micrograms per day of selenium for an average of four and a half years caused no toxic side effects in nearly seven hundred men. All it did was cut their death rate from cancer by half.

Fatty Acids

Gamma-Linolenic Acid (GLA)

RDI: None determined.

Dosage: Usually 160 to 320 milligrams of GLA per day from evening primrose oil (EPO) or other GLA-rich oils like borage and black currant oil. According to EFA expert David Horrobin, your body may need extra magnesium, zinc, and vitamins B_3, B_6, and C to efficiently process supplemental GLA.

Cost: Moderate.

Cautions: GLA may aggravate epilepsy or worsen some psychiatric disorders, especially mania; it may disagree with people genetically adapted to diets very low in plant food; and it may not, according to Wong et al., mix well with phenothiazine-type antipsychotic drugs like Haldol, or with nonsteroidal anti-inflammatory drugs, corticosteroids, beta-blockers, or anticoagulants.

Alpha-Linolenic Acid (ALA)

RDI: None determined.

Dosage and administration: Usually 1 teaspoon to 2 to 4 tablespoons of fresh, unrefined linseed oil (LSO) per day, depending on body weight and your response as you gradually increase the dosage. Freshly ground or cooked flaxseeds (about 50 percent linseed oil) are also a rich source of phytoestrogens and other nutrients. (The whole, uncooked seeds are poorly digested.) Taking at least part of your LSO prescription this way is a good idea. However, high phytoestrogen intake can dampen the thyroid and may cause other ill effects.

Too much LSO can worsen your symptoms, according to LSO guru Donald Rudin. After several months to a year or two, your body will have soaked up all it can use, and overload reactions like sleepiness, achy muscles, skin problems, or depression will occur if you don't cut down to a maintenance dosage.

Cost: Whole or ground flax: cheap; oil: pricey.

Side effects: Though usually calming, LSO also can trigger "racing thoughts." Occasionally it provokes euphoria, hyperactivity, or mania; and it appeared to trigger rapid cycling in one bipolar depressive treated by Rudin.

Cautions: People with serious conditions should be medically monitored while taking therapeutic doses of LSO, Rudin cautions. Rudin also recommends backing up LSO with a fruit-, vegetable-, and fiber-rich diet, a multi, and extra vitamin C and E to ensure that it's safely and efficiently metabolized. Extra magnesium (which abounds in ALA-rich whole foods, like flaxseeds, but isn't found in the oil) may help prevent mood destabilization and other side effects. So may GLA, which very often is prescribed to balance LSO and other omega-3 supplements. Some people may respond better by augmenting LSO with the preformed long-chain omega-3 fatty acids found in fish oil. While taking LSO, megadoses of B vitamins may have to be lowered, because their potency, Rudin finds, can be exaggerated in an ALA-enriched body.

Eicosapentanoic Acid (EPA) and Docosahexanoic Acid (DHA)

RDI: None determined.

Dosage: One teaspoon to several tablespoons (5–40 milliliters) of fish oil per day or the equivalent of about 5 to 10 grams of EPA and DHA. (Fish *liver* oils have too much vitamins A and D to be safe in high doses.) As with ALA, the body will gradually get its fill and need a lower maintenance dose.

EPA- and DHA-rich food sources basically are wild or domestic animals that feed on omega-3s themselves (not grainfed livestock or farmed fish) and are, to some extent, exposed to cool or cold temperatures: wild game, grazing livestock, and fatty fish and seafood, such as anchovies, salmon, herring, mackerel, sardines, trout, eel, cod, and carp.

Cost: Fish oil: cheap to moderate; special EPA and DHA-rich products: pricey.

Side effects: Mild gastrointestinal upset (mostly loose stools) at high dosages.

Cautions: Fish oil has upset blood-sugar control in insulin-dependent diabetics. Being a strong blood thinner, it may lower your requirement for similar medications (including aspirin) and be contraindicated before surgery. To prevent harmful oxidization of high doses of fish oil in your body, take extra vitamin E.

Amino Acids

General Considerations

Except for the tragic outbreak of EMS among tryptophan users, amino acids have enjoyed a good safety record. "In all the years I have been treating depression with amino acids, I have never had to discontinue the treatment because of side effects," writes UCLA psychiatrist Priscilla Slagle. But Slagle warns that large doses may be contraindicated if you have severe liver or kidney disease. She also recommends that long-term users following a low-protein diet—and children—take a balanced amino acid supplement, the soluble kind you take with meals, to prevent induced deficiencies of the other amino acids.

It may also be a good idea to try to balance a high dose of any aminos. Because these aminos compete for passage across the blood-brain barrier, high doses of one may induce a brain shortage of the others. Feeling wired on tyrosine or phenylalanine, for example, could be due to a lack of soothing serotonin's precursor, tryptophan. SAMe could falter for lack of amino acids to methylate into neurotransmitters.

Tyrosine and Phenylalanine

RDI: None established; the estimated requirement for tyrosine and L-phenylalanine (LPA) combined is 14 milligrams per kilogram of body weight, or about 1 gram per day for a 150-pound person.

Dosage and administration: Tyrosine: 100 milligrams per kilogram—about 6 to 8 grams for the average adult—has been the norm in studies. But in clinics like Braverman's and Slagle's, much lower doses, as low as 500 milligrams per day, seem to suffice. LPA has worked across a very wide dose range, from 250 milligrams per day (as an adjunct to L-deprenyl, in one study) up to a dozen or more grams a day in some studies. Depressives usually respond to between 500 milligrams and 6 grams per day. In clinical trials, depressives have responded to dosages of DL-phenylalanine (DLPA) or D-phenylalanine (DPA) as low as 75 milligrams and 50 milligrams, respectively, with 100 to 200 milligrams per day being the usual range. In one study, a measly 100 milligrams per day of DPA boosted urinary PAA (the breakdown product of PEA) by a stunning 1,300 percent, nearly twice as much as the tricyclic antidepressant imipramine did at the same, low-average dosage. For some reason, American doctors like Arnold Fox and Andrew Weil typically prescribe much higher doses of DLPA, on the order of 750 to 1,500 milligrams, either in divided doses or in one morning wake-up shot. These higher dosages might also boost NE and, perhaps, dopamine and thyroid hormones too, although LPA or tyrosine would be a more natural way to do that.

A comparatively low dose of these aminos will suffice when taken on a "protein-free stomach," that is, at least forty-five minutes before or three hours after eating a high-protein meal or snack. This is when blood levels of other amino acids that compete for passage across the blood-brain barrier are low.

Depressives often improve within just a few days to a week or two on DLPA or LPA. Tyrosine seems to take longer. Interestingly, in a small study by José Yaryura-Tobias and associates, most depressives were able to stop taking DLPA or DPA soon after they recovered, without relapsing. Arnold Fox also has his patients stop DLPA when they've been well for a week and resume it only if their symptoms begin returning.

Cost: Cheap to moderate.

Adjunctive supplements: A good diet and multi should provide the nutrients required to process tyrosine and phenylalanine safely and efficiently. Extra vitamin B_6 might cause too much conversion of these amino acids to dopamine and NE outside the brain. This has been reported in people taking the dopamine precursor L-dopa for Parkinson's disease and by Mouret et al. in some people taking tyrosine for depression. Perhaps this also explains why in one trial of

LPA by Sabelli et al. (1986) in which a high dose of adjunctive B_6 was administered—200 milligrams per day—the patients required as much as 14 grams of LPA to relieve their depression. It may therefore be prudent to take no more B_6 than you get in your multi when trying out tyrosine or phenylalanine and to take the multi at a different time of day. Later, you can see if higher doses of B_6 add any benefit.

Side effects: Irritability, aggression, feeling tense or wired, agitation, restlessness, headache (if chocolate gives you headaches, phenylalanine may too), constipation, nausea or upset stomach, difficulty falling asleep if taken at night, mania or hypomania. One man experienced a suicidally depressive crash following a rapid euphoric reaction to LPA, on two separate occasions ("idclub," 1997).

Cautions and contraindications: Use with caution (especially phenylalanine), or avoid, if you have a history of aggressive behavior, mania (these amino acids may retrigger it), hallucinations, delusions, schizophrenia, migraines, cardiac arrythmia, high blood pressure, or mitral valve prolapse. These aminos may raise blood pressure, especially if combined with MAOIs that come with dietary restrictions. Theoretically, large doses may promote an involuntary movement disorder (tardive dyskinesia) in some users of phenothiazine antipsychotic drugs (Gardos et al.) or worsen malignant melanoma (Slagle). Avoid phenylalanine if you have phenylketonuria (PKU) or are pregnant (your fetus could have PKU).

SAMe (S-Adenosylmethionine) and Methionine

RDI: None established. The estimated requirement for methionine and cystine (a related amino acid) combined is 13 milligrams per kilogram of body weight, or about 1 gram per day for a 150-pound person.

Dosage and administration: SAMe is a very unstable compound. Unless a brand contains stabilized, enteric-coated SAMe, it may be inert. Currently, Nature Made's SAMe, which is imported from Italy, is the gold standard.

Oral SAM: Despite the high dosage of 1,600 milligrams per day used in most clinical trials, anecdotally, some people seem to respond to as little as 200 milligrams per day. Columbia University psychiatrist Richard Brown usually finds 400 to 800 milligrams effective, especially for mild to moderate depression. For severe depression, he says the higher doses may be required, alone or with other anti-depressants. Brown recommends taking SAMe about half an hour before meals (unless it gives you heartburn), starting at 400 milligrams for the first two weeks (200 milligrams if you tend to be sensitive to medications), then doubling the dosage if you have little or no response.

For Brown's patients and many other users, oral SAMe usually works fast: "On average," Brown and associates write, "SAM-e begins to relieve depression in seven days, although some people may need more time."

L-methionine: Usually 1 to 2 grams per day.

For safe and efficient utilization of methionine and SAMe, a generous intake of vitamins B_6 and B_{12}, folic acid, magnesium, and calcium is essential. A high-potency multi should fill that need, though an additional milligram of folic acid per gram of methionine (and perhaps SAMe) would also be advisable.

Cost: Methionine: moderate; SAMe: very expensive (more than $3.00 per day).

Safety and side effects: According to Brown et al., SAMe has been associated with fewer side effects than placebos in clinical trials, causing "almost no one" to drop out, despite the high dosages used. Typically mild and transient, SAMe's side effects include dry mouth, thirst, nausea, vomiting, gas, bloating, diarrhea, urinary delay, blurred vision, headache, sweating, anxiety (especially in people with panic disorder), rapid heart beat, insomnia (if taken in the evening), and restlessness. One user tells me his excellent reponse to SAMe has been marred by numbness and burning in his extremities and "a flushed feeling and pounding heart," even at very low doses.

SAMe can also induce hypomania or mania—usually transient, but sometimes persisting even after discontinuing the supplement—in about 10 to 15 percent of users, mostly bipolar depressives. Bipolars should use SAMe "under cover" of mood stabilizers like lithium and tryptophan and with medical supervision.

Methionine's negligible, but little known, side effects (Braverman et al. report flatulence and uneasy feelings) likely resemble SAMe's.

One case of serotonin syndrome (see page 177 in chap. 13 for a description) was reported by Iruela et al. It was triggered by injec-

tions of SAMe in a woman already taking the strong serotonin reuptake inhibitor, clomipramine (Anafranil). For this reason, SAMe
(and methionine) should only be combined cautiously with
strongly serotonergic drugs, as well as lithium, tryptophan, 5-HTP,
and other supplements that may boost serotonin (e.g., omega-3s, St.
John's wort, and *Ginkgo biloba*). That said, Brown has used SAMe
safely "with nearly every antidepressant available" except MAOIs,
and claims it only improves his patients' response to the drugs.

Brown et al. also believe the literature suggests SAMe is probably
safe during pregnancy and lactation.There are a few other safety
considerations. In a study by N. Orentreich et al., a lifetime of severe methionine *restriction* completely stunted the growth of rats,
but it increased their lifespans by 30 percent. Although it doesn't
follow that methionine supplements would shorten human lifespan, we do know that extra methionine without extra folic acid
(and to a lesser extent vitamins B_6 and B_{12}) to prevent the accumula-
tion of its dangerous metabolite homocysteine would promote life-
shortening diseases.

Animal studies by Charlton and Crowell suggest excessive methylation by SAMe fosters the degenerative process underlying Parkinson's disease. This seems to conflict with evidence cited by Brown et
al. that SAMe levels are extremely low in people with PD (L-dopa,
the principal treatment for Parkinson's disease, uses up SAMe), and
clinical studies in which therapeutic doses of SAMe as high as 3,300
milligrams per day improved depressive and even neurologic symptoms in patients with Parkinson's disease. Perhaps, in Parkinson's
disease, there is a therapeutic window for SAMe. Too little leads to
insufficient synthesis of dopamine and serotonin, both of which are
lacking in the disease. Too much leads to increased catabolism
(breakdown) of these neurotransmitters. Judging by the clinical research, therapeutic dosages of SAMe (and perhaps methionine, with
protective nutrients on the side) fall safely within that window.

Tryptophan and 5-HTP (5-hydroxytryptophan)

RDI: None established. The estimated requirement for tryptophan is
3.5 milligrams per kilogram of body weight, or about 250 milligrams per day for a 150-pound person.

Dosage and administration: Tryptophan: usually 1.5 to 6 grams per day, slightly higher for bipolar depression and up to twice as much for mania. 5-HTP: usually 50 to 600 milligrams per day. On a "protein-free stomach" (see above), much lower doses of tryptophan (and possibly 5-HTP) may suffice, perhaps as low as one-third, if your stomach is also "carbohydrate-rich" (carbohydrates increase tryptophan's passage into the brain). Lower doses also are optimal when combined with antidepressant drugs, but these combinations must be taken with care (see below).

Both tryptophan and 5-HTP appear to have a therapeutic window. In fact, at very high doses, tryptophan becomes enough of a downer to relieve acute mania. 5-HTP may well have a therapeutic window. "In some patients the effect of *l*-5-HTP hinges on 10 to 25 milligrams per day more or less," observes L. J. van Hiele, a most meticuluous prescriber of 5-HTP. To avoid overshooting this sliver of a window, the Dutch psychatrist slowly builds up each patient's dosage by just 10 milligrams every three to seven days. When the right dosage is found (usually between 200 and 300 milligrams), marked improvement often occurs within days. Similarly, fixed dosages in the 200 to 300 milligram range have been the norm in 5-HTP's many successful clinical trials.

Herman van Praag, a pioneer in the field, has observed that within a month or two, 5-HTP's effect wanes for about 20 percent of responders. In these people, something else wanes: 5-HTP's ability to boost norepinephrine and dopamine. Adding tyrosine usually restores response to 5-HTP (van Praag, 1984).

Because of unresolved safety concerns (see sidebar on page 160), Ray Sahelian, M.D. recommends that 5-HTP users (a) stick to the low end of the therapeutic dose range, (b) not take 5-HTP every day, and (c) take a month or two off at least every three months (raysahelian.com). Unfortunately, these very cautious restrictions would render 5-HTP ineffective for many depressives.

Cost: Tryptophan: expensive; 5-HTP: pricey.

Side effects, cautions, and contraindications: Especially at low/moderate dosages, tryptophan and 5-HTP are very well tolerated by most users. Side effects associated with tryptophan include gastrointestinal upsets (dry mouth, nausea, vomiting, heartburn, constipation, diarrhea), transient drowsiness or lethargy after taking a dose, diuresis, headache, reduced appetite, dizziness or lightheadedness, loss of balance, tremors, blurred vision, elation, agitation, sexual disinhibition, and (paradoxically) hostility or aggressiveness. 5-HTP, which has a similar side effect profile, is more likely than tryptophan to provoke mania or hypomania or to worsen anxiety. Its most common side effects are gastrointestinal upsets and acute sedation. Not so common: sexual dysfunction (reduced drive, performance, or ability to achieve orgasm, as with serotonergic drugs like the SSRIs), fatigue, increased depression, feeling wired, insomnia when taken at night (though 5-HTP more often helps people sleep), vivid dreams and nightmares, stuffy or runny nose, headache, sweating, chills, and difficulty breathing. There have been a very small number of cases of eosinophilia-myalgia syndrome (EMS), EMS-like syndromes, eosinophilia, and dermatitis in 5-HTP users (see sidebar on page 160).

The most common side effects of tryptophan and 5-HTP—the gastrointestinal effects—are largely eliminated by taking them with food or using enteric-coated capsules of 5-HTP, which may be obtained from some compounding pharmacies or European sellers.

Mostly on theoretical grounds, Thomas Sourkes recommends caution using tryptophan (perhaps 5-HTP too; Sourkes was only writing about tryptophan) if you have hypoglycemia or liver disease. To err on the safe side, Sourkes also recommends against long-term, high-dose supplementation with tryptophan for children and pregnant women, women taking estrogen, and anyone with chronic bladder irritation, a lack of stomach acid, overgrowth of gastrointestinal microorganisms, upper bowel malabsorption, or a history of any sclerodermalike condition (again, this probably should apply to 5-HTP too), diabetes, or cancer.

Although combining tryptophan or 5-HTP with other serotonin-boosting drugs or lithium can be highly synergistic, it could also trigger a dangerous serotonin syndrome (described on page 177 in chap. 13). In theory, St. John's wort and other supplements that may strongly boost serotonin (SAMe, methionine, omega-3 fatty acids, folic acid, *Ginkgo biloba*, progesterone) might also need to be used cautiously when taking tryptophan or 5-HTP. In practice, however, some clinicians freely mix serotonergic drugs (but rarely MAOIs, which are the riskiest) and tryptophan or 5-HTP, because they can work wonders and seem to have a good safety record.

Are Tryptophan and 5-HTP Safe?

Few if any authorities doubt that the crippling, sometimes deadly out-break in 1989 of the eosinophilia-myalgia syndrome (EMS) in thousands of tryptophan users was entirely due to contamination by a major manufacturer, Showa Denko of Japan.

Unfortunately, that's not the whole story. There have also been sporadic reports of serious EMS-like syndromes or symptoms—eosinophilia, skin disorders, life-threatening pulmonary hypertension—in people using other sources of tryptophan and 5-HTP. In a study by Blauvelt and Falanga, while six of seventeen people with the rare EMS-like syndrome of *eosinophilic fasciitis* (Shulman's syndrome) had been using contaminated Showa Denko tryptophan, five others had used other sources. In another report by Michelson et al., a Showa Denko–like impurity known as "peak X" was identified in the 5-HTP used by three members of a family exhibiting EMS-like signs and symptoms.

In 1998, soon after 5-HTP became a best-selling supplement in North America, researchers from the Mayo Clinic reported that they had detected peak X and other contaminants in six commercial brands of 5-HTP, albeit at levels just 3 to 15 percent of those found by Michelson et al. several years earlier. The FDA soon confirmed the findings. Even brands containing 5-HTP extracted from *Griffonia simplicifolia* seeds were affected. (In parts of Africa, crushed 5-HTP-rich *Griffonia* seeds are a time-honored tranquilizer for children.) But when several National Nutritional Foods Association (NNFA) members had their 5-HTP products independently tested with the sensitive Mayo Clinic technique, although a distinct impurity was found, it wasn't the dreaded "peak X." (Drugs and supplements are allowed to contain minimal impurities.) In April 1999, the NNFA claimed its members had instituted routine screening of 5-HTP for peak X.

Meanwhile, 5-HTP remains on the market. Despite its continuing popularity, as of November 1999, there have been no further reports of EMS or EMS-like syndromes.

Unfortunately, contamination isn't the only concern. Tryptophan and (to a much lesser extent) 5-HTP have normal metabolic products which, in excess, could be (and in some cases have been) harmful in ways reminiscent of EMS (fibrotic skin and lung diseases) and, theoretically, in other ways too (AIDS dementia, Parkinson's disease, cataracts, bladder tumors).

These metabolic mishaps are elusive, because in many millions of patient years of use only a few dozen severe reactions have been reported, though many others may have gone unnoticed. One unsettling possibility is that the most serious complications of the banned serotonin-releasing drugs fenfluramine (the "fen" in "fen-phen") and dexfenfluramine (Redux)—primary pulmonary hypertension (PPH) and heart valve damage—might also occur at an elevated rate among 5-HTP or (much less likely) tryptophan users. A 1995 study by K. Wessel et al. offers some reassurance to the contrary. Even at a whopping dosage of 1,000 milligrams of 5-HTP per day for ten months, thirty-nine neurological patients showed no signs of harm, despite being subjected to a battery of tests, including echocardiograms, which would have spotted heart valve damage.

This is not entirely surprising, for the body has ways of safely handling tryptophan, 5-HTP, and their metabolites. And we can help it do an even better job.

The 1 or 2 grams of tryptophan most of us consume every day are either incorporated into proteins or metabolized along several other pathways. The major pathways lead either to NAD (the active form of vitamin B_3) or to a much, much lesser extent (about 10 milligrams of tryptophan a day), to serotonin and melatonin, and finally to these compounds' excretable breakdown products. But excesses of some of the intermediate compounds and of serotonin itself can irritate or damage certain tissues and organs. One way these biochemicals can build up is if there is a shortage of the nutrients that help metabolize them fully. For example, deficiencies of vitamins C and B_6 can foster a bladder tumor-inducing glut of a tryptophan metabolite called 3-hydroxyanthranilic acid.

A generous intake of these other nutrients should lessen the metabolic hazards while maximizing the conversion of tryptophan (and possibly 5-HTP) to serotonin and (in the case of tryptophan) NAD, which, as we saw in chapter 6, can be an antidepressant in its own right. A reasonable guesstimate might be to balance every 500 milligrams of supplementary tryptophan (and perhaps every 50 milligrams of 5-HTP) with at least 5 to 10 milligrams of B_6 (up to 50 to 100 milligrams per day, but probably no more than 25 to 50 milligrams with 5-HTP) or 1 to 2 milligrams of pyridoxyl-5-phosphate (up to 10 to 15 milligrams per day—again, possibly much less with 5-HTP), 25 milligrams of B_3 (up to 100 to 200 milligrams per day), 100 micrograms of folic acid (up to 1 to 2 milligrams per day), 100 milligrams of vitamin C, 50 IU of vitamin E, and possibly 25 to 50 milligrams of methionine or SAMe. A good diet and a well-endowed multivitamin and mineral supplement can fill much or all of this prescription (except for SAMe), while rounding it off with other nutrients that may also be needed to process tryptophan or 5-HTP safely and efficiently.

There are special considerations when it comes to adjunctive vitamin B_6. If lots of B_6 is present when 5-HTP is taken, a potentially harmful excess of serotonin, which cannot cross the blood-brain barrier, could be synthesized in the liver before the 5-HTP has a chance to enter the brain. On Internet newsgroups, Steven Harris, M.D., has for several years cautioned that not only would this peripheral (outside the brain) serotonin be useless as an antidepressant, in excess it could be damaging, notably to the right heart valve. Harris argues, on theoretical grounds, that doses of 5-HTP greater than 50 milligrams a day could raise peripheral serotonin enough to cause damage even without extra B_6. Defenders of 5-HTP, like James South, have fiercely rebutted these speculations. Their strongest argument is that such reactions have never been reported in the many thousands, if not millions, of people who have taken 5-HTP over the years, including many who have used it with high doses of B_6. But some cases of gradual sclerosis of the right heart valve or lungs could have gone unnoticed or unattributed to 5-HTP.

Another potential safety strategy would be to take 5-HTP with a drug like carbidopa that blocks 5-HTP's peripheral conversion to serotonin. This has been the common practice in Europe since the 1970s, not for safety, but for efficiency. Yet surprisingly, a 1988 review by Zmilacher et al. found the combination has tended to be slightly less effective and much less user-friendly than 5-HTP alone. More to the point, and no less surprising, it seems that only (or mostly) people taking carbidopa have suffered those rare sclerodermalike reactions to 5-HTP. Investigators like P. Joly et al. now wonder if carbidopa is the real culprit.

And then there is the report by Sternberg et al. in which high blood levels of the noxious tryptophan metabolite *kynurenine* were implicated as the cause of scleroderma in people taking 5–HTP. Kynurenine was also high in people with scleroderma who *weren't* taking 5-HTP. Ironically, the body's antidote to kynurenine is vitamin B_6.

So it would seem that, for users of 5-HTP, playing it safe means taking neither too much B_6 (perhaps no more than 50 to 100 milligrams per day) nor too little (perhaps no less than 10 to 25 milligrams per day), and taking the vitamin at a different time of day than the 5-HTP.

By the time you read this, the issue may be less confused than it is now. Check with supplement-savvy doctors, relevant Internet newsgroups (search the archives at deja.com) or websites (e.g., www.escape.ca/~sgb, www.fda.gov, raysahelian.com, lef.org), or other up-to-date sources.

A few other measures may minimize the hazards of tryptophan and 5-HTP:

- Several dietary amino acids compete with tryptophan (and possibly 5-HTP) for seats on the molecular bus that carries them across the blood-brain barrier. Timing your intake of tryptophan and 5-HTP with respect to food as described on page 159 will maximize synthesis of serotonin in the brain, not outside.
- To reduce the risk of contamination, buy only pharmaceutical-grade tryptophan and 5-HTP or seed-extracted 5-HTP made by reputable companies.
- Negative ionizers (see chap. 2) can markedly reduce elevated peripheral serotonin levels and lift some people's moods in the process. Using a negative ionizer after taking 5-HTP could, theoretically, minimize peripheral serotonin synthesis. It may even lower the dose of 5-HTP you need.
- Until and unless 5-HTP is cleared of the valve damage concern, ask your doctor about having an echocardiograph done periodically if you're taking 5-HTP long-term.

Other Nutrients

Choline

RDI: 425 to 550 milligrams.

Dosage: For acute antimanic effect, usually 250 to 2,000 milligrams of choline, 10 to 100 grams of lecithin (the stimulating inositol in lecithin might counteract the choline somewhat), or 2 to 20 grams of phosphatidylcholine per day. An animal study by A. Koppen et al. suggests that much lower doses may suffice if large or megadoses of niacinamide (a tranquilizerlike form of vitamin B_3) are taken too.

Cost: Choline and lecithin: moderate; phosphatidylcholine: pricey.

Side effects: Gastrointestinal upset; fishy body odor (choline).

Caution: Large doses can worsen depression; may be contraindicated if you have ulcers or Parkinson's disease; will be counterproductive if you're taking anticholinergic drugs like atropine or diphenhydramine.

Inositol

RDI: None. Diets usually provide about one gram a day, mostly from fruit, nuts, grains, and beans.

Dosage: Clinical trials have used megadoses of 10 to 18 grams per day, with researchers even wondering if 20 to 30 grams might work better. Anecdotally, people have benefited from as little as 500 to 650 milligrams two or three times a day. The higher the dosage, the better it is to use pure inositol powder dissolved in liquid (it's sweet).

Cost: Moderate at low-moderate dosages.

Side effects: Based on minimal clinical experience, inositol is usually very well tolerated. But (usually at very high dosages) it can provoke mania or hypomania (as little as 3 grams a day), aggravate attention deficit disorder, and possibly cause mild psychotic symptoms, weakness, tremor, burning skin, nausea, or flatus.

L-Carnitine and L-Acetylcarnitine

RDI: None.

Dosage: L-carnitine and L-acetylcarnitine: 1 to 3 grams per day.

Cost: Expensive.
Side effects: Mild diarrhea. "L-carnitine is a safe and very well tolerated medicine," according to A. V. and S. Plioplys of Mercy Hospital in Chicago.
Contraindications: Possibly uremia.

Phosphatidylserine

RDI: None.
Dosage: Usually 100 milligrams, three times a day. Because phosphatidylserine is gradually incorporated into cellular membranes, after a month or so the body will tend to be full of it, and a lower maintenance dose (usually 100 milligrams per day) will be adequate.
Cost: Most brands are expensive.
Side effects: Reportedly very well tolerated.
Contraindications: None reported.

CHAPTER 12

Guidelines for a Healthy Antidepressant Diet

In the last few chapters on nutrition, we've covered a lot of ground. In this chapter, I'd like to offer something simpler: a few very basic dietary guidelines. (For a more detailed treatment, see psychiatrist Abram Hoffer's recent books on orthomolecular nutrition or Rudolph Ballentine's classic, *Diet and Nutrition*.)

These guidelines are based on the best of what nutritional science and complementary and alternative medicine have to tell us about eating for good health in general, and for mental health in particular. Don't feel pressured to follow them to the letter (I don't). Just give them your serious consideration and take from them what you will.

➤ *Favor whole foods over "food fractions."* Although food fractions are the stuff of which nutritional supplements are made, not all food fractions are created equal. Most of our diet-related health problems come from the indiscriminate, industry-driven use of food fractions—sugar, sodium, refined fats and oils, refined grains—and the junk-food and convenience-food products that typically are reconstituted, like Dr. Frankenstein's monster, from these dead food parts. Food fractions and Frankenfoods promote nutritional deficiencies and imbalances and contain many additional chemicals that can promote adverse psychological reactions in sensitive individuals. Although doctors and dietitians now recommend a diet high in whole foods to prevent major physical diseases, it's just a matter of time before they add affective illness to the list.

❧ *Minimize your consumption of foods and food products that have been traumatically processed or prepared.* Once again, I have to blow the whistle on some of your favorite foods and mine. Frying, barbecuing, and other cooking methods that burn or brown food create billions of mutant molecules that can be toxic or carcinogenic. Aggressive commercial food processing—the refining of oils and grains, for example—typically devitalizes, nutritionally depletes, contaminates, and chemically alters the wholesome starting materials.

❧ *Look for food that's clean, pure, and uncontaminated.* Again, as much as you can, pass on commercial foods laden with artificial additives. Wash your produce thoroughly to remove pesticides and other chemical residues (see the procedure on page 49 in chap. 3). Consider buying organic, unsprayed produce or avoiding the most pesticide-heavy foods, as detailed in David Steinman's *Diet For a Poisoned Planet.*

❧ *Eat a diverse balance of the different tissues and organs of plants and/or animals: roots, seeds (that includes nuts, grains, and legumes), leaves, flowers (like broccoli), stalks, shoots, stems, fruits; and if you eat meat: muscles, viscera (organ meats), and even bones and marrow (as in soup stocks).* Because every tissue is rich in some nutrients, deficient in others, an anatomically well-rounded diet is a nutritionally well-balanced diet. The more your diet looks like a rainbow, the more you've captured both the nutritional and the "nutraceutical" diversity of food.

❧ *Maximize your consumption of fresh food—and don't neglect raw.* Not only does the nutritional value of food fall rapidly after harvest or slaughter, but microbial decay sets in immediately, creating unwholesome, even toxic, new compounds.

Raw foods may have certain medicinal benefits that cooked foods lack. Herbert Newbold cites some old clinical research that suggests raw nuts, seeds, and unrefined oils can raise low hormone levels. As we saw in chapter 2, this could be just what many depressives need.

❧ *Beware of compulsive food preferences or of foods you eat day in, day out, all year round.* As we've seen in chapter 3, some doctors consider this to be a recipe for food allergies that can adversely affect brain and mood.

✺ *Respect your appetite, nose, taste buds, and eyes, and let them help guide what you eat, how much you eat, and when.* This is tricky. It only applies where wholesome, natural foods are concerned; and even then it's subject to the exception of "addictions" that can arise when natural seasonal variations in food availability are erased by industry and commerce.

The more that foods have been processed, cooked, seasoned, or otherwise transformed into something that tastes, smells, and looks like what they are not, the more our genetically naive senses can be led astray. Suddenly we find ourselves satisfying our yen for starch with potato chips, for fruit with pie, for protein with greasy cheeseburgers. When a wide variety of strictly natural foods are on the menu, studies have reportedly shown that animals and human infants instinctively select a balanced diet. There may be hope for us too.

Respecting your appetite also means not eating when you don't have one. Pleasure in the smell and taste of food facilitates digestion. Its absence invites indigestion, malabsorption, and food allergy. Of course, if severe depression has eliminated your appetite, following it could eventually eliminate you. But this could be a good time for a medically supervised fast to see if food allergies are why you're depressed in the first place.

✺ *Consider eating in accordance with* who, what, when, *and* where *you are—that is, eating idiosyncratically, ancestrally, seasonally, and geographically.* Eating idiosyncratically (according to who you are) means listening to your body and respecting your appetites and food preferences—within the confines of a wholesome diet, of course. It could also mean eating in accordance with your constitutional type, as prescribed by ayurvedic medicine, for example.

Eating ancestrally is based on the idea that the diet that suited your ancestors' genes (assuming you know what they ate) probably suits you too. As mentioned in chapter 8 on fats, Canadian physician C. E. Bates and others have found that when Northwest Coastal Native Americans return to their traditional, salmon-based diets, they experience remarkable relief from the multiple disorders that plague them on the modern Western diet, including suicidal depression.

Eating seasonally and geographically is based on the idea that different seasons and geographic/climatic conditions stress us in different ways. By eating plants and/or animals adapted to these conditions we can adapt better ourselves. This could be why research suggests the oils of cold-adapted fish and plants protect people in northern and temperate industrialized countries from the diseases of civilization, while heat-adapted saturated fats, which are consumed with impunity in the tropics, do just the opposite.

Eating seasonally/geographically also appears to influence seasonal and geographic mood disorders, such as recurrent winter and summer depression. As we saw in chapter 8, there is evidence that cold-adapted omega-3 fatty acids prevent and treat winter depression. Would a diet high in fresh fruits and vegetables have a similar effect on summer depression?

Part 3

———— ❦ ————

Other Substances, Other Energies

Just a hop, skip, and jump away from nutritional medicine lies the verdant field of herbalism. The golden flowers of St. John's wort almost singlehandedly pollinated herbal psychiatry in the 1990s. Among the antidepressant's mainstream champions was Norman Rosenthal, the National Institute of Mental Health psychiatrist who turned his profession on to bright light therapy in the early 1980s. Recently, the equally prominent psychiatrist in charge of NIMH's $4.3 million clinical trial of St. John's wort, Duke University's Jonathan Davidson, published favorable research on homeopathy, a practice that still makes most of his colleagues wince or guffaw with disbelief. Complementary and alternative medicine—and a healthy new respect for the therapeutic potential of natural forces like light and magnetism—is infiltrating the mainstream. In the next four chapters we'll look at some exciting psychiatric applications.

CHAPTER 13

———— ❦ ————

St. John's Wort and Beyond: The Herbal Antidepressant Pharmacy

Working on the first edition of this book in the early nineties and pressed for space, I contemplated omitting the small, scientifically weak chapter on herbal antidepressants. In the end, I kept it in, largely because at least one obscure herb could boast of some preliminary clinical research to support its traditional reputation as an antidepressant. The herb? St. John's wort.

A year after the first edition appeared, St. John's wort (SJW) was on its way to becoming the natural Prozac of the nineties. As it turned out, there had been far more clinical research on SJW tucked away in German-language medical journals than virtually any North American expert had known.

Which says a lot about the difference between American and European medicine. Here, until very recently, doctors have shunned herbal remedies like old wives' tales. There, especially in Germany, they have prescribed them freely and unself-consciously. Even before doctors here knew a St. John's wort from a plantar wart, German MDs were writing twenty-five times as many prescriptions for SJW as Prozac. In 1993 alone, they wrote nearly three million prescriptions, Klaus Linde and associates noted in the 1996 *British Medical Journal* meta-analysis of twenty-three trials of SJW for depression that helped make the herb a household name in the English-speaking world. That landmark study persuaded many American psychiatrists it was time for a reality check. So the National Institute of Mental Health set out to fund its own study: a $4.3 million, twenty-six-week multicenter trial comparing SJW with the popular "Prozaclike" Zoloft and a placebo. The results won't be in until after this book comes out. But one result is in.

Herbalism has arrived in North America. It's knocking at the gates of psychiatry. And St. John's wort is its messenger.

St. John's Wort

"St. John's wort has been like a miracle for me . . . I am constantly thinking to myself, 'Is this how other people have always felt? How wonderful!'"

"All I know is that I've tried nine antidepressants . . . they've all made me very sick. SJW doesn't."

"I could not reach orgasm on Prozac but am able to do so regularly on SJW."

Such are the testimonials SJW has received from depressives on Internet newsgroups, mailing lists, and elsewhere. Like other antidepressants, SJW has also been panned—usually for lack of effectiveness, seldom for side effects. At deja.com, a major website where netsurfers can rate anything rateable, SJW was tied with Prozac in late August 1999 for second place in a field of twenty-six antidepressants. Its eighty-three users scored it 3.4 out of 5, second only to Zoloft's 3.6.

SJW is clearly making a big difference in many people's lives. And research suggests it's no mirage.

The *British Medical Journal* (*BMJ*) meta-analysis looked at twenty-three randomized controlled trials of SJW for depression, twenty of them double-blind. There were 1,757 patients, most of them with mildly to moderately severe cases of depression, a mixture, probably, of dysthymia and major depressive disorder. The patients received either SJW, a drug (usually an antidepressant), or a placebo, usually for four, six, or eight weeks. Compared to placebo in thirteen trials, SJW was a resounding success: 55 percent responded to SJW; 22 percent to placebo. In three trials comparing SJW with an antidepressant drug, SJW also had a slight edge: 64 versus 59 percent response. And in two trials comparing SJW combined with valerian (a relaxing herb that may also be an antidepressant) to antidepressant drugs, the edge was 68 to 50 percent. In fact, SJW performed about as well as drugs normally do, while the drugs, prescribed in these studies at the low end of their dose range, didn't.

SJW has continued to pile up victories, equaling Prozac in a large German trial (Harrer et al.), proving its mettle against recurrent fall/winter depression in several others (Wheatley, 1999). In a multi-center trial by Vorbach et al., SJW—at twice the usually recommended dosage—finally went to bat against severe major depression, with a normal-dosage antidepressant as its competition. It proved only slightly less effective than the drug, a first-generation antidepressant named imipramine—still considered the gold standard for severe depression. But imipramine and its ilk are plagued by unpleasant side effects and some serious risks. Not so SJW.

The *BMJ* meta-analysis revealed that SJW was not only much better tolerated than the drugs, it was even associated with fewer side effects than the placebos. Probably SJW reduced, rather than fueled, the background noise of people's everyday ills. This is not surprising, given that SJW can also relieve such depression-related aches and angsts as anxiety, insomnia, and (possibly) alcoholism and drug dependence, eating disorders, premenstrual syndrome, chronic pain, and migraine and tension headaches. And some people feel they handle stress better with SJW.

It's beginning to look as if SJW is a contender for any kind of depression. Only its effect on melancholic, psychotic/delusional, and bipolar depression is still little known.

Using St. John's Wort

The most commonly recommended dosage of SJW for depression is 900 milligrams per day (usually in three doses) of an SJW extract standardized to contain 0.3 percent hypericin. In practice, dosages as low as 200 or 300 milligrams and as high as 1,800 or 2,700 milligrams have been used successfully. Some people do poorly on the lower dosages and fabulously on the high ones; for others it's just the opposite, as if SJW has a therapeutic window. Some SJW users feel dramatically better almost from the start. More commonly the herb works as slowly as most other antidepressants, taking a month or two to peak.

Quite a few people find they may do well on one brand of standardized SJW and poorly on another. As with all herbs today, what's on the label isn't necessarily what's inside. Studies in the late 1990s suggested that the hypericin content of standardized brands tended to be substantially less than 0.3 percent.

Even when two brands of SJW truly do contain 0.3 percent hypericin, they may be significantly different in other ways. This is important, because it turns out hypericin likely has little to do with SJW's antidepressant effect. Research suggests another of its dozens of potential active ingredients, *hyperforin*, is a much stronger contender. At least one product—Movana—is standardized for hyperforin.

Traditional herbalists maintain that any honestly prepared SJW product can be effective for depression. But unless a product comes well recommended, the safest bet is to buy the "as used in clinical trials" LI 160 extract. It's sold in North America by its German manufacturer as "Kira." But it's also available in other products that use strictly "research-grade hypericum" (*Hypericum* is the Latin name for SJW), such as the inexpensive "joypills" sold by Peter McWilliams, coauthor of *Hypericum & Depression*, the book that broke the SJW story in North America. That book can be read free of charge on McWilliams's website (hypericum.com), where you can also order his joypills. Movana, which has performed well in several controlled trials, also seems a good choice. If any of these products work for you, you can experiment with other, perhaps cheaper, brands.

Safety, Side Effects, Cautions, and Contradications

In the years since SJW has become popular in North America, it has gradually become apparent that when it comes to safety, side effects, and even efficacy, there are two kinds of SJW: the research-grade hypericum commonly used in Europe, and the dog's breakfast of unregulated products sold here.

The literature on SJW's safety has, so far, been predominantly European. There, SJW has been extraordinarily well tolerated in trials and drug-monitoring studies involving thousands of users. When psychiatrist Harold Bloomfield and Peter McWilliams published their book on SJW in 1997, they assured readers that after millions of patient-years of use by European men, women, children, and even pregnant women, there had been no published reports of fatalities, serious side effects, or adverse drug interactions. In an extensive review, Ernst et al. also concluded: "The data suggest that hypericum is well tolerated, with an incidence of adverse reactions similar to that of placebo."

But no sooner had the good news about SJW hit North America than Internet SJW users began reporting side effects with a frequency, and sometimes intensity, that belied the European experience. Headaches—rarely reported by European users—were often reported by users of North American SJW products. There was concern that SJW's reputed monoamine oxidase inhibiting (MAOI) effect would make it dangerous to combine with a host of foods, beverages, and drugs that MAOI users must avoid. These combinations can (rarely) lead to skyrocketing blood pressure and even strokes. Severe headaches are a typical symptom of these "hypertensive crises." And the headaches some SJW users were reporting were "terrible," "raging," "hellacious," "mind blowing." A few reported high blood pressure when they had their headaches while paying no heed to MAOI food and drug restrictions. Some also reported a stiff neck or pain at the base of the skull; rapid heart beat; palpitations; severe chest pains or spasms; sweatiness; and/or weird, spaced-out feelings, sometimes in near-syndromic combinations. These reports were vaguely suggestive of minor hypertensive crises or "serotonin syndrome"—theoretically a very remote risk when taking SJW alone, but not when in combination with other serotonin-boosting drugs or supplements like 5-HTP.

Most disturbing was a report in November 1997 by Mary Arneson, M.D. Shortly after beginning to take an unspecified brand of SJW, an elderly patient of Arneson's experienced a hypertensive crisis that led to a nonfatal hemorrhagic stroke. She had been taking a MAOI-contraindicated bladder medication at the time.

There is good reason to believe that such reactions are absent from the European literature because the most popular SJW products there, like LI 160 and the product known here as Movana, are methanol or CO_2 extracts. According to Camilla Cracchiolo, a registered nurse whose online "FAQ" or monograph on SJW may be the world's most meticulous treatise on SJW, studies very strongly indicate that such extracts possess vanishingly little MAOI activity. The same assurance cannot be made for the water or oil extracts that may be used in many North American products. Even ethanol extracts are suspect. According to Cracchiolo, "Christopher Hobbs [a respected herbalist] states that an ethanol tincture CAN contain an MAOI." Perhaps this is why in a trial by Harrer et al. of a new ethanol extract of SJW—LoHyp-57—there were not that many fewer adverse reactions and withdrawals from the study on SJW than there were on a low dose of Prozac.

What follows is a list of side effects reported by SJW users (brand and type are usually unspecified). Some of these reactions (or coincidental symptoms) have undoubtedly occurred in people using the finest research-grade or methanol- or CO_2-extracted hypericum. Culled from anecdotal reports on the Internet, private communications, and the published literature, they are listed in apparent decreasing order of frequency (very roughly): gastrointestinal upsets, particularly gas, nausea, and stomach pains (often relieved by taking SJW with food), and one case of paralytic ileus (temporary paralysis of the intestine); headaches (including mild, seemingly not hypertensive ones); muscle fatigue, aches, or spasms; extreme drowsiness (SJW is approved for insomnia in Germany) or (at the other extreme) sleeplessness if taken in the evening; feeling wired, restless, nervous, irritable, jittery, or even mildly manic; loss of sex drive, of genital sensitivity, or of ability to achieve orgasm (rarely, compared to many antidepressant drugs); dry mouth; breakthrough seizures in an epileptic on Dilantin; feelings of hostility, anger, suspicion, or alienation; feeling strange, spaced-out, dazed, or "in a dream"; absent-mindedness, mental fuzziness; trembling or shaking; emotional numbness; light-induced itch, rash, or transient neuropathy (painful nerve damage); weird sunburns; mania or hypomania; increasing depression; depressive "crashing" when trying to quit; transient, mild dizzy spells; poor heat tolerance, sweatiness; shortness of breath; diarrhea; heartburn; swollen feet; and breakthrough bleeding in women on low doses of oral contraceptives.

The list may sound alarming, but I am aware of only a few cases of most of these reactions—in some cases just one. My impression is that few people actually experience significant side effects that don't pass with continued use or go away when they lower the dosage or switch to a different brand.

SJW also comes with some other real and theoretical risks.

In theory, SJW's ability to significantly inhibit serotonin reuptake, not to mention the MAOI effects some SJW extracts likely possess, could trigger a so-called serotonin syndrome in sensitive users if the herb is combined with other strongly serotonergic agents, notably MAOIs (phenelzine), SSRIs (Prozac, etc.), nonselective SRIs (venlafaxine, some tricyclics, trazadone), lithium, tryptophan, and 5-HTP. The risk would be much lower with milder serotonin boosters like SAMe, methionine, *Ginkgo biloba*, ginseng, yohimbe, and perhaps other anti-depressant herbs.

Much feared, but seldom seen, the serotonin syndrome is a mild to severe attack of twitchy, jerky, spasmy, shivery, sweaty, staggering confusion. In very rare cases, it rapidly escalates to a feverishly fatal pitch. "In the mouth, myoclonus [one of the main symptoms] can feel like a rapid fluttering of the soft palate, tongue, or throat, often only on one side," Cracchiolo notes.

So far, only a very few cases suggestive of mild serotonin syndrome in people on SJW—taken alone or with serotonergic antidepressants—have come to light. At least one person reported other side effects when combining SJW with an SSRI: extreme aggression, light sensitivity, and migraines. More typically, people are safely combining SJW with SSRIs and other non-MAOI antidepressants. When a close, eighty-two-year-old family member began to slide emotionally one fall, I cautiously added a very small dose of SJW to her regime—which includes the SRI Effexor and a low augmenting dose of serotonergic lithium—and arranged for more light in her kitchen. Within days she was back to normal, and over a year later, the combination has caused no apparent side effects.

Another theoretical hazard of SJW is cataracts. Bright light can turn light-sensitive hypericin into a damaging free radical. The fact that SJW is also rich in antioxidants and can, as Cracchiolo points out, "convert oxygen to the strong antioxidant enzyme superoxide dismutase *in the presence of light*" (emphasis mine) may make this a hollow threat—assuming that therapeutic doses of SJW even result in enough hypericin in the eyes in the first place. Still, users of SJW might consider limiting themselves to no more mood-lifting bright light than they need, wearing wraparound sunglasses and a hat if necessary, and consuming lots of eye-protective antioxidants like vitamins C and E. It's worth noting that photosensitization is a property of most antidepressant drugs—but *they* don't come with antioxidants.

Even more theoretically, test tube studies indicate that *at extremely high concentrations* (seemingly equivalent to thousands of capsules per day) SJW can interfere with male and female fertility. So if you want to conceive, limit yourself to no more than a few bottles of SJW per day.

Not so theoretical is the slight risk of provoking mania or hypomania. Bipolars in particular should be cautious.

Conservatively, some authorities, like Wong et al. and Cracchiolo, recommend against using SJW during pregnancy or lactation. Psychiatrist Jonathan Zuess, author of a popular book on SJW, is even more cautious. He also recommends against SJW for people with heart failure and for children under twelve, and he says to use the herb only under medical supervision if you have liver or kidney disease or high blood pressure. With the possibility of adverse MAOI interactions or serotonin syndrome in mind, Zeuss warns of potential interactions with other antidepressants and many other psychotropic drugs, diet pills, nasal decongestants, cold and hay fever medications, asthma medications (cromolyn sodium and steroid inhalers are okay), "illicit drugs or narcotics," and even our friends phenylalanine and tyrosine. Zeuss also insists on a complete washout period before replacing any antidepressant drug with SJW. Some psychiatrists, however, fade SJW in while fading the drug out—unless it's an MAOI (too risky).

How Does It Work?

Until a few years ago, SJW's mechanism of action seemed clear. Early research had suggested that one of the herb's major ingredients, hypericin, was a *monoamine oxidase inhibitor* (MAOI), in common with some of the most powerful antidepressant drugs. But later studies indicated that hypericin itself is not an MAOI and that SJW as a whole has a far weaker MAOI effect than is required to single-handedly relieve depression. Indeed, research-grade methanol and CO_2 extracts of SJW seemed to have little or no MAOI effect at all.

As if on cue, new research began pointing to a more credible active ingredient called *hyperforin* and to other mechanisms of action: suppression of excessive cortisol release from the adrenal glands, reduction of depressives' high levels of interleukins (a sign of immune system dysregulation), stimulation of receptors for the calming neurotransmitter GABA (like Valium), and a more classically antidepressantlike effect: inhibition of the neuronal reuptake of serotonin, norepinephrine, and dopamine. Most antidepressant drugs appear to work by inhibiting the reuptake of just one or two of these neurotransmitters. SJW seems to inhibit them all about equally. Altogether it has the unique pharmacological profile of a super-antidepressant *and* tranquilizer. Were SJW's MAOI effect truly strong, it would also be a super-dangerous antidepressant. Instead, St. John seems to have blessed his namesake herb with a synergy that is highly safe and remarkably effective.

Beyond St. John's Wort

As miraculous as SJW has been for so many depressives, it would be an even greater miracle if it were the only herb that could perform such antidepressant wonders. What sets SJW apart from the rest of the pack is that a German company saw its potential, developed a proprietary extract called LI 160, and funded studies that made their product acceptable to the medical community. There undoubtedly are other St. John's worts, and some of them are sure to be found among the dozens of other plants herbalists have used for centuries to treat depression.

In Western herbalism, these herbs are collectively classified as *nervines*, with a subclass called *nervous restoratives* or *nervine tonics* being the nervines of choice for depression. Taken daily for weeks or months, say herbalists like Simon Mills, these brain-nourishing plants bring "slow but real improvement" to depressed and debilitated users.

Some nervous restoratives are relatively tranquilizing. These include ashwagandha, gotu kola, lavender, lemon balm, licorice, marjoram, skullcap, and vervain. They tend to work best for depressives for whom insomnia, anxiety, irritability, aches, and pains are prominent. Other nervous restoratives, like basil, ginseng, *Ginkgo biloba*, rosemary, and sage, tend to be stimulating. They're better suited for depressive lethargy, apathy, and retardation.

Some nervines are stimulating without being "restorative" or "nourishing." They provide the spark, but only as long as you supply the fuel. These stimulants, which include black tea, kola (cola nut), damiana, green tea, safflower, saffron, yerba mate, and yohimbe, can help depressives "reassert vitality and activity," Mills says. But, he cautions, they must be used in moderation, under cover of nervous restoratives, good diet, and supplements that feed and replenish the brain, like the amino acid neurotransmitter precursors and omega-3 fatty acids. Otherwise these stimulants can simply drain you.

Coffee is an example of the mixed blessings of a strong herbal stimulant. Some touted it as a mild antidepressant. Research suggests that many depressives instinctively use it and other caffeinated beverages for that very purpose. But skeptical scientists point out that most of the experiments validating caffeine's pick-me-up effect have used caffeine-deprived addicts as subjects. In controlled studies using non-coffee drinkers (e.g., Veleber and Templer), large doses of caffeine have worsened many subjects' moods, as stimulants often do. A number of investigators, like Veleber and Templer and psychologist Larry Christensen, have also reported adverse neuropsychiatric effects—headaches, nervousness, insomnia, anxiety, depression, mental confusion—among people who drink lots of coffee, and relief from those symptoms when they quit (after weathering the withdrawal, of course).

Depending on your symptoms, a little bit of nervine from "column A" and a little from "column B" might suit you better than putting all your stock in just one or two. You may, for example, take stimulating nervines or a stimulant like *Ginkgo biloba*, ginseng, or green tea early in the day and tranquilizing ones like valerian or gotu kola in the evening. Or an herbalist, taking stock of all your symptoms, conditions, and possibly your constitutional type, may recommend a traditional formula or compound a prescription just for you.

The following herbs are most likely to help when you're depressed. Although the clinical evidence is mostly anecdotal, so, not long ago, was the evidence for St. John's wort.

From Black Cohosh to Yohimbe: A Guide to Other Herbal Antidepressants

Black Cohosh: Herbal HRT?

According to a review of herbs in psychiatry by University of Toronto psychiatrist Albert Wong and his colleagues, European studies support the traditional North American aboriginal prescription of black cohosh for "women's problems." In a randomized trial, a popular brand of this mimicker of ovarian hormones, Remifemin, equaled hormone replacement therapy for the menopauselike symptoms of hysterectomy. In another trial, Remifemin actually bettered estrogen for physical and psychological menopausal distress. There is evidence that black cohosh can relieve PMS too.

At a typical dosage of 40 to 200 milligrams per day, black cohosh usually takes up to two weeks to work, according to Wong et al. Possible side effects, they note, include upset stomach, throbbing headache, *worsened* mood, and depressed heart function. If you're taking ovarian hormones or their precursors (pregnenolone, DHEA), you may have to cut down when taking black cohosh. It's not recommended if you're pregnant or lactating.

Damiana: A Touch of Testosterone

For its part, damiana appears to be a mimicker of testosterone. This would account for its reputation as an aphrodisiac and as a mood tonic, helpful for "depression and debilitated states in both sexes," according to Mills.

Ginkgo Biloba: *Happy Smart Pill*

Every day, millions of North Americans take a standardized extract of the herb *Ginkgo biloba* to sharpen their mental faculties or to treat or prevent senile dementia or stroke. In Europe, ginkgo is a "smart drug" prescribed by doctors as often as many best-selling actual drugs.

Dozens of controlled clinical trials and preclinical studies suggest ginkgo's stew of natural chemicals preserves and protects the brain in a multitude of ways (Kleijnen and Knipschild, 1992). Ginkgo may, for example, counteract some of the age-related decline in serotonin. Other studies suggest ginkgo, like SJW, shares the major properties of antidepressant drugs: reuptake inhibition of serotonin, norepinephrine, and dopamine, as well as reversible MAO inhibition (much safer than irreversible MAOI drugs). Gingko even appears to stimulate the release of neurotransmitters (as stimulants do) and to inhibit adrenal steroid synthesis (which is excessive in severe depression). As with SJW, these effects must be relatively weak or buffered by others. Otherwise ginkgo would be a dangerous herb—and a powerful antidepressant. Instead, research suggests it's safe, but mild.

According to Wong et al., a repeated finding in trials of ginkgo for senile dementia and cerebral insufficiency (age-related mental decline) has been improvement in depression, anxiety, fatigue, and other psychological and psychosomatic symptoms. In a German study cited by Wong et al. and described in detail by naturopath Michael Murray in *Natural Alternatives to Prozac*, forty patients aged fifty-one to seventy-eight had a primary diagnosis of mild to moderate depression and weren't responding to antidepressant drugs. Half were prescribed adjunctive ginkgo, half adjunctive placebo. The placebo group barely improved, but those on ginkgo saw their depression scores drop by half after the first four weeks, and by another 36 percent by the end of the eight-week trial. Murray, who says ginkgo "tends to promote . . . an improved outlook on life," recommends the herb to all his patients older than fifty.

But what about younger depressives? For accountant Robert Sealey, ginkgo hit the spot when he was just a babe of forty-four. Sealey had been haunted by the blues since his teens. By his early forties, his depression became so severe it launched him on a course of antidepressant drug therapy. A year later, his condition had only deteriorated. Then he read about ginkgo. "After trying small doses of *Ginkgo biloba* for a few days," Sealey writes, "I was surprised and pleased when my depression improved." Ginkgo became the centerpiece of a natural regime that ended Sealey's long bout with the blues.

In a lone negative trial, gingko was no better than placebo at preventing fall/winter depression, or SAD (Lingaerde et al.).

But the herb has another ace up its sleeve. Backed by extremely favorable research from the University of California at San Francisco by A. J. Cohen and B. Bartlik, some psychiatrists (uhs.bsd.uchicago.edu/dr-bob/tips/split/SSRI-sexual-dysfunction.html) are confirming that ginkgo can alleviate the sexual dysfunction that haunts users of SSRIs and other antidepressants. The UCSF group reported a roughly 80 percent success rate in thirty men and thirty-three women.

The usual dosage of ginkgo is 40 to 80 milligrams, three times a day, of an extract standardized to contain 24 percent glycosides and (sometimes) 6 percent terpenes. Although very uncommon, side effects include gastrointestinal upset, skin rash, headache, overactivation, dizziness or lightheadedness, tinnitus, peripheral visual "shimmering," and (very rarely) spontaneous bleeding, including subdural hematomas and retinal hemorrhage in aspirin users. (Ginkgo is a blood thinner, like aspirin, so users may need to lower their dosage of blood thinners or use with caution if they have a bleeding disorder.) At Harvard's Neurology WebForum (neuro-www.mgh.harvard.edu/forum), two people reported becoming depressed or relapsing into depression on ginkgo and then returning to normal after discontinuing the herb. Others found gingko helpful for depression.

Ginseng: The Most Time-Honored Tonic

Ginseng—both the Asian *Panax* variety and the Siberian *Eleutherococcus* type—has a mythic reputation as an invigorating panacea for the frail, the weary, and the senescent. It's also said to be useful for depression.

According to ginseng scholar Stephen Fulder, modern research gives some credence to these claims. In double-blind studies from Maudsley and St. Francis's hospitals in London, Korean ginseng boosted the performance of nurses and patients. And in an uncontrolled German study, it elevated the mood of ninety-five nursing home residents.

"Siberian ginseng . . . along with being an energy tonic, has a positive effect on stress and depression," writes supplement guru Earl Mindell. It "has become the anti-fatigue supplement 'par excellence' in Russia, and is given to cosmonauts, Olympic athletes, and workers doing heavy physical work," prominent herbalist Michael Tierra notes on his website (www.planetherbs.com). "Perhaps no other material," Tierra adds, "has as long and successful a history of helping this problem."

Ginseng is often characterized as an *adaptogen*, an herb that, by mimicking the adrenal stress hormone cortisol, helps people adapt to stress. To anyone familiar with the biology of depression, the thought of an herb mimicking cortisol may sound an alarm bell. Severely depressed people typically have too much in their bloodstreams, enough to actually cause brain damage. But ginseng appears to be a kind of good-fairy cortisol. Not only does ginseng lower high levels of human cortisol, its sterling reputation as a stress reducer and senility preventer suggests its adaptogenic phytocorticosteroids pose no threat to the body.

For treating depression, Michael Murray recommends a dose of *Panax ginseng* that contains at least 5 milligrams of *ginsenosides*, one to three times a day. Side effects such as overstimulation and high blood pressure are possible, especially if you're a hot-blooded type, in which case the cooler American ginseng might be more suitable. Some herbalists recommend that the stimulating Siberian ginseng only be taken in thirty-day courses, with a pause of a week or two in between.

According to Wong et al., possible side effects of ginseng include insomnia, restlessness, anxiety, euphoria, diarrhea, and high blood pressure. Use ginseng with caution if you have diabetes or hypertension, or if you're taking psychotropic drugs (drugs that affect the brain; ginseng may increase the effects of MAOIs, caffeine or other stimulants, or Haldol, causing headaches, tremors, or even mania). Ginseng may increase your requirement for the blood thinner Coumadin, decrease your need for corticosteroid medications or estrogens, and interfere with digoxin.

Gotu Kola: Keeping a Cool Head

If ginseng is the fire in the belly of Chinese herbalism, gotu kola is the cerebral third eye of India's ayurvedic herbalism. It is revered in India as an enlightening, brain hemisphere–balancing rejuvenant for the nervous and immune systems that increases intelligence, combats senility, and relieves sundry psychiatric ills, including depression.

"Tibetan monks use it for calming, as an aid to meditation," says Jacques Bradwejn, chairman of psychiatry at the University of Ottawa (Sherman, 1998). In controlled studies by Bradwejn and others, gotu kola has reduced stress-induced anxiety and acutely dampened the startle response in animals and humans. It also made people feel less "energetic," confirming its reputation as a sedative. A very similar ayurvedic herb that shares the same common name—*brahmi*—is *Bacopa monniera*. It may be more specifically helpful for depression.

Kava Kava to Make You Calmer

A soothing, relaxing, "what me worry" nervine, kava kava typically gives users a mellow buzz. Double-blind studies have repeatedly demonstrated kava root's effectiveness for anxiety disorders, including the nerviness, depression, and other symptoms of menopause (Warnecke, 1991).

"It is probably the most powerful anxiolytic [anxiety buster] available without a prescription," says Jerry Cott, director of the Adult Psychopharmacology Program at the National Institute of Mental Health (Sherman, 1998B). Cott is one of many mainstream authorities who are giving kava a big thumbs up. In part, this is because kava imitates the calming neurotransmitter GABA, similar to prescription tranquilizers. Unlike those drugs, research shows it doesn't dull people's faculties; if anything it heightens them. But then kava also inhibits the reuptake of norepinephrine, a stimulating effect shared by many antidepressants.

A powerful muscle relaxant and social lubricant, kava could spell relief if you're just in a tense, hostile, depressed mood or maybe take the anxious, sleepless edge off a full-blown depression. According to herbalist Michael Tierra, it could also help you keep your cool while withdrawing from caffeine, tobacco, or other drugs. A friend finds a bedtime dose allows her to sleep better and face her frequent nightmares with empowering calm and detachment.

Kava plays second fiddle only to St. John's wort in Tierra's formulas for depression. "I know from personal experience that this herb can restore peace of mind and tranquility, and can promote a feeling of well-being," testifies Earl Mindell.

Kava's usual dose range is about 50 to 200 milligrams of kavalactones per day, from a kavalactone-standardized extract. Some people who don't respond to capsules find alcohol extracts effective, usually 30 to 90 drops per day.

Too much kava makes people sluggish and drowsy, even stuporous. It has even caused a coma when combined with the tranquilizer alprazolam. Other side effects only seem to occur in very long-term abusers of very high doses.

Because kava can counteract the get-up-and-go neurotransmitter dopamine, it could deepen depressive passivity or inertia, if dopamine boosters like tyrosine and NADH aren't also on the menu. For the same reason, kava could worsen Parkinson's disease. Germany's Commission E (the agency that regulates herbs) recommends against taking kava for endogenous depression.

Lemon Balm (Balm, Melissa): The Gentle Nervine

Herbalists of yore listened to nervines the way psychiatrists today listen to Prozac. "Melissa causeth the mind and heart to become merry, and driveth away all troublesome cares and thoughts arising from melancholy," declared Thomas Culpeper. Modern herbalists like Simon Mills and the British Herbal Medicine Association still extol this gentle, stomach-calming nervine as a relaxing antidepressant, particularly well suited to children.

Although balm appears to inhibit thyroid hormone secretion, it has never been known to cause hypothyroidism, according to expert Michael Castleman.

Oats to Make You Stronger

The humble oat is a time-honored nervous restorative in Western herbalism. It's particularly well suited for depressions of the run-down, exhausted, and debilitated variety, according to the *Herbal Pharmacopoeia* of the British Herbal Medicine Association and other authorities. "Oat tea" has also been reputed to help beat drug addiction.

A tincture of fresh, milky oat seeds is the preferred prescription, but according to Simon Mills, oat straw and even oats themselves (the kind you eat with a spoon) are also effective nervous tonics.

Valerian: Another Mood Stabilizer?

An ever-popular sleeping pill, valerian has traditionally found much broader application as a calming nervous restorative for the very anxious, distraught, mad (psychotic, manic), and depressed. The influential nineteenth-century American physician Samuel Thomson declared valerian "the best nervine known." During the First World War, it was to valerian that doctors turned to calm shell-shocked soldiers. And in 1950, this notoriously smelly root was still listed as a sedative in the U.S. *Pharmacopoeia and National Formulary* (Castleman).

At least one modern study suggests valerian really can calm people under stress (Wong et al.). In an uncontrolled trial, fifteen out of twenty patients "with major depression, generalized anxiety, insomnia, or other psychiatric symptoms . . . rated themselves as very much improved" after just two weeks (Sherman, 1998B).

Preclinical research reviewed by Wong et al. suggests valerian's natural chemical stew has multiple effects on the nervous system, including Valium-like effects on GABA and possibly serotonergic effects too, with hypnotic (sleep inducing), anticonvulsant, and both antidepressant and (probably at much higher doses) CNS depressant effects. In rats, valerian has antidepressantlike behavioral effects similar to those of imipramine (Sakamoto et al.).

Valerian may, therefore, be an atypical antidepressant, like the tranquilizers alprazolam and clonazepam, with high-anxiety depressives being most likely to benefit. Like clonazepam, it might also be a mood-regulating downer for mania. But for some depressives, valerian may be nothing *but* a downer—or just a good sleeping pill.

Valerian has no known drug interactions and few recorded side effects (headache, morning grogginess), despite its frequent prescription in Europe (Sherman, 1988B). Still, one should be cautious combining it with strong sedatives. Paradoxically, overdoses have made people restless, agitated, and even hallucinatory (Castleman). Some herbalists believe that valerian can become toxic or depressant after a few weeks of use and that it should be avoided by immunocompromised individuals. There also, according to Wong et al., have been a few "reports of hepatotoxic effects, although the offending preparations often contained a mixture of ingredients, making it difficult to draw definitive conclusions."

Vitex Agnus-Castus L.: Women's Problems? No Problem

With a mouthful of a moniker like that, it better be worth pronouncing. And for women with breast pain, irregular periods, menopausal symptoms, PMS, postpartum depression, or infertility, *Vitex* is. Also known as chaste tree or agnus-castus, *Vitex's* kindness to women has been known since ancient times. According to Wong et al., modern scientists have found that *Vitex* counters excess prolactin (a pituitary hormone) and mimics the get-up-and-go neurotransmitter dopamine. In a recent randomized, double-blind trial by C. Lauritzen et al., a German standardized extract of *Vitex* was compared to 200 milligrams per day of vitamin B_6 in 175 women with PMS. Although 60 percent of the women who took the vitamin for three menstrual periods felt it improved their depression and other premenstrual symptoms, 77 percent were just as pleased with the herb. Twice as many doctors (24.5 percent) rated *Vitex* as "excellent." Mind you, more than twice as many *Vitex* users had side effects (13 percent). None, however, were serious, unless you count the five pregnancies, evidence of the fertility-enhancing effects of the herb.

Yohimbe: Herbal Viagra and More

Yohimbe is an herbal stimulant in more ways than one. This African bark is perhaps the closest thing there is to herbal Viagra. For the many depressives who have lost their sexual groove on today's popular SSRI antidepressants, yohimbine (the active ingredient in yohimbe) is a sometimes successful antidote (Jacobsen, 1992). Studies indicate yohimbine (and probably the whole herb too) can also relieve two of the most problematic side effects of first-generation antidepressants: dry mouth and orthostatic hypotension (faintness upon standing).

When psychiatrists Mark Pollack and Paul Hammerness at Massachusetts General Hospital prescribed yohimbine to one of their depressed patients, they were hoping only to relieve her drug-induced sexual dysfunction. The fifty-year-old woman had suffered from dysthymia and recurrent major depression since adolescence. She was highly drug-resistant and markedly depressed when the doctors put her on 5.4 milligrams per day of yohimbine. At first, as yohimbine often does, it simply made her anxious. So they halved the dosage. Three days later, the first thing the woman noticed was her mood. "I feel better than I have in thirty years," she declared. Sixteen months later, her sexual function and her mood were still normal, despite a bout of rocky family life.

"This case suggests that the addition of adjunctive yohimbine to an antidepressant trial may provide another potentially effective intervention for the treatment-refractory depressed patient," Pollack and Hammerness wrote.

It wasn't the first time—or the last—that psychiatrists would try to augment antidepressants with yohimbine. But like stimulants in general (including amphetamines), the good results have tended to be canceled out by negative ones. Reading between the lines, it seems likely that yohimbine—or yohimbe—in a careful, less-is-more dosage can be a useful augmentor for a minority of depressives. (Women with "maternity blues" might be in that minority, a biochemical study suggests.)

As a stimulant, excess yohimbine has been known to aggravate psychosis and make people anxious, nervous, restless, agitated, sleepless, tremulous, irritable, even manic. Indeed, yohimbine is used experimentally to provoke panic attacks. Physically, it can also boost heart rate and blood pressure; provoke seizures; be toxic with alcohol; and potentially increase some of the side effects of antidepressant drugs. Combining it with other stimulants, Albert Wong and associates warn, can push things right over the top. Because yohimbe appears to have some MAOI effect (Cracchiolo, 1998), users may need to heed the drug and dietary precautions recommended for MAOI drugs.

Many more herbs are reputed to have antidepressant effects. These include ashwagandha, basil, bee pollen, black haw, borage, cramp bark, kola (cola nut), lady's slipper, lavender, licorice, mugwort, rosemary, thyme, and vervain. In the next few years, we likely will be hearing a lot more about them.

Holistic Herbalism

Conditioned by modern medicine, most of us transfer our preconceptions about treating specific disorders with specific drugs to herbs. We go from Prozac to St. John's wort; from Valium to valerian. But when we do, we soon find that the adage "your mileage may vary" applies to herbs too. What works like a charm for one depressive can flop for another. In traditional medical systems that employ herbalism, mileage is not left so much to chance or trial and error.

"We diagnose holistically," explains Janna Weiss, Ph.D., a licensed acupuncturist and practitioner of traditional chinese medicine (TCM). In TCM, Weiss continues, "one depression may be diagnosed as 'liver qi congestion,' another as 'liver heat,' and another as 'spleen cold and deficient,' etc." For each subtype of depression, with its distinct profile of signs and symptoms, the herbal prescription will be anywhere from slightly to diametrically different.

And in Chinese medicine, as in ayurvedic medicine and Western naturopathy, the tendency is to prescribe not one herb or two, but a complex cocktail to harmoniously address the totality of a person's symptoms. Even for depression, herbs other than nervines may be prescribed: detoxificational herbs for a "toxic" depression, digestive herbs to optimize absorption of nutrients and rejection of allergens, or herbs to neutralize the unwanted side effects of the others. Thus, as Weiss notes, a formula for one depressed person might be quite different for another.

How different from Western medicine. Weiss recalls a case in an Israeli hospital where she consults. "One patient with severe depression had dark purple lips—'blood stagnation' in TCM." But when Weiss told the resident psychiatrist, he responded matter-of-factly: "We don't treat it. She gets the same [antidepressant] meds everyone else does."

Trial-and-error use of herbs like St. John's wort has worked wonders for many people. But one shouldn't underestimate the herbal practitioner who can perhaps treat the whole of you more specifically, safely, and effectively.

Using Herbs

Can You Believe the Label?

As herbs have exploded in popularity, the herb industry has come under increasing scrutiny—and it hasn't always come out smelling like lavender. Studies have found that what's listed on the bottle is not always what's inside. In surveys of major brands, the dosage or percentage of active ingredients has often varied wildly from label claims.

Fortunately, public demand will likely ensure that it will soon be possible to buy any herb, confident that it's exactly what it says it is. In the meantime, good word of mouth and company reputation are the best we have to go by. If brand X doesn't work for you, it's possible brand Y of the "same" herb will.

To Standardize or Not to Standardize?

As herbalism enters the new millennium, it faces another burning issue: to standardize or not to standardize. The making of a standardized extract begins when a manufacturer uses water, alcohol, CO_2, or oil to extract a complex chemical soup from the crude plant. By measuring the ingredient the extract is to be standardized for, the manufacturer can formulate a precisely standardized product—0.3 percent hypericin for SJW, for instance.

But as we've seen, experts now believe hypericin is not the active antidepressant ingredient in SJW. This is one reason many herbalists distrust standardization. Besides, even if hypericin were "the active ingredient," such herbalists worry that unscrupulous manufacturers would "standardize" by spiking inferior material (cheap stalks instead of flowers, for instance) with pure hypericin. This would not make a proper herbal medicine, for herbalists believe many chemicals contribute to an herb's safety and efficacy. Hence their preference for high-quality herbs or extracts that contain a harmonious balance (standardized by nature, as it were) of major active and minor supportive ingredients.

Ironically, that may be why at least one manufacturer's SJW (the LI 160 used in most clinical trials), though standardized to contain 0.3 percent hypericin, has proven to be such an effective antidepressant. Very likely, Lichtwer Pharma has simply been using high quality SJW: The hypericin content has merely been a marker of quality and potency, just as sweet and crunchy is a marker of ripe and fresh in some fruits.

The moral? Standardized extracts by honest manufacturers are likely to retain the holistic chemical balance found in high-quality herbs while ensuring specific concentrations of ingredients that may very well be key to the herb's medicinal value.

Playing It Safe

The more an herb becomes a hit, the more we discover its dark side. Most herbal antidepressants are not bestsellers, and so we have little more than tradition and minimal research to guide us. We must be vigilant and consult up-to-date references and experts—even doctors and pharamacists. As with all supplements, start with a low dosage and increase gradually into the therapeutic range, watching for side effects as you hope for relief.

CHAPTER 14

Subtler Substances: Homeopathy, Aromatherapy, and Flower Remedies

The brainchild—by way of Hippocrates and early medical sages—of an iconoclastic German physician named Samuel Hahnemann (1755–1843), homeopathy is one of the most widely practiced medical systems on earth today. It is also perhaps the most reviled by skeptics.

On the surface, it has good reason to be. The substances that homeopathic remedies are made from give healthy persons the very symptoms they are supposed to relieve. But then by the time these materials (from sodium chloride to snake venom) have been diluted and shaken over and over again into homeopathic form, the most potent homeopathic remedies rarely, if ever, contain even a single molecule of the original substance.

As fantastic as homeopathy may sound, few healing arts have inspired as much admiration from as many admirable devotees the likes of Goethe, William James, Mark Twain, Gandhi, Pope Pius X, and Mother Teresa. In Britain, where nearly 50 percent of doctors admit to referring patients to homeopathic colleagues, a survey cited by Dana Ullman suggests most patients are happier for it.

In the past decade, two major medical journals have published reviews of the surprisingly ample body of clinical research on homeopathy. In a 1991 review in the *British Medical Journal*, Jos Kleijnen and associates found 105 controlled clinical trials, 75 of them double-blind.

Homeopathy proved significantly better than placebo or as effective as standard medical treatments in 81, including 15 of the 22 most rigorous trials. "Based on this evidence we would be ready to accept that homeopathy can be efficacious, if only the mechanism of action were more plausible," the University of Limburg epidemiologists concluded.

Six years later, England's other august medical journal, *The Lancet*, published a meta-analysis of eighty-nine placebo-controlled trials of homeopathy. No matter how Klaus Linde et al. sliced and diced the studies (e.g., including only the most rigorous, or only those with the entire sample corrected for publication bias), a statistically and clinically powerful effect for homeopathy remained.

Finally, in a 1998 review of more than three hundred studies for the European Union, M. Van Wassenhoven not only concluded homeopathy is not a placebo, but wrote that basic research is finally hinting at the secrets of its implausible mechanism of action. In contrast, negative academic reviews of homeopathy have been comparatively few and small.

Homeopathy in Psychiatry

Homeopaths strive to treat the whole person. Although there have been few controlled trials for psychiatric disorders, most have turned out positive (Kleijnen et al.). For example, homeopathy won its only controlled match with depression.

Naturopaths like Robert Ullman and Judyth Reichenberg-Ullman are typical of the professionals who practice homeopathy in North America today. In their book *Prozac-Free*, they write that none of the natural healing modalities they are trained to use has proven so consistently rewarding as homeopathy for depression and other psychiatric ills. Although their evidence is purely anecdotal, the Ullmans describe many patients with chronic or recurrent psychiatric disorders who typically have responded very gradually to a course of homeopathic remedies and fared well through years of follow-up. This is the gold that homeopathy goes for: not a quick fix—a bandage you have to replace every few months or years—but a slowly wrought transformation that amounts to a "cure" or a remission with but few, easily treatable relapses.

Treating Depression Homeopathically

At last count, there were roughly two thousand homeopathic remedies (*any* material can be made into a homeopathic remedy). But most homeopaths, even classical homeopaths with years of formal training under the belt, use only a fraction.

The challenge for the classical homeopath is to find the one remedy whose total "symptom picture" (the same symptoms crude doses provoke in healthy people) comes closest to that of the patient's. That symptom picture consists not just of the patient's depression, but of her particular kind of depression and her other symptoms and idiosyncrasies too, like getting a headache in a stuffy room, hating tight clothes, avoiding people, or craving greasy foods in the morning. Making the match—finding the so-called *similimum*—can take several tries and many hours of careful (and expensive) case-taking. And as the patient recovers, the similimum can change.

A secretive loner, depressed by unresolved grief, yet averse to consolation, might be matched with homeopathic table salt, *Natrum mur*, especially if he has trouble peeing before an audience. A suicidal depressive who alternates between agitation and apathy and has turned uncommunicative and indifferent to her loved ones might be a candidate for *Sepia* (homeopathic cuttlefish ink), especially if the smell of food turns her stomach.

It's possible to buy one-size-fits-all homeopathic combination remedies for depression. These contain a medley of homeopathy's favorite antidepressant hits (there are, perhaps, no more than a dozen or two of these). But most classical homeopaths frown on the practice.

Homeopaths also tend to discourage self-prescribing anything more ambitious than a low-potency remedy for a depressed mood. If you're clinically depressed, an ill-matched high-potency remedy, they warn, could make you sicker or harder to treat. And if you're severely depressed, even an appropriate choice could trigger an acute aggravation of your symptoms or a healing crisis that could be dangerous if you're potentially suicidal.

Obviously, serious depression calls for a skillful homeopath. Most homeopaths are medical doctors, naturopaths, osteopaths, chiropractors, practitioners of traditional Chinese or ayurvedic medicine, or clinical psychologists. Homeopathy is more often a specialty than a distinct profession.

The following letters after a homeopathic practitioner's name indicate a high level of homeopathic training (often three or four years): DHt (Diplomate in Homeotherapeutics), DHANP (Diplomate of the Homeopathic Academy of Naturopathic Physicians), and/or CCH (Certified in Classical Homeopathy). But as the National Center for Homeopathy in Alexandria, Virginia, points out, "the practitioner's level of competence in homeopathy often has little to do with his or her type of licensure." At least as important is how much the person actually practices or specializes in homeopathy and how much skill and talent she has acquired, especially in treating people with your kind of problem.

The NCH can help you find a homeopath in your area ([703] 548-7790; fax: [703] 548-7790; www.healthy.net/pan/pa/homeopathic/natcenhom/index.html).

How *Can* It Work?

At first blush, the idea of medicines so dilute that not a single molecule of active ingredient remains sounds like a practical joke. At second blush, it still does for most skeptics.

In fact, homeopathy involves a combination of dilution and very vigorous shaking (succussion). This act of succussion, homeopaths and researchers believe, is where the apparent magic of preparing a homeopathic remedy occurs.

The prevailing theory is that succussion physically imparts the unique identity of the diluted material to the impressionable dilution medium: distilled water. As the molecules of diluted material grow fewer and fewer, their "memory" in the water—which current theory and research suggests is stored in an electromagnetic and/or fluid crystalline form—grows stronger. The more dilute and "potentized" a homeopathic remedy becomes, the less it behaves like a drug, dependent on mass chemical action, and the more it becomes a discrete *informational signal*, like an image or odor. The medium (potentized water) becomes the message. And the message, as homeopaths see it, is a wake-up call to the self-healing system of the patient, the very same system to which it has so carefully been matched.

Aromatherapy

"The way to health is to have an aromatic bath and scented massage every day," Hippocrates said, apparently to his wife after a long, hard day at the clinic. As usual, Hippocrates had a nose for good medicine.

Today, the evidence that scent can relax, heal, and uplift is mounting. Consider just a few examples:

✣ At the University of Vienna, the smell of lavender and other reputedly sedative fragrances slows mice right down, even when they're hopped up on caffeine (Buchbauer et al.). In Ireland, aromatherapy so effectively cuts hospital patients' need for sleeping pills that the coronary care unit of one hospital adopted it to lighten their own stress load (Cannard).

✣ In Reading, England, 112 patients admitted to an ICU are randomly given either a single session of aromatherapy massage with lavender oil, a scentless massage, or a rest period. When they leave the hospital, all are feeling better, but the aromatherapy group is the least anxious and blue (Dunn et al.).

✣ In Japan, psychiatrists and immunologists led by R. Fujiwara report that certain scents, notably citrus and lemon, restore disturbed immune function and have antidepressantlike effects on stressed-out rats. In a small uncontrolled study, depressed humans are exposed to the smell of citrus, and their immunologic and neuroendocrine functions normalize too. Their need for antidepressant drugs plummets (Komori et al.).

Few of these findings would come as a surprise to aromatherapists. For millennia, healers have been freshening the air of sickrooms and rubbing fragrant plant oils into people's skin. Today, although little controlled research is to be found in peer-reviewed journals, scientists like M. Lis-Balchin of South Bank University in London believe aromatherapy truly is psychoactive. Its clearest effect, it seems, is to encourage healing by relieving stress and lifting mood.

Mood-Lifting Scents

"I have had amazing results with true melissa, rose otto, and marjoram," Colleen K. Dodt, author of *The Essential Oils Book*, tells me of her experience treating depression with essential plant oils. For Dodt personally, melissa is the ticket. When she feels a depression coming on, she dabs some on her sleeve to sniff herself into a better mood.

But what about clinical depression? In her book *The Fragrant Mind*, prominent aromatherapist Valerie Ann Worwood promises only that "essential oils . . . which have been traditionally shown in aromatherapy to be effective in the treatment of depression . . . will not provide a magic cure but will definitely support and complement any other therapy." (See table 14.1.)

To aromatherapy practitioners and connoisseurs, different essential oils have personalities as distinctive as their scents. "Someone might talk about needing geranium," Worwood writes, "as one might need a dear friend or partner, to offer comfort and solace after a hard day. . . ." Lavender is like a strong mother; ylang-ylang, a "gentle seductress."

Inevitably, the idea of matching essential oils' "personalities" with people's arises. Worwood delves into great detail. For example:

❧ Melissa gives strength and comfort with her cheerful, nurturing personality. She is a "bubbly, fizzy" carefree lover of life, propelled by her indomitable curiosity and enthusiasm to keep exploring ever-new interests and activities. But negative partners and relationships can slow her down to a dull, depressive crawl.

❧ Orange is a dynamic, kindhearted lug who inspires self-confidence, courage, and good cheer with his sunny disposition. He is a popular people person: touchy-feely, funny, even flamboyant. But depressing circumstances or surroundings can gradually, almost imperceptibly, drag Orange down into a mire of depression or obsessive-compulsive behavior.

❧ Clary Sage can be sage one minute, oafishly funny the next. Artistically creative, romantic, and nonjudgmentally kind and considerate, she is psychologically androgynous, sexually keen, and not averse to "experimentation." But she can break under pressure, becoming hypersensitive, suspicious, burned out, and possibly obsessive-compulsive or addictive.

Table 14.1 Essential Oils Commonly Used for Depression

Essential Oil	Additional Psychological Effects
Bergamot Clary sage Lemon Mandarin Marjoram Melissa Nutmeg Orange Orange blossom *Osmanthus* Petitgrain Rose maroc Rose otto	Relieves anxiety, anger, pain, and insomnia
Grapefruit *Helichrysum* Jasmine Patchouli Ylang-ylang	Relieves anxiety, anger, pain, and insomnia; relatively stimulating
Chamomile, Roman *Eucalyptus citriodora* Frankincense Geranium Lavender Neroli	Relieves anxiety, anger, pain, and insomnia; relatively stimulating in high doses
Sandalwood Thyme	Relatively stimulating

A key to aromatherapeutic matchmaking is smelling to see if an essential oil agrees with you. Aromatherapists place great stock on leading with your nose.

Aromatherapy How-To

The most popular aromatherapy technique is to mix essential oils with a neutral carrier like almond oil, and massage. Depending on the oil, the ratio can vary from 5 to 50 drops per 100 milliliter of carrier. Aromatherapists also recommend many other techniques, including the following:

❧ A few drops of essential oil can be dabbed on a hot surface (a radiator, a bowl of hot water), dissolved in water and sprayed from a mister, sprinkled in your bath water, or placed in the medication well of a vaporizer. You can even sniff the oil directly from the bottle or from something you've dabbed it on, like a handkerchief or cotton ball carried in an airtight bag.

❧ Some oils, like lavender and orange blossom, can be used as perfumes after diluting them in jojoba oil or vodka. Any oil can be mixed with a scentless lotion or cream for topical application.

❧ Some aromatherapists recommend drinking essential oils—a few drops dissolved in water—but only those safe for internal use. This obviously is more like herbalism than "aroma"therapy.

A few cautions:

❧ Don't use an oil "neat" (on the skin, but undiluted), internally, or in the bath, unless you know it can be safely used that way.

❧ Some people are instantly allergic to contact with certain essential oils; others become sensitized only after prolonged exposure. One man developed eczema after using aromatherapy candles for a year. His apartment was so contaminated, it had to be gutted. Ironically, aromatherapy may not have been the culprit. Department store "aromatherapy" candles are notorious for using cheap synthetic scents instead of real—and costly—essential plant oils.

Aromatherapists tend to limit their *materia medica* to pure, essential plant oils, and look down their noses at artificial scents. However, the smell of incense is considered psychotherapeutic in ayurvedic medicine, and the fresh smells of nature can obviously be uplifting too.

The Bach Flower Remedies

Psychological negativity, believed Edward Bach (1886–1936), a mystical English medical doctor and homeopath, was the root of all illness. The antidote was something that could hardly be purer and sweeter: the essence of flowers, extracted with distilled water.

By the time of his death, Bach believed he had intuited the unique spiritual essence or "personality" of thirty-eight common Welsh and

English countryside flowers, and the specific negative psychological quality each one could alleviate. Healing was simply a matter of matching a patient's negative psychological state with the appropriate flower extract. As chronicled by Bach's biographer Nora Weeks, all manner of ills, including depression, responded like a charm to Bach's gentle medicine.

Today, Bach's remedies—and dozens of other flower essences developed by his followers (in theory, every flower has a positive quality to offer)—are a popular alternative therapy available in most health food stores and prescribed by some 60,000 alternative health practitioners, and some mainstream ones. Some have undergone extensive training and certification by the Flower Essence Society in Nevada City, California (1-800-736-9222; fax: [916] 265-0584; http://www.flowersociety.org).

Although there is very little controlled research on the Bach remedies, some psychiatrists have become converts based on clinical experience alone. According to author Jane Heimlich, Herbert Fill, formerly the New York City Commissioner of Mental Health, considers the remedies an excellent substitute for psychotropic drugs. Another psychiatrist cited by Heimlich reports that after three to six months, the remedies benefited thirty-two out of forty patients.

Patricia Kaminski, codirector of The Flower Essence Society, writes that "flower essences have outstanding and even astonishing success with children." The reason, she believes, is that children are not yet as psychologically convoluted as are adults. It's easier for a child's essence to be matched with a flower's essence and respond to it.

Kaminski writes that many practitioners find the essences remarkably synergistic with psychotherapy. The essences seem to catalyze a gradual process that begins modestly with symptomatic relief, proceeds to insight, and—if client and therapist are sufficiently committed—culminates in personal transformation, positive lifestyle changes, and spiritual growth.

As psychiatrist John Diamond contends in Weeks's book, "Used wisely and with respect, the [Bach] remedies can be of inestimable value."

CHAPTER 15

Elementary Healing: Darkness and Light, Heat and Cold

F or some people, the relationship between darkness and despair, light and joy, is more than metaphoric. For others, the kind of "heat" they can't stand is literally measured in degrees. For all these people, treating depression can be quite elementary.

Shedding Light on the Blues

In the early 1980s, psychiatrist Norman Rosenthal and his associates at the National Institute of Mental Health, spurred on by an insightful patient, rediscovered an old truth about depression and nature's flashiest stimulant, bright light.

Every fall and winter when the days shorten and the cold chases people indoors, some people slide into a torpor. Only with the light of spring do they recover—even becoming hyperactive, euphoric, or manic in some cases. But in the dark of winter, just set these people down next to a sunny bright artificial light box for a few hours each day, and soon most of them snap back to life.

Since the early 1980s, many dozens of studies have shed further light on recurrent fall/winter depression, commonly known as SAD (seasonal affective disorder), but best described as winter depression, for short. It now seems that wherever the days get much shorter in winter, most people experience at least some symptoms of winter depression, however mild. The full-blown syndrome strikes 5 to 10 percent of people (depending on latitude and sunshine levels), while a milder, subsyndromal form afflicts three times as many. Atypical depressives are especially vulnerable, as are people prone to recurrent brief depressions year round.

Extreme lethargy, acute mental dullness, and (sometimes) suicidalness are the major symptoms of winter depression. Typically, sufferers oversleep in the morning and pack on five, ten, or more pounds by indulging their pronounced seasonal craving (especially at night) for sweets and other carbohydrates.

In dozens of controlled trials, bright light therapy (BLT), also known as phototherapy, has usually entailed sitting for thirty minutes to two or three hours a day—depending on the brightness of the light box—near a commercially designed, tabletop bright-light box. Rapidly (usually within a week or two), BLT has brought clear improvement or recovery to 60 to 70 percent of winter depressives, including children. People with the most typical symptoms—oversleeping, carbohydrate-craving, feeling worst late in the day or night—have proved most responsive. Pulling the plug has quickly led to relapse.

Mild subsyndromal winter depression has also responded to phototherapy, as has winter premenstrual syndrome. Indeed, there is more and more evidence that if you have a symptom or condition that flares up during the dark season—obsessive-compulsive disorder, panic disorder, anorexia—BLT may make it better.

With research suggesting that winter depression is at least partially a syndrome of low serotonin, serotonergic drugs like Prozac have become the most commonly prescribed alternatives to bright light. Still, in a five-week trial by S. Ruhrmann et al., bright light brought full remission to twice as many depressives as Prozac. However, many winter depressives find it necessary to use drugs (or supplements like tryptophan, 5-HTP, or St. John's wort) as adjuncts or substitutes for BLT.

You Don't Have to Be Seasonal

"Most patients with depression should receive bright light treatment in addition to any medicines or psychotherapy they may be receiving," says Daniel Kripke, a veteran light researcher and psychiatrist at the University of California in San Diego. Kripke isn't just talking about people with winter depression. "Light's value for nonseasonal and seasonal depression are comparable," Kripke said at an American Psychiatric Association symposium in 1997. Indeed, BLT is as effective for nonseasonal depression as drugs, Kripke asserted—in the short run, at least. In the many controlled trials Kripke cited, BLT had usually lasted just a week, never more than a month. Compared to placebo (typically dim light), it fared as well as drugs typically do compared to their placebos after months.

But in these brief trials of BLT, typically only one in every four or five depressives have recovered. BLT's brightest prospects for nonseasonal depression would therefore seem to be as an adjunct to other therapies. And the research leaves little room to doubt that. In studies reviewed by Kripke, a dash of BLT has significantly hastened response to slow-acting antidepressant drugs, converted drug nonresponders into responders, and sustained response to a normally very short-lived antidepressant we'll meet in chapter 18, *partial sleep deprivation* (PSD). Bright light even seems to augment psychotherapy. And, Kripke adds, "many depressed patients benefit from incorporating bright light into their long-term living patterns." Research suggests those nonseasonal depressives most likely to benefit are light-deprived, have a history of recurrent winter depression, or have winter depressionlike symptoms.

For Rapid Cyclers Too?

Ironically, for a treatment that must be used with extreme caution for bipolar depression, BLT could be a potent remedy for the rockiest bipolar disorder: rapid cycling.

In Japan, normalizing aberrant circadian (daily) body rhythms is the subject of considerable research. Psychiatrist Ichiro Kusumi and his associates wondered if rapid cycling bipolar disorder—which is practically synonymous with run-amok circadian body rhythms—could benefit from a combination of mild morning BLT (two hours at 3,000 lux) and megadoses of methylcobalamin (vitamin B_{12}), another circadian rhythm normalizer. They chose two highly drug-resistant inpatients for their subjects.

It worked. Within just a few days, the sleep-wake patterns of both men normalized and their bipolar symptoms began to remit. Though both had been bipolar for over ten years and rapid cyclers for three, just three weeks of the combination therapy sparked a nearly two-year (at last count) recovery in one. The second patient returned to work after three months and remained well after he discontinued BLT two months later. Both men remained on their mood-stabilizing medications throughout.

Because neither had responded previously to methylcobalamin, the researchers suspected BLT was the key. "We expect," they concluded, "that this chronobiological therapy will provide another approach to treatment-resistant rapid cycling affective disorders."

Taking the Light Cure

Successful BLT depends on a number of factors:

The kind of light. Research suggests any bright light source—fluorescent, incandescent, or natural—can be effective, though full-spectrum light may have an edge. Most of light's antidepressant power seems to be packed into the cool, blue-green end of the spectrum.

There are quite a few manufacturers and sellers of light therapy devices. The Sunbox Company (1-800-548-3968; members.aol.com/sunbox) designed the light boxes used in most of the early research. It currently offers a range of full-spectrum boxes, visors, and dawn simulators. Amjo Corp (877-BUY-AMJO; www.sadlight.com) sells the powerful (10,000 lux), but low-wattage, inexpensive, and very well-shielded parabolic "Satellite Light." Tools For Exploration (1-800-456-9887, toolsforexploration.com) sells a wide variety of light therapy devices. Sunnex (877-7-SUNNEX; www.sunnexbiotech.com) offers a unique low-intensity green wavelength light box. It's as effective as bright white light boxes, in the experience of many users and a few studies, but less likely to damage the eyes or provoke adverse reactions, according to its codesigner Murray Waldman (Baumel, 1998).

Of course, the sun is the ultimate light therapist. The snow on a sunny winter day vastly outshines any light box. And the cold (as we'll see in a moment) could be an antidepressant in its own right. The exercise you'd get trying to keep warm certainly is. In the only study so far to test Mother Nature's Lightbox, a one-hour walk every morning brought full remission to 50 percent of SAD patients within just one week (Wirz-Justice et al.). Even indoors, sitting right next to a big sunny window is like sitting next to a moderate intensity, 2,500-lux light box.

Brightness. Light therapy seems to work, at least in part, by suppressing the pineal gland's secretion of the soporific hormone melatonin. For most people, ordinary indoor light (about 200 to 400 lux) doesn't quite cut it. Outdoor light, even on an overcast day, and the light near a 2,500 to 10,000 lux light box does. But so should the light from an ordinary shaded lamp or a brightly lit, light-colored surface, if your eyes are right next to it. Try burying your head in a book with a powerful desk lamp right over it. *Very bright!*

The amount of light. One to three hours a day of phototherapy was the norm in early clinical research with moderately bright light boxes (2,500 lux). But as little as fifteen to forty minutes has sufficed in more recent trials with much brighter 10,000 lux boxes, usually in the morning—the earlier the better. In fact, half an hour a day at 10,000 lux has become a kind of "standard dosage," though some people do better on more, or less.

The time of day. The morning sleepiness of most winter depressives suggests they have what you will come to know in chapter 19 as a "phase-delayed circadian rhythm." Morning bright light is a capital remedy for that, and winter depressives usually respond to it best.

Early morning light has also worked well for nonseasonal depressives. Theoretically, it would be best suited for those who are wakeful late at night. This is a very common problem in the elderly, especially if they're depressed or demented. Brief morning BLT has been investigated as a treatment for this "sundowning" syndrome, with preliminary success. Nonseasonal depressives with the opposite circadian dysfunction (sleeplessness early in the morning) would likely benefit more from evening BLT.

Safety

BLT is not without side effects. Some people become overactivated. A few become hyperirritable, even manic. (Even mellow dawn simulation makes some people mildly manic.) But most side effects, though quite common, are minor—headaches, eyestrain, nausea, insomnia, hot flushes (rare)—"dose related," and tend to abate with time. Because bipolar persons seem particularly sensitive to light, they may fare best on a "bright-light lite" regime to prevent mania. They may also be at increased risk of a much more serious, though rare, side effect.

Three winter depressives, two of them bipolar, have attempted suicide or become extremely tempted to within a week of beginning BLT at a major SAD research center. N. Praschak-Rieder et al. suspect BLT did what antidepressant drugs sometimes do: give a suicidal depressive the drive to act on the impulse before lifting his mood. Kripke reports that one depressive actually did commit suicide soon after beginning to wear a bright light visor (a mini-light box you wear on your forehead).

To minimize the risk of eye damage during long-term BLT, experts recommend ocular prescreening and monitoring. A high intake of eye-protective antioxidants like vitamins C and E is a good idea, especially if you're also taking a photosensitizing antidepressant drug (most of them are). To protect your skin, use only UV-filtered light boxes. To prevent overexposure to fluorescent lights' magnetic field, use a shielded light box.

Dawn Simulation

Clinical studies by David Avery and associates at the University of Washington and by others suggest an entirely different kind of light therapy can treat winter depression, though perhaps with a slightly weaker effect. Early every morning, around the time the sun begins to rise in the summer, a small, computer-controlled light comes on in the patient's bedroom. Gradually, as the patient sleeps, the faint light brightens until, by rising time, the room is fully lit.

"Dawn simulation" usually lasts one or two hours, though in one study a ten-minute special was nearly as effective. Curiously, simulations that peak at very bright levels appear less effective (and less agreeable) than those that get no brighter than an average artificially lit room.

Dark Therapy

Light stimulates, darkness sedates. If it took Norman Rosenthal to bring light to modern psychiatry, his NIMH colleague Thomas Wehr is bringing the darkness.

In 1998, Wehr and several associates published what appears to be the first (and so far only) trial of "darkness therapy." It was really just a return to nature's normal daily cycle of light and dark. As Wehr et al. observed, "the modern practice of using artificial light to extend waking activities into the nighttime hours might be expected to precipitate or exacerbate bipolar illness."

The problem with bright light at night is that it interferes with the normal evening rise in melatonin, the mellow lights-out hormone secreted by the pineal gland. For most of us, this may do little more than keep us up late. (More seriously, epidemiologic studies suggest this may also increase our risk for cancer. As an antioxidant, melatonin is one of the body's natural cancer fighters.) But for people with bipolar disorder, a little bit of insomnia can go a long way. Sleeplessness precedes most manic episodes and even seems to trigger them. Thomas Edison's most famous invention could be hazardous to bipolars' mental health.

Wehr and associates persuaded a rapid cycling patient to spend fourteen hours in bed every night (which they later reduced to ten hours) in darkness. They followed him up closely for several years on the darkness regime and off. Off, his sleep time and darkness exposure fluctuated in time with his mood swings. But on the darkness regime, his rapid cycling stabilized. Significantly, not just his manic episodes, but his depressive episodes too were prevented.

The Hot and the Cold of It

The temple priests of ancient Greece had a rough and ready remedy for people who clung too tenaciously to depression: They dumped them in cold water. The Chinese have long had similar inclinations: "In the mentally tired, the emotionally inhibited and listless depressives, a brief moment of cold water bathing can revitalize mental spirits and enhance the mood" asserts a traditional text (Chang, 1985). In Europe, Emil Kraepelin, a founder of modern psychiatry, had a similarly elemental remedy for depression: cold baths.

Cold therapy might well have remained in the deep freeze of medical history were it not for those same intrepid NIMH investigators who saw the light and the dark. Some of their patients, Thomas Wehr and his associates noticed in the 1980s, regularly become clinically depressed every summer. Cool weather, trips north, or the arrival of fall restore their spirits. Indeed, come the fall or winter, many become manic or hypomanic, though a few become depressed again in the winter.

It was winter depression in reverse, another kind of SAD.

One of these patients was struggling with her fifteenth consecutive summer depression when Wehr and associates had a bright idea. They gave her the keys to an air-conditioned home and a prescription for frequent cold showers. Five days later her depression had all but vanished. When they sent the lady back home, she quickly relapsed.

The Chinese don't think you have to be seasonal to benefit from a cold antidepressant. Here's their traditional prescription (not recommended if you have "fever, acute or subacute diseases, or serious heart disease"): Gently and gradually, briefly expose yourself every day to cooler and cooler air or water, but never so cold that you shiver, let alone freeze. In time, you should be able to enjoy a daily, brief (as little as a few minutes), bracing, cold-water swim, shower, or bath, or just a "cold air bath." And that should be as bracing for your mood as it is for your body (Chang, 1985).

CHAPTER 16

Healing Fields, Happy Currents: The Promise of Electromagnetic Mood Medicine

I t's quite painless, it seems safe, and—in the words of one depressed patient—it feels like having Woody Woodpecker on your head. "We're excited," says psychiatrist Robert M. Berman, director of Yale University's Mood Disorders Research Program. "It has the potential to make ECT [electroconvulsive/shock therapy] obsolete"(Katz). The excitement is shared by dozens of investigators around the world, at the National Institute of Mental Health, Harvard Medical School, the Medical Research Council in the United Kingdom, and elsewhere. The excitement is electromagnetic.

Transcranial Magnetic Stimulation (TMS)

Studies have shown that when we're worried or depressed there's a change in the electrical weather of our brains. Specifically, there's a reduction of neuroelectrical activity in the *left prefrontal cortex*—the gray matter just behind the left forehead. Simultaneously, the activity in the *right prefrontal cortex* under our right foreheads increases. But if we're very happy, optimistic, euphoric, or even manic, the pattern is just the opposite.

An inoffensive way, scientists have discovered, to influence this electrical activity is to expose the cortex to a powerful pulsing magnetic field at the surface of the skull. The field is thousands of time stronger than the earth's magnetic field at the surface of the earth, but about equal to the field used in MRI scanners.

The best results have been obtained when the small hand-held electromagnetic coil that has become the tool of the trade is repeatedly turned on and off, a technique called *repetitive transcranial magnetic stimulation*, or *rTMS*. When the on-off frequency is fast—usually ten or twenty times a second (10 to 20 Hertz)—electrical activity in the underlying neurons is stimulated. When the rate is slow—usually once every two or four seconds (0.25 to 0.5 Hertz)—it's actually inhibited.

It may sound like mad scientist stuff, but most studies—as recently reviewed by Mark S. George of the Medical University of South Carolina and his associates—have found that rTMS really works, and almost painlessly: no need for anesthesia, no seizures, no confusion, and no memory loss. It even works for depressed rats. Most impressively, rTMS sometimes works for the toughest human cases.

Perhaps because the technique resembles ECT, researchers have focused on testing it on patients who normally are candidates for that aggressive intervention: depressives who have proven resistant to drugs and, usually, are very severely or psychotically depressed.

In a 1995 pilot study by Mark George and associates, one such patient enjoyed a complete remission—the first in three years. In 1996, a much more sophisticated study was published in the prestigious British medical journal *The Lancet*. The researchers, led by another rTMS pioneer, A. Pascual-Leone, chose seventeen medication-resistant psychotic (delusional) depressives. Most had responded only to ECT in the past.

The study was complex. Each patient received five five-day courses of rTMS—one per month—focused over three different brain areas. In the "sham rTMS" courses, the magnetic coil was held not flat, but at a 45-degree angle to the head to weaken the magnetic effect, presumably into the placebo range. As the researchers expected, only one of the courses—full, level stimulation of the left prefrontal cortex—had more than a minor effect. It brought improvements of roughly 30 to 60 percent in both self-rated and psychiatrist-rated depression to eleven of the patients.

"This remarkable result," George et al. commented in their 1999 review, "was superior to what could be expected with any medication regimen, or even ECT." But most of the improvement lasted only two weeks, indicating that five days of rTMS would not be an adequate treatment. (A course of ECT, it should be said, usually lasts a few weeks.)

Researchers have also explored using *low-frequency* rTMS to inhibit the overactive right prefrontal cortex of depressives. In a pilot study by D. L. Menkes et al. from the University of Louisville, eight sessions significantly relieved depression in eight patients over a six-week period. That was nothing compared to the largest double-blind study of rTMS to date, by psychiatrist Ehud Klein and his associates at the Technion-Israel Institute of Technology. The subjects were sixty-seven patients with recurrent major depression. Of the thirty-five randomly assigned to ten sessions of slow rTMS over two weeks, seventeen enjoyed a 50 percent or greater reduction in their depression. Just eight of the thirty-two patients assigned to sham rTMS did.

As we've seen, in mania, the prefrontal brain activity imbalance is opposite to that of depression. In theory, low-frequency rTMS over the *left* prefrontal cortex of manic patients should be therapeutic. So far, researchers have only tried the complementary approach. In a small double-blind trial by N. Grisaru et al., rapid rate rTMS over the right prefrontal cortex had a significantly greater antimanic effect than rapid rTMS over the left.

The evidence that rTMS's antidepressant effect quickly fades raises the question of whether it could be used, like thyroid hormone and lithium, to augment drugs or other long-term treatments. In a controlled study by A. Conca et al., after just three sessions depressives assigned to rTMS plus an antidepressant drug were already recovering at a significantly greater pace than those on the drug alone.

In addition to "last resort" depressives, preliminary research suggests rTMS can also be of benefit for winter depression, for depression in people with multiple sclerosis, for chronic depression following head injury, and for depression during pregnancy. Psychiatrists are just beginning to study whether rTMS can also be used as a long-term treatment and maintenance therapy for depression.

rTMS still needs work if it is to become a proven source of safe and lasting relief from depression. It also needs the approval of the FDA and the health regulatory agencies of other countries if it is to emerge from the research clinic. Low-frequency rTMS, which carries a very low risk of provoking seizures, may be first to gain that approval. Eventually, perhaps a new generation of rTMS units will be approved for in-home use as self-care devices, not unlike light boxes, negative ioniz-ers, and rTMS's first cousin, which we'll soon meet: *cranial electrotherapy stimulation* (CES) devices.

At the forefront of rTMS research, Mark George and his associates be-lieve the verdict on rTMS for depression should be in very soon, perhaps by the time you read this. In a letter to the *American Journal of Psychiatry* in 1999, they noted that fifteen double-blind trials of rTMS for depres-sion were underway. One of those studies was a U.S. multicenter trial large enough "to completely settle the issue of transcranial magnetic stimulation's putative antidepressant effect within the next two years."

In the meantime, those trials need subjects. Your psychiatrist should be able to tell you if any are going on in your area. Online, the Interna-tional Society of Transcranial Stimulation (www.ists.unibe.ch/ists) has a list of research centers looking for subjects.

Can Therapeutic Permanent Magnets Relieve Depression Too?

People have been using permanent magnets for healing since antiquity, but lately the practice has exploded. The publication in 1997 of a well-controlled double-blind study from Baylor University by Carlos Vall-bona and associates undercut many doctors' skepticism. The study found that permanent magnets were highly and significantly more ef-fective for acute relief of postpolio pain than nonmagnetic lookalikes. The efficacy of rTMS raises the possibility that permanent magnets could be used to relieve depression too.

"There are numerous anecdotal reports about the therapeutic bene-fits of magnets and lodestones [magnetic rocks] to relieve depression," writes UCLA neurologist Ron Lawrence, president of the North Ameri-can Academy of Magnetic Therapy. But there are no clinical trials. How-ever, Lawrence and his coauthors do describe "a carefully designed double-blind study" from the Menninger Clinic. Tibetan monks medi-tated with magnets suspended over the top of their heads. "When the field was north-up," Lawrence et al. write, "male subjects tended to be physically and emotionally energized, and females tended to be physi-cally and emotionally inhibited." The results were reversed when the field was south-up.

The top of the head, according to Michael Tierra, a distinguished ex-pert on Eastern and Western natural medicine, is a major site for magnetic treatment of mental illness. It corresponds both to the crown *chakra* of Hindu mysticism and the *Governor 20* point in acupuncture. Tierra has observed that the north-seeking pole of magnets is calming or *yin* in effect, while the south-seeking pole is stimulating or *yang*. "Applying the South pole at this point," Tierra writes on his website (www.planetherbs.com), "will stimulate mental activity and physiological processes. . . . The North pole will calm mental agitation and relieve depression." Judging by the Menninger study, that prescription may have to be reversed for women.

Tierra's observations raise the question of whether applying therapeutic magnets over the left or right prefrontal cortex could have effects similar to rTMS. North-pole magnets would be used like slow-frequency rTMS to inhibit brain activity; south-pole magnets, like high-frequency rTMS, to excite it. (Would those polarities be opposite for women?) But so far this is purely conjecture.

Some of the strongest anecdotal evidence for magnet therapy comes from people with fibromyalgia, a condition marked by chronic pain, muscle tenderness, fatigue, insomnia, and depression. Some claim that sleeping on magnetic mattress pads relieves their symptoms, sometimes dramatically. People who owe their depression to any chronic pain condition should find their mood lifting when and if magnet therapy relieves their pain. Such was the case for a fifty-four-year-old man whose pains were complicated by insomnia and depression. "It is such a relief," his wife wrote, "to see him laugh and joke, which he has not done for years. Bioflow [a magnetic therapy product] has changed his whole outlook on life."

Is Magnetic Therapy Safe?

In short-term human and animal studies, rTMS has appeared safe and extremely well tolerated. There have been few side effects: mostly brief, mild to moderate headaches, transient muscle twitches, and discomfort at the site of stimulation (intense enough, it should be said, to have caused two out of twenty-five patients to drop out of one study).

But while magnetism is a force of nature, it would be stretching it to call rTMS a natural technique. The pulsed magnetic fields employed in rTMS bear some resemblance to the weak, alternating current power-line magnetic fields implicated in adverse health effects, including depression and suicide. They bear little resemblance to the Earth's weak (on its surface) magnetic field or to the stronger magnetic fields of therapeutic permanent magnets, which are still several orders of magnitude weaker than the fields used in rTMS. On the positive side, the adverse effects from weak power-line magnetic fields are associated with chronic exposure. A course of rTMS typically exposes a person for only a few minutes a day for just a week or two.

As far as therapeutic permanent magnets are concerned, though well tolerated and long assumed safe, they've never been proven to be free of hidden long-term hazards either.

Gentle Electric: Mental Relief by Cranial Electrotherapy Stimulation

"The healing power of electricity" may sound like a carnival pitch from nineteenth-century quack medicine, but it's long been part of the high-tech arsenal in modern pain clinics. There, it goes by the highly uncatchy name of *transcutaneous electrical nerve stimulation* (TENS). Recalling the ancient use of electric eels to relieve pain, today's portable TENS devices deliver weak electric currents to where it hurts or relevant acupuncture points. What few people know is that similar devices that apply minute electric current to the head have been investigated and used since the beginning of the twentieth century, primarily for neuropsychiatric disorders, including depression. Animal studies indicate that these *cranial electrotherapy stimulation* (CES) devices boost endorphins *and* the major mood-modifying neurotransmitters, serotonin, norepinephrine, and dopamine.

In a 1995 meta-analysis, Sidney Klawansky and associates from the Harvard School of Public Health found eighteen "carefully conducted randomized controlled trials of CES versus sham treatment." Though none of the trials were for depression, the meta-analysis did suggest that CES is significantly effective for anxiety. Less rigorous studies have usually supported other indications for CES, including depression (e.g., Krupitsky et al.). The most popular, heavily researched and recommended CES device—the Alpha-Stim—has been approved by the FDA for treating pain, and its manufacturer is allowed to claim efficacy for anxiety, insomnia, and depression.

The Alpha-Stim (available only by prescription in the United States, but over the counter everywhere else) and other more affordable, non-prescription CES devices sell for about $300 to $600 (Tools for Exploration, listed on page 302, is a major seller). They have no known side effects. Treatment is as simple as clipping the leads from the Walkman-sized, battery-powered units to your earlobes and letting the juice flow for about twenty to sixty minutes a day.

Part 4

Saved by the Body:
From Bodywork to Working Out

If the eyes are the windows of the soul, the body is its home. We normally think that the body reflects and expresses the state of the person inside, but it works both ways. Changing the state of the body can change the mood of the mind. Putting on a happy face, as psychologist William James argued, can reflexively make you feel happy. Massaging the stress from muscles can knead the tension from a worried mind. The list of body-over-mind effects goes on, as we'll see in the next four chapters.

CHAPTER 17

Bodywork: Working the Body
to Free the Mind

Massage, acupuncture, therapeutic touch, Rolfing, Reiki, yoga—
the list of bodywork techniques keeps growing and growing.
What all or most of these practices have in common is the assumption that working the body can work out blocks to health and well-being: chronic muscle tension, "energy blockages," spinal misalignments, and so on. Most of these techniques have never been scientifically tested for anything, let alone depression. But some have enough evidence of an antidepressant effect to bear singling out here, though others may be just as worthy.

With the exception of acupuncture, none of these techniques seems powerful or reliable enough to bet on as a sole treatment for moderate to severe depression. But they all seem like reasonable adjuncts for clinical depression and, in most cases, excellent long-term investments in building a more depression-proof self.

Massage: Mother of all Stressbusters

Massage cuts through stress like a hot knife through butter, relaxing muscles; lowering heart rate, blood pressure and stress hormones like cortisol; enhancing blood circulation; and even boosting immune function and modulating neurotransmitter levels. "My guess," says Stanford University neuroscientist Robert Sapolsky, "is that massage mechanically forces your muscles to relax, and once you do that, your brain does the same" (Epstein, 1997).

And massage, quite simply, *feels good*. But is that enough to make it good for depression too?

Research—most of it by psychologist Tiffany Field and her associates at the Touch Research Institute at the University of Miami School of Medicine—suggests it is, but only in a modest way. In controlled studies, Field et al. have repeatedly documented massage's salutary effect on depressed moods and on ills often associated with depression, like fatigue, pain, stress, and bulimia. Courses of massage therapy have had an immediate and, in some cases, a slight, cumulative antidepressant effect.

In one of the only studies to test massage therapy on depression itself (also by Field et al.), the subjects were sixteen dysthymic adolescent new mothers. Although a thirty-minute full body massage promptly cut their self-rated depression by roughly 50 percent, five weeks later when they arrived for their tenth and final rubdown, they were still as depressed as ever. But that last massage again cut their blues in half.

So massage may have a mood-lifting effect that's as short as it is sweet. Done frequently, however, it might augment slower-acting antidepressants—or at least make the wait easier to bear.

That massage can loosen not just muscles but tongues and emotions is the basis of psychotherapeutic bodywork. There are many such techniques, but most hearken back to the insights and practices of a few Western pioneers and the legacy of such Eastern bodywork systems as *hatha yoga* and *qigong*.

From Character Armor to Bioenergetic Therapy

Early in his career, Wilhelm Reich (1897–1957), the psychoanalyst and renegade student of Sigmund Freud, made a painful discovery. Try as he might to connect with his patients, he kept butting up against a brick wall of "character armor." Clenched jaws, glazed eyes, stiff necks, braced shoulders, rigid pelvises—these and other defensive body habits prevented his patients from even recognizing, let alone expressing, many of their deepest feelings.

To breach this barrier, Reich rolled up his sleeves and began chipping away at it with his bare hands. Soon he evolved a method of digging into one rigid musculoskeletal "band of character armor" after another, from head down to pelvis. As he poked away, Reich would bid his patients to groan, kick, hit, scream—do whatever their untrammeled inner selves desired. As his patients came alive with emotion and buzzed with memories of long-suppressed traumas, Reich could finally help them put body and soul back together again.

Reichian bodywork and analysis, also known as medical orgonomy (*orgone* was Reich's term for the universal life force), is still practiced. In her book *The Magic of Touch*, Sherry Suib Cohen quotes a patient who says the experience "changed my life. My whole body is more relaxed and my mind too. If you want me to sum up what I got, I'd say: relief, insight, and the capacity for greater joy in life."

The American College of Orgonomy in Princeton, New Jersey ([732] 821-1144; fax: [732] 821-0174; www.acoreich.org), can refer you to psychiatrists or other doctors trained in medical orgonomy.

Reich's most influential student, the American psychiatrist Alexander Lowen, brought a more explicitly spiritual perspective to Reich's system, along with elements of traditional Chinese medicine. If you have images of people "in therapy" swinging towels and kicking pillows, Lowen is one of the senior me-generation psychiatrists you have to thank for it. But, with a nod to *tai chi* and other traditional Chinese medicine practices, Lowen also included gentler "bioenergetic" movement and breathing exercises.

In his thoughtful book *Depression and the Body*, Lowen equates psychological depression with bioenergetic depression. Depressed people, he writes, are typically deadened, cut off through loss of faith in life and despair from their own life force. To help them reconnect with their vital bodily selves, Lowen and his followers (1,500 at last count) engage depressives in exercises that physically ground and center them.

"Getting feelings into the belly so that a person can sense his guts and into his legs so that he can sense them as mobile roots is called grounding the individual," Lowen explains. And a grounded person, Lowen maintains, can more easily become a centered person, breathing from the depths of her belly and living life to the fullest. As with Reich's approach, insight-oriented psychotherapy is a necessary accompaniment to this gradual process.

Although lacking controlled clinical trials, bioenergetic therapy has its share of contented customers. "People who have undergone the therapy—and there are quite a few—swear by it," writes Cohen. They say "it brings the body and mind greater aliveness and life itself a greater wholeness."

The International Institute for Bioenergetic Analysis in New York ([212] 532-7742; fax: [212] 532-5331; www.bioenergetic-therapy.com) can help you find a certified bioenergetic therapist.

Rolfing

Bad posture, the biochemist-turned-mindbody-therapist Ida Rolf (1896–1979) concluded, is the root of much evil. Her solution—*structural integration*, commonly known as "Rolfing"—was to manually dig into the connective tissue surrounding every muscle in the body and work it like putty until the body could assume its naturally ideal stance: poised, balanced, and erect.

Often an acutely painful process that lasts for at least ten weekly sessions, Rolfing can unleash buckets of psychic baggage as deep tensions are released. Rolfing has been popular since the seventies. But Rolfers nowadays seem to focus most on the athletic, orthopedic, and other physical benefits.The Rolf Institute of Structural Integration in Boulder, Colorado (1-800-530-8875; fax: [303] 449-5978; www.rolf.org) estimates that more than one million people have been Rolfed, including many celebrities and Olympic athletes. "Many say that Rolfing has a soothing effect on personality and behavior comparable to the effect of practicing yoga over a long period," writes Cohen. "The release acts as a catharsis and one is less bound by unconscious pain and conflicts." The Rolfed body is commonly experienced by its owners as a tower of free-flowing energy (often literally taller by an inch or two) and incredible lightness of being.

The Alexander Technique: You Are How You Move

F. M. Alexander (1869–1955) was an Australian actor who, like Reich, Lowen, and Rolf, believed something was seriously wrong with the way people "used" their bodies. But instead of attacking the problem with his hands, Alexander taught his students to solve it with their minds—to sense and move their bodies with unique self-awareness and efficiency.

The reward, after many weeks or months of training was the ability to be as poised, relaxed, and efficient, at rest or in motion, as a cat.

Alexander's technique is summed up by an instruction that all students are taught to give themselves whenever they catch themselves "misusing" their bodies: "Let my neck be free, to let my head go forward and up, to let my torso lengthen and widen, to let my legs release away from my torso, and let my shoulders widen."

The message may sound obscure, but thousands of certified Alexander Technique (AT) teachers have a touch and a way (the product of 1,600 hours of training) of making it make sense to the average pupil's slack, uptight, or otherwise misused body. And according to testimonials such as those in *The Alexander Technique* by AT teachers Judith Leibowitz and Bill Connington, as a student's body gets the message, he or she typically experiences a newfound sense of physical ease, lightness, confidence, and pleasure. When Alexanderites give their bodies the "let . . ." message in real-life moments of depressive collapse or tense apprehension, many report it breaks the spell. As one puts it: "I can't think my directions and be depressed at the same time."

In his book *The Alexander Principle*, Wilfred Barlow contends that a person who chronically slouches, for example, collapsing her chest and rounding her shoulders, is fertile postural soil for depression. To illustrate, the British physician displays before and after pictures of a depressed woman. Collapsed, posturally and psychologically, in the first shot, she stands erect and emotionally uplifted in the second after a few weeks of Alexander training.

Testimonials suggest the technique's forte lies in making people less depression-prone. Barlow himself professes that the high recurrence rate among recovered depressives would plummet if AT were put on the menu.

The American Society for the Alexander Technique (1-800-473-0620; www.alexandertech.com) can help you find a certified AT teacher.

Hatha Yoga:
Bending the Body and Mind Back into Shape

More than just an exotic stretching system, *hatha yoga* is, in significant ways, a forerunner to the bodywork of Reich, Lowen, Rolf, and

Alexander. What Reich called character armor resembles what psychotherapeutically oriented yoga teachers like Maureen Lockhart refer to as *kleshas*: chronic, maladaptive psychological tendencies that distort posture and disturb body function. The purpose of hatha yoga is to bend, stretch, and twist these kleshas out of your system. A 1992 position paper by the International Society of Sport Psychology notes that three studies have shown that "exercise has helped yoga participants to be less anxious, tense, depressed, angry, and confused."

There are two major types of klesha, each a departure in one direction or the other from the ideal, *sattvic* posture. A sattvic person has the gracefully erect bearing of someone who has been Rolfed or mastered the Alexander technique.

A person with the *rajasic* klesha has the bearing of a drill sergeant. Back overarched, chest and butt pushed out, muscles stiff and tight, he's inclined to rigidity, compulsiveness, and emotional insensitivity.

In contrast, the *tamasic* klesha type has the slack, downcast bearing associated with low self-esteem or depression. With droopy head, rounded shoulders, and sunken chest, she is, according to Lockhart, afraid to embrace life and "gives up easily and tends toward self-pity, carrying the burdens of the world on the shoulders." If the rajasic person tightens or explodes under stress; the tamasic slackens or implodes.

Whichever klesha you may be inclined to, *asanas* (yoga postures) that bend or stretch your body in the opposite direction are the antidote. Thus, for the rigid rajasic person, forward-bending asanas, like the *sitting forward bend* in which you slowly fold yourself up like a closed book, are the ticket. With their navel-gazing self-intimacy, these asanas gently bring the stoical raja type face to face with her soft underbelly—perhaps her suppressed grief, shame, or tenderness. Although these same asanas might intensify a tamasic person's passivity and introversion, in small doses they may simply soothe and relax him. But the mainstay of treatment for the collapsed tamasic are the rajasic asanas. These arch the back, puff out the chest, and flatten the shoulders. To adopt these asanas—such as the cobra, locust, bow, or dancer—is to feel the vibrant, outgoing thrust of rajasic energy: assertiveness training, yoga-style.

Breathing and Breathwork

Traditional Eastern bodyworkers have always said so, and now contemporary Western bodyworkers—even some scientists—concur: Most of us don't breathe well. We chronically inhale shallowly from the top of our chests when we should, at least from time to time, let our bellies bulge so the air can be sucked right down to the bottom of the lungs, where the blood flow is greatest.

Deprived of *prana*, the universal life force that permeates the air we breathe, we are less vital and alert, say the yogis. Starved for oxygen, the scientists explain, and a little green around the gills from unexpired carbon dioxide, we weaken our immune systems, lower our energy, and become easier prey for anxiety and depression. It may be no coincidence that people with clinical breathing disorders are exceptionally prone to anxiety and depression.

When we inhale fully, the belly balloons to let the muscle layer at the bottom of the chest cavity, the diaphragm, drop a few inches, giving the lungs maximum breathing room. This *diaphragmatic breathing* is "one of the most powerful methods of eliminating stress and producing more energy in the body," writes naturopath Michael Murray. It's also a major tool—and goal—of Lowen's bioenergetic therapy. And it's on natural health guru Andrew Weil's shortlist of most vehemently recommended health tips.

It's very easy to evoke diaphragmatic breathing. Just rest a hand or two on the top of your belly and feel it balloon as you inhale. Next, let the wave of inhalation inflate your chest and finally raise your shoulders as you suck down every last drop of air. Pause briefly, then, as you exhale, feel your shoulders sag, your chest collapse, and your belly slowly contract like a squeeze box to pump all the stale air out of your lungs.

In his book *Body, Mind, and Sport*, chiropractor and ayurvedic practitioner John Douillard strongly recommends a diaphragmatic breathing technique called *ujjayi pranayama*. The trick is to make a raspy, snorelike, "Darth Vader" throat sound while breathing slowly through your nose. This forces your belly to pump in and out for all it's worth. A typical five- or ten-minute session, Douillard claims, "is very effective in times of stress and has been reported to be helpful in states of anxiety, fear, worry, and insomnia."

It's obviously not feasible (or even healthy, I suspect) to walk around breathing diaphragmatically all day. But doing it for just a few minutes a day, say enthusiasts like Sheldon Hendler and Weil, can really calm you down and recharge your batteries. It's a minor mood stabilizer that's never more than a breath away.

Recently, a type of *kriya* yoga (kriya yoga focuses on breathing) called *sudarshan kriya yoga* has been investigated at the National Institute of Mental Health and Neuroscience in India. In two small, uncontrolled studies by P. J. Naga Venkatesha Murthy and associates, the effect of thirty minutes of breathing practice per day was swift and strong, not just for the mildly depressed, but for many severely, melancholically depressed patients too. In one study, after just a month, twenty-two out of thirty patients (fifteen dysthymics and fifteen melancholics) were fully recovered.

Bodywork, Chinese-Style: Tai Chi and Qigong

In China, where exercise is a favored method of psychotherapy, the graceful, focused "meditation in motion" movements of *tai chi* are the exercise of choice for depression. Here in the West, tai chi has become almost as popular as an all-round tonic.

In Australia, studies by psychologist Putai Jin confirm that a sixty-minute session of tai chi acutely boosts vigor and lowers tension, anxiety, anger, confusion, and depression. It also lowers that arch stress hormone cortisol. Jin's studies suggest tai chi relieves stress about as effectively as moderate aerobic exercise.

For clinical depression, tai chi Grand Master S.-C. Man, M.D., of the University of Manitoba, has told me that the long form of tai chi, which usually takes forty-five minutes, is therapeutically preferable to the short form. Man, who often recommends tai chi for depressed patients, finds it usually takes three to four months to fully work. This, he believes, makes it most suitable as an adjunct to faster-acting therapies and a long-term prevention strategy.

As popular, perhaps, in China as tai chi, *qigong* is an eclectic discipline that incorporates movement, posture, breathing, self-massage, and meditation. It's also catching on big in the West.

There is very little research on qigong. But in *The Way of Qigong*, Western qigong master Kenneth S. Cohen describes two large studies of the psychological benefits that were presented at a qigong conference in the 1990s. One was a large Chinese study that found that people who had practiced qigong for more than two years were significantly healthier mentally—less depressed, less anxious, and so on—than those who had practiced for less than two years. (It's possible, however, that people who stuck with the program were just mentally healthier to begin with.) In another large but less rigorous study, "Qigong was found to engender emotional stability, increased joy of life, decreased selfishness, more open-minded attitudes, increased enthusiasm and willpower, and greater caring for others."

Acupuncture

If depression has given you a guilty craving for punishment, the prickly art of acupuncture might seem like just the right medicine for you.

In China, acupuncture—especially electroacupuncture, in which a mild electrical current is passed through the needles—has long been a popular prescription for nervous exhaustion and depression. Russian psychiatrists have also used it for decades. And the World Health Organization recognizes it as a legitimate treatment for depression. Even in the United States, acupuncture is being investigated as an antidepressant by the National Institutes of Health.

As early as 1980, psychiatrist Louise Wensel of the Washington Acupuncture Center in Washington, D.C., had already treated 872 depressives with a regime combining acupuncture and orthomolecular therapy. Of those patients, 686 (79 percent) had enjoyed "significant" improvement, 183 (21 percent) "slight" improvement, and just three, no improvement. Wenzel's patients had typically begun to feel better after the very first of six to ten daily acupuncture sessions. Maintenance treatments then came every week or two, and later every few months.

Traditional acupuncture uses very fine needles to stimulate or sedate key points along the vital energy channels said to flow throughout the human body. The related arts of moxibustion and acupressure do this with heat and very strong finger pressure, respectively. But other stimuli work too. In a recent paper, George Ulett of the University of Missouri and S. and J. S. Han of Beijing Medical University concluded that electroacupuncture is superior to plain needles and that it works just as well when the minute current is passed through a smooth skin-patch electrode—no need to be prickly. Other investigators claim cold lasers and magnets can work too .

According to research cited by J. S. Han, acupuncture can stimulate major mood-regulating neurochemicals, such as serotonin, norepinephrine, and the endorphins. In a controlled study in the 1980s at Beijing Medical University by Han's group, five weeks of daily electroacupuncture brought complete or near-complete relief to most of forty-seven severely depressed patients. Because there were no side effects, Han rated electroacupuncture superior to the competition, the tricyclic antidepressant amitriptyline.

Han's colleagues H. Luo et al. have confirmed these findings in two large, randomized, double-blind multicenter trials. The NIH has taken notice. Recently, a well-designed pilot study funded by the National Center for Complementary and Alternative Medicine (NCCAM) yielded a 64 percent remission rate in thirty-four women with major depression (Sherman). This prompted the NCCAM to fund a much larger trial, still in progress, and a smaller trial for a condition many are loathe to medicate with drugs: depression during pregnancy.

Therapeutic Touch

Something miraculous is happening to the nursing profession. Encouraged by their academic journals, professional organizations, and many of their professors, thousands of nurses are learning to heal by the laying on of hands—an inch or two *above* the body, to be exact. And many are learning this technique, called *therapeutic touch* (TT), at nursing school. Indeed, some are learning it at New York University from the professor of nursing who helped devise/revive the instinctual healing practice herself, Delores Krieger.

TT is a modern-day revival of healing through goodwill, through channeling tender loving care from one person's presumed energy field to another's. Typically, for half an hour or so, the recipient of TT has the undivided attention of a well-meaning person who passes her hands over his body in a gentle, meditative act of smoothing and clearing the troubled waters of his energy field.

A hit among nurses and patients in many hospitals, and popular among bodyworkers in general, TT's most conspicuous benefits are subjective: It makes troubled people feel better. Even a recent highly critical paper by Linda Rosa and her associates found that only twenty-three out of seventy-four quantitative studies of TT prior to 1997 "were clearly unsupportive." Most drugs couldn't claim a better record.

CHAPTER 18

Sleep Cures: Sleep Therapy and Sleep Deprivation

S how me a depressed person and I'll show you someone who in all likelihood has trouble in the sleep department. Whether it's trouble falling asleep, staying asleep, getting up in the morning, or staying awake in the daytime, sleep is a problem that helps define most every depression. And while chronic sleep disorders such as severe insomnia and sleep apnea can promote depression in their own right, usually disturbed sleep is just a symptom of being depressed.

Who, then, would have thought that going out of your way to sleep *too much*, or not to sleep *at all*, or to sleep at "the wrong time" could all be effective ways of *treating* depression?

Rest Cure, Anyone?

When the world is too much upon them, some people know just what to do: They take a nap. Studies by psychologist Suzanne R. Daiss and associates at Texas A&M University and by others confirm that these pit stops from the daily grind do indeed freshen people's moods and perk up their performance.

But what to do when you're so burned out, it seems as if the kind of nap you need could last maybe a year? Go for it.

Sleep therapy is one of those common-sense healing techniques, like light and cold therapy, that keeps cropping up in the psychiatric traditions of the world. In India, ayurvedic psychiatrists prescribe rest cures of up to fifteen hours a day. In Nigeria, medicine men treat their mentally disturbed patients to marathon, drug-induced sleep sessions. In the United States, the rest cure was championed a century ago by the distinguished neurologist Weir Mitchell.

In some parts of Europe—the former Soviet Union in particular— sleep therapy (ST) was still going strong as recently as the 1960s when a Soviet psychiatrist named B. V. Andreev wrote a monograph on the subject. ST, he noted, works best for patients who look and feel as if they need it. Typically, Andreev observed, such persons can't stand "noise, bright light, and social intercourse"; they're foundering at work; they long for "peace, quiet, and solitude;" and they're *very, very tired.* Those who benefit most from ST, Andreev and others found, are burned out and depressed, often in the wake of a toxic or infectious brain disease. In a series of eighty-seven patients treated at Andreev's clinic for one to three weeks, more than 50 percent were "cured" or markedly improved.

Many such people would be diagnosed today with chronic fatigue syndrome (CFS). Some people with CFS *do* find oversleeping helpful. In an interview on CBC radio in 1989, Dr. Stuart Rosen of Charing Cross Hospital in London reported that a majority of three hundred CFS patients responded well to ST, combined with measures to counteract their tendency to hyperventilate.

Sleep therapy may be an overlooked antidote for the manic phase of bipolar disorder. Not only is mania accompanied by sleeplessness, it usually is preceded—and perhaps precipitated—by it. As we saw a couple chapters ago, persuading a rapid cycler to spend ten to fourteen hours in bed every night prevented both his manic and depressive mood swings. Using safe, natural sleep aids like tryptophan, 5-HTP, GABA, melatonin, valerian, hops, hot baths, relaxing music, and sleep tapes could make this mood-stabilizing discipline more accessible. Preventing an episode of mania, with its huge expenditure of energy, can prevent the depressive "payback" that often follows.

Despite sleep therapy's common-sense appeal, it is virtually unheard of in modern Western medicine. This may be more than just an aversion for simple, natural treatments. In the late 1970s, a horror story of medical malpractice came to light in Australia. At the Chelmsford Private Hospital near Sydney, psychiatrists had for years been subjecting patients to days and weeks of barbiturate-induced "deep sleep therapy," accompanied by frequent electroshock therapy, sexual abuse, and in some cases, psychosurgery. Scores of patients died, committed suicide after being released, or were left scarred for life. For most doctors, the Chelmsford scandal, and a similar one at the Allen Memorial Institute near Montreal, may have put a deep chill on anything remotely connected with sleep therapy.

Taking the Rest Cure

Catching some extra sleep at night or napping during the day could be all the sleep therapy you need. A full-blown rest cure is another matter.

At Charing Cross Hospital, the procedure, according to Dr. Rosen, is "to sleep the patient out for a few days, fifteen, sixteen, seventeen hours a day . . . basically having several days where they just have nothing but their batteries recharged by a good sleep." After that, ST continues on a more modest scale. Eventually, patients very gradually return to a normal schedule.

In Andreev's clinic, patients would usually sate themselves on eleven to seventeen hours of sleep a day for one or two weeks. Because they found very prolonged sleep disagreeable, they would get their extra sleep by napping from 10 A.M. to 2 P.M. and 3 P.M. to 7 P.M. Bedtime was from 10 P.M. to 8 A.M.

Quiet, peaceful surroundings are *de rigueur* for a rest cure. For other depressives, something completely different may be indicated.

Sleepless Therapy

It's one of psychiatry's best kept secrets. In many dozens of studies conducted around the world since the 1970s, when depressed patients have been deprived of sleep for all or half of a night, 50 to 60 percent have felt markedly better—even sprightly or back to normal—the next day. (For a good review see Leibenluft and Wehr, 1992.)

But there's a hitch: What sleep deprivation (SD) giveth, sleep restoration taketh away. After a good night's sleep or two most responders plunge down into the dumps again. Few enjoy lasting improvement.

But all is not lost. Studies have shown that by repeating a night of *partial* (half a night) sleep deprivation (PSD), usually once a week or so, some depressives—perhaps one in every three or four—can obtain relief that lasts. Repeat PSD, suggests D. A. Sack and his associates at NIMH, "might provide a clinically useful alternative treatment for depression, particularly in patients who cannot tolerate or do not respond to conventional antidepressant therapies."

But there's more! More than half a dozen controlled studies suggest SD can augment the gradual therapeutic effect of antidepressant drugs and lithium to produce a rapid and sustained response. In one study, psychiatrists R. C. Shelton and P. T. Loosen of Vanderbilt University began a trial of antidepressant drug therapy for twenty patients right after a night of total SD (TSD). Nine of the patients took the usual few weeks to respond, the other eleven responded immediately and didn't look back. Similarly, at the University of Pittsburgh, the usually tardy antidepressant drug response time in elderly depressives was shaved from thirteen weeks to just two in eight out of thirteen seniors. Their trial of Paxil had been launched with a night of TSD (Bump et al.).

When it comes to augmentation of lithium by SD, the most eligible depressives are obviously bipolars. In an extremely encouraging study from the University of Milan, F. Benedetti et al. subjected forty bipolar depressives to three nights of TSD over a nine-day period. Those who had been on lithium for at least six months responded markedly better than those who were drug free. Remarkably, over the next three months, thirteen of the twenty patients on lithium compared to just two of the others remained depression-free.

SD has also converted antidepressant drug nonresponders into responders. The usual procedure is to repeat TSD or PSD a few times for a week or two, then once a week in the longer trials. In at least fourteen trials, this has worked for about 40 percent of more than 400 patients.

In principle, SD's synergy with antidepressant drugs and lithium should extend to other natural antidepressants like St. John's wort, 5-HTP, and SAMe.

For people who suffer from very brief depressions (including premenstrual depression), SD's transient effect may not be a problem. Such people have sometimes been able to nip their depressions in the bud or prevent them (if they follow a predictable pattern) with well-timed SD.

Is Sleep Deprivation for You?

Studies have shown that if you have a relatively severe, typical (endogenous, melancholic) form of depression, you have about a 67 percent chance of benefiting from SD. If yours is an atypical depression, you have about a 45 percent chance. Melancholic depression is especially responsive, and so, it seems, is bipolar depression. Mild depression is least responsive.

How-To

Partial sleep deprivation seems to be as effective as total. And *late* PSD—that is, missing the second half of your night's sleep by getting up four hours early—has usually been more effective than early PSD. Those early morning hours would be an apt time to enjoy the synergy of exercise, bright light, and a big high-protein breakfast. Just don't nap. Even a catnap can wipe out SD's effect.

A small percentage of depressives, usually atypical ones, feel worse after SD. After a night of recovery sleep, even some responders take a brief dip.

Because SD can trigger mania in bipolar or rapid cycling depressives, it's best taken under cover of lithium or other mood stabilizers. SD can also worsen the condition of schizophrenic or psychotic/delusional depressives.

If you're a good candidate for sleep deprivation, you're probably a good candidate for phase advance of the sleep-wake cycle too. Read on.

CHAPTER 19

———— ❧❦ ————

Healing Rhythms:
Getting Your Body Clock
Back in Sync

Nature is full of things that ebb and flow, expand and contract, revolve, rotate, or fluctuate rhythmically in other ways. Everything from planets and stars to hearts and brain cells has rhythm. And it's largely through rhythm that the different parts of the natural world synchronize with each other. The earth's rhythmic revolution around the sun creates the seasons, which set the pace of life on Earth. And Earth's daily rotation cues our own circadian (daily) body rhythms.

Which brings us back to depression. Scientists have found that many, perhaps most, seriously depressed persons have disturbed circadian rhythms. It's as if they were severely jet lagged. Symptomatically, "typical" depressives usually have the kind of jet lag you get after flying west across five or six time zones. Their circadian rhythms are often five or six hours ahead of schedule—*phase advanced* five or six hours, in chronobiological parlance. This is probably why they typically wake up so early every morning.

In the 1970s, Wehr and his colleagues at NIMH had an idea. If phase-advanced depressives would ignore the clock on the wall and listen instead to their jet-lagged circadian clock (the master timepiece in the brain), they would become more in sync with their jet-lagged body rhythms. And perhaps this would ease their depression.

Enlisting a handful of bipolar depressives as their guinea pigs, Wehr et al. had them go to bed and get up six hours early. After just two days, one patient had recovered, two had enjoyed partial improvement, and the fourth was so buoyed he became manic.

But there was a snag. The recovered patient relapsed after two weeks, and though she responded again to another six-hour phase advance, she soon relapsed again. Subsequent phase advances no longer helped her.

Fleeting though it was, the antidepressant effect of this phase advance of the sleep-wake cycle (PASWC) has since been confirmed in all but one of about ten studies by Wehr's group and others, most recently by M. Berger et al. in Germany. And as with its equally eccentric cousin, sleep deprivation therapy, most of these studies have shown that PASWC's future likely lies in combining it with other antidepressants. For example, Wehr's group has used PASWC to convert four antidepressant drug nonresponders to responders in just one week (Sack et al.). The patients gradually returned to a normal sleep schedule soon after they recovered, yet remained well for up to a year. At the University of Freiburg in Germany, a night of sleep deprivation followed by PASWC and a gradual return to a normal sleep schedule in just one week sprung eleven of seventeen drug-resistant melancholic depressives from hospital within weeks (Vollmann and Berger).

In contrast, the kind of jet lag that *atypical* depressives have suggests they've been flying east, not west. Their circadian clocks, Alfred Lewy and his associates observe, are phase *delayed*. Typically young and not too severely depressed, these patients tend to be bushy-tailed at bedtime, dead tired in the morning. For them, going to bed and getting up hours later, not earlier—phase delaying their sleep-wake cycles— might be the ticket, Lewy (a pioneer in light, sleep, and rhythm therapy research) and his associates suggest. A radical phase delay procedure for chronic night owls (going to bed later and later every night until they're actually bunking down at a normal hour) has usually relieved their depressiveness. Unfortunately, the practice has also caused some night owls' circadian rhythms to become completely unhinged, or "free running."

But there's another way. Instead of adjusting the sleep schedule to match the wayward circadian rhythms, one can adjust the rhythms themselves.

Shifting Body Rhythms

Circadian rhythms are programmable. The circadian clock takes its cue from the natural, social, and behavioral rhythms of our lives. Researchers have found that by tightly scheduling these rhythms—in particular the compelling chiaroscuro of bright light and darkness—we can reset our circadian clocks. We can bring our daily body rhythms back into sync with the daily schedules we must follow. In research by Rosenthal et al. at NIMH, this has worked for night owls. And Lewy's group suspects it can benefit depressives too.

The circadian clock is most keenly receptive to resetting in the middle of the night, around 4:00 or 5:00 A.M. If you persistently stimulate it (with bright light, exciting activities, coffee, etc.) *earlier* than that— that is, as late at night as you can—it will think the night is still young, and reset itself accordingly. The clock on the wall may say midnight, but your circadian clock will tell your body it's only 9:00 or 10:00. If you stimulate it not too long *after* its peak receptive hours—that is, very early in the morning—it will start thinking about what to have for lunch.

Studies show that a few nights or early mornings of timed bright light can be all it takes to shift your depressively jet-lagged body rhythms "halfway around the world," east or west.

Here's the deluxe approach: If you need to delay your circadian rhythms because they're phase-advanced (you're waking up early every morning), schedule stimulating activities and influences at night, especially late at night: high-protein meals, loud music, stimulating herbs and beverages, stimulating antidepressants like phenylalanine, tyrosine, SAMe, thyroid hormone, exercise, and cold therapy, and (most of all) *bright light*. "Dusk simulation" (to coin a therapy), which would consist of dawn simulation (as described in chap. 18) in reverse, starting when you go to bed and lasting until 3:00 or 4:00 A.M., might also be an effective phase delayer. (Some dawn simulators can do this.) Early in the day, schedule nonstimulating activities and influences: low/no protein meals, nonstimulating antidepressants like tryptophan, vitamin C, calcium, magnesium, kava kava, meditation, and massage, and *dim light* or *darkness*.

If you need to advance your body rhythms because they're phase-delayed (you're wakeful late at night and sleepy in the morning), do the exact opposite. A dawn simulator timed to wake you up earlier and earlier every morning can also do the trick.

You'll know you've shifted your body rhythms far enough when your feelings of sleepiness and wakefulness are in sync with your desired/imposed sleep-wake schedule. To avoid shifting your rhythms any further, you'll need to moderate what you're doing. Exposure to bright light at night probably should not be done long-term. It will suppress melatonin, possibly putting you at increased risk for cancer. However, a low-dose melatonin supplement at night might compensate.

Chemical Clock Setters

Two natural chemicals show promise as safe, effective means of bringing wayward circadian rhythms into line: *melatonin* and *methyl-cobalamin*.

Melatonin is the pineal gland's "lights out" hormone. It spills into the bloodstream in the dark of night and ebbs in the morning light. It's a popular over-the-counter sleeping pill. Researchers have had variable success using well-timed doses of melatonin to reset circadian clocks desynchronized by jet lag, shift work, or other causes.

To date, no one has explicitly tried using such strategic doses of melatonin to lift depression by normalizing circadian rhythms. In a study by Dolberg et al. that came close, melatonin at bedtime helped depressives on Prozac sleep better, but it didn't seem to make them any less depressed.

In theory, depressives who are phase delayed could benefit from as little as a few hundred micrograms of melatonin as their desired bedtime approaches. A slow-release preparation might minimize early awakening—a side effect for some users. A trickier proposition: Phase-advanced depressives might benefit from a pinch of melatonin when they wake up hours early in the morning—tricky, because melatonin could be a downer in the daytime.

Potentially, melatonin could have more to offer for bipolar disorder. The condition's ups and downs are very often heralded by insomnia or other sleep-wake disturbances. One ten-year-old boy had suffered from treatment-refractory bipolar disorder since the age of five. On the eve of a sleepless manic phase, his psychiatrists gave him melatonin at night, and both his insomnia and mania were promptly aborted. "He has continued to take melatonin and adjunctive alprazolam [a tranquilizer and mild antidepressant] for fifteen months without recurrence of insomnia or mania," J. M. Robertson and P. E. Tanguay report.

However, in a study by Leibenluft et al., a twelve-week course of nightly melatonin didn't benefit five patients with rapid cycling bipolar disorder. But the dosage was so high (10 milligrams) that a free-running sleep-wake cycle was triggered in one patient after discontinuation. Doses of less than 1 milligram are usually recommended today.

Methylcobalamin poses no known problems, other than finding a store that sells it (see page 138). Dozens of reports, mostly from Japan, suggest that megadoses of this most active form of vitamin B_{12} (taken any time of day, it seems) often can normalize delayed sleep phase syndrome and possibly other circadian disturbances too. Alas, one double-blind trial by Okawa et al. found methylcobalamin no better for delayed sleep phase syndrome than a placebo.

CHAPTER 20

———— ✿ ————

Exercising to
Exorcise the Blues

W hen *The Joy of Running*, a seminal book on exercise as psychotherapy by Thaddeus Kostrubala, dashed its way onto the bestseller lists in 1976, it seemed as if the fitness craze had hit its wackiest stride. Visions of goateed psychoanalysts padding down running tracks in Vienna U track suits, their faithful patients straggling behind them, rolled comically across the mind's eye:

DOC: *Now* do you see vy you haff alvays envied your cousin Harold?

PATIENT: Yeah, Doc, I can see (huff, huff) it all so clearly now. . . . Why, it's as if a curtain—yeah, that's it, a *curtain*—has been lifted from my eyeeeEE . . . aWOOoooooo . . . ArrrRRR! My *SHIN*!!!

DOC: Let me haff a look at zat. . . .You know, Herr Schwartz, Doctor Freud always said zer are *no accidents*. . . .

If there was ever any doubt back then about the legitimacy of exercising to exorcise your demons, there's little left now. In consensus statements, position papers, and scholarly reviews, the National Institute of Mental Health, the International Society of Sport Psychology (ISSP), and other authorities have proclaimed that exercise is good for our mental health. The evidence is overwhelming. In 1998, Edzard Ernst and associates at the University of Exeter found more than a thousand trials "relating to exercise and depression" alone. Those studies and others have shown that exercise is a ward against negativity, fear, worry, anger, and tension. Practiced regularly, regardless of age, it brings improved self-image, greater self-confidence, less neuroticism, enhanced mental performance and creativity, greater composure under stress, better sleep—and *less depression.*

Studies suggest exercise is at least as fit an antidepressant as any other for mild to moderate depression, and that it's a sensible adjunct for treating or preventing any kind of depression. As naturopath Michael Murray puts it, "regular exercise may be the most powerful natural antidepressant available."

In an impressive study by psychologists Jeffrey Fremont and Linda Craighead, aerobic exercise proved as effective as cognitive therapy, the gold standard psychotherapy for depression. The fifty-four mainly sedentary female volunteers were all mildly to moderately depressed. Of those randomly assigned to a light, supervised walk/jog/run program, most had already improved or recovered after just four weeks (only two of the nineteen dropped out). By the end of the ten-week study, eleven were nearly or completely depression-free, and months later most were still running to keep their blues at bay.

Exercise has also helped more serious cases. In a study by Martinsen et al. in Norway, twenty-four hospitalized patients with major depression were randomly assigned to adjunctive aerobic exercise. After nine weeks, their self-rated depression fell significantly more than controls randomly assigned to adjunctive occupational therapy, even though twice as many of the latter were taking antidepressant drugs. "Our results are in accordance with eight other experimental studies on clinically depressed patients," Martinsen et al. later wrote. Although most experts are skeptical about exercise for severe major depression, in one successful study all the patients were severely depressed (Doyne et al., 1983).

Depressives may feel like running in the opposite direction at the very mention of "tennis, anyone?" but people with chronic fatigue syndrome (CFS) only wish they could. But there's really no need to run. Therapeutic exercise programs always build gently from an easy-does-it level of activity.

It was just such a graded aerobic exercise program that Kathy Fulcher and Peter White decided to try on 33 patients with CFS in a randomized controlled trial. The patients' self-rated improvement was twice as high as a flexibility and relaxation control group.

Exercise Rx

For years, researchers assumed that the kind of exercise that's good for your body's health—the sustained, deep-breathing *aerobic* kind—is the kind that's good for your head too. But a small number of studies have also suggested that nonaerobic exercises like weightlifting confer similar psychological benefits. As far back as 1987, Elizabeth Doyne and her associates at the University of Rochester showed that running and weightlifting were equally effective for young, clinically depressed women. It now seems that almost any regularly practiced exercise can be a clinically useful mood normalizer, stress reliever, and brain booster. However, the great bulk of evidence suggests that the surest bet is good, old-fashioned aerobic exercise. Strength and flexibility training on the side could make for an ideal balance—when researchers get around to testing it.

Going Aerobic

What exactly is aerobic exercise? It's any activity that conditions your body's ability to extract oxygen from the air (aerobic means *with oxygen*) and distribute it to the working muscles. If it makes you breathe deeply and rapidly and gets your heart racing, it's aerobic. If it makes you breathless, you're pushing yourself into *anaerobic* (without oxygen) metabolism, and you'd better back off.

Exercise physiologists have a formula to gauge whether you're exercising at an optimal aerobic pace. First, subtract your age from the number 220. This is your age-adjusted maximum heart rate. Now multiply this number by 60 percent and then by 85 percent. If your pulse during exercise is anywhere between these two target heart rates, you're in the aerobic "target zone." If you have heart disease or other medical conditions, you might have to work out near the bottom of this zone.

Be physically active at this pace for at least fifteen to thirty minutes (the lower the heart rate, the longer the workout), three or four days a week, and you'll soon be enjoying the many benefits—physical and psychological—of being aerobically fit.

But don't try to become an athlete overnight. In order to stay in the aerobic "target zone," depressives in running programs normally spend most of their time just walking; for the first few weeks, they jog only in spurts. Yet according to running therapy pioneers Roger Eischens and John Greist, "most . . . begin to feel better within a week and feel virtually well within three weeks."

The Aerobics Menu

Any kind of aerobic (and perhaps nonaerobic) exercise can relieve depression, most experts assume, not just the walk/jog/run programs employed in most clinical studies.

Physiologically, the most efficient aerobic activities include cross-country skiing, running, jogging, aerobic "power" walking, uphill hiking, swimming, aerobic dancing, cycling, rowing, canoeing, boxing, skipping rope, and running on the spot; squash, handball, racquetball, lacrosse, soccer, basketball; digging, shoveling, or other repetitive weight-moving activities (if you're strong enough to keep up); and working out on a treadmill, trampoline, stationary bicycle, or a rowing or skiing machine. Lighter activities like ice skating and roller-skating, walking, gardening, lawn mowing with a hand mower, *tai chi*, and most popular dances are perfect if you're not in great shape. Stop-and-start activities like volleyball, tennis, badminton, downhill skiing (short runs), and fencing must be performed for up to an hour or so to yield comparable aerobic effects.

Different exercises have different "personalities," just like the people who are attracted to them. This could account for their psychotherapeutic benefits too. Jogging, for instance, is very conducive to introspection or reverie. Dance is social, sensual, and emotionally engaging. An absorbing, competitive sport like racquetball distracts you from worries. When you select from the aerobics menu, consider these psychotherapeutic perks:

⤳ Many aerobic activities bring you together with other people in a spirit of camaraderie.
⤳ Most allow you to get better and better at something, increasing your self-esteem.

Runner's High

Perhaps you're wondering if the antidepressant effect of exercise has anything to do with runner's high. There is little or no evidence that the endorphins that appear to fuel this euphoric state have any sustaining antidepressant effect, or that exercise has to get you high to get you up from depression. The modest workouts that relieve depression aren't even conducive to runner's high. But then, neither do they promote runner's *addiction*, which can create problems of its own.

What modest workouts do achieve, according to numerous studies, is an acute antidepressantlike boost of serotonin and other mood-regulating neurotransmitters. This not only helps explain why exercise works, it suggests that exercise could biochemically augment other antidepressants. For many people, that's just what exercise seems to do. One woman who had been depression-free on the antidepressant Zoloft and regular exercise for two years summed up the synergy for writer Peter Jaret this way: "The drug helps make me feel normal again. But it's the exercise that really makes me feel good."

- ✤ Many are playful. They can lighten you up, reconnect you with your "inner child" or trickster.
- ✤ Many are conducive to emotional release or expression. You can, for example, exercise predator/prey instincts (chasing and fleeing, as in playing soccer, or attending a soccer match), channel aggression (hitting, kicking, as above), or move expressively (dancing).
- ✤ Some activities are productive (gardening, housework), rewarding you with a sense of accomplishment.
- ✤ Many are monotonous (walking, jogging, rowing), leaving your mind free for inner work: meditation, autosuggestion, Walkman therapy, and so on.

⚘ Many provide a diverting change of scenery: a sightseeing walk or bike ride, a swim at the lake.

⚘ If you exercise outdoors you can also partake in bright light therapy, and sometimes cold therapy too.

Safe Exercising

Exercise can be risky if you have certain medical conditions like cardiovascular disease, poorly controlled asthma, or diabetes; or risk factors like smoking or using certain drugs, including some antidepressants. (An ample intake of magnesium may be key to preventing adverse cardiac reactions to exercise.) Intense exercise can even trigger panic attacks in people with panic disorder. No matter how healthy you are, if you're over thirty-five, the American College of Sports Medicine recommends you consult your doctor before embarking on an exercise program.

The golden rule for exercising safely is *take it easy and don't overdo it.* Neglecting to spend a few minutes warming up and cooling down with light exercise before and after a workout is a prescription for aches, pains, muscle fatigue, nausea, dizziness, fainting, injuries—even life-threatening cardiac arrhythmia. Plugging on despite suspicious symptoms, like chest pains, faintness, or pallor, can endanger your life. Exercising too long, too hard, and too often not only invites injuries, it may paradoxically, as the International Society of Sports Psychology warns, "lead to fatigue, anxiety, and depression."

Part 5

———— ❧ ————

Saved by the Psyche: Psychotherapies and Medicines of the Mind

Not so long ago, most people assumed there was only one kind of help for depression: psychotherapy. Today, the danger lies in believing only pills can work. This is ironic, for the last two decades have seen an unprecedented surge of controlled trials establishing that depression—even the severe "major" kind that can convincingly look and feel like a purely chemical imbalance—can respond as well to certain psychotherapies as it can to antidepressant drugs.

The success of these psychotherapies should open our minds to the potential of other psychotherapeutic techniques and practices, such as imagery, suggestion, meditation, and art therapies.

CHAPTER 21

Psychotherapies for Depression That Work

There are more than two hundred different kinds of psychotherapy. And although most, if not all, purport to relieve depression, very few have been formally put to the test. Here's what those tests tell us:

➤ *Psychoanalysis,* the Freudian method of long-term, insight-oriented "couch therapy" that most of us know only from parody, has never actually been subjected to a controlled clinical trial. Even Freud felt impotent before the inertia of what we would now call severe endogenous or melancholic major depression. Contemporary psychoanalysts like Hans Strupp and associates concur that what evidence there is suggests analysis is of little acute benefit for major depression. But whether this lengthy and expensive excavation of the unconscious can, as many psychoanalysts claim, free patients from deep-seated hangups that make them *prone* to depression remains an open question.

In recent years, analytically trained psychiatrists have begun using *brief dynamic therapies* for depression. These focused, short-term variations on psychoanalysis have been tested in at least seven controlled trials. In a recent review by M. Balslev Jorgenson and associates, brief dynamic therapies equaled cognitive-behavioral therapies (CBTs)—the gold standard of depression psychotherapy—in four of these trials, but didn't measure up in the rest. But taking potential researcher bias into account, Balslev Jorgenson et al. argue it's possible Freud-in-a-cup is as effective as CBT. It may even be a better choice than drugs if your depression is relatively mild. Surprisingly, as reviewed by Balslev Jorgenson et al., meta-analyses of clinical trials have usually found brief, focused psychotherapies (focused on relieving the depression rather than transforming the patient) of any kind to be mildly to markedly superior to medication.

❧ At the opposite end of the spectrum from psychoanalysis, traditional *behavior therapies* that pay little or no attention to thoughts and feelings and focus on manipulating behavior are relatively weak antidepressants. In fact, nowadays the term *behavior therapy* is hardly used, except as a synonym for the cognitive-behavioral therapies that have succeeded them.

CBTs work simultaneously on thoughts, attitudes, and behaviors, and are powerful antidepressants. They include *cognitive therapy* (chap. 23), *problem-solving therapy* (chap. 25), *self-control therapy, interpersonal therapy, social skills training* (chap. 24), and *cognitive-behavioral marital therapy* (chap. 24). A 1993 meta-analysis for the U.S. Department of Health and Human Services (USDHHS) revealed that in many dozens of controlled clinical trials, CBTs proved about 20 percent more effective than antidepressant drugs. However, as Balslev Jorgenson et al. point out, the patients in these studies tended to be less than severely depressed, and the researchers biased toward psychotherapy.

❧ *Interpersonal psychotherapy* (not to be confused with the CBT *interpersonal therapy*) is a brief, focused, supportive talk therapy that combines the old-fashioned goals of healing through insight and emotional release with a touch of pragmatic problem-solving and other cognitive-behavioral interventions. As discussed in chapter 24, research suggests IPT is effective for treating and preventing depression and for augmenting drugs in severe depression. In the USDHHS meta-analysis, IPT performed 12 percent better than drugs.

IPT and CBTs are very well tolerated. Usually just 5 to 15 percent of patients drop out during a typical three- to four-month course, about half to one-third the dropout rate for antidepressant drugs. Typically, these therapies bring major improvement from nonbipolar, nonpsychotic major depression (the usual diagnosis in these studies) within two to four weeks. By the end of the treatment course, depression levels usually have fallen 65 to 75 percent, with more than half the patients fully recovered. Psychiatrists Michael

Thase and Edward Friedman of the University of Pittsburgh School of Medicine note that even patients with what many would pigeon-hole as a biological or endogenous depression—including melancholic depression—commonly enjoy some degree of improvement, while a minority fully recover. Drugs do seem to have an edge for such patients, but it's not an outstanding one.

Who Responds to Psychotherapy?

Whereas brief, focused psychotherapies, especially CBTs and IPT, are well-established treatments for major depression, chronic mild depression, or *dysthymia*, appears somewhat less responsive and may need a more "chronic" course of therapy. Still, in a 1996 study by Dunner et al., CBT proved as effective for dysthymia as Prozac.

There is very little research into psychotherapy for the most severe or "biological" forms of depression: *melancholic, psychotic/delusional,* and *bipolar depression.* This is largely because psychiatrists are pessimistic that psychotherapy has much of a chance here. In a 1999 review of the subject, Thase and Friedman describe a study in which twelve weeks of social skills training (a CBT) worked very well for three out of four melancholic depressives. Of two responders who were followed up long-term, one needed an antidepressant drug to stay well. The other, who received nothing but monthly maintenance sessions of CBT, relapsed only after two years. In another study, tricyclic antidepressants (TCAs)—the gold standard for melancholic depression—were only slightly more helpful for melancholics than cognitive therapy.

Still, Thase and Friedman conclude there just isn't enough evidence to abandon the widespread conviction that the more melancholic or endogenous and recurrent a depression is, the more likely it is to require somatic (physical) therapy. But, they add, "When a nonpsychotic, nonsuicidal patient presents with a melancholic episode in the absence of past recurrent depressive episodes, and expresses a strong preference for psychotherapy alone, it may be feasible to first try the psychotherapy if a skilled therapist is available."

In recent years, there has also been a growing movement to bring counseling and psychotherapy to bipolar disorder, not as a primary treatment but as an adjunct to drugs. *Psychoeducation* seeks to teach bipolars and (usually) their families about the nature of their condition, the need to stick with their medications to prevent relapse, and practical ways to remain on the straight and narrow. Several studies suggest that a few sessions of psychoeducation can go a long way, according to a review by Sagar V. Parikh and his associates. In a controlled study, just six sessions resulted in much greater lithium compliance and significantly fewer hospital admissions down the road.

Spousal family therapy has yielded similar benefits. In a controlled study also reviewed by Parikh et al., six sessions prior to release from the hospital translated into significant improvements over the next eighteen months in all aspects of the lives of female, but not male, bipolars.

Some of the most sensational benefits have been noted for group psychotherapy, though the studies have been uncontrolled and methodologically weak, according to Parikh et al. In a two-year study of interpersonal group therapy, hospitalization dropped from 16.8 weeks per year to just 3.6, while steady employment rose.

Although the evidence is scant, Parikh et al. note that some experts believe cognitive-behavioral therapy may even be a useful treatment for bipolar depresssion.

Perhaps no group of depressives stands to gain more by choosing psychotherapy over drugs than children. A meta-analysis in 1995 by P. Hazell et al. found that tricyclic antidepressants were only very, very slightly, but not significantly, more effective than placebos for these young patients. There have been so few studies of other antidepressants, like the SSRIs usually prescribed to young depressives today, that none of these drugs are FDA-approved for childhood depression.

In contrast, CBTs *have* been well investigated in youngsters with clinical depression, though mostly of mild to moderate severity. A 1998 meta-analysis by Richard Harrington of the Royal Manchester Children's Hospital and his associates found that CBTs were consistently superior to control conditions, including active controls like relaxation training and family and supportive therapy in three of the six randomized trials. Overall, 129 out of 208 (62 percent) children aged eight to nineteen recovered fully on CBTs compared to 61 out of 168 (36 percent) in the control groups.

Psychotherapy as Maintenance Therapy

As we'll see in chapters 24 and 28, research suggests that long-term prescriptions for antidepressant drugs can be replaced or effectively supplemented by booster sessions of psychotherapy. Remarkably, it may not even be necessary to keep attending those booster sessions. A few good ones can last a long time, judging by a provocative study by psychiatrist Giovanni Fava of State University of New York and his associates.

The subjects were forty patients who had just recovered on drugs from an episode of recurrent major depression. Typically, most had some residual symptoms, like anxiety or irritability, which are a common risk factor for relapse. Over a twenty-week period, the patients were very gradually withdrawn from their antidepressant medications by Fava, who saw them every other week for thirty minutes. Fava also treated half with a cognitive-behavioral approach consisting of cognitive therapy, lifestyle advice to lessen the risk of relapse (get enough sleep, avoid overwork, etc.), and a final few sessions of a morale-boosting intervention he calls "well-being therapy." The control group received only "support and advice if necessary" from Fava during their visits.

At the end of the twenty weeks, the CBT group had enjoyed a much greater lessening of their residual symptoms. But it was the two-year follow-up period that proved most revealing. Off drugs, the control group (as expected) quickly began dropping like flies, 80 percent eventually relapsing and requiring a new prescription. But in the equally drugless CBT group, only 25 percent relapsed. With just ten hours of preventive psychotherapy, Fava had accomplished what it usually takes years of maintenance psychotherapy or drug refills to achieve.

The Biology of Psychotherapy

If clinical research suggests psychotherapy can be at least as effective a treatment for most depressions as drugs, laboratory studies suggest its effects are no less biological. To give one example, blood levels of the thyroid hormone precursor thyroxine (T_4) commonly are high during depression and normal after successful biological (drugs, ECT) treatment. When psychiatrist Russell Joffe and associates did a before-and-after study of T_4 levels in thirty major depressives treated for twenty weeks with cognitive therapy alone, they made a remarkable finding. T_4 fell significantly in the seventeen responders and rose in the others.

Which Therapist?

No less important a consideration than which psychotherapy is which psychotherapist. According to psychiatrist E. Fuller Torrey, studies conducted since the 1950s suggest that the effectiveness of a therapist is strongly correlated with three bedside-manner virtues: *"accurate empathy, nonpossessive warmth, and genuineness"* (italics mine). According to psychoanalyst L. Luborsky et al. (as quoted by Torrey), "the major agent of effective psychotherapy is the personality of the therapist, particularly the ability to form a warm, supportive relationship."

But, as Torrey writes, it's not just the personal qualities of the therapist that matters, "but how these interact with the personality characteristics of the client." So if the chemistry between yourself and a therapist is poor, it doesn't augur well, and you'd best look for someone else.

Is Psychotherapy Safe?

Psychotherapy can be hazardous to your mental health. Although the established psychotherapies for depression appear tame and without reports of treatment casualties, there are risks inherent to psychotherapy in general and to some therapies (including the other two hundred plus) and therapists in particular:

❧ A small minority of psychotherapies/ists take an aggressive, confrontational approach to a client and his problems. This can push some clients beyond their breaking point.

❧ Even with a gentle approach, the excavation by some psychotherapies of emotionally loaded unconscious material—taboo feelings and impulses, memories of abuse or trauma—can bring acute, destabilizing anguish or, if managed poorly, lasting clinical deterioration.

⚹ A therapist can foist ideas or values on a client that violate the client's integrity. Psychoanalysts, for instance, have traditionally pressured incest survivors to interpret their actual memories as wish-fulfillment fantasies. (I believe they've recently mended their ways.)

⚹ In therapy, clients often develop a childlike dependence upon or awe toward their therapists, converting them into surrogate parents or gurus. Some unethical or emotionally unstable therapists seize this opportunity to seduce or exploit their clients. Typically, this winds up eroding the client's self-esteem and mental health even more.

⚹ Even the most innocuous psychotherapies can be dangerous if the therapist is incompetent, irresponsible, or unscrupulous. To some extent, a therapist's competence can be ensured by choosing one who is well trained and certified, registered, or licensed. Her integrity can be checked by contacting her professional association or disciplinary body (if she has one) to ask if there have been any complaints or legal actions against her.

As with finding any healthcare provider, good word of mouth is worth its weight in gold.

Bibliotherapy: Therapy in a Book

In the early 1980s, some cognitive-behavioral therapists thought of a nifty control condition for a study of their "Coping with Depression" course: Just give the subjects a how-to book on the course, with no more than fifteen minutes a week of telephone time to touch base with an actual therapist. There was just one problem: The control group did almost as well as the group that got the real thing.

And so was born bibliotherapy for depression.

By 1997, when P. Cuijpers published the first and only meta-analysis of six small, but high-quality, controlled studies, the results were clear. As expected, four to eleven weeks of CBT with a live therapist proved very effective. But so did spending the time with a CBT book. In fact, bibliotherapy was slightly better. And the books didn't put anyone to sleep: Only 7of 102 subjects dropped out.

To be fair, most studies had provided the bibliotherapy participants with one or two face-to-face instruction/orientation sessions with a real therapist and up to five, ten, or fifteen minutes each week over the phone. And the subjects were all mildly to moderately depressed community volunteers (recruited by ads), not "patients." But it was a strong hint that popular self-help books like *Feeling Good* by cognitive therapist David Burns and *Control Your Depression* by CBT therapists Peter Lewinsohn and associates may not be making hollow promises on their dust jackets. In fact, these very books were successfully used in four of the studies.

What sets books like these (including works by Martin Seligman, Michael Yapko, and Mary Ellen Copeland, among others) apart from so many is that they provide a practical course of self-help activities and exercises. They are, quite literally, biblio*therapy*. This isn't to say that other books that attempt to inspire and motivate can't help too. In her struggle with depression, writer Jennifer Cawthorne found *Life 101* and other books by Peter McWilliams—himself a depressive—to be a real treasure (and cheap, because they can be read free at the author's website: www.mcwilliams.com). Other depressives have found great comfort and validation in the autobiographical accounts of fellow sufferers, like those by Redfield Jamison, Tracy Thompson, and William Styron (*Darkness Visible*). For many depressives, these books are ideal for another kind of bibliotherapy: presents for their loved ones to show them what depression really is.

CHAPTER 22

Being More Active to Become Less Depressed

When we're psychologically depressed, we're behaviorally depressed. Life no longer sweeps us up so easily into its swirl of activities. Expecting more pain than gain— impervious even to pleasure in the worst cases—we retreat. But the more we withdraw—the less we do, achieve, enjoy—the more persuaded we become of our terminal unfitness for life. And that depresses us even more. How perfect a vicious cycle. And how simple the antidote: Just *be more active*.

"Just!" Of course, this goes completely against the grain. But rare is the depression that doesn't contain the seeds of renewed activity.

Psychotherapists of virtually every stripe, from behaviorists to psychoanalysts, agree on at least one thing: What depressives lack, but need in order to feel whole again, is the sense of being competent, productive, self-fulfilling human beings.

Psychotherapy only succeeds, the influential social learning theorist Albert Bandura maintained, when it imparts or restores to the patient a sense of *self-efficacy*. "The depressed patient," writes psychoanalyst Michael Franz, "should have the experience of finding that he or she can still function successfully." "The depressed patient should have the experience of finding that he or she can still function successfully," echoes psychoanalyst Michael Basch. "The most powerful antidepressant," cognitive-behaviorist Peter McLean joins in, "is successful performance."

Easy for them to say. But they have a secret weapon. As Richard Dreyfuss's pop psychiatrist told Bill Murray's patient-from-hell in *What About Bob?*, it's summed up in a two-word mantra: *Baby steps.*

Cognitive-behavioral therapists (including cognitive therapists) are the specialists in the art of baby steps. Most, if not all, of their therapies for depression feature strategies to help derailed depressives get on track again, one step at a time. Even the success of cognitive therapy is believed by its practitioners to be very largely due to this behavioral component of its program.

Helping depressives be more active is the focus of *interpersonal therapy* (IT), a cognitive-behavioral program for depression developed at the University of British Columbia in the 1970s by Peter McLean and his associates. In two controlled studies, IT outperformed traditional all-talk, no-action psychotherapy, relaxation training, and antidepressant drugs for moderately depressed patients. Remarkably—considering how aversive activity can be for depressives—the dropout rate was a mere 5 percent.

The Art of Being More Active to Become Less Depressed

The art of being more active to become less depressed is also spelled out in the self-help books of cognitive-behavioral therapists. As we've seen, studies suggest these books can be just as effective as the real thing for nonseverely depressed readers. Here are the basics.

Developing an Inventory of Activities

Baby steps demand that you follow a systematic course if you're eventually to get anywhere. The first step is to come up with a so-called "inventory," or list, of schedulable activities. A good way to do this is to relax and brainstorm possibilities, recording them on paper or computer.

Brainstorming is an important first step in any creative problem-solving process. It means temporarily binding and gagging your inner critic and going for the gross, not the gold: going for *quantity* and *variety* of ideas (in this case, things to do), not quality. It means happily, uncritically, jotting down even the silliest ideas that come to mind. These silly notions can speak volumes about your truest feelings and desires. With a bit of thoughtful, postbrainstorming adjustment, they often can be applied to real life. "I feel like flying to the moon," for example, could lead you to buy a telescope or take a course in astronomy. Here are some aids to help you brainstorm:

❧ *Sentence completions.* Pick any of the following that appeal and then keep repeating the first words to trigger a growing list of completions. Every sentence begins with "I would like to . . ." or "I want to . . ." and continues with: know . . . learn . . . understand . . . make . . . build . . . design . . . find . . . discover . . . invent . . . go . . . play . . . be with . . . talk to . . . see . . . hear . . . feel . . . smell . . . taste . . . tell . . . say . . . show . . . explain . . . fix . . . clean . . . improve . . . get . . . buy . . . give . . . help . . . be able to . . . or any other suggestive verb you can think of.

Or just try an open-ended "I would like to . . ." Also:

❧ God (my Higher Self, the Universe, Jesus . . .) would like me to (wants me to) . . .

❧ I should (ought to, need to, have to) . . . This sentence completion is mainly intended to get some of the guilty thoughts out of your head and onto paper. You'll probably feel better for it. As to whether you eventually act on these shoulds, evaluating them in light of what you learn in the next chapter on cognitive therapy "should" help you decide if you really *must.*

❧ Visualize yourself in your current state. Ask: "What can that person do to help himself/herself?" Consider asking a "benign inner figure" (as discussed in chap. 28 on healing imagery) what he or she recommends.

Now that you've generated a list of activities, it's okay to ungag your inner critic. He or she can now help convert this raw material into an inventory of doable, schedulable activities. Although any activity is likely to counteract your depression, the activities most likely to help will probably fulfill criteria like the following:

❧ They're inherently pleasurable or uplifting for you.

❧ They engross you and distract you from your worries.

❧ They enhance your self-esteem: they make you feel decent, lovable, capable, admirable.

❧ They bring approval, especially from significant others.

❧ They help you achieve personal goals, dreams, or wishes.

❧ They help resolve the very problem(s) you may be depressed about. (Chap. 25 is devoted to *that*.)

❧ They help further the treatment of your depression or are antidepressants themselves (e.g., scheduling an appointment with a doctor, taking a sunny walk, or planning your antidepressant program, as discussed in the conclusion of this book).

❧ They're on your to-do list, even though that list may have grown a six-inch layer of moss. Doing them lightens your guilt load, enhancing your sense of (drum roll) *self-efficacy*.

Scheduling Activities

Now that you have an inventory of activities, the best way to ensure that some actually get done is to *schedule them*. Cognitive-behavioral therapists recommend scheduling activities a week at a time, *for every hour of the day*. "When you're depressed, you're unfocused, indecisive, overwhelmed," writes one such compulsive cognitive therapist, Gary Emery. "What you need most is structure, since poor use of time is symptomatic of depression."

On your detailed schedule, include routine activities like washing and eating, obligatory activities (work, school), passive ones (napping, watching TV), blocks of free time, and, above all, *time to keep working on the schedule itself*. Feel free to schedule on more or less than a weekly basis, if that suits you, and to make your schedule more or less structured (e.g., to schedule alternative activities for the same time period).

It's important not to feel stifled by the schedule. Think of it as a provisional itinerary you can alter as you go along, not some Prussian rule book.

"Accomplishing even a part of your scheduled activities," cognitive therapist David Burns promises, "will in all probability give you some satisfaction and will combat your depression." Finally, every day make an effort to record how much pleasure or discomfort you get from each activity, on a scale of −5 to +5. On a separate scale, record how good or relieved you felt simply *for having done it*. High-scoring activities can be promoted to a short list for frequent repetition.

Working on Your Resistances

It's hard work defying depressive inertia and the demons that drive it. In the next chapter, we'll explore some tried-and-true cognitive counter-measures. Here you might like to try a powerful sentence completion my friend Anna Olson has taught in her creative writing workshops: "I want (would like) to [name the activity you're having trouble doing], but I can't because _____." Complete the sentence, on paper or computer, with whatever comes into your head and heart at least a dozen times. It often takes that long to get to the bottom of things.

Making It Easy for Yourself

Here are a few more cognitive-behavioral strategies to make it easier to baby-step your way to a better mood.

- ☇ *Always reward yourself* for performing your scheduled activities, especially the hard ones. Rewards can be in the form of money, time (to do as you please), "points" (redeemable in dollars or time), and/or simply taking a moment to pause, savor your victory, and sincerely pat yourself on the back. Patting yourself on the back is actually the key ingredient of *self-control therapy*—a very effective CBT for depression developed by psychologist Lynn Rehm and associates at the University of Houston. It can also be immeasurably helpful if loved ones join in. If they understand the kind of mountains you're climbing (get them to read those autobiographical books mentioned on page 261), their enthusiasm may even be stronger than yours.
- ☇ Break down large or complex activities into bite-size, schedulable steps. Reward yourself for each step—don't wait for the finish line.
- ☇ Schedule activities "on time," not "by the job." In other words, from 9:00 to 9:30 A.M. Tuesday, don't schedule "repair the ozone layer" or "write that first novel." Schedule "work on fixing the ozone layer," or "sharpen pencils." When you schedule "on time" you always win just for showing up and giving it a shot. These small victories are the stuff that will help lift you up from depression.
- ☇ Don't be dismayed if "pleasurable activities" aren't as pleasurable as they used to be. You're an injured athlete, easing your battered body

back into training. It'll be awhile before you can play with your old vim and vigor.

❧ Don't get down on yourself for breaking your schedule. Depression being the dead weight it is, you'll often deserve top marks just for tugging yourself out of bed in the morning. But do try to adjust your schedule so it's never too far out of reach.

❧ Regard your lapses as opportunities to become more aware of the headstuff that may be getting in the way. Which brings us to our next chapter.

CHAPTER 23

———— ⚜ ————

Reasoning with Yourself: The Cognitive Approach to Depression

D epressives are notoriously, stubbornly, negative. Try telling them life isn't really *that* bleak, that they aren't really such horrible persons, that their fate isn't sealed, that they *will* get better—and what do you get? Disbelief: "That may be true for other people, but not for me. . . . You can't imagine how rotten I really am. . . . My situation *is* hopeless—I know it with every fiber of my being."

Aaron Beck was no stranger to this airtight negativity of depression. As a clinical psychiatrist who had written a minor classic on depression in the 1960s, he had been sparring with it for years. Yet he believed that if you could just *reason* with depressives persistently enough—or, better yet, *get them to reason that way themselves*—you might be able to break the stranglehold of their negative thinking and free them from depression itself.

Beck was right. The program for reasoning your way out of depression that he and his associates developed in the 1960s and '70s at the University of Philadelphia is today the most intensively investigated of all psychotherapies, not just for depression but for many, many other conditions too. In dozens of controlled clinical trials, *cognitive therapy* (CT) has almost always brought relief or recovery to a majority of clinically depressed patients within just a few weeks. Typically, by the end of a full twelve- to twenty-week course of CT, one hour per week, the average patient has enjoyed a greater than 70 percent reduction in depression. And that's equal or even better than the control group's response to other effective psychotherapies or antidepressant drugs.

CT has a broad antidepressant range. In 1999, in the first randomized, controlled trial of any psychotherapy for atypical major depression (a large, double-blind endeavor by Jarrett et al.), CT convincingly equaled the gold standard—a powerful MAOI antidepressant—and proved twice as effective as placebo. In another trial, CT's low dropout rate gave it a decisive edge over Prozac for dysthymia (Dunner et al.). CT has even proved irresistible to the severely depressed subgroup of inpatients in some studies (Robins and Hayes).

CT is also an effective alternative to drugs for preventing depression. In a three-year study by Jarrett et al., just ten sessions of CT during the eight months after recovery cut the relapse/recurrence rate roughly by half compared to a no-CT control group. In another two-year maintenance study by Blackburn and Moore, seventy-five patients had all recovered from recurrent major depression. The conventional wisdom is that people like these need drugs as a diabetic needs insulin. Yet for them, including those who had recovered on drugs, maintenance CT actually proved superior to maintenance drug therapy.

I Think, Therefore I Am (or *Am Not*) Depressed

The Greek Stoic philosopher Epictetus summed up the philosophy of cognitive therapy long ago: "Men are disturbed not by things, but by the view which they take of them." "There is nothing either good or bad but thinking makes it so," Shakespeare's Hamlet added, centuries later.

The cognitive prescription is to *think otherwise*, to change our point of view. CT teaches us to become more critically aware of the negative thoughts and attitudes that make us or keep us depressed. It teaches us to systematically challenge them and replace them with more reasonable and constructive alternatives. By persisting this way (and with the help of "baby-step" behavioral techniques to help get us back into the swing of things), we can gradually lift ourselves out of depression. And maybe even gain some new mental reflexes in the process, to help keep future episodes at bay.

As we saw in chapter 21, studies suggest that people who are mildly to moderately depressed (and not suicidal or delusional) can success-fully practice CT with self-help guidebooks like those by David Burns. If you'd like an actual therapist, the Center for Cognitive Therapy at the University of Pennsylvania ([215] 898-4100; www.med.upenn.edu/psy-cct) can help you find one.

So how does cognitive therapy work?

Getting in Touch with Your Depressing "Automatic Thoughts"

Between what happens to us at point A and our depressive reaction to it at point B lie the thoughts that get us there. This is the core insight of cognitive therapy. And this is insight number two: Typically, these thoughts, which can be in words, images, or both, proceed quite auto-matically, with little or no critical scrutiny on our part. So hypnotized are we by these *automatic thoughts* (as cognitive therapists call them) that we barely realize we've just

✖ flung some soul-withering epithet at ourselves;
✖ accused ourselves without benefit of legal counsel of some repug-nant sin;
✖ swallowed blindly some dark vision of doom and gloom; or
✖ just thought ourselves into a depressive corner in some other way.

The first order of business in CT is to become fully conscious of these depressing automatic thoughts, to yank them out of the shadows of semiconsciousness and expose them to the light of reason. We can do this at any time—not just when we're in the thick of them. When-ever we like, we can reflect on a depressing circumstance or situation in our lives and recall, recreate, or anticipate the automatic thoughts asso-ciated with it.

Think of a depressing problem or situation in your life. What thoughts pass through your mind as your mood goes south? Write them down. If they're hazy or ill-defined, bring them into focus. If they're nonverbal (images, sensations), try to put them into words.

Working on Your Depressing Automatic Thoughts

Now you're ready to talk back to those automatic thoughts, one at a time, to challenge their reasonableness, fairness, even truthfulness, and see if you can't replace them with kinder, gentler, more constructive alternatives. It's best to do this on paper or computer. "Negative ideas are so powerful," cognitive therapist Gary Emery warns, "that if you try to answer them in your head, they'll immediately erase the answers."

Here is the ammunition you can bring to your automatic thoughts:

❧ What evidence do I really have to support this idea?
❧ Are there any other ways I could view this situation? Am I taking it too personally? How would other people—or a fly on the wall, an extraterrestrial, a personal hero of mine, or God—see it?
❧ Am I overgeneralizing? Jumping to conclusions? Exaggerating or (as psychologist Albert Ellis would say) "catastrophizing"—making an abyss out of a pothole?
❧ Am I wearing blinders? Am I screening out the positive and looking for the cloud behind every silver lining?
❧ Am I thinking in rigid, all-or-nothing, black-or-white terms?
❧ Am I guilty of what Ellis calls "musturbatory thinking," of dogmatically and self-frustratingly insisting things *must* or *should* be a certain way?
❧ Am I tyrannizing myself? Would I treat another person this way?
❧ Is this thought helping me or hindering me on my life's path?
❧ Assuming I am right in my negative view, is the situation really that bad? Am I underestimating my ability to solve or cope with the problem? Am I forgetting that "this too shall pass"?
❧ Can I test the reality of this thought? Is there something I can do, someone I can ask?

Rooting Out the Maladaptive Assumptions That Underlie Automatic Thoughts

Why do we have such depressing automatic thoughts in the first place? According to cognitive therapists, it's because, deep down, we subscribe to equally negative or self-destructive beliefs about ourselves or the world. Our automatic thoughts are just a manifestation of these *maladaptive assumptions*, which are so deeply ingrained we've usually forgotten they're even there.

Typically, we've absorbed (or been force-fed) these maladaptive "tapes," "programs," unwritten rule books for living during our most impressionable formative years. We may, for example, implicitly believe:

❧ I can't be happy unless everybody likes/loves/admires/respects me.
❧ If I fail at ____, I'm a failure.
❧ It's shameful to be weak or seem so.
❧ I must be outstanding to be acceptable.
❧ If I'm good to people, they must be good to me.
❧ I could never cope with catastrophe.
❧ I'm nobody if or unless _____.

Becoming aware of our maladaptive assumptions, and then challenging and replacing them with more adaptive ones, is a major goal of cognitive therapy. And well it should be, for research by psychologist Anne Simons and associates indicates that if we recover from depression, yet continue to harbor many maladaptive assumptions, we are that much more likely to relapse. Our unchallenged maladaptive assumptions lie in wait, ready to trigger a new volley of depressing automatic thoughts the next time circumstances rub them the wrong way.

There are several ways to recognize our maladaptive assumptions. One powerful method is described by cognitive therapist David Burns in his popular book *Feeling Good*. Pick one of your depressing automatic thoughts and assume it's true. Now ask yourself: "Why would that be so bad?" When you've got an answer, ask: "Why would that be so bad?" Keep querying until you can go no further. Each answer uncovers a deeper assumption.

Sentence completions are another powerful tool:

❧ I can't (don't deserve to) be happy (content, pleased with myself) unless _____.
❧ I'm not lovable (likable, respectable, a good person) unless _____.
❧ I deserve to be depressed because (if) _____.

While thinking of something that's depressing you, repeatedly complete the following sentences: I should _____. I shouldn't _____.

The assumptions we identify by using these techniques should . . . I mean *must* . . . I mean . . . Ah well, let's just say it would be nice for us to cognitively take them to task, as we do our automatic thoughts. When we question and weigh them in the balance, can we make them more adaptive, more life-affirming? Can we reject or reformulate them so that they sit well with our reasoned, conscious values, allowing us to live, breathe, and grow?

If maladaptive assumptions are toxic unconscious waste, those we've revised into *adaptive* assumptions can be beamed back down to our core, therapeutically, as *affirmations*. More on those in chapter 27, "Word Medicine: Suggestions for Self-Help."

CHAPTER 24

The Social and Spiritual Dimensions of Depression and Their Treatment

In 1993, researchers at the Medical College of Virginia turned 680 pairs of identical and nonidentical female twins into a window into the etiology of depression. After careful study of the women's histories, Kenneth Kendler and his associates identified nine factors that seemed to account for 50 percent of their vulnerability to major depression.

As expected, genetic factors ranked high. But they only came in second. Number one was a risk factor that was already going "out of style": *stressful life events*. Most other risk factors were cut from the same psychosocial cloth:

- lack of parental warmth;
- loss of a parent in childhood or other past traumas;
- recent hassles; and
- lack of social support.

Only neuroticism (as in an anxious or depressive personality) and a history of previous episodes of major depression hinted at other genetic or constitutional causes.

Depression *is* a chemical imbalance. But it needs a match to ignite it. Kendler's group are among many who have confirmed the incendiary role of psychosocial influences.

What happened to us when we grew up (losing a parent, being abused by a parent), when we were older (assault, rape, war), or just recently (unemployment, marital conflict) is in very large part the stuff depression is made of. Even what most experts regard as the most chemically unbalanced of all mood disorders—bipolar disorder—is exquisitely sensitive to life's ups and downs (Parikh et al.)

The most important and potentially most remediable psychosocial influence on depression is *relationships*. Social isolation is one of the most potent promoters of depression. Bad relationships may be even more depressing, according to research by University of Washington psychologist Neil S. Jacobson and others. But good relationships—close confidantes, supportive spouses—protect us from depression, research shows. Not surprisingly, relationships are a major focus of most psychotherapies for depression.

Marital Therapy

No relationship is more often the cause of depression than a troubled marriage, research by Jacobson's group and others show. Even if you're depressed for some other reason, if your partner is unsympathetic or unsupportive you'll have a harder time recovering, and an easier time relapsing after you do. A supportive partner will have just the opposite effect.

It's enough to make you think that some sort of therapy that would help depressives and their partners get along better—teach them to communicate and resolve conflicts more effectively, be intimate more supportively—would be a capital treatment for depression. And it is.

In three studies, including two by Jacobson's group, a cognitive-behavioral approach to marital therapy has been as effective for maritally distressed depressives as cognitive therapy and has produced greater long-term marital satisfaction. Noncognitive-behavioral marital therapy has had similar success. Cognitive therapy founder Aaron Beck has written a self-help guide to cognitive marital therapy called *Love Is Never Enough*.

Assertiveness Training and Social Skills Training

Social ease and depression don't go together. When we're depressed we're typically withdrawn, uncommunicative, unassertive, at pains to enjoy ourselves socially. Overcoming these causes or consequences of depression, cognitive-behavioral therapists maintain, can be a key to overcoming depression itself. "[W]hen patients learn to ask for what they want, resist unwelcome requests or exploitation from others, initiate conversations, and develop more intimate relationships, therapeutic gains are impressive," writes the distinguished psychologist Arnold Lazarus. Learning those skills is a cognitive-behavioral process commonly called *assertiveness training* (AT) or *social skills training* (SST). AT/SST has proven an effective antidepressant or adjunct in most controlled trials. In one twelve-week study, a comprehensive SST package developed at the Medical College of Pennsylvania by Allan Bellack and his associates was put to the test. It outperformed both a tricyclic antidepressant drug and analytic psychotherapy in 125 moderately to severely depressed women.

AT/SST is not unlike being coached in acting or a sport. Commonly, it begins with you, the student, describing a problem area in your social life and then acting it out, with the therapist or other members of an AT/SST group playing the other roles. Next, the therapist or a group member plays or "models" your part, only closer to the way you'd like to play it. With that for inspiration, you try again. And, usually, again and again.

This is all done in a relaxed, even playful manner, with lots of gentle, constructive advice and praise for every baby step that you and your fellow students take toward greater social ease. If internal doubts and resistances—automatic negative thoughts, for example—cramp your style, advice on dealing with them cognitively is usually available.

AT and SST are a component of cognitive-behavioral therapy. If your need for them is great, a CB therapist can simply spend more time with you on them.

Talking to Someone

Clinical trials of antidepressant therapies have been haunted by not one, but two, placebo effects. Not only have sugar pills (placebos) often performed nearly as well as drugs or supplements, but often placebo versions of psychotherapy have also put on an embarrassingly good show. Typically, this has occurred when the placebo psychotherapy has provided an opportunity for the patient to spend some quality time each week talking to a nice, supportive professional.

It's a clue that you can't underestimate the healing power of self-disclosure to someone who makes you feel heard and understood. So therapeutic, in fact, is a good listener that in an oft-cited 1979 study by Hans Strupp and S. W. Hadley, even college professors with a reputation for forming understanding relationships were just barely less effective for young psychiatric patients than highly experienced psychotherapists.

Interpersonal Psychotherapy

One type of psychotherapy goes out of its way to provide depressives with a sympathetic, supportive confidante. Developed in the 1970s at Cornell University Medical College by two prominent authorities on depression, Gerald Klerman and Myrna Weissman, *interpersonal psychotherapy* (IPT) posits that depression is always caused or fueled by interpersonal problems—loss, conflict, role problems, or social skills deficits. IPT therapists help clients single out one or two such problems in their lives that they can potentially resolve within a few months. Therapy involves not just talking, but freely expressing your feelings; not just gleaning old-fashioned insight into your problems, but getting some cognitive-behavioral-style tips on solving them. The focus is obstinately on *now* and the future, not on the past.

Originally developed as a treatment for major depression, IPT has been adapted for dysthymic disorder, depression during pregnancy, and several other psychiatric conditions, including bipolar disorder. Several studies suggest IPT may be as effective as drugs and cognitive-behavioral therapies for mild to moderate major depression.

IPT has had one close call. But then it was one of those "the emperor may have no clothes" moments for all of psychiatry. The context was the National Institute of Mental Health Treatment of Depression Collaborative Research Program. When the much anticipated results of this major multicenter clinical trial came out in 1989, it turned out that IPT combined with a placebo pill was just barely more effective for major depression than the placebo pill plus that warm and fuzzy placebo we talked about earlier. In the NIMH study, that placebo consisted of weekly twenty- to thirty-minute visits with a supportive and encouraging psychiatrist. In fact, when only the nonseverely depressed patients were considered, IPT was not *at all* better than the placebos. But then neither was cognitive therapy plus a placebo. And neither was an antidepressant drug plus the nice psychiatrist placebo. It wasn't that the active treatments weren't effective. The problem was that the double-placebo special was very effective too—with one exception.

For patients whose depressions were relatively severe, the placebos didn't measure up to IPT and fell far short of the drug. (Although the same couldn't be said of cognitive therapy, in a subsequent critique, Jacobson and Hollon noted that most of the cognitive therapists in the study were inexperienced and poorly trained.)

A recent mega-analysis by Thase et al. of six clinical trials yielded a similarly mixed veredict. For relatively mild depression, IPT had little or nothing to add to drug therapy. But for relatively severe and recurrent depressives, the combination brought full recovery to 43 percent, a better rate than drugs alone usually achieve and much better than that of IPT alone.

Researchers have also been grooming IPT as a maintenance treatment, especially for recurrent depression. It makes sense that a technique that helps people nip potentially depressing problems in the bud should help avert new episodes. A study by Charles Reynolds and associates supports that case. The subjects were 107 elderly people with recurrent depression who had just recovered from a major episode on a combination of IPT and a commonly prescribed antidepressant. The three-year "survival rate" rose steeply from 10 percent in those randomly assigned to placebo alone, to 36 percent in the placebo plus monthly maintenance IPT group, to 57 percent for drug maintenance alone, and to a formidable 80 percent in the drug plus IPT group.

IPT has one problem: Outside of a few big cities, there are still relatively few therapists trained to do it.

Strength in Numbers: Support Groups

If talking to one sympathetic listener can be helpful, talking to a group can be even better. Support groups and group therapy provide unique opportunities for interpersonal healing:

⚜ Mutual self-disclosure—people opening up to each other—is of the essence in such groups. Letting down our guard satisfies a deep hunger we all have to know and be known, accept and be accepted, for who we and others really are.

❧ Groups tend to be egalitarian. This can be more inviting and empowering than psychotherapy where, typically, self-disclosure is one-sided and the therapist is perceived as an authority figure rather than a peer.

❧ Groups are workshops in social skills training, rife with opportunities for enhancing one's interpersonal sensitivities and skills.

❧ In groups whose participants all share the same problem, two great healers are abundantly available: empathy and understanding.

By far the most popular and accessible group is the support group. Dozens, if not hundreds, can be found in any city. For depressives, there are two major support-group organizations:

❧ Based in Chicago, the National Depressive and Manic-Depressive Association (NDMDA: 1-800-826-3632; www.ndmda.org) provides information and support to people with mood disorders and their families. Although it encourages medical treatment, according to a survey by L. F. Kurtz, what members value most is the emotional support and acceptance they obtain through NDMDA's "rap groups," public meetings, lectures, and telephone assistance.

❧ Also based in Chicago, Recovery, Inc. ([312] 337-5661; www.recovery-inc.com) sponsors support groups around the world (over 700 at last count) based on the cognitively oriented teachings of the late psychiatrist Abraham Low. At meetings, members with any psychiatric condition describe distressing feelings or experiences and everyone pitches in to "spot" the underlying maladaptive attitudes. The longer people stick with Recovery, Inc., a survey by Marc Galanter suggests, the better they feel and the less professional help they seek.

The granddaddy of all support groups is Alcoholics Anonymous (AA). Today there are AA-style twelve-step groups for virtually every compulsive or addictive behavior (Overeaters Anonymous, Gamblers Anonymous) and for the victims of those behaviors (Adult Children of Alcoholics, Incest Survivors Anonymous). Emotions Anonymous ([651] 647-9712; EmotionsAnonymous.org) attracts many people whose primary problem is depression. At last count, there were more than twelve hundred EA chapters worldwide.

In twelve-step meetings, people share their stories and help each other apply the twelve steps: a graded path toward moral and spiritual recovery that focuses on seeking guidance from one's "higher power" and becoming reconciled with the people in one's life.

Twelve-step groups are supportive, but not necessarily curative for depression. Even Bill W., the cofounder of AA, openly acknowledged that the twelve steps weren't enough to free him of his own depression.

Fido Rx: The Therapeutic Benefits of Pets

Our fellow humans are not the only warm bodies that can comfort us in our times of need. In some ways, animal companions may do an even better job. Having a pet around can shield us with "a protective armor against much of the pain of living . . . that few human beings can give with such unvarying constancy," write Alan Beck and Aaron Katcher. Pets can even help shield us against depression. Beck and Katcher describe how Oregon psychiatrist Michael McCulloch studied the effects of family pets on thirty-one of his depressed patients. Most of the patients reported that the pets were a mood-lifting distraction that made them feel less lonely, less worried, and more "secure and needed." Similarly, a large-scale study from the University of Kentucky reported by Barbara Culliton revealed that "among the elderly bereaved who were without friends, a pet apparently helped stave off depression."

Pets can also tame the savage breast. At the Loma State Hospital for the Criminally Insane in Ohio, psychiatric social worker David Lee "has found that patients with pets are less depressed, less violent, less suicidal, and less in need of drugs than patients in wards without pets" (Cusack and Smith).

Spirituality and Depression

Karl Marx disparagingly called it the opiate of the masses. But opium is a powerful drug, and so, it seems, is religion. "Scientific studies," writes Dale Matthews, M.D., of Georgetown University, "show that religious involvement helps people prevent illness, recover from illness, and—

most remarkably—live longer. The more religiously committed you are, the more likely you are to benefit." One of those benefits is a greater freedom from depression.

When L. Miller and associates of Columbia University studied 81 women and 151 of their children over a ten-year period, the most religious women suffered 81 percent fewer depressions than the least religious. The religious women's grown daughters were 60 percent less vulnerable to depression. Those who shared their mothers' religiosity were 71 percent less vulnerable; the mothers' religious sons, 84 percent.

A year later, in a much-publicized 1998 study from Duke University Medical Center by psychiatrist Harold Koenig and his associates, physically sick and depressed elderly people got over their depressions 70 percent faster if religious faith and practice was a guiding force in their lives.

Koenig et al.'s study offers hope to those of us who aren't formally religious, but at least have a spiritual pulse. Religious behaviors alone, even private prayer, had no significant antidepressant effect. A religious *attitude*, it seemed, was key. But not just any religious attitude. In another large study published that year, Koenig et al. found that only "positive" religious coping behaviors and attitudes correlated strongly with good physical and mental health, including less depression, in 577 hospital patients older than fifty-five. It was just the opposite for "negative" religious coping behaviors and attitudes, such as believing in a punitive God or demonic forces, pleading for direct intercession, and having a negative attitude toward God, the church, or other church members. Positive religious attitudes and behaviors included believing in a benevolent God, trying to connect and "collaborate" with God, seeking support from clergy or fellow church members, and "giving religious help to others."

No one is quite sure what it is about religion that seems so incompatible with depression. Is it, as studies like Koenig's suggest, having faith in a loving God or Higher Power, in oneself, and in one's fellow man and woman? Is it that religious people may give and receive more social support through their congregations and their religious leaders and by volunteering in the community? Is it a reward for striving to lead a moral life? Is it being able to say "the Lord works in mysterious ways" when bad things happen to good people? And to what extent is religious faith simply the result of a sunnier, more optimistic disposition or a lighter legacy of hard knocks?

Do we have to believe in God to have a faith that protects us from depression? Can a secular humanist or a Buddhist who puts his faith in the higher, better reaches of human nature be saved too?

Harold Koenig simply advises us to "be open to the notion of religion and spirituality." "Ask yourself," he says, "'Have I really given spirituality a chance?' Even if you've dismissed it before, be open to the role that spirituality or God might play in your life" (Parker, 1998).

My own bias is that spirituality can't be pinned down to any specific belief system. Rather, it corresponds to that dimension of our being that—sometimes more, sometimes less—strives to live in accord with the highest, most meaningful values, and purposes we can comprehend. Whether such spirituality—which very often is informed by or leads to religious, social, or political commitments—is "good or bad for depression," I can't be sure. But I think it's the best game in town, existentially—so it has to be good! Even the depressive crises that may arise from it are good too, as long as we get through them.

CHAPTER 25

---※---

Creative Problem-Solving for the Causes of Your Depression

As I suggested in the introduction to this book, whenever we become depressed we become depressed about *something*—something in our lives we find intolerable, a problem we feel *must* be solved. The problem may be sharp and focused—a broken marriage, the death of a loved one—or vague and diffuse—"I can't get anything done," "I can't enjoy myself anymore." Its causes may be psychosocial, biophysical, or both. But the problem is why we're depressed, and an obvious way to get undepressed is to deal with it.

There's an art to that, and it can be learned.

For decades, psychologists have been teaching people how to solve their practical and professional problems the way an Einstein or a Da Vinci might. In the 1980s, some of them brought their problem-solving courses to the clinic. They began teaching people how to apply these creative problem-solving techniques to their personal problems, the ones that make them anxious, depressed, addictive, violent. And what they came up with—*problem-solving therapy* (PST)—may be as effective a treatment for depression as any other.

In the late eighties, psychologist Arthur Nezu and his associates conducted two controlled trials of PST for patients with mostly moderate to severe depression. The response was quite remarkable. Just eight or ten weeks of PST in small weekly group sessions lasting one to one and a half hours each brought recovery or marked improvement to all but two of the twenty-five subjects randomly assigned to PST. In contrast, only four of the twenty-six control-group subjects fared so well. Months later, the response persisted.

In England, a simpler version of PST called *problem-solving treatment* (PSTr) has also performed well in clinical trials. With government support, PSTr is being groomed—mostly by L. Mynors-Wallis and associates at Oxford University—as a cost-effective alternative for mildly to moderately depressed patients not ill enough to require psychiatric referal. PSTr is also being evaluated in major European Union and American multicenter trials.

The buzz about PSTr is that it's as fast and cheap as psychotherapy can get (Sherman, 1999). Primary care physicians, psychologists, and even nurses are being taught to administer PSTr for just *two to three hours* per patient, spread out over four to six half-hour sessions. Evidently, a little bit of PSTr can go a long way.

In a study published in 1995 by Mynors-Wallis et al. in the *British Medical Journal*, the subjects were ninety-one primary care patients suffering mild to moderate major depression. They were randomly assigned to one of three treatments: PSTr; the tricylic antidepressant amitriptyline (at a respectable 150 milligrams per day dosage) plus standard clinical management (STM); or a placebo plus standard clinical management. STM was a nonspecific control condition during which the patients could talk with their doctors without getting any actual psychotherapy. There were just six biweekly thirty-minute sessions of PSTr or STM, except for the first session, which lasted an hour.

After six weeks, the PSTr group had already improved by more than 50 percent, slightly more than the drug group and significantly more than the placebo group. At the end of the twelve-week study period, the recovery rate in the three groups was 60, 52, and 27 percent. Remarkably, the patients had received just three and a half hours of PSTr from GPs who had learned the technique in almost as little time (I exaggerate slightly). All the patients said they found PST helpful.

With such cost-effective results, problem-solving training could soon become widely available. Problem-solving *therapy*, which isn't widely available, is usually taught by clinical psychologists, one-on-one or in groups. Even though it may sound like a demanding therapy, the dropout rate in clinical studies has been close to zero.

There appears to be no self-help books on PST or PSTr. But books on PST for professionals by Thomas D'Zurilla, Arthur Nezu, and their associates contain the same information (albeit at a premium price). Problem-solving therapists also recommend self-help books on creative problem solving in general, like the highly influential classics by Sidney Parnes. Here's a primer on PST you may find useful in its own right.

Getting in the Problem-Solving Mood

Creative problem solving evolves in consecutive steps and stages, though considerable backtracking and leapfrogging normally take place. Perhaps the most critical step when we're feeling depressed and discouraged is the first one: overcoming the fear of trying, pessimism, self-doubt, and other mental obstacles. When this step was deliberately omitted in a clinical study of PST by Nezu and Perri, the antidepressant effect was cut in half.

So how do you get into the problem-solving mood?

➤ Try thinking of your problems not as threats, but as challenges or opportunities. If you're oppressed by visions of failure, close your eyes, relax, and force yourself to imagine what it would be like to succeed. Promise yourself that even if you don't attain your goal, you'll probably learn a thing or two in the process and that no sincere effort is really wasted.

➤ Don't aim too high (remember: baby steps). Don't think, "Now I'm going to solve all my problems." Just schedule a convenient amount of time—half an hour, one hour—to follow the problem-solving process. Reward yourself or give yourself a thumbs up, and schedule another session.

➤ Take advantage of the other antidepressant strategies discussed in this book to put you in a more positive and clearheaded frame of mind.

Taking Stock of Your Problems

Before you choose a specific problem to work on, it's a good idea to pause and take stock of the range of problems on your plate. Ask yourself: Where am I hurting? Where is my life not working? That's where your problems are.

In writing, try to describe or classify each problem you identify in more than one way, from more than one angle. Different descriptions (I don't have a job . . . I have too much idle time . . . People think I'm lazy . . .) will suggest different kinds of solutions.

One problem often results from another. And many little problems can result from the same big one. To identify these underlying problems, ask *why?*—repeatedly. Why did my business fail? Because I didn't have enough drive. Why didn't I have enough drive? Because I didn't think I had what it takes. Why didn't I . . . ?

Selecting a Problem

Now that you've identified and listed more problems than you ever thought you had, the next question is: Which one first? It can help to rate the candidates according to criteria like these:

➤ How responsible for your depression does the problem seem to be?
➤ How solvable do you think it is?
➤ How much would resolving it improve your life *in general*?
➤ How bad would it be for you *not* to resolve it?

Clarifying Your Problem

Once you've chosen a problem, the next challenge is to examine it much more closely than you probably have until now.

Is it really what you think it is? Use the cognitive therapy approach to find out. Subject the problem to the same kinds of questions you would ask of an "automatic thought": *What evidence do I have that this is true? Am I jumping to conclusions?* . . . (For more interrogations, see page 272.)

Do research, if necessary. For example, observe your problem in action, read about it, or ask knowledgeable people for their advice.

Now that you have a clearer take on your problem, the next step is to formulate one, or, better yet, several *goal statements* for its solution: *How can I ____? What can I do to ____?* The greater the diversity of goal statements you can come up with, the more alternative solutions you'll be able to think of later.

It's still not too late to identify deeper, perhaps more significant problems. Ask *why?* of each goal statement: *Why do I want to _____, anyway?*

Coming Up with Alternative Solutions

Now it's time to brainstorm (see sidebar on page 291) in high gear, to generate as many "wild and crazy" alternative solutions for your goal statements as you can.

A potent technique for generating original ideas is metaphorical or analogous thinking. Say your goal statement is, "How can I find a mate?" Metaphorically, you might redefine it as, "How does a flower attract bees?" Analogously, "How would I find new clients for my business?" Metaphors and analogies work best when they're derived from things you know well. If you're a gardener you might ask, "How would I find new flowers for my garden?" A lawyer: "How would I find better ways to chase ambulances?"

Or try sentence completions: "To meet a mate I could _____."

Or think of how other people might solve the problem. "How would Joe Cool meet prospective partners?"

Choosing Solutions

Now that you're done brainstorming, you can ungag your inner critic. You need him now to help evaluate your alternative solutions. Do any of the crazy ones contain a kernel of inspired lunacy that can be converted into something useful? Which ones really *are* crazy?

As you begin to formulate would-be solutions, it helps to rehearse them in your imagination or with real people. When you've amassed a collection of contenders, rate them according to such criteria as potential effectiveness, degree of difficulty, fringe benefits, and costs and risks.

Perhaps you can't come up with any viable solutions, even after redefining your problem. In that case, you might ask someone you trust for help. Or just pick another problem to work on. You *do* have more than one problem, don't you?

Implementing Your Solution Plan

Unless your problem is really simple, you'll probably want to tackle it with more than one strategy. Each strategy will probably have to be broken down into small, easily accomplishable steps—steps you can schedule (on paper) and reward yourself for doing. As we saw in chapter 22, the activity alone can help lift your depression, especially if you accept that it's the quality of your effort that counts most—the outcome is in the hands of the gods.

When you try to implement your solution strategies, internal obstacles—automatic thoughts, white-knuckle panics—may rear their ugly heads. You may be able to mitigate them with the strategies recommended earlier for getting in the problem-solving mood. Or you can treat them as problems to be solved in their own right. (How can I stop procrastinating? How can I overcome my fear of _____?)

A good idea is to let at least one other person in on what you're doing, someone supportive who can cheer you on. Or find a "buddy" who has a problem or two she'd also like to solve.

Evaluating Your Efforts

Well, is it working? It helps to keep a before-and-after record or score sheet of problem-related feelings, behaviors, or other criteria. Take some time to figure out what those should be and how you could rate them.

If your strategy isn't working, you can go through the problem-solving steps again. If you keep getting nowhere, choose another problem, reserving the right to return to the first one later.

Trying Is What Counts

Ironically, in the end, actually solving our depressing problems may not be critical to relieving our depression.

As I suggested in the introduction to this book, problems alone don't cause depression. Feeling helpless to solve them or unwilling to

Problem-Solving Tools and Techniques

Problem-solving therapists recommend a number of strategies to facilitate the creative problem solving process.

- *Get into a creativity-enhancing state.* No, don't reach for those recreational substances. Relaxation and meditation tools and techniques, such as those described in chapter 26, can get you there safely and lucidly.
- *Brainstorm.* The fertile soil from which creative problem-solving grows is ideas—mass quantities of ideas. Enter *brainstorming*, the most seminal of all creative problem-solving strategies.

  More an attitude than a technique, brainstorming simply means tying and gagging your inner critic as you open the floodgates of your imagination. It's the opposite of getting all squinched up mentally, worrying about finding the one and only right answer. Creative problem-solving experts teach that right answers often come dressed in the wrong clothing. They look "impossible," "irrelevant," or "silly" at first glance. So when you brainstorm, every weird or homely idea—"the wilder the idea the better," say PST founders Thomas D'Zurilla and Arthur Nezu—is welcomed like royalty and duly recorded. Later, a little creative tailoring can make even some of the strangest birds look like a million bucks.
- *Externalize.* You're working with lots of ideas. So you don't lose any—and to leave room in your head for new ones—"externalize" them right away onto paper or computer.
- *Go with the creative flow.* Our minds tend to bring forth their ideas and insights in a nonlinear way. Their tendency is to hop from *a* to *g* to *b* to *x* to *c* and then suddenly to *347*. And like spirals, they keep wanting to circle back over old ground to deposit new insights. We can get a lot further faster if we go with this flow rather than try to progress in a nice straight line. Which is why it's critical to leave lots of white space between and around all of your "externalizations."
- *Use your imagination.* Don't just think in words and concepts. Use as many of your senses as you can. Also, examine things from exotic points of view other than your own: animal, vegetable, and mineral.
- *Translate the general to the specific, the abstract to the concrete, and vice versa.* Whenever you find yourself using an abstract or general concept (love, success, failure), translate it into specific, concrete examples ("I want to make my father proud of me"). These are much easier to work with and act on. On the other hand, when you find yourself immersed in a maze of concrete specifics (My nose is too long . . . I have too much cellulite in my nose . . .), see if you can infer the general principles (I seem to be obsessed with my appearance) or abstract concepts or values (I put a high stake on looks) at work.

accept them is what brings us down. By reengaging in the effort to solve or come to grips with our problems—even if we only chalk up a few small victories—PST can be an antidote to that aura of helplessness and irreconciliation. It can restore our all-important sense of self-efficacy, bringing us peace and hope. And that can be all the antidepressant we need.

CHAPTER 26

✦

Journeys Out of Stress: Relaxation and Meditation

There is a dizzying variety of stress-busters in today's self-care marketplace. Yet nearly all of them share a common ingredient: relaxation.

Relaxation is the opposite of the tense, "fight or flight" state provoked by stress. What stress perturbs, relaxation restores. Teach people to relax or meditate, studies show, and their health tends to improve; their need for potentially depressing medications for conditions like insomnia, epilepsy, hypertension, and anxiety to diminish or disappear; their spirits to rise. They even live longer, a study by Alexander et al. suggests.

Relaxation for Mood Stabilization

It might seem odd to suggest we need to relax when we're depressed. Aren't we wet blankets "relaxed" enough as it is?

Well, not exactly. Studies show what many of us know: Passive or withdrawn on the outside, underneath, we may be seething with tension, our autonomic nervous systems on overdrive. Not only is anxiety an extremely common symptom of depression, many depressives suffer from full-blown anxiety disorders like panic disorder and social phobia. We may seem "still," but we're not serene. We're just stuck with problems we can't resolve: struggling with them one moment, collapsing in despair the next. Real relaxation can help break this vicious cycle in several ways:

❧ When we relax, we relax the high-strung, sweaty, jaw-clenching, sympathetic side of our autonomic nervous systems. The "what, me worry?" parasympathetic side, which facilitates recovery from the effects of stress, takes over.

❧ Deep relaxation is a facilitator of inner work. It makes it easier for us to know our minds, to paint healing imagery, and to let therapeutic suggestions sink in deeply. As we wind down toward the still center of our being, we may even enjoy moments of forgetting our everyday selves and awakening to a bedrock of blissful being.

A modest body of controlled clinical research supports the relaxation prescription for depression. A study by G. E. Murphy and associates involved thirty-seven patients with relatively mild major depression. Daily sessions of deep relaxation (taught by experts) were pitted for sixteen weeks against two strong antidepressants: cognitive behavioral therapy (CBT) and tricyclic antidepressants. Remarkably, relaxation brought recovery to fully 73 percent of the depressives, a performance just shy of CBT and more than double that of the drugs.

Most research, however, suggests relaxation is a pretty mild antidepressant that would be a sensible adjunct to any antidepressant program. In a study from the University of Iowa, Wayne Bowers compared antidepressant medication combined with daily relaxation to medication alone in thirty hospitalized depressives. The combination was significantly more effective, nearly equaling the drug combined with cognitive therapy.

Relaxation would seem an even more obvious antidote for mania. Martha Sanbower reports that if she's alert to her "early warning sign"—speeding as if she's had too much coffee—she can nip an incipient manic episode in the bud. "At the first sign of this feeling, I make myself take a break from whatever I am doing and relax. Usually lying down and listening to one of my relaxation tapes is enough to stop the 'speediness.' "

If Sandower catches on too late, she resorts to stronger medicine: a day or two in bed, relaxing to the max. "This," she writes, "takes care of the problem and my energy returns to normal."

How to Relax

Relaxing doesn't mean collapsing into your favorite easy chair to watch the evening news through clenched teeth. To really relax it's not enough just to sit still. We also have to let go of the residual tensions in our bodies and minds. Our muscles and wills are always reaching, grasping, pushing, resisting. To relax, we have to cool this down. There are many tools and techniques that can help. Some work mainly through the body, some through the mind; but all relax us as a whole. The following are some of the most popular and effective.

Progressive Muscle Relaxation

A relaxed body begets a relaxed mind. This is the premise of *progressive muscle relaxation* (PMR), probably the most prescribed and tested of all relaxation techniques. In PMR you sit or lie down, close your eyes, and progressively relax each and every one of your muscle groups, from head down to toes, or vice versa.

At first it helps to exaggerate the tension. Before trying to relax your jaw, clench it for a few moments. Then let it go for twenty to thirty seconds. After you've done this a few times your jaw might still feel like a battering ram, but if you keep practicing these PMR scales twice a day (as recommended), it should soon begin to soften. Indeed, according to Martha Davis and associates, authors of *The Relaxation & Stress Reduction Workbook*, after a few weeks or months, many people can turn their bodies into rag dolls in moments.

Suggestion and Imagery

A powerful way to get your mind-body to relax, suggests prominent holistic physician C. Norman Shealy, is to ask it. As you inhale diaphragmatically (see page 229), mentally say "I am . . ." As you exhale, say ". . . relaxed," feeling the tension drain out of you.

Images can speak louder than words. Saying "relax, relax, *relax already!*" to your obstinately stiff neck may not get you far. But if you picture it as a thick, wire-wound cable and then patiently imagine the strands snapping and unwinding, your neck may take the hint. Or perhaps it's more like a poker that needs melting. Or a steel beam—you get the picture.

Here's a technique of my own. Close your eyes and let your attention go to any tense or uncomfortable part of your body. Using your instincts as a guide, ask yourself what you can mentally "apply" to that spot to make it feel better (e.g., light, warmth, touch, a sound, or a substance). Apply it and move onto the next trouble spot.

Here are a few more relaxation images, courtesy of mind-over-body pioneer Maxwell Maltz. Lie down, picture yourself in a peaceful place, and . . .

❧ Imagine you're a marionette, your head and limbs sprawled loosely in all directions.
❧ Imagine your body parts are made of concrete, sinking, sinking, sinking . . .
❧ Imagine your body parts are balloons. Let the air out, one balloon at a time.

Relaxing Clenched Attitudes

Another way to relax is to release the tension in mental muscles taut with anger, worry, shame, resentment, craving, frustration, anticipation, or dread. You can loosen the grip of these symptoms just by recognizing them.

While mentally repeating the words "I accept," "I recognize," or "I understand," let some inner tension fill your consciousness until you can identify and name it. (I accept . . . I accept . . . I accept *that I wish I weren't growing old.*) Keep repeating the process. Every time you recognize and name an inner tension, you relax a little more. (This exercise is inspired by psychologist Eugene Gendlin's powerful self-help technique, *focusing*, described in his book by the same name.)

Meditation: Relaxation in a Higher Key

Every day millions of North Americans meditate, often because their doctors told them to, for research suggests meditation is a stress-relief tool par excellence—good for whatever ails you, and then some. Psychologically, meditators tend to become less tense, less neurotic, less addictive; more empathic, loving, flexible, intelligent, creative, and productive. And less depressed.

Meditation, Patricia Carrington and other therapists report, can be particularly helpful for people who suffer chronically from mild depression or dysthymia. Controlled studies have generally concurred. In a well-designed trial from Princeton University, Carrington and her associates taught a simple mantra meditation technique modeled after transcendental meditation (described below) to seventy-six overstressed, mildly depressed subjects. Within six weeks, most had improved markedly on a variety of psychological and psychosomatic measures. Several months later, their depression was down nearly 70 percent—twice the improvement measured in the no-treatment control group, and significantly better than that of a group taught progressive relaxation.

Meditation's value for major depression is less clear-cut. Psychiatrists Bernard Glueck and Charles Stroebel found transcendental meditation (TM) unhelpful for severely depressed patients who were very slowed down or retarded, but highly effective for those who were agitated.

How to Meditate

The common denominator among the varied forms of meditation is *focus* or *attention*. The common goal is to shift that focus from the objects of attention to the source: the still center of the self. The health benefits are extras.

The most popular forms of meditation—and the subjects of almost all clinical research—are mantra meditation and mindfulness meditation.

Mantra Meditation

In the East, "mantras" (actually, *mantra* is the plural, *mantram* the singular) are regarded as sacred sounds. "The mantram," writes Eknath Easwaran, a leading Indian exponent of mantra meditation, "is the living symbol of the Lord. As it penetrates the deeper levels of consciousness it comes to stand for the highest we can conceive of, the highest we can aspire to, the highest we can love." Mantra meditation, he argues, is a way to follow Christ's precept to "seek ye first the kingdom of heaven, and all else shall be added unto you."

Hindu gurus carefully pick an appropriate mantra for each student. TM also provides each meditator with her own sacred Sanskrit mantra,

Some Popular Mantras (or Mantra Equivalents) from Various Traditions

Hindu: *Ram* (pronounced rohm). *Rama* (*roh*-ma). *Om* (aum). *Ommani padme hum. Omnamah Shivaya.*

Christian: *God is Love. My God and my all. Jesus. Lord Jesus Christ, have mercy upon me* (this Prayer of the Heart may make a better mantra if shortened to *Lord have mercy* or, simply, *Mercy*). *Hail Mary. The Lord is my Shepherd. Kyrie eleison.*

Judaic: *Shalom* (shah-*lom*—peace). *Adonai* (uh-doh-*nye*—God). *Elohim* (eh-loh-*heem*—God). *Adonai Elohenu, Adonai Ehad* (The Lord our God, the Lord is One).

Muslim: *Allah* (God). *La ilaha illa 'llah* (There is no God but God).

Secular: *Peace. Love. Hope. Faith. One.*

Others: *In God (All, One) are we all. God (All, The Creator) and I are one. God be my guide.*

but according to some former TM teachers, it's selected by formula from a very limited stock. Most Western meditation enthusiasts, like Carrington and Harvard's Herbert Benson, simply advise people to pick *any* traditional Eastern or Western mantra, word, or phrase that appeals or to invent one that resonates with their personal values and preferences. Traditionalists like Easwaran recommend you stick with a mantra you like after you've started using it, for the relationship grows deeper and better with age.

A Pocket Guide to Mantra Meditation

Pick a time when you're reasonably alert. Sit (preferably with your back straight and legs uncrossed), close your eyes, relax, and gently begin thinking your mantra. Let the pace, volume, intonation, or other qualities of the mantra vary as they will. When your mind wanders, gently return it to the mantra.

As you follow the mantra, your stream of consciousness will continue like a sideshow. But the contents may become more vivid and compelling. If anything disturbs or engrosses you, let it flow or stay with it until it breaks up like a cloud. Be similarly laid back about twitches, vocalizations, tears, or other signs of stress release. But if meditation stirs up more muck than you can handle, give it a pass or consult a specialist.

Don't strive for spiritual or mystical effects. Mantra meditation is about being, not doing; letting, not willing. Efforts to micromanage things inhibit the flow.

After ten or twenty minutes, stop thinking the mantra and take a minute or so to gently emerge from your mild trance by slowly stretching, rubbing your eyes, and so forth.

Mindfulness Meditation

Zen "sitting meditation" (*shikan-taza*) and the *vipassana* mindfulness-insight meditation of Theravadan Buddhism are major examples of meditation that focuses not on a mantra but on the meanderings of the mind itself. Beginners are usually advised to start by focusing on the ins and outs of their breath. To get a taste of what the more advanced practice is like, close your eyes and simply witness whatever is happening in your mind—the passing thoughts, sensations, emotions, impulses—without losing yourself in the show. Whenever you catch yourself getting caught up, witness that too, and then witness the next turn of the kaleidoscope.

Mindfulness meditation is a subtle gateway to freedom from our usual state of blindly following our automatic thoughts, feelings, and impulses. At the University of Massachusetts Medical Center, Jon Kabat-Zinn and associates teach it to patients suffering from stress-related conditions. Their research suggests mindfulness meditation greatly reduces tension, anxiety, and depression, though to my knowledge they've never investigated it in clinically depressed patients. Importantly, most people who learn the technique stick with it for years.

Other groups are verifying in randomized controlled trials that mindfulness meditation "may represent a powerful cognitive behavioral coping strategy for transforming the ways in which we respond to life events," and "have potential for relapse prevention in affective disorders" (Astin). For Oxford psychologist John Teasdale and his associates, mindfulness is the perfect antidote to the mindless automatic thoughts that lead people down the slippery slope to depression. Mindfulness, they argue, can also alert a person when those thoughts are too compelling to overcome without help.

The next time you catch yourself caught up in depressing thoughts, try *the mindfulness meditation test*: For at least five or ten minutes, stop actively thinking—or passively going along with—the thoughts, and instead just witness them and anything else that comes up. See if this mindful "time out" doesn't break the spell.

How Much Meditation?

Spiritual aspirants, under the guidance of a guru or teacher, sometimes meditate all day for long periods of time. But for people who are not living in a cave or on a mountaintop, the usual prescription is two fifteen- to thirty-minute sessions a day. Adverse reactions to meditation (see below) are "dose-related." Because even a few minutes a day can rub some people's noses in too much unconscious muck, Carrington recommends people meditate very briefly until they're sure it agrees with them. It helps to have access to a therapist in case overly disturbing material comes up.

Although meditation can sometimes produce a phenomenal state of bliss, that soon passes. The lasting benefits of meditation are said to unfold subtly over weeks, months, and years, as the mind-body sloughs off years of stress and becomes conditioned to function in an ever more stable, poised, and clear-headed manner.

Techno-Relaxation

In addition to various disciplines of relaxation and meditation, there are gadgets and gizmos that can help you relax.

Floating

In many cities, you can find a health club, a tanning salon, or a "flotation center" where you can park your body inside a flotation tank: a lightless, soundless, womb-temperature chamber where you float in peace on a sea of mineral water. With sensory stimulation and gravity pared to a minimum, floaters commonly drift off into a blissful state of disembodiment. This liberating state, according to research and testimony described by Michael Hutchison and A. and M. Barabasz, is one in which floaters can more readily tackle personal problems, break bad habits, shed physical pain or mild depression, or enjoy other benefits.

Biofeedback

Portable and affordable electronic biofeedback devices allow you to eavesdrop on your body's subtlest tension signals, such as sweating, muscle tension, and frenetic brain wave activity. Some people find this feedback helps guide them to exceptionally deep levels of relaxation.

Mind Machines and Psychoacoustic Recordings

When we relax, our brain waves relax too, becoming slower, steadier, stronger, and more synchronized between one part of the brain and another. Studies have shown that light or sound pulsing forcefully at these same low frequencies can entrain our brain waves, like a Pied Piper, to follow these relaxing frequencies. The rest of us then follows. This technique is used in most so-called "mind machines."

The simplest mind machines, which are about as small and cheap as a good Walkman, come with headphones and/or goggles to convey the relaxing frequencies to your brain. Some self-help tapes and CDs do the same thing, usually with therapeutic suggestions (often subliminal), affirmations, or guided imagery, with a pleasant musical score to boot.

Electro-Relaxation

As we saw in chapter 16, *cranial electrotherapy stimulation* (CES) devices are scientifically quite well-established as relaxation aids—and more.

The Mind/Body-Tech Marketplace

Mind/body tools and toys can be purchased from self-improvement stores and mail-order and online companies. The California company

Tools For Exploration has long specialized in the field (1-800-456-9887; toolsforexploration.com). In some cities, you can rent time on mind machines at "brain spas" or "mind gyms."

Other Ways to Relax

Let's not forget the relaxation aids discussed elsewhere in this book: bodywork (massage, yoga, therapeutic touch), relaxing music, exercise, and tranquilizing herbs and scents, among others. For more relaxing words and imagery, see chapters 27 and 28, respectively.

Is It Safe to Relax?

Ironically, relaxation and meditation can themselves be stressful. The release of chronic tensions can create transient aches, pains, spasms, nightmares—even crying or screaming—and temporarily worsen health problems, including depression. Clinicians and researchers like Patricia Carrington and Deane Shapiro, Jr. have documented that some people are even driven temporarily psychotic when destabilizing psychic material works its way out of their unconscious minds like a splinter. Others are dislocated by meditation-induced changes in self-image and consciousness. For many long-term transcendental meditators, a study by Shapiro suggests, the benefits are marred by at least one or two negative effects: psychological or psychosomatic symptoms (e.g., increased depressiveness), interpersonal conflicts, or addiction to meditation. People who meditate the most and the longest seem particularly prone to these mixed reactions, perhaps because they may tend to be more disturbed to begin with.

Evidently, deep relaxation and meditation are psychoactive activities that must be used with some caution and moderation.

CHAPTER 27

Word Medicine:
Suggestions for Self-Help

When a hypnotist says "Your eyelids are getting heavy," he is giving you a *suggestion*. But as he would be the first to admit, anything you hear, see, or read is a suggestion that can influence you for better or worse, including the suggestions you give yourself.

When we're depressed, our autosuggestions (including our automatic thoughts) are overwhelmingly negative. Positive suggestions—auto or otherwise—we're inclined to discount, negative ones to welcome like old friends.

There are two ways we can put our suggestions on a more positive course:

➤ We can attempt to defuse the negative ones, as in cognitive therapy.
➤ We can determinedly love-bomb the dark corners of our psyches with *positive* suggestions.

Cognitive therapy has demonstrated the effectiveness of the first approach. But what about the second?

The Antidepressant Power of Suggestion

Hypnotherapy could be defined as the art of imparting positive suggestions to a relaxed and receptive mind. A century ago, the eminent French neurologist Hippolyte Bernheim claimed hypnosis could heal "depression of the spirit" (Pratt et al., 1988). Hypnotherapists today still consider their craft an effective antidote to the blues, although usually as an adjunct to other therapies if the depression is more than mild.

Research on hypnotherapy for depression is surprisingly hard to find. Ironically, the hardest evidence for the antidepressant effect of suggestion comes from a field viewed by many skeptical scientists with the same disdain they once reserved for hypnosis itself: *subliminal suggestion.*

Subliminal suggestions or messages are too faint or fleeting to register consciously, but just strong enough to make their presence felt subconsciously. Most clinical studies of subliminal suggestion have explored the effects of the feel-good message: "Mommy and I are one." The theory, rooted in psychoanalysis, is that this message, when perceived subliminally, can subconsciously evoke "symbiotic fantasies" of reunion with "the good mother" of infancy. And that should be chicken soup for the soul.

In 1990, psychologist R. Hardaway found nearly sixty placebo-controlled clinical trials of the subliminal symbiotic prescription to include in a meta-analysis. The studies involved some 2,500 subjects, 110 of whom were primarily depressed.

"Mommy and I are one" and, to a lesser extent, other subliminal symbiotic suggestions like "Daddy and I are one" tended to be very beneficial indeed. Among other things, they significantly relieved depression and anxiety, improved academic performance in students, and soothed schizophrenics. Remarkably, in most of these studies, the Mommy message was flashed before the subjects' eyes less than a dozen times over a few weeks—less than a tenth of a second's worth of subliminal psychotherapy!

Evidence that subliminal *auditory* suggestions, the kind found on self-help tapes, work is much more limited (Urban). In one double-blind study, depressed psychotherapy clients improved more with real subliminal tapes than placebo ones. But in studies involving other conditions like being overweight and drug dependency, placebo tapes sometimes have equaled subliminals.

Working with Suggestions

Probably the best time to work with suggestions is when we're as relaxed as can be. (Deep relaxation is the basis of hypnotic "trance.") In our ordinary waking state, our minds tend to be focused outward, and suggestions may have a hard time getting in. But if we close our eyes, relax, and focus inward, suggestions can more readily penetrate to the depths, where our beliefs and values are rooted. It's also easier to calmly contemplate negative autosuggestions when we're relaxed.

The twilight state, when we haven't quite fallen asleep at night or fully awakened in the morning, is also considered a good time for working with suggestions. It may even be possible to soak up positive suggestions or affirmations while we're asleep.

Working with Your Depressing Autosuggestions

When you're relaxed and receptive, here are some exercises you can try. Although their purpose is to lighten one's burden, stop if you find they're making you more disturbed or depressed, or try them with a supportive confidante standing by.

❧ Focus on a depressing trouble spot in your life that you don't have a good handle on. Immerse yourself in the feelings and sensations, and then let your felt sense of the situation verbalize itself. The words may come suddenly. But more likely it will be a gradual process in which your heart, guts, and all the rest of you searchingly fine-tune the language until the match feels just right. This may well evoke a deep sigh of relief, as the nonverbal and verbal sides of your being arrive at a mutual climax of understanding.

But don't stop there. Keep allowing more images and feelings to emerge, and verbalize them too. As you continue in this way, invite positive images, feelings, and suggestions to emerge, as they probably will, like rays of sunshine when the clouds part. (This exercise is inspired by psychologist Eugene Gendlin's focusing technique, the subject of his 1981 book, mentioned earlier.)

❧ Try some sentence completions. Use them like probes to awaken feelings and images, repeating them again and again to draw new endings out of your subconscious.

I can't ____. I won't ____. I can't accept ____. I must ____. I'm sorry (I regret) ____. I admit (confess) ____. I'm afraid ____. I resent ____. I'm mad (angry) ____. I dread ____. I don't care ____.

See if you can temper the negativity of some of these suggestions by reflecting on them or cognitively challenging them as described in chapter 23. Some can be converted into affirmations just by changing a word or two.

❧ Many negative autosuggestions are actually internalizations of other people's criticisms or harsh values. The next time you catch yourself replaying one of these old tapes, ask yourself: "Who wants me to believe _____?" If you can identify the culprit(s) or simply imagine someone who would fit the bill, you can mentally confront them. You can argue or reason with them; exhort them to be kind; ask why they're picking on you. You can even get inside *their* skin for a change and disarm them with compassion.

Working with Positive Suggestions

Sentence completions can also be a source for positive autosuggestions. When you're depressed, you may draw a blank at first, but if you keep at it, the opening words will gradually kindle a positive response, however modest (I'm glad . . . I'm glad . . . *I'm glad I have all my limbs*). Black humor is welcome. Gradually, the sentences will become more genuinely positive, and so, probably, will your mood. The best can become personal affirmations.

I'm glad _____. I forgive _____. I thank _____. I accept _____. I can _____. I will _____. I look forward to _____. I like _____. I love _____. I believe _____. I revere _____. I admire _____. I respect _____. I'm a good (fine, lovable, likable, respectable, admirable) person because _____. God (Jesus, my Creator) loves me because _____.

Affirmations

Affirmations are inspiring, life-enhancing sayings. "Mommy and I are one" is an affirmation. So is Emil Coue's famous autosuggestion: "Every day in every way, I am getting better and better." Many great sayings, prayers, and mantras can be made into affirmations, sometimes with a little modification or streamlining: *The kingdom is within. I am true.* Some of the best affirmations are the ones you fashion, eyes closed, relaxed, using your body and feelings as a touchstone.

Probably the best way to work with affirmations is to savor them, flowing with the imagery they provoke, changing the words to your taste, and opening wide to their benign influence.

Here are some affirmations:

The essence of me is goodness. (Or more simply: Essence is good. Our subconscious mind best absorbs messages that are short and sweet.)

Love surrounds me and fills me. (Love surrounds.)

God is All; All is God. (God is All is God is All is God . . .)

In the arms of God (Jesus, my beloved) I rest. (I rest.)

God's (my beloved's) caress consoles me.

I am renewed (restored, reborn).

I breathe universal love. (Breathe love.)

I forgive and am forgiven.* (Forgive, all forgiven.)

I bless and release all those who have caused me pain. (Blessings.)

God (Jesus, Mary, the Creator) and I are one. (One.)

God be my Guide.

I let go and let God.* (Let God, let good.)

God grant me the serenity to accept the things I cannot change, the courage to change the things I can, and the wisdom to know the difference. (This is the serenity prayer of the twelve-step movement.)

My broken heart is an open heart.* (Open heart.)

I release the past and embrace the now. (Embrace.)

I will be happy. (Happy.)

---

*Adapted from *Words That Heal*, by Douglas Bloch.

CHAPTER 28

———— ❧ ————

Imaginary Healing: Therapeutic Imagery for the Blues

For three days, the two small groups of winter depressives spent three hours each morning undergoing bright light therapy. As expected, the treatment worked. But while the depressives in one group sat in front of an actual light box, the others spent the whole time with their eyes closed, hypnotized to imagine the bright light.

Does this mean people have been wasting their money on light boxes?

Probably not. After the three days were up, the seven depressives who sat before the real thing continued to improve for the next ten days, but the moods of the seven visualizers darkened. Nor were these typical depressives. They had all been selected by psychiatrist Paul Richter and associates because they were highly hypnotizable.

Still, the study was an object lesson in the axiom, expressed by Errol Korn, that "imagery is the basis of human thought processes, and is therefore the appropriate language for communicating with the human biocomputer." Certainly the monks of Tibet would not disagree. When Harvard Medical School cardiologist Herbert Benson, a distinguished leader in the field of behavioral medicine, led a team of researchers to Tibet to verify the monks' legendary feats of visualization, the scientists got an eyeful of unforgettable imagery themselves. Benson et al. repeatedly bore witness that certain "monks could indeed dry icy, wet sheets on their naked bodies in temperatures of 40 degrees Fahrenheit." Thanks to years of training in focusing their imaginations, "within three to five minutes of applying the dripping three-by-six-foot sheets to their skin, the sheets began to steam! Within thirty to forty minutes, the sheets were completely dry, and they were able to repeat this process two more times."

The imagination is a much-employed therapeutic tool. It's a staple of hypnotherapeutic suggestion; the language that makes most relaxation techniques work; a frequent aid in cognitive-behavioral therapies, and the very operating room for two of the most effective treatments for fears and phobias, *systematic desensitization* and *implosive therapy*. Transpersonal psychotherapists, Jungian analysts, and New Age therapists of every stripe routinely enlist the power of the imagination to heal.

If imagining a disaster can knot up our stomachs and make us sick with fear, why shouldn't good imaginings make us better? A modest body of research suggests they can.

In more than half a dozen studies, therapeutic imagery has usually brought acute relief from depression; and in some studies, long-term relief too (Schultz, 1984). In a four-week randomized trial by B. L. Rees, relaxation therapy with guided imagery reduced depression and anxiety and increased self-esteem significantly more than relaxation therapy alone in sixty women during the first demanding month following childbirth. Even a few minutes a day of imagery can be therapeutic, according to experts like Gerald Epstein. Too much, however, can be disorienting. If you have any problem keeping your feet on the ground, it may be best not to get into imagery without professional guidance.

In some studies, imagery has enriched verbal psychotherapy. One such study, by L. Rebecca Propst, addressed a key issue for therapeutic imagery and psychotherapy in general: Should the content be adjusted to suit the sensibilities of the individual?

The subjects were mildly depressed college students who also were religious Christians. All were undergoing cognitive therapy. While one group was taught nonreligious imagery to help them cope with their negative thoughts and feelings, another group was taught religious imagery: for example, imagining themselves being filled by the Holy Spirit while struggling with an issue, or using the following autosuggestion: "I can visualize Christ going with me into that difficult situation in the future as I try to cope."

After four weeks, only 14 percent of the students randomly assigned to the religious imagery group were still depressed, while 60 percent of the nonreligious imagery students were. In fact, the latter group fared no better than a third group of students assigned to a waiting list.

Working with Imagery

Often referred to generically as "visualization," therapeutic imagery can involve any of the senses, and words too, which can help both to evoke images and to integrate them with our conceptual minds.

Inevitably, therapeutic imagery also involves emotions—sometimes very strong ones. As Mike and Nancy Samuels write in their classic, *Seeing with the Mind's Eye*, psychotherapists from Freud on have observed that giving these feelings vent is integral to healing with imagery. The most powerfully healing images, the Samuels write, are those that arise from our "inner center." Throughout our lives, our egos alternately inflate us with grandiose fantasies and deflate us with catastrophic ones. But, the Samuels argue, our healing inner center—if we pay it attention—will stabilize and balance us with its pure energy.

Imagining Your Depression

As an example of their inner-center theory, the Samuels quote Carl Jung, the influential psychoanalyst. Whenever Jung uncovered the images "concealed" within his troubled feelings, he wrote, he became "inwardly calmed and reassured."

"Start[ing]," as Jung did, "with your point of trouble," writes Gerald Epstein, is a time-honored method in therapeutic imagery. The following "point of trouble" exercise could make you feel worse. So "use with caution."

Start by letting your depression engulf you: Really feel it, be it. Then let a symbolic image of your state take shape—a thing, a place, a soundscape, a tactile image, or a self-image. You can prompt yourself by repeating "I feel like . . . I feel like . . ." When you get an image, take your time to mold it until it really fits, until you and it are one.

Now let the image change. Let it unfold organically, with nothing more than your will-to-wellness to nudge it, if necessary, toward something more positive, affirmative—a resolution. Because your state of mind and the image are one, as the image changes, so will your state.

Say your image is a desert. Perhaps your inner center, seeking a dramatic release of tension, would start by making the sun grow hotter and hotter, until it literally incinerate or vaporize the desert, leaving you suspended in a cool, dark vacuum. Then, drops of heavenly rain might condense in the darkness, bathing you in a refreshing mist, while, down below, a lush valley slowly springs to life.

Imaginary Activities

In our imaginations we can do anything, including therapeutic or cathartic things. We can "destroy Tokyo" like Godzilla, to vent rage. We can immolate ourselves to release powerful feelings of guilt or despair. We can seek succor at the breast of a giant Earth Mother.

❧ Imagine something dirty, fouled, broken, or dilapidated. Clean or repair it.

❧ Imagine *yourself* dirty, fouled, broken, wounded, or dilapidated. Imagine a spring, a pond, or a cloud, filled with the purest water or magical cleansing elixir. Bathe or shower in it.

❧ Imagine yourself encrusted in an incredibly thick, dry, old skin. Feel the weight and stiffness of a thousand years of decrepitude. Now feel it flaking and peeling, revealing a smooth new skin beneath. Dress up in the finest new threads and go out and have a good time.

❧ Imagine a badly wounded creature. Tend to it.

Working with Inner Selves, Healers, and Other Figures

A very popular imagery technique is getting in touch with "inner figures"—inner healers, spirit guides, power animals, or other entities, real or imaginary. This may be a way of channeling goodwill from unconscious or transpersonal sources to our conscious selves.

A popular class of inner figures are benign: deities and spiritual heroes; moral or intellectual heroes; inner healers; archetypal sages, tricksters, and power animals; or wise extraterrestrials.

Another class of inner figures are subselves. Life-cycle subselves include wounded inner children for us to listen to and reparent; bright-eyed youths who can refresh us with their passion and idealism; and aged, deathbed selves who can bring the wisdom of hindsight to our current problems. There are fearsome shadow selves to greet with loving courage and depressed and dysfunctional selves in need of support. There are healthy, functional selves who can care for our weaker subselves. And there are ideal or idealized subselves in need of review. In our imaginations, we can also have heart-to-heart encounters with real people, alive or dead.

A spontaneous way to contact inner figures is to focus inward and either wait for one to "appear" or search one out. You're more likely to conjure a relevant inner figure if you imagine you're somewhere that resonates with the way you're feeling (or would like to feel) or somewhere the figure might be—a childhood haunt for an inner child, a forest for a power animal, a sacred place for a spiritual figure.

It's as inappropriate to "give your power" to inner figures as to anyone else. Use all of your marbles to weigh and filter the significance of these special encounters.

Emotional Images and Memories from the Past

Psychiatrists have long known that when someone emotionally relives a traumatic experience, she is likely to experience a therapeutic release, a *catharsis*. Shell-shocked soldiers were rehabilitated this way during the Second World War. Today, some therapists use hypnotic age regression to return people to the scene of past traumas, as far back as infancy, birth, life in the womb, or even life *before* the womb—supposed past lives. Real or imaginary, these intense, personal psychodramas reportedly can help heal the past to resolve current psychological problems.

Using Words as a Trigger

A single word can evoke a thousand pictures—and a wealth of feeling—if you focus on it like a mantra. Words that can magnetically conjure up mood-lifting images and feelings as you thoughtfully contemplate them include *faith, trust, hope, love, courage, patience, confidence, acceptance, serenity, cheerfulness, enthusiasm,* and *joy.*

CHAPTER 29

—————— ✹ ——————

The Healing Arts:
From J. S. Bach to Journaling

Outside a theater where a particularly evocative film about World War II has just been screened, a young man of twenty approaches a man nearly four times his age. "Did you fight in the war?" he asks. The elderly man nods, and the youngster walks over and embraces him. Both men dissolve in tears.

Whether it's a movie or a play that breaks the ice surrounding a sensitive subject, or the echo of one's heartbeat in another person's music, or the soul-satisfaction of speaking your mind with a brushstroke, a sound, or a movement, art (and craft) is one of the highest forms of medicine. Soulstuff made tangible, the essence of the human experience given shape and form, art, in turn, shapes, forms, and sometimes heals the souls of those who make or behold it.

When we're depressed, art can heal in a number of ways:

- ✹ That escapist novel we're reading or that doodad we're making can engross us, lifting us out of our depressed selves and returning us later, as a renewed person.
- ✹ Making art and crafts can restore our sense of self-efficacy by helping us feel creative or productive again.
- ✹ Art can reach into our hearts, sometimes through walls of denial, and help transform troubled feelings into peaceful ones.
- ✹ Art can be an outlet for thoughts and feelings we may not express any other way.
- ✹ The physical act of making arts and crafts brings body and soul together when we may otherwise be coming apart at the seams.

❧ Art can reveal ourselves to ourselves and to each other, replacing alienation with reconciliation.

❧ The arts shine at provoking two of our healthiest coping mechanisms: laughter and tears.

Although clinical research is sparse, it seems clear that the arts can be powerful antidepressants for at least a minority of people, and valuable adjuncts for any depressed person. Here are just a few ways to use art to fight depression.

Videotherapy

In 1964, the distinguished editor Norman Cousins was stricken with a mysterious, paralytic illness. Suspecting ankylosing spondylitis, one of his doctors gave Cousins only a 1 in 500 chance of recovering. Ever the optimist, Cousins decided to treat himself with megadoses of vitamin C—and comedy.

Bedridden, the middle-aged man of letters laughed his way through reels of his favorite Marx Brothers movies and *Candid Camera* episodes. As he later wrote in his influential classic, *Anatomy of an Illness as Perceived by the Patient*, the belly laughter relieved his pain, gave him sound sleep, and may well have accounted for his gradual recovery.

Whether it's comic relief, escapist adventure, or tearful catharsis, the effects of "videotherapy" can be as chemical as a drug. In a controlled study by T. W. Buchanan et al., thirty healthy young subjects watched a funny and exciting thirty-minute video. Not only did it activate them and brighten their moods, it significantly lowered the stress hormone cortisol. High cortisol is almost synonymous with severe depression.

Music Therapy

Music's healing powers are the stuff of legend. David's lyre relieved King Saul's melancholy. Greek bards salved the sorrows of spent Homeric warriors. In modern hospitals and institutions, music is still used to lift people's moods, ease pain, and break through walls of isolation.

Limited research has affirmed music's psychotherapeutic benefits. In an interesting study by Eifert et al., people were exposed from a distance to the animals they feared. Those who were serenaded by music they liked got over their phobias more easily than those who faced their fears in silence.

Most people would think that bright, cheerful music would be the obvious prescription for the blues. But when depression runs really deep, "happy music" can be a rude noise. Music that resonates with our "diminuendo" feelings may help us get through them better. As one melancholic music lover told psychiatrist Roberto Assagioli: "When I hear sad music composed by a man who suffered, as did Chopin, Beethoven, and Tchaikovsky, I feel that I am 'seconded,' and in feeling the beauty of that music I forget I am not well." No wonder. Such music often embodies the composer's successful efforts to work through these feelings himself. So, as music therapist Hal Linderman advises, "Let music come into you, music that will stir you and at the same time will act as a clearing agent that will take and absorb the feelings you release into it."

Writing as Therapy

For some people, private writing or "journaling" is a healing routine for exploring and expressing their most intimate thoughts and feelings. Psychologists like James Pennebaker even prescribe journaling as therapy.

In a seminal study by Pennebaker's group, university students poured their most painful secrets into private journals for just fifteen minutes a day, four days in a row. Immersing themselves, as instructed, in their worst memories was initially very disturbing. But later the students felt lighter, happier, more in touch with themselves. Their visits to the student health center dropped by half. Other students who had been told to write about superficial matters or to dryly recount the details of their problems enjoyed no such benefits, nor did students told to simply vent their feelings on paper without thought or reflection.

Therapeutic writing should be done unself-consciously, without pressure to write well. It's the process, not the product, that counts.

Writing Your Hurts Out

This is Pennebaker's "confessional writing approach," as described in *Opening Up*. Pick a personal issue that's so sensitive you may have trouble just thinking about it. Write about it for at least fifteen minutes, frankly exploring the exact details and your related thoughts and feelings.

Putting Images to Words

"It is a common experience among diarists," writes Tristine Rainer, "to find that anxiety or depression disappears once they have found an image to express it in writing." Rainer suggests you search yourself for an image that corresponds to how you're feeling (see also chap. 28). Explore and express that image in prose or verse.

Letters from the Edge

Here's your chance to speak your mind to a significant other—to loosen that bitten tongue—in a letter you'll never send. The significant other can even be yourself.

In her writing workshops, my friend Anna Olson recommends a powerful technique for dealing with ambivalence. Clear the decks with a no-holds-barred "angry letter," then follow with an appreciative "love letter."

Points of View

Think of an important area of conflict or confusion in your life. Write about it from the point of view of the conflicting parties or parts of yourself. Does anyone else have something to contribute? Write about it from her point of view too.

Reading as Therapy

Even if we don't face our demons in our own writing, others have. And their best efforts have been published for us to share.

"We all have times of trouble in our lives when hearing or reading just the right words can remind us that peace, calm, and tranquility do exist, and they can be ours to enjoy again," writes Jennifer Cawthorne. Seeking out inspiring, comforting, and often humorous writings proved to be a key ally in Cawthorne's own struggle with a severe midlife depression.

Visual Art

For years, art therapist Janie Rhyne's new client had sat atop a corked volcano of rage and despair. At her request, the chronically depressed psychiatric social worker painted his torment out on a large sheet of paper, attacking it with red and black paint, while muttering about "blood and guts" and "horror, terror, fury, nothingness." He covered sheet after sheet, and as he vented his pent-up feelings, his palette gradually softened, his images became less and less chaotic. In that single all-out session, the man later told Ryan, he expressed more of himself than he had in a year of psychotherapy.

Here are a few approaches to art therapy.

Drawing on Your Imagination

Your subject can be anything important to you, whether it's before your eyes or in your mind's eye. Freely bend or distort its appearance to express your feelings about it. Alternatively, clip images from magazines, newspapers, or other sources and paste up a collage, again using your feelings to guide you.

Abstract Expression

Here is where you break free from the real world and express yourself with abstract (nonrepresentative) shapes, colors, patterns, and textures. Fluid media—brush and ink, paints, oil pastels, computer paint programs—will best help you speak your mind with strokes, splatters, smudges, blobs, and other self-satisfying marks and forms.

In a very black and alienated mood, a student of Rhyne's set out to paint an entire sheet of paper black. "Painting in black and giving in to

The Art of Laughter and Tears

Laughter is a load-lightening reflex that often goes flat when we're depressed. Similarly, crying is a healing spring that can become blocked under an iceberg of depressive numbness. The arts excel in provoking these complementary coping responses.

Laughing and crying are the only healthy convulsions (other than sneezing and orgasm) that humans, almost uniquely among animals, experience. Perhaps they're our reward for the more complex burdens we carry. Polar opposites, they share the same stress-relieving mission. Laughter makes us feel better by rising above, almost detaching from, that which might otherwise disturb us. Crying makes us feel better by entering the heart of darkness and emerging lighter and fresher.

Humor is the appropriate antidote when we're taking something too seriously. It can transform overblown mountains into comical molehills. It's our expansive spirit laughing at the antics of our uptight selves. A spontaneous form of cognitive therapy, humor can help free us from dysfunctional "shoulds," "musts," and "don'ts," from false values and sacred cows, and from groundless or petty shame, worry, hostility, or inhibition. As Bill Cosby puts it, "If you can laugh at it, you can survive it." Laughter even boosts your immune system and lowers stress hormones, according to Patty Wooten, a nurse, clown, and leader of the laughter-as-medicine movement.

Studies have shown that people who use humor to cope with stress are less likely to become disturbed, depressed, or immunologically compromised. But can this coping style be taught?

Laughter missionaries like Wooten believe it can. In a controlled study, Wooten and her associates gave a "six-hour humor training course" to a large group of nurses. The nurses—whose profession is notorious for its stress and burnout rate—"were given permission and techniques for appropriate use of humor with patients and coworkers." Six weeks later, a psychological test revealed they had developed a significantly greater sense of internal control over circumstances—the opposite of the helpless, hopeless, "external locus of control" mindset that often goes with depression.

Crying is the perfect homeostatic complement to laughter. It's what we need when we're not taking things seriously *enough,* when it's not a sense of humor we lack, but a sense of tragedy. Crying makes molehills seem like the mountains they really are, carrying us right into the center of the volcano, allowing it to erupt, flow, and be spent.

"The expression 'to cry it out' might literally be true," says William H. Frey II, a biochemist known for his research on the psychobiology of crying (Kopecky, 1992). Frey has found that emotional tears contain two pituitary stress hormones. "[T]ears may be an adaptive response to stress, serving to remove these built-up hormones from the body," Frey speculates.

According to physician and biochemist Sheldon Hendler, research has also shown that crying has a marked normalizing effect on both low and high testosterone levels in men. This not only seems to confirm that weeping can tenderize a stoically macho male, but it belies fears it might make a soft man wimpy. As we saw in chapter 2, both low testosterone and (in dysfunctionally macho men) high testosterone are conducive to depression. Crying could be a guy's ticket to the testosterone "zone."

Can we cry or laugh too much? Stanford University psychologist Susan Nolen-Hoeksema finds that people (usually women) who can't stop crying take longer to get over a depression than those (usually men) who distract themselves with pleasant or problem-solving activities (Kopecky, 1992). Laughter can be such a distraction, but not if it's nothing but a distraction. That's the problem for people who compulsively laugh to distance themselves from hurts and pains they need to touch base with emotionally and release through tears.

So, it would seem, people who cry or laugh the least stand to benefit from crying or laughing the most. The thousands of tear-jerkers and side-splitters that line the shelves of book, music, and video stores are a convenient place to fill that prescription.

my feelings seemed to have a very liberating effect on my black mood," she commented. "In a sense, I painted my way out of the corner and as my mood brightened, my colors brightened."

A Separate Peace

The world of geometric forms and patterns is one of order, calm, and stability. It is perhaps the closest thing in art to meditation, with its focus on a dimension more stable, more primal than the chaotic "phenomenal world." An easy way to enter this peaceful realm is with a compass, the kind you make circles with.

Set the radius of your compass to about ½ to 1 inch. Draw a circle (circle A) in the center of a roughly 8-by-11-inch or larger piece of paper. Next, put the point of the compass at the top of the circle and draw another circle (circle B). Then put the compass point on each of the points where circle B intersected circle A and draw new circles. Now draw circles at each of the new intersection points. Finally, draw a circle at the last intersection point. See what forms take shape when you connect the intersection points on circle A in different ways.

Extend the drawing by continuing to draw circles with their centers at the intersection points outside of circle A. (Keep the radius of the compass constant.) Continue discovering new forms and patterns by connecting different intersection points.

Depending on how you shade or color the multitude of forms and patterns that organically grow from these circles and lines, dramatically different drawings or paintings will emerge.

Part 6

―――――✦✦――――――

"Unnatural" Antidepressants: Antidepressant Drugs and Electroconvulsive Therapy

With such a diversity of effective, user-friendly natural antidepressants to choose from, do we really need antidepressant drugs and electroconvulsive therapy (ECT)? The answer is probably . . . *yes.*

Even Abram Hoffer, one of the fathers of orthomolecular psychiatry, finds it useful to pull out the old prescription pad, or even order a course of ECT, on occasion.

But Hoffer and others in his progressive wing of the medical profession typically use drugs as short-term crutches. Their goal is to get their patients to live a drug-free (or nearly so) life, with natural therapies and lifestyle changes making up the bulk of their treatment.

More and more depressives are striving to achieve that same goal. For them, drugs are becoming the alternative, not the other way around. But sooner or later, you may need to pursue that alternative, or even have to face the prospect of ECT. The next chapters will help you understand what you're dealing with.

CHAPTER 30

Drugs for Depression

The major advantage that antidepressant drugs (ADs) have over natural treatments is economic: Much more money has gone into establishing their safety and efficacy in well-controlled research (underwritten by drug companies) and selling doctors on their virtues. The disadvantage is that they're artificial substances, designed for profit by drug companies, not for constructive biological purposes by nature. Usually they produce annoying side effects, and sometimes they're responsible for very serious or (rarely) fatal ones. Their long-term effects are essentially a mystery.

Yet the side effects of being severely depressed can be dire in their own right. There are times when the right drug may be just what the doctor ordered.

Most of the roughly two dozen ADs on the market today belong to one of three families. By far, the most popular are the *selective serotonin reuptake inhibitors*, or SSRIs: Prozac (fluoxetine), Zoloft (sertraline), Paxil (paroxetine), Luvox (fluvoxamine), and Celexa (citalopram). Dating back to the 1950s are the *tricyclic and other cyclic antidepressants*, such as Tofranil (imipramine), Elavil (amitriptyline), Anafranil (clomipramine), and Norpramin (desipramine). The other classic antidepressants are the *monoamine oxidase inhibitors* (MAOIs), like Nardil (phenelzine), Parnate (tranylcypromine), and the newer Aurorix (moclobemide).

A new class, *selective norepinephrine reuptake inhibitors*, is under development. These drugs, of which Reboxetine has been the first to hit the market, are to the natural antidepressants tyrosine and phenylalanine what the SSRIs are to tryptophan.

Belonging to none of these classes are ADs like Effexor (venlafaxine), Serzone (nefazadone), Desyrel (trazodone), Wellbutrin (bupropion), BuSpar (buspirone), and Remeron (mirtazapine).

One way or another, all these ADs boost the activity of one or more of the neurotransmitters thought to be key to keeping us content: *serotonin* and *norepinephrine*. Although these drugs usually have other neurochemical effects, such as boosting dopamine, phenylethylamine, and/or GABA, and blocking acetylcholine, most theorists believe their net serotonergic (serotonin boosting), noradrenergic, and possibly dopaminergic effects are key.

Despite the widespread belief that Prozac and other newer ADs are more effective and much better tolerated than cyclics and MAOIs, research has consistently indicated otherwise. The latest review of more than three hundred clinical trials for the U.S. Agency for Health Care Policy and Research found no evidence that any ADs, new or old, were significantly better than any others for the most commonly investigated forms of depression, notably major depression in adults. Nor were there any significant differences in how well tolerated the ADs were. Different drugs had different side effects, but for the average patient, one drug was about as tolerable as another (Dermott).

This doesn't mean that ADs are perfectly interchangeable. An AD that is one depressive's nightmare is another's salvation. With just about every new one that hits the market, a few more people find a pill with their names on it.

How Doctors Use Drugs to Treat Depression

Despite the evidence that all ADs are roughly equal, most first prescriptions today for depression are for the relatively expensive SSRIs or for other pricey late-model ADs. In part, this is a case of doctors succumbing to the latest drug promotions (or pressure from their patients). It can also be pragmatic. Initially, it's easier to safely manage a patient on most of the newer ADs than on most of the first-generation ones.

Most depressives experience side effects. For about 15 to 40 percent, these are so annoying or serious that they discontinue the AD. Of those who don't, about 60 to 70 percent begin to improve within two or three weeks and respond (i.e., enjoy a 50 percent or greater reduction in their symptoms) within a month or two. But of those responders, only about half completely recover. The others are at substantial risk of relapsing, or of having to get by with a half-recovery instead of a full one, unless they receive additional treatment.

If AD number one doesn't work, doctors who take a strictly psycho-pharmacological approach (as most do) have several options:

- ⚚ They can push the dosage, hoping the patient will respond before the side effects become unbearable.
- ⚚ If there has been a partial response, a doctor may try another AD from the same class, because people who respond a little to one can respond a lot to another.
- ⚚ Particularly if the first drug has been a complete bust, doctors can switch to an AD with a different profile of neurotransmitter effects, for example, from a serotonin-boosting SSRI to a norepinephrine-boosting tricyclic, like desipramine, or to an AD like Wellbutrin that boosts norepinephrine and dopamine. Or they can add the comple-mentary AD to the first one.
- ⚚ If the first drug was highly selective (e.g., an SSRI), they can switch to an AD that isn't—to a "broad spectrum" AD that substantially boosts two or more neurotransmitters, like Anafranil, Effexor, or one of the MAOIs, although usually at the price of more side effects or risks.
- ⚚ An often fast and effective strategy is to augment the first AD with an established augmentor like lithium, thyroid hormone, or tryptophan.

Studies indicate that any of the above strategies will likely bring re-covery to about 25 to 30 percent of the patients who tolerate them and partial recovery to another 25 to 30 percent. This still leaves a substan-tial percentage of depressives—perhaps 30 to 50 percent—who are still as depressed as ever, or not fully recovered and at considerable risk of sliding back down the slope in the next weeks and months.

Sadly, most doctors will still stick to the pharmacy. They won't con-sider reasonably well-established alternatives or adjuncts like brief psy-chotherapy, exercise, neurotransmitter precursors, SAMe, St. John's wort, gonadal or adrenal hormones, bright light therapy, or sleep depri-vation. Some will recommend electroconvulsive therapy (ECT) if the patient is severely or psychotically depressed. Or they may try yet a third or a fourth or an *n*th AD, alone or in a combination/augmentation strategy. Or they may resort to some of the more experimental or anecdotal drug alternatives or adjuncts for treatment-resistant depression: the Valiumlike Xanax (alprazolam), which has some mood-lifting effect; an anticonvulsant mood stabilizer, like Tegretol (carbamazepine) or Neurontin (gabapentin); the beta-blocker pindolol; a psychostimulant, like dextroamphetamine or Ritalin; or an atypical antipsychotic, like clozapine or risperidone.

To my knowledge, there is no research to indicate what percentage of depressives can be brought to full recovery aggressively employing only drugs, ECT, and the few natural substances widely used by mainstream psychiatry. But it likely falls well short of 100 percent. As University of California psychiatrist Stephen Stahl laments: "Although over 90 percent of depressed patients will eventually 'respond' to one or a combination of different drugs, up to half of these will never remit, and for those who do, up to 30 percent do not remain well in the first eighteen months following remission." Stahl urges his colleagues to stop settling for "response" and "go for the gold" of remission with each and every one of their patients.

How much more likely would doctors be to win that gold if they enriched their armamentarium with the complete garden of natural antidepressants? Almost every one of these can boast of having worked for some people who "tried everything." And most are not only safe for long-term use, they typically come with more side benefits than side effects: preventing heart disease, cancer, premature aging, and so forth.

Take-Home Messages for Antidepressant Drug Users

There are many subtleties to the art of prescribing antidepressant drugs successfully. Psychiatrists, particularly those who specialize as psychopharmacologists or work in mood disorder clinics, are much better equipped than general practioners (GPs) to prescribe them effectively.

Books like *The Essential Guide to Psychiatric Drugs*, by psychiatrist Jack Gorman, and *Prozac and the New Antidepressants* by Harvard psychiatrist William Appleton, and many online sources, can give you more on the pros, cons, and fine print on ADs. Online, the newsgroup alt.support.depression.medication is a good place to read what real people have to say about their experiences with ADs (synthetic and natural) and join in the conversation. Finally, here are a few more facts about ADs to help you choose, use—or refuse—them wisely.

➣ ADs are strikingly superior to placebos—about two to three times better—for major depression, when it's very severe. But the milder the depression, the smaller the advantage; and in the mildest depressions, they appear little or no more effective for the average depressive than a placebo.

➣ Some research suggests the effectiveness of ADs has been systematically exaggerated in clinical trials. R. P. Greenberg and associates argue that the conspicuous side effects of antidepressant drugs (especially the old ones) interfere with the blindness of researchers in double-blind clinical studies, allowing those biased in favor of the drugs (the usual case) to consciously or unconsciously rate them as more effective than they really are. When Greenberg et al. analyzed the literature circa 1992, they found that the blinder the studies really were, the smaller the advantage ADs had over the placebos. In the blindest studies, that advantage all but disappeared in the patients' own ratings.

➣ Although researchers have been at pains to find any significant differences in clinical efficacy between different ADs for depression in general, this doesn't seem to be the case for certain kinds. For instance, cyclic antidepressants seldom work for atypical depression, but MAOIs very often do. The SSRIs also show promise.

When it comes to very severe or melancholic depression, SSRIs tend to be less effective than cyclic ADs and MAOIs, which boost both serotonin and norepinephrine. In one study, Swartz and Guadagno found that nine out of nine depressives who became melancholically depressed while taking an AD were taking an SSRI. Switched to a complementary norepinephrine- and/or dopamine-boosting AD (or, in two cases, to ECT, which also boosts multiple neurotransmitters), they all recovered rapidly. Likely one would see similar problems in depressives treated with NE reuptake inhibitors, like Reboxetine. Of the newer generation ADs, only Effexor, which strongly boosts serotonin and norepinephrine, rivals the old guard's ability to treat the severest depressions. If there is a lesson here,

Stephen Stahl suggests, it's an old one that predates the age of Prozac: If boosting one neurotransmitter doesn't work, try boosting the other—or just boost both. This can readily be done with drugs, with supplements, or both. It can also be done with other neuroactive natural antidepressants like exercise, hormones, and acupuncture.

❧ Some ADs are not just ineffective for some depressives, they're hazardous. For people with a personal or family history of bipolar disorder, cyclic ADs can be a disaster, worsening their depression or provoking a severe, rapid-cycling bipolar disorder.

Elderly persons are more susceptible to serious adverse AD effects like heart attacks and strokes, falling after getting up suddenly, severe sodium deficiency, and delerious or psychotic reactions.

❧ A small minority of people complain that certain side effects, like sexual dysfunction and cognitive impairment, have persisted long after they've stopped taking an AD, typically an SSRI.

❧ Don't be eager to be the first kid on your block to try the new drug. In recent years, two antidepressants—zimelidine and nomifensine—had to be pulled from the market because of very serious side effects not reported in premarketing studies.

❧ Extreme drowsiness, dry mouth, and many of the other often prohibitively annoying side effects of cyclic antidepressants usually subside after the first few weeks. People who stick with these drugs often become quite comfortable with them. With SSRIs, the pattern tends to be the opposite. Side effects gradually emerge and persist, especially insomnia, weight gain, and impaired sexual function (loss of genital sensitivity and inability to reach orgasm or extremely delayed orgasm). Sexual dysfunction is also a problem with strongly serotonergic cyclic and MAOI ADs. The herbs *Ginkgo biloba* and yohimbe/yohimbine often can allay these side effects.

Some people on selectively serotonergic ADs—SSRIs, lithium—eventually complain of another side effect: emotional flatness or apathy. This is in stark contrast to the complaint of many people on Wellbutrin, which selectively boosts norepinephrine and dopamine, of irritability, anger, or rage. The moral seems to be that too polarized or "selective" an antidepressant can have an unbalancing effect. The SSRI blahs can be relieved by drugs like Wellbutrin and Pamelor and probably by similar natural agents like thyroid hormone, tyrosine, phenylalanine, NADH, and SAMe. The Wellbutrin willies might be allayed by an SSRI, lithium, tryptophan, acupuncture, or possibly SJW, 5-HTP, omega-3s, or magnesium.

✕ Sometimes prescribed for anxious depression, alprazolam (Xanax) is a benzodiazepine tranquilizer, like Valium, that can become a habit that's extremely hard to break. Unfortunately, some of the newer ADs, notably Effexor and Paxil, also are notorious for withdrawal symptoms, even in people who quit very, very gradually. Some people have simply stopped trying. Anecdotally, weaning temporarily to Prozac has sometimes helped. Possibly, weaning to amino acid neurotransmitter precursors, vitamin C, and acupuncture would help too.

✕ Most depressives become less suicidal on antidepressants, but some become more suicidal or suicidal for the first time, and a few become homicidal, obsessive, unbearably agitated, or psychiatrically worsened in other ways. The SSRIs may be the worst offenders, but almost any antidepressant drug (and, theoretically, natural substitutes) can have this effect. Defenders of ADs maintain these symptoms are coincidental. But after careful study, Martin Teicher and his associates at Harvard Medical School arrived at what I believe is a more incisive conclusion: "Antidepressants may redistribute suicide risk, attenuating risk in some patients who respond well, while possibly enhancing risk in others who respond more poorly."

Regardless of the cause, the occurence of such symptoms is an obvious sign that the treatment isn't working and should immediately be reviewed by patient and doctor.

CHAPTER 31

Electroconvulsive Therapy

A barbaric procedure for shocking incorrigible mental patients into a state of vegetablelike compliance—that's the image many people still have of "shock therapy" (electroconvulsive therapy, ECT), a legacy of its indiscriminate use (and abuse) in previous generations and its portrayal in movies. But as normally administered today, ECT is one of the most effective and, arguably, safest mainstream treatments for suicidal, psychotic, or severe treatment-resistant depression.

ECT is like a computer reset that more or less erases the troubling contents of RAM (recent memory) in the course of five to ten sessions over a few weeks. The majority of depressives not only forget their depression, research suggests their neurochemistry receives an antidepressant druglike makeover too. For some people, nothing else seems to work. Even orthomolecular psychiatrists like Abram Hoffer and Harvey Ross occasionally recommend it.

Yet ECT remains controversial. Safe enough for most people who are too old or ill to handle many antidepressant drugs, it has yet to shake its dark reputation of causing permanent memory loss—even brain damage.

Proponents of ECT insist that, at worst, it only erases memories for the time around which it was administered, a small price to pay. But some people swear it has permanently wiped out precious older memories. I have seen this myself in a close relative for whom ECT was almost magically effective (at least the first time). Although controlled studies have yet to corroborate these complaints, even proponents like Murray Enns and Jeffrey Reiss of the University of Manitoba admit insensitive research methodology may be to blame.

But if ECT is to be employed as a last resort, it must really be one. Patients, families, and their doctors should first consider other reasonable options, such as cautiously augmenting (or replacing) antidepressant drugs (ADs) with thyroid hormone, lithium, tryptophan, 5-HTP, St. John's wort, steroid hormones, sleep deprivation, light therapy, or other adjuncts, including the promising ECT alternative, rTMS (chap. 16). As Enns and Reiss point out, augmentation strategies can be as rapidly effective in drug-resistant depressives as ECT. And unlike ECT, they can easily be continued as maintenance therapy for these high-risk patients.

Softer options like diet, exercise, acupuncture, and psychotherapy should not be underestimated, especially when one's eye is on the prize of long-term recovery and not just a quick and dirty "computer reset."

Recently, Giovanni Fava and his associates at the University of Bologna in Italy did the unthinkable. They took nineteen major depressives who had just flunked trials of at least two consecutive ADs and, instead of upping the psychopharmacological ante or referring them to the ECT clinic, they treated them with cognitive-behavioral therapy. The results were remarkable. Although three of the patients dropped out, twelve recovered fully, eight of them eventually discontinuing their drugs. Two years later, only one had relapsed. "Drug refractory," Fava et al. argued, should not be confused with "treatment resistant" until "a psychotherapeutic effort has been made."

If you do have to resort to ECT, research suggests memory problems can be minimized without compromising efficacy if:

❧ ECT is administered bifrontally (Letemendia et al.).
❧ A moderate dose of anesthetic is used, and concomitant psychotropic drugs are avoided.
❧ The lowest dose of brief pulse current necessary to provoke an adequate seizure is used.
❧ ECT is administered no more than two or three times a week (Gangadhar et al., 1993).
❧ A few hours are spent resting in a dark, quiet room after coming to (Suedfeld et al.).

Anecdotally, psychiatrist Abram Hoffer (1987) claims megadoses of vitamin B_3 before, during, and after can also prevent ECT-induced memory loss.

CONCLUSION

Putting It All Together: "Growing" Your Depression Recovery Program

We've covered *a lot* of ground in this book. The big question now is how to choose from among this plethora, this cornucopia of treatment possibilities that even I have trouble keeping track of. How to devise a program for recovery from depression for yourself?

I say *program* (nervously mindful that the word, with its implication of structured routine, may cause many a gulp or groan), because unless there is a single identifiable cause for your depression with a 100 percent effective treatment, it would be imprudent to pin your hopes on just one—or even two or three—antidepressant therapies. An antidepressant program that can get you over your current depression and continue working for you in the years ahead should be more like a full-course meal than a single entrée. It should be an antidepressant lifestyle.

So now is the time to plunge in and make some choices or to elaborate on those you've already made. You may already have some ideas of which antidepressants you'd like to try, based on the evidence, their suitability or appeal to you, and their ease of use, safety, cost, or other criteria.

Regarding the first and most critical of those criteria, one of the problems in choosing among natural antidepressants is the highly variable quality of the evidence. In the table on page 341, I've ventured to evaluate that evidence for each of the antidepressant strategies discussed in this book, whether as major acute treatments, as adjuncts, augmentors, or team players, or as long-term maintenance and prevention strategies. A ✓ means I consider the evidence to be strong; a ○ means I think it's either moderately good, or strong but very limited in quantity; a ● means I think the evidence is scientifically very weak, preliminary, or nonexistent, although the anecdotal evidence may be encouraging. My standards are toughest for the main course treatments, because these are the ones we invest most of our hopes in for acute relief. My standards are easier for the adjunctive and preventive practices, because, like broccoli and brown rice, these tend to be good for you anyway.

In fact, some of these latter antidepressants are so safe, well founded, and fraught with side benefits, that I believe they deserve special mention here. I suggest you incorporate as many of them as possible into your daily antidepressant feast, your diversified portfolio of investments in your affective well-being. Individually, only a few are likely to cure many cases of clinical depression. Even a plateful may not have the force to budge a deeply entrenched depressive disorder. But the more of them you swallow, the healthier you will be in general, and the less need you're likely to have for the heavier hitters like drugs and even powerful supplements of uncertain long-term safety.

Have a thorough medical workup to catch any depressing physical illnesses you may have.

The older you are or the less responsive you've been to antidepressant therapies, the more likely this measure will bear fruit. But even children can suffer from cryptic physical causes, like Wilson's disease or chronic lead poisoning. Be sure your doctor doesn't fast-forward through this step.

Clean up your act.

A toxic brain breeds a depressed mind. Look critically at the quality of everything you eat and breathe. With the help of chapter 3 on toxic depression and the chapters on diet (especially chaps. 4 and 12), get as much of the junk out of your body as you can.

Eat right to feel right.

Good food is our body's most basic and user-friendly medicine. As a general rule, minimize your consumption of processed foods and maximize your intake of a colorful variety of fresh, whole foods, cooked and raw.

Don't forget to take your vitamins.

A well-balanced, broad-spectrum, medium- to high-dosage multivitamin and mineral supplement is cheap "insurance" against depressing deficiencies and even treatment for some. It's also an essential foundation for any antidepressant supplements you're taking in high doses.

Get your RDA of bright light and exercise.

Chronic lack of bright light in the daytime will dim almost anyone's spirits, any time of the year. Physical activity is one of the pillars of mental and physical health. Put them together and you have a natural antidepressant that is both pleasant and potent.

Get regular.

Irregular sleep, wake, and activity patterns are conducive to irregular moods, even including descents into depression and flights into mania. Strive for a schedule that provides you enough sleep at night (augmented by daytime naps, if necessary) to fire on all cylinders during the day, with a bedtime and rising time that varies little from day to day.

Stop the world and get off . . .

One or two daily periods of alert, yet relaxed detachment from your usual preoccupations are a unique stress medicine, dubbed by Harvard behavioral medicine luminary Herbert Benson "the relaxation response." Deep relaxation techniques and meditation (chap. 26) are the most scientifically tested of such breaks. But any life-affirming "re-creation" that stops the world for you and gets you in that state of "flow" when you're like a child with a new toy can likely fulfill the same function.

. . . but don't get off the treadmill altogether.

There is a vicious cycle between depression and inactivity. Try to remain involved in purposeful activities for at least a small part of every day, even if it's just doing housework, paying the bills, or keeping in touch with friends (see also chap. 22).

Be connected.

We are social animals, and for lack of close, supportive relationships we wilt. Being socially connected is one of those things, like being active and eating well, that bears a nonvicious healing cycle relationship with mood.

If you've become disconnected, support groups of kindred spirits are seldom far away, no matter where you live. Even online support groups can fill some of that need, and so can companion animals.

Practice mental hygiene.

Our thoughts are like food that can nourish us or make us sick. We're the farmers, the cooks—and the ones who have to eat the meal.

Cognitive techniques (chap. 23), positive suggestions (chap. 27), and/or healing imagery (chap. 28) can help create an internal atmosphere of nourishingly constructive and compassionate thoughts. It's not necessary to deny difficult realities. But it's essential not to let them bury us under a mountain of negative rumination.

Open up.

Whether to a confidante, a therapist, or even a journal, expressing how you feel—telling your story—is as essential for mental health as breathing. If you're "plugged," bodywork (chap. 17), psychotherapy, and the healing arts (chap. 29) are some things that can help.

Cultivate your spirituality.

The fourteenth Dalai Lama of Tibet is a Buddhist, and therefore an atheist. Yet few would doubt his dynamic spirituality.

Spirituality is the dimension of our personality that breathes the fine air of meaning, value, and purpose. The more we inhale and exhale it in our daily lives, the less fitting hosts we become for depression. Although crises of meaning, value, or purpose may befall us, resulting in that ebb of the spirit we call depression, the answer is to breathe spirit even deeper, not to hold our breath or rummage frantically for a gas mask. (Don't rely solely on spirit, however, if your depressive crisis is severe.)

Try to find at least one potent antidepressant that works for you.

You probably won't have to use it (or them) all the time, if you're following a balanced diet of other antidepressants. But it's a lifejacket you should have on hand.

No antidepressant program, no matter how great, will succeed if you can't follow it. That's why it's important (in keeping with our culinary theme) not to bite off more than you can chew. So start easy, and think "baby steps."

For most of us, that can mean taking pills, although not so many that we can't keep track of them. It can mean easing into an exercise routine every day or two. It can mean taking one or two breaks a day to relax, meditate, or otherwise "re-create." It can mean making basic brain-friendly modifications to our diet, deferring the more demanding reforms for later. It can mean adding an hour or two of sleep every twenty-four hours if we've been pushing ourselves to function on less than we need.

The chances are good that if you take just a few such steps, within weeks you'll be feeling substantially better—perhaps even well. You'll then be strong enough to raise the bar, if necessary, and go for the gold of a complete and lasting recovery.

But if you're not feeling better after a month or two, discouragement can arise, making the effort much more difficult. Now more than ever, it can be crucial to have one or more strong and caring people to support you. Reaching out for that help may require a special effort if you don't have anyone of the sort nearby. If you're not receiving professional care, this could be the time to seek it out. If your depression is severe—or threatening to become so—you owe it to "the well person inside you dying to get out" to seek professional help as soon as possible.

After a month or two (at most), any pills you're taking should be at or near their maximum dosage, in which case lack of improvement argues for trying alternatives or adjuncts. For example, if you started with St. John's wort, you could switch to or add phenylalanine or tyrosine in the morning and tryptophan or 5-HTP at night (barring any contraindications). Or you could ask your doctor to add some thyroid, lithium, or (if indicated) natural steroid hormone(s) like estrogen or DHEA. (Of course, you must always be mindful of possible adverse interactions.) If you've been exercising every day or two, you could add other strategies like supplements, acupuncture, or bibliotherapy with a self-help book that appeals to you. There is no shortage of possibilities, and your perseverance is sure to be rewarded.

Here are just a few more practical and tactical suggestions:

⤳ Review chapter 22 on being more active to become less depressed and chapter 25 on creative problem solving. Most of the ideas on brainstorming, planning and scheduling activities, rewarding yourself, and so on are highly applicable to designing and maintaining your natural antidepressant program.

⤳ Be patient. When you've been depressed for a long time, recovery is usually a slow, bumpy process—two steps forward, one step back. The backward steps can be bitterly disappointing and threaten your progress if you "catastrophize" and believe they're permanent. They very rarely are, although major retooling may be necessary if your recovery really stalls. Similarly, if you plateau at a partial level of recovery, don't give up: Keep pushing for the gold.

⤳ After you've recovered, continue following your complete program for at least a few months to prevent relapse. Then, if you like, you can take a month or two to scale down to a lighter maintenance program to prevent recurrences. Continuing full-strength, however, will afford the most protection if you have a history of many major depressions.

⤳ If you don't feel up to "doing the program thing" just yet, just do whatever you can. Pick an antidepressant, any antidepressant (unless it's contraindicated, of course)!

Well, that's it. School's out! We've finally arrived at the end of our journey together. From here on, the journey for you should get better and better. No matter how hard it may be to believe that, the odds are solidly in your favor.

So, as someone who has been there—and probably will again before my time is up—I wish you freedom from depression (except for when you really need a small dose) and the energy and freedom to be the best "you" you can be.

Rating the Antidepressants

LEGEND
✓ a good to excellent bet
○ a moderately good bet
✚ little or no scientific evidence—but may be worth a try
✳ could be a good choice for certain subgroups of people with depressive or bipolar disorders, as noted in the relevant chapters
❏ not enough known about long-term safety to give an unequivocal thumbs-up for use as a maintenance therapy: best to use long-term only if you must

Antidepressant Treatment or Intervention	As Sole or Major Acute Treatment	As Adjunct/ Augmentor or "Team Player"	As Maintenance and Prevention Strategy
Complete medical examination	✳	✓	As needed
Hormones			
thyroid hormones	✳	✓	❏
DHEA	✳ ○	○	❏
pregnenolone	✳	○	❏
estrogen	✳	✳	❏
progesterone	✳	✳	❏
testosterone	✳	✳	❏
Allergic depression	✳	○	○
Toxic depression	✳	✓	✓
Candida syndrome	✳	✳	✳
Mercury amalgam dental fillings	✳	○	○
Negative ions	✳	○	○
Orthomolecular and Nutritional Approaches			
medium- to high-potency multi-vitamin and mineral supplement	○	✓	✓
vitamin B$_1$*	✚	○	○
vitamin B$_2$*	✚	○	○
vitamin B$_3$: niacin or NADH*	○	○	○
vitamin B$_6$*	✳	○	○

Orthomolecular and Nutritional Approaches *(continued)*

folic acid*	○	✓	✓
vitamin B$_{12}$*	✳ ○	○	○
vitamin C*	○	○	○
vitamin E*	✚	✚	✚
balancing sodium and potassium	✳ ○	✓	✓
magnesium*	✳ ○	✓	✓
calcium*	✳ ✚	✳	✳
calcium restriction (for mania and bipolar disorder)	✚	○	○
zinc*	✳	✳	?
iron*	✳	✳	?
selenium*	○	✓	✓
lithium	✓ (bipolar) ○ (unipolar depression)	✓	❏
rubidium	✓	✓	❏
omega-3 fatty acids	○	✓	✓
gamma-linolenic acid	✳	○	○
a good-fat diet	○	✓	✓
SAMe	✓	✓	❏
methionine	○	○	❏
tryptophan	○ ✓ (winter depression)	○	❏
5-HTP	✓	✓	❏
tyrosine	✓	✓	❏
L-phenylalanine	✓	✓	❏
DL-phenlylalanine	✓	✓	❏
GABA	✳	✳	❏
glycine	✳	✳	❏
threonine	✳	✳	❏
L-dopa	✳	✳	❏
choline, lecithin	○ (mania)	✓ (mania, bipolar)	✓ (bipolar)
inositol	○	○	○ (also for bipolar)

Orthomolecular and Nutritional Approaches (continued)

acetylcarnitine, carnitine	O	O	❏
phosphatidylserine	O	O	❏
euglycemic diet	✳	✓	✓
a wholesome antidepressant diet	✚	✓	✓

Herbal Antidepressants

St. John's wort	✓	✓	❏
Ginkgo biloba	✳ ✚	O	❏
ginseng	✳ ✚	O	❏
gotu kola	✚		❏
kava kava	✚	O	❏
other herbs	✳ ✚	O	❏
Aromatherapy	O (for very mild depression or "the blues")	O	O
Homeopathy	✚	O	O
Bach Flower Remedies	✚ O (for very mild depression or "the blues")	O	O

Healing Fields

rTMS	✓	✓	?
Magnet therapy	✚	✚	✚
CES	O	O	O
Bright light therapy	✓ (winter depression) O (nonseasonal depression)	✓	✓
Dawn simulation	O (winter depression)	O (winter depression)	O (winter depression)
Darkness therapy	O (bipolar, mania)	O (bipolar, mania)	O (bipolar, mania)
Cold therapy	✳ ✚ (summer depression)	O	O
Heat therapy	✚ (mania)	✚ (mania)	As needed
Sleep therapy	✳	✳	As needed
Sleep deprivation	O (especially if repeated periodically)	✓	O (especially if repeated periodically)

Healing Fields (continued)

Circadian rhythm therapy	✚	✓	✓
Exercise	✓ (mild to moderate depression) ○ (severe depression)	✓	✓

Bodywork

massage	✚	○	○
medical orgonomy (Reichian analysis)	○ (mild depression)	○	○
bioenergetic therapy	○ (mild depression)	○	○
Rolfing (structural integration)	○ (mild depression)	○	○
Alexander technique	○ (mild depression)	○	○
Hatha yoga	○ (mild depression)	○	○
good breathing	✚	○	○
T'ai chi or qigong	✚ ○ (mild depression)	○	○
acupuncture	✓	✓	✓
therapeutic touch	✚ ○ (mild or brief depression)	○	○
Relaxation techniques	○ (mild to moderate depression)	✓	✓
Meditation	○ (mild to moderate depression)	✓	✓

Psychotherapies and Psychotherapeutic Practices

being more active	○ (mild to moderate depression)	✓	✓
cognitive therapy	✓ (mostly for mild to moderate depression)	✓	✓
problem-solving therapy	✓ (mostly for mild to moderate depression)	✓	✓

other cognitive-behavioral therapies (including CB-marital therapy and assertiveness/social-skills training)	✓ (mostly for mild to moderate depression)	✓ ✓	✓ ✓
interpersonal psychotherapy	✓ (mild to moderate depression)	✓	✓
brief dynamic (analytic) psychotherapy	○ (mostly for mild to moderate depression)	○	
supportive psychotherapy	○ (mostly for mild to moderate depression)	○	○
other psychotherapies (psychoanalysis, gestalt therapy, etc.)	✚	○	○
bibliotherapy (using cognitive-behavioral books)	✓ (mild to moderate depression)	✓	✓
bibliotherapy (using other books)	✚ ○ (mild depression)	○	○
talking to someone	✚ ○ (mild depression)	✓	✓
spirituality	✚	○	✓
support groups	✚ ○ (mild depression)	✓	✓
pet therapy	✚	✓	✓
word medicine (suggestion and affirmations)	✚ ○ (mild depression)	✓	✓
therapeutic imagery	✚ ○ (mild depression)	✓	✓
the healing arts	○ (mild depression)	✓	✓
antidepressant drugs	✓	✓	❏
ECT (Electro-convulsive Therapy)	✓	✚	❏

* These ratings are for doses larger than those obtained by taking a medium- to high-potency multivitamin and mineral supplement.

References

Abbey, L. C. "Agoraphobia." *Journal of Orthomolecular Psychiatry* 11, no. 4 (1982): 243–259.

Abou-Saleh, M. T., and A. Coppen. "The Biology of Folate in Depression: Implications for Nutritional Hypotheses of the Psychoses." *Journal of Psychiatric Research* 20, no. 2 (1986): 91–101.

Abraham, G. E. "Nutritional Factors in the Etiology of the Premenstrual Tension Syndromes." *Journal of Reproductive Medicine* 28 (1983): 446–464.

Addy, D. P. "Happiness Is: Iron." *British Medical Journal* 292 (April 12, 1986): 969–970.

Airola, Paavo. *Hypoglycemia: A Better Approach.* Phoenix, AZ: Health Plus Publishers, 1977.

Alexander, C. N., et al. "Transcendental Meditation, Mindfulness, and Longevity: An Experimental Study with the Elderly." *Journal of Personality and Social Psychology* 57 (December 1989): 950–964.

Alvir, J. M., and S. Thys-Jacobs. "Premenstrual and Menstrual Symptom Clusters and Response to Calcium Treatment." *Psychopharmacology Bulletin* 27, no. 2 (1991): 145–148.

American Psychiatric Association. *Task Force Report #7: Megavitamin and Orthomolecular Therapy in Psychiatry.* Washington, D.C.: American Psychiatric Association, 1973.

Amodio, J. V. "Mood Makers." *Good Housekeeping* 227 (November 1998): 53.

Ananth, J., and R. Yassa. "Magnesium in Mental Illness." *Comprehensive Psychiatry* 20 (September/October 1979): 475–482.

Andreev, B. V. *Sleep Therapy in the Neuroses.* New York: Consultants Bureau, 1960.

Anisman, H., and R. M. Zacharko. "Depression as a Consequence of Inadequate Neurochemical Adaptation in Response to Stressors." *British Journal of Psychiatry* 15 (Supplement, February 1992): 36–43.

Anon. "Inositol Hexaniacinate." *Alternative Medicine Review* 3 (June 1998): 222–223.

APA Task Force on Meditation. "Position Statement on Meditation." *American Journal of Psychiatry* 134 (June 1977): 720.

Appleton, William. *Prozac and the New Antidepressants.* New York: Plume, 1997.

Arneson, Mary. "Regulatory Weakness Cost 'Grandma' the Use of Her Right Side, and I'd Like to Know Why." *Minneapolis Star-Tribune,* November 19, 1997.

Aronson, R, et al. "Triiodothyronine Augmentation in the Treatment of Refractory Depression: A Meta-analysis." *Archives of General Psychiatry* 53 (September 1996): 842–848.

Assagioli, Roberto. *Psychosynthesis.* Harmondsworth, Middlesex, England: Penguin, 1976.

Astin, J. A. "Stress Reduction Through Mindfulness Meditation: Effects on Psychological Symptomatology, Sense of Control, and Spiritual Experiences." *Psychotherapy and Psychosomatics* 66, no. 2 (1997): 97–106.

Atkins, Robert C. *Dr. Atkins' Health Revelations* 3 (June 1995).

Avery, D. H., et al. "Dawn Simulation Treatment of Winter Depression: A Controlled Study." *American Journal of Psychiatry* 150 (January 1993): 113–117.

Azorin, J. M., et al. "L-Tyrosine and L-Tryptophan Membrane Transport in Erythrocytes and Antidepressant Drug Choice." *Biological Psychiatry* 27 (April 1990): 723–734.

Baldewicz, T., et al. "Plasma Pyridoxine Deficiency Is Related to Increased Psychological Distress in Recently Bereaved Homosexual Men." *Psychosomatic Medicine* 60 (May–June, 1998): 297–308.

Baker, E. L., et al. "Environmentally Related Disorders of the Nervous System." *Medical Clinics of North America* 74 (March 1990): 325–345.

Baker, E. R., et al. "Efficacy of Progesterone Vaginal Suppositories in Alleviation of Nervous Symptoms in Patients with Premenstrual Syndrome." *Journal of Assisted Reproduction and Genetics* 12 (March 1995): 205–209.

Baldessarini, R. J., et al. "Effects of Lithium Treatment and Its Discontinuation on Suicidal Behavior in Bipolar Manic-Depressive Disorders." *Journal of Clinical Psychiatry* 60, no. 2 (Supplement, 1999): 77–84.

Ballentine, Rudolph M. *Diet and Nutrition: A Holistic Approach.* Honesdale, PA: Himalayan Institute Press, 1979.

Balslev Jorgenson, M., et al. "The Efficacy of Psychotherapy in Non-Bipolar Depression: A Review." *Acta Psychiatrica Scandinavica* 98 (July 1998): 1–13.

Banki, C. M., et al. "Aminergic Studies and Cerebrospinal Fluid Cations in Suicide." *Annals of the New York Academy of Sciences* 487 (1986): 221–230.

Barabasz, A., and M. Barabasz, eds. *Clinical and Experimental Restricted Environmental Stimulation.* New York: Springer, 1993.

Barlow, Wilfred. *The Alexander Principle,* rev. ed. London: Gollancz, 1990.

Barnes, Broda. *Hypothyroidism: The Unsuspected Illness.* New York: Thomas Y. Crowell, 1976.

Basch, Michael Franz. *Understanding Psychotherapy: The Science Behind the Art.* New York: Basic Books, 1988.

Bassman, Lynette, ed. *The Whole Mind.* Novato, CA: New World Library, 1998.

Bates, C. E. "Racially Determined Abnormal Essential Fatty Acid and Prostaglandin Metabolism and Food Allergies Linked to Autoimmune, Inflammatory, and Psychiatric Disorders Among Coastal British Columbia Indians." *Medical Hypotheses* 25 (1988): 103–109.

Bauer, M., et al. "Treatment of Refractory Depression with High-Dose Thyroxine." *Neuropsychopharmacology* 18 (June 1998): 444–455.

Baumel, Syd. *Natural Antidepressants.* Los Angeles: Keats Publishing, 1999.

———. "New Light on Light Therapy: You Don't Have to Be SAD to Benefit." *The Aquarian* 5 (Winter 1998): 1, 12–14. Also published online at www.aquarianonline.com.

———. *Serotonin: How to Naturally Harness the Power Behind Prozac and Phen/Fen.* Los Angeles: Keats Publishing, 1997.

Beard, T. C., et al. "Randomised Controlled Trial of No-Added-Sodium Diet for Mild Hypertension" *Lancet* (August 28, 1982): 455–458.

Beck, Aaron T. *Love Is Never Enough.* New York: Harper & Row, 1988.

Beck, Alan, and Aaron Katcher. *Between Pets and People: The Importance of Animal Companionship.* New York: Putnam's, 1983.

Beckmann, H. "Phenylalanine in Affective Disorders." *Advances in Biological Psychiatry* 10 (1983): 137–147.

Behan, P. O., et al. "Effect of High Doses of Essential Fatty Acids on the Postviral Fatigue Syndrome." *Acta Neurologica Scandinavica* 82 (September 1990): 209–216.

Bell, I. R. "Allergens, Physical Irritants, Depression, and Shyness." *Journal of Applied Developmental Psychology* 13 (April–June 1992): 125–133.

Bell, I. R., et al. "Vitamin B_1, B_2, and B_6 Augmentation of Tricyclic Antidepressant Treatment in Geriatric Depression with Cognitive Dysfunction." *Journal of the American College of Nutrition* 11 (April 1992): 159–163.

Bell, I. R., et al. "Vitamin B_{12} and Folate Status in Acute Geropsychiatric Inpatients." *Biological Psychiatry* 27 (January 15, 1990): 125–137.

Bell, K. M., et al. "S-Adenosylmethionine Treatment of Depression: A Controlled Clinical Trial." *American Journal of Psychiatry* 145 (September 1988): 1110–1114.

Bella, R., et al. "Effect of Acetyl-L-Carnitine on Geriatric Patients Suffering from Dysthymic Disorders." *International Journal of Clinical and Pharmacological Research* 10, no. 6 (1990): 355–360.

Bellack, A. S., et al. "A Comparison of Social-Skills Training, Pharmacotherapy and Psychotherapy for Depression." *Behavior Research and Therapy* 21, no. 2 (1983): 101–107.

Bellak, Leopold, ed. *Disorders of the Schizophrenic Syndrome.* New York: Basic Books, 1979.

Belmaker, R. H., et al. "Behavioral Reversal of Lithium Effects by Four Inositol Isomers Correlates Perfectly with Biochemical Effects on the PI Cycle: Depletion by Chronic Lithium of Brain Inositol Is Specific to Hypothalamus, and Inositol Levels May Be Abnormal in Postmortem Brain from Bipolar Patients." *Neuropsychopharmacology* 19 (September 1998): 220–232.

Benedetti, F., et al. "Ongoing Lithium Treatment Prevents Relapse After Total Sleep Deprivation." *Journal of Clinical Psychopharmacology* 19 (June 1999): 240–245.

Benson, Herbert, with Marg Stark. *Timeless Healing.* New York: Fireside, 1996.

Benton, D., et al. "Thiamine Supplementation Improves Mood and Cognitive Functioning." *Psychopharmacology (Berlin)* 129 (January 1997): 66–71.

Benton, D., et al. "Vitamin Supplementation for 1 Year Improves Mood." *Neuropsychobiology* 32, no. 2 (1995): 98–105.

Benton, D., and R. Cook. "The Impact of Selenium Supplementation on Mood." *Biological Psychiatry* 29 (June 1, 1991): 1092–1098.

Berger, Diane, et al. *We Heard the Angels of Madness: A Family Guide to Coping with Manic Depression.* New York: Quill, 1992.

Berger, M., et al. "Sleep Deprivation Combined with Consecutive Sleep Phase Advance as a Fast-acting Therapy in Depression: An Open Pilot Trial in Medicated and Unmedicated Patients." *American Journal of Psychiatry* 154 (June 1997): 870–872.

Berube, B. "Depression, Virus Link." *Medical Post* 23 (June 2, 1987): 1, 12.

Birkmayer, W., et al. "L-Deprenyl Plus L-Phenylalanine in the Treatment of Depression." *Journal of Neural Transmission* 59 (January 1984): 81–87.

Blackburn, I. M., and R. G. Moore. "Controlled Acute and Follow-Up Trial of Cognitive Therapy and Pharmacotherapy in Out-Patients with Recurrent Depression." *British Journal of Psychiatry* 171 (October 1997): 328–334.

Blauvelt, A., and V. Falanga. "Idiopathic and L-Tryptophan-Associated Eosinophilic Fasciitis Before and After L-Tryptophan Contamination." *Archives of Dermatology* 127 (August 1991): 1159–1166.

Bloch, Douglas. *Words That Heal: Affirmations & Meditations for Daily Living.* New York: Bantam, 1988.

Bloch, M., et al. "Dehydroepiandrosterone Treatment of Midlife Dysthymia." *Biological Psychiatry* 45 (June 15, 1999): 1533–1541.

Blonz, E. R. "Is There an Epidemic of Chronic Candidiasis in Our Midst?" *Journal of the American Medical Association* 256 (December 12, 1986): 3138–3139.

Bloomfield, Harold H., and Peter McWilliams. *Hypericum & Depression.* Prelude Press, 1997. Also published online at hypericum.com.

Bloomfield, Harold H., et al. *TM: Discovering Inner Energy and Overcoming Stress.* New York: Dell, 1975.

Booth, A., et al. "Testosterone and Men's Depression: The Role of Social Behavior." *Journal of Health and Social Behavior* 40 (June 1999): 130–140.

Bourgoin, B. P., et al. "Lead Content in 70 Brands of Dietary Calcium Supplements." *American Journal of Public Health* 83 (August 1993): 1155–1160.

Bowers, W. A. "Treatment of Depressed In-Patients: Cognitive Therapy Plus Medication, Relaxation Plus Medication, and Medication Alone." *British Journal of Psychiatry* 156 (January 1990): 73–78.

Braam, A. W., et al. "Religiosity as a Protective or Prognostic Factor of Depression in Later Life: Results from a Community Survey in The Netherlands." *Acta Psychiatrica Scandinavica* 96 (September 1997): 199–205.

Bratel, J., et al. "Potential Side Effects of Dental Amalgam Restorations. (II). No Relation Between Mercury Levels in the Body and Mental Disorders." *European Journal of Oral Sciences* 105 (June 1997): 244–250.

Braverman, Eric. R., et al. *The Healing Nutrients Within.* New Canaan, CT: Keats Publishing, 1997.

Breneman, James C. *Basics of Food Allergy,* 2d ed. Springfield, IL.: Charles C Thomas, 1984.

Brent, D. A., et al. "A Clinical Psychotherapy Trial for Adolescent Depression Comparing Cognitive, Family, and Supportive Therapy." *Archives of General Psychiatry* 54 (September 1997): 877–885.

Bressa, G. M. "S-Adenosyl-L-Methionine (SAMe) as Antidepressant: Meta-Analysis of Clinical Studies." *Acta Neurologica Scandinavica—Supplement* 154 (1994): 7–14.

British Herbal Medicine Association. *British Herbal Pharmacopoeia 1972.* London: British Herbal Medicine Association, 1971.

Brostoff, Jonathan, and Linda Gamlin. *The Complete Guide to Food Allergy and Intolerance*. New York: Crown, 1989.

Brown, D. R., et al. "Chronic Psychological Effects of Exercise and Exercise plus Cognitive Strategies." *Medicine and Science in Sports and Exercise* 27 (May 1995): 765–775.

Brown, M., et al. "Food Allergy in Polysymptomatic Patients." *Practitioner* 225 (November 1981): 1651–1654.

Brown, Richard, Teodoro Bottiglieri, and Carol Colman. *Stop Depression Now*. New York: Putnam's, 1999.

Brown, R. S., et al. "The Prescription of Exercise for Depression." *Physician and Sportsmedicine* 6 (December 1978): 34–45.

Brush, M. G., and M. Perry. "Pyridoxine and the Premenstrual Syndrome." *Lancet* (June 15, 1985): 1399.

Brusov, O. S., et al. "Thrombocytic Serotonergic Markers in Therapy-Resistant Patients with Endogenous Depression Undergoing Alpha-Tocopherol Treatment" (in Russian). *Zhurnal Nevropatology Psikhiatrii Imeni S. S. Korsakova* 95, no. 6 (1995): 72–76.

Bryce-Smith, D., and R. I. D. Simpson. "Anorexia, Depression, and Zinc Deficiency." *Lancet* (November 17, 1984): 1162.

Bryce-Smith, D., and R. Stephens. "Sources and Effects of Environmental Lead." In *Trace Elements in Health*, edited by J. Rose, 83–131. Stoneham, MA: Butterworths, 1983.

Buchanan, T. W., et al. "Cortisol Fluctuates with Increases and Decreases in Negative Affect." *Psychoneuroendocrinology* 24 (February 1999): 227–241.

Buchbauer, G., et al. "Fragrance Compounds and Essential Oils with Sedative Effects upon Inhalation." *Journal of Pharmaceutical Sciences* 82 (June 1993): 660–664.

Bump, G. M., et al. "Accelerating Response in Geriatric Depression: A Pilot Study Combining Sleep Deprivation and Paroxetine." *Depression and Anxiety* 6, no. 3 (1997): 113–118.

Burke, E. "NADH Energizes Mental and Physical Performance." *Nutrition Science News* (January 1998). Published online at www.nutritionsciencenews.com/NSN_backs/Jan_98/nadh.html.

Burns, David D. *The Feeling Good Handbook*. New York: Plume, 1999.

———. *Feeling Good: The New Mood Therapy*. New York: New American Library, 1980.

Burton, Robert. *The Anatomy of Melancholy*. Kila, MT: Kessinger Publishing, 1997.

Calabrese, J. R., et al. "Fish Oils and Bipolar Disorder: A Promising but Untested Treatment." *Archives of General Psychiatry* 56 (May 1999): 413–414.

Cannard, G. "The Effect of Aromatherapy in Promoting Relaxation and Stress Reduction in a General Hospital." *Complementary Therapies in Nursing and Midwifery* 2 (April 1996): 38–40.

Cappiello, A., et al. "Yohimbine Augmentation of Fluvoxamine in Refractory Depression: A Single-Blind Study." *Biological Psychiatry* 38 (1995): 765–767.

Carman, J. S., et al. "Calcium and Calcitonin in Bipolar Affective Disorder." In *Neurobiology of Mood Disorders*, edited by Robert M. Post and James C. Ballenger, 340–355. Baltimore: Williams & Wilkins, 1984.

Carney, M. W. P., et al. "Thiamine, Riboflavin and Pyridoxine Deficiency in Psychiatric Inpatients." *British Journal of Psychiatry* 141 (1982): 271–272.

Carrington, P., et al. "The Use of Meditation-Relaxation Techniques for the Management of Stress in a Working Population." *Journal of Occupational Medicine* 22 (April 1980): 221–231.

Carrington, Patricia. *Freedom in Meditation*. Garden City, NY: Anchor Press, 1977.

Cass, Hyla. *St. John's Wort: Nature's Blues Buster*. Garden City Park, NY: Avery Publishing Group, 1998.

Castleman, Michael. *The Healing Herbs*. Emmaus, PA: Rodale Press, 1991.

Cawthorne, J. "Healing Words." *The Aquarian* 6 (Fall 1999): 1, 12–15. Also published online at www.aquarianonline.com.

Chandler, J. D., and J. E. Gerndt. "The Role of the Medical Evaluation in Psychiatric Inpatients." *Psychosomatics* 29 (Fall 1988): 410–416.

Chang, Edward C., trans. *Knocking at the Gate of Life and Other Healing Exercises from China: The Official Handbook of the People's Republic of China*. Emmaus, PA: Rodale Press, 1985.

Charlton, C. G., and B. Crowell, Jr. "Striatal Dopamine Depletion, Tremors, and Hypokinesia Following the Intracranial Injection of S-adenosylmethionine: A Possible Role of Hyper-methylation in Parkinsonism." *Molecular and Chemical Neuropathology* 26 (December 1995): 269–284.

Charney, D. S., et al. "Desipramine-Yohimbine Combination Treatment of Refractory Depression: Implications for the Beta-adrenergic Receptor Hypothesis of Antidepressant Action." *Archives of General Psychiatry* 43 (December 1986): 1155–1161.

Chouinard, G., et al. "A Pilot Study of Magnesium Aspartate Hydrochloride (Magnesiocard) as a Mood Stabilizer for Rapid Cycling Bipolar Affective Disorder Patients." *Progress in Neuro-Psychopharmacology and Biological Psychiatry* 14, no. 2 (1990): 171–180.

Chouinard, G., et al. "Estrogen-Progesterone Combination: Another Mood Stabilizer?" (letter). *American Journal of Psychiatry* 144 (June 1987): 826.

Chouinard, G., et al. "A Controlled Clinical Trial of L-Tryptophan in Acute Mania." *Biological Psychiatry* 20 (May 1985): 546–557.

Christensen, Larry. "Food and Mood: The Sugar- and Caffeine-Free Diet for Depression." In Bassman, 1998, pp. 273–284.

Christensen, L., et al. "Dietary Alteration of Somatic Symptoms and Regional Brain Electrical Activity." *Biological Psychiatry* 29 (April 1, 1991): 679–682.

Christensen, L., et al. "Impact of a Dietary Change on Emotional Distress." *Journal of Abnormal Psychology* 94 (November 1985): 565–579.

Cleary, John P. "The NAD Deficiency Diseases." *Journal of Orthomolecular Medicine* 1, no. 3 (1986): 149–157.

Cohen, A. J., and B. Bartlik. "Ginkgo Biloba for Antidepressant-Induced Sexual Dysfunction." *Journal of Sex and Marital Therapy* 24 (April–June 1998): 139–143.

Cohen, B. M., et al. "Lecithin in the Treatment of Mania: Double-Blind, Placebo-Controlled Trials." *American Journal of Psychiatry* 139 (September 1982): 1162–1164.

Cohen, Kenneth S. *The Way of Qigong*. New York: Ballantine Books, 1997.

Cohen, Sherry Suib. *The Magic of Touch*. New York: Harper & Row, 1987.

Conca, A., et al. "Transcranial Magnetic Stimulation: A Novel Antidepressive Strategy?" *Neuropsychobiology* 34 (1996): 204–207.

Conners, C. Keith. *Food Additives and Hyperactive Children*. New York: Plenum Press, 1980.

Connor, D. J. "Thiamine Intake and Monoamine Oxidase Activity." *Biological Psychiatry* 16 (September 1981): 869–872.

Cooke, R. G., et al. "T_3 Augmentation of Antidepressant Treatment in T_4-Replaced Thyroid Patients." *Journal of Clinical Psychiatry* 53 (January 1992): 16–18.

Copeland, Mary Ellen. *The Depression Handbook*. Oakland, CA: New Harbinger, 1992.

Coppen, A. J. "The Chemical Pathology of the Affective Disorders." In *The Scientific Basis of Medicine Annual Reviews*, 189–210. London: Athlone Press, 1970.

Coppen, A., et al. "Folic Acid Enhances Lithium Prophylaxis." *Journal of Affective Disorders* 10 (January–February 1986): 9–13.

Coppen, A., et al. "Potentiation of the Antidepressive Effect of a Monoamine-Oxidase Inhibitor by Tryptophan." *Lancet* 1 (1963): 79–81.

Corvaglia, L., et al. "Depression in Adult Untreated Celiac Subjects: Diagnosis by the Pediatrician." *American Journal of Gastroenterology* 94 (March 1999): 839–843.

Cousins, Norman. *Anatomy of an Illness as Perceived by the Patient*. New York: Bantam Doubleday Dell, 1991 (reissue of the 1979 original).

Cowley, Geoffrey. "The 'Sammy' Solution." *Newsweek* (March 22, 1999).

Cox, I. M., et al. "Red Blood Cell Magnesium and Chronic Fatigue Syndrome." *Lancet* 337 (March 30, 1991): 757–760.

Cracchiolo, Camilla. "FAQ on St. Johns Wort (Hypericum Perforatum and Hypericum Augustifolia), V. 3.1k." December 10, 1998. Published online at www.primenet.com/~camilla/STJOHNS.FAQ.

Crayton, J. W. "Effects of Food Challenges on Complement Components in 'Food-Sensitive' Psychiatric Patients and Controls." *Journal of Allergy and Clinical Immunology* 73 (Supplement 1, 1984): 134.

Cronkite, Kathy. *On the Edge of Darkness.* New York: Doubleday, 1994.

Crook, William G. *The Yeast Connection.* New York: Vintage, 1986.

Cuijpers, P. "Bibliotherapy in Unipolar Depression: A Meta-Analysis." *Journal of Behavior Therapy and Experimental Psychiatry* 28 (June 1997): 139–147.

Culliton, B. J. "Take Two Pets and Call Me in the Morning." *Science* 237 (September 1987): 1560–1561.

Cusack, Odean, and Elaine Smith. *Pets and the Elderly: The Therapeutic Bond.* New York: Haworth Press, 1984.

Cutler, P. "Iron Overload and Psychiatric Illness." *Canadian Journal of Psychiatry* 39 (February 1994): 8–11.

Czeisler, C. A., et al. "Bright Light Induction of Strong (Type O) Resetting of the Human Circadian Pacemaker." *Science* 244 (June 16, 1989): 1328–1333.

Dadd, Debra Lynn. *The Nontoxic Home.* Los Angeles: Tarcher, 1986.

Daiss, S. R., et al. "Napping versus Resting: Effects on Performance and Mood." *Psychophysiology* 23, no. 1 (1986): 82.

Davidson, J. R., et al. "Homeopathic Treatment of Depression and Anxiety." *Alternative Therapies in Health and Medicine* 3 (January 1997): 46–49.

Davis, Martha, et al. *The Relaxation & Stress Reduction Workbook,* 3d ed. Oakland, CA: New Harbinger Publications, 1988.

Dean, Ward. "VRP's Response to Flawed Androstenedione Study in *JAMA.*" *Vitamin Research News* (July 1999): 1, 7, 11. Available online at www.vrp.com.

Demott, K. "Tolerability Is Similar for Tricyclics, SSRIs." *Clinical Psychiatry News* 27, no. 5 (1999): 8.

Denicoff, K. D., et al. "Glucose Tolerance Testing in Women with Premenstrual Syndrome." *American Journal of Psychiatry* 147 (April 1990): 477–480.

Dietch, J. T., and M. Zetin. "Diagnosis of Organic Depressive Disorders." *Psychosomatics* 24 (November 1983): 971–979.

Diegoli, M. S., et al. "A Double-Blind Trial of Four Medications to Treat Severe Premenstrual Syndrome." *International Journal of Gynaecology and Obstetrics* 62 (July 1981): 63–67.

Dismukes, W. E., et al. "A Randomized, Double-Blind Trial of Nystatin Therapy for the Candidiasis Hypersensitivity Syndrome." *New England Journal of Medicine* 323 (December 20, 1990): 1717–1723.

Dodt, Coleen K. *The Essential Oils Book.* Pownal, VT: Storey Communications, 1996.

Dolberg, O. T., et al. "Melatonin for the Treatment of Sleep Disturbances in Major Depressive Disorder." *American Journal of Psychiatry* 155 (August 1998): 1119–1121.

Dommisse, J. "T_3 Is at Least as Important as T_4 in *All* Hypothyroid Patients" (letter). *Journal of Clinical Psychiatry* 54 (July 1993): 277–278.

Douillard, John. *Body, Mind, and Sport.* New York: Harmony Books, 1994.

Doyne, E. J., et al. "Running versus Weight-Lifting in the Treatment of Depression." *Journal of Consulting and Clinical Psychology* 55 (1987): 748–754.

Doyne, E. J., et al. "Aerobic Exercise as a Treatment for Depression in Women." *Behavior Therapy* 14 (1983): 434–440.

Draper, Harold H., ed. *Advances in Nutritional Research,* Vol.4. New York: Plenum, 1982.

Dubrovsky, B. "Natural Steroids Counteracting Some Actions of Putative Depressogenic Steroids on the Central Nervous System: Potential Therapeutic Benefits." *Medical Hypotheses* 49 (July 1997): 51–55.

Dunn, C., et al. "Sensing an Improvement: Experimental Study to Evaluate the Use of Aromatherapy, Massage and Periods of Rest in an Intensive Care Unit." *Journal of Advanced Nursing* 21 (January 1995): 34–40.

Dunner, D. L., et al. "Cognitive Therapy versus Fluoxetine in the Treatment of Dysthymic Disorder." *Depression* 4, no. 1 (1996): 34–41.

D'Zurilla, Thomas J., and Arthur Nezu. *Problem-Solving Therapy*. New York: Springer, 1986, 1999.

Easwaran, Eknath. *The Mantram Handbook*. Berkeley, CA: Nilgiri Press, 1977.

Echeverria, D., et al. "Neurobehavioral Effects from Exposure to Dental Amalgam Hg(o): New Distinctions Between Recent Exposure and Hg Body Burden." *FASEB Journal* 12 (August 1998): 971–980.

Eckmann, F. "Cerebral Insufficiency—Treatment with Ginkgo-Biloba Extract: Time of Onset of Effect in a Double-Blind Study with 60 Inpatients" (in German). *Fortschritte der Medizin* 108 (October 10, 1990): 557–560.

The Editors of East West. *Meetings with Remarkable Men and Women*. Brookline, MA: East West Health Books, 1989.

Edwards, D. A. "Depression and Candida" (letter). *Journal of the American Medical Association* 253 (June 21, 1985): 3400.

Edwards, N. "Mental Disturbances Related to Metals." In *Psychiatric Presentations of Medical Illness*, edited by Richard C. W. Hall, 283–308. Jamaica, NY: Spectrum Publications, 1980.

Edwards, R., et al. "Omega-3 Polyunsaturated Fatty Acid Levels in the Diet and in Red Blood Cell Membranes of Depressed Patients." *Journal of Affective Disorders* 48 (March 1998): 149–155.

Egger, J., et al. "Controlled Trial of Hyposensitisation in Children with Food-Induced Hyperkinetic Syndrome." *Lancet* 339 (May 9, 1992): 1150–1153.

Egger, J., et al. "Oligoantigenic Diet Treatment of Children with Epilepsy and Migraine." *Journal of Pediatrics* 114 (January 1989): 51–58.

Eifert, G. H., et al. "Affect Modification Through Evaluative Conditioning with Music." *Behavior Research and Therapy* 26, no. 4 (1988): 321–330.

Eischens, R. R., and J. H. Greist. "Beginning and Continuing Running: Steps to Psychological Well-Being." In *Running as Therapy*, edited by Michael L. Sachs and Gary W. Buffone, 63–82. Lincoln: University of Nebraska Press, 1984.

Ellis, Albert. *How to Stubbornly Refuse to Make Yourself Miserable About Anything—Yes, Anything*. New York: Carol Publishing, 1988.

Ellis, F. R., and S. Nasser. "A Pilot Study of Vitamin B_{12} in the Treatment of Tiredness." *British Journal of Nutrition* 30 (1973): 277–283.

Emanuels-Zuurveen, L., and P. M. Emmelkamp. "Individual Behavioural-Cognitive Therapy v. Marital Therapy for Depression in Maritally Distressed Couples." *British Journal of Psychiatry* 169 (August 1996): 181–188.

Emery, Gary. *A New Beginning: How You Can Change Your Life Through Cognitive Therapy*. New York: Simon & Schuster, 1981.

Emslie, G. J., et al. "Nontricyclic Antidepressants: Current Trends in Children and Adolescents." *Journal of the American Academy of Child and Adolescent Psychiatry* 38 (May 1999): 517–528.

Engstrom, G., et al. "Serum Lipids in Suicide Attempters." *Suicide and Life Threatening Behavior* 25 (Fall 1995): 393–400.

Enns, M. W., and J. P. Reiss. "Electroconvulsive Therapy." *Canadian Journal of Psychiatry* 37 (December 1992): 671–678.

Epstein, Gerald. *Healing Visualizations*. New York: Bantam, 1989.

Epstein, R. H. "Bodywork: TLC or Therapy?" *Vegetarian Times* 236 (April 1997): 32.

Erasmus, Udo. *Fats That Heal, Fats That Kill*. Burnaby, BC, Canada: Alive Books, 1993.

Ernst, E., et al. "Adverse Effects Profile of the Herbal Antidepressant St. John's Wort (Hypericum Perforatum L.)." *European Journal of Clinical Pharmacology* 54 (October 1998): 589–594.

Ernst, E., et al. "Complementary Therapies for Depression: An Overview." *Archives of General Psychiatry* 55 (November 1998): 1026–1032.

Esterling, B. A., et al. "Empirical Foundations for Writing in Prevention and Psychotherapy: Mental and Physical Health Outcomes." *Clinical Psychology Review* 19 (January 1999): 79–96.

Estroff, T. W., and M. S. Gold. "Psychiatric Misdiagnosis." In *Advances in Psychopharmacology: Predicting and Improving Treatment Response*, edited by Mark S. Gold, et al., 33–66. Boca Raton, FL: CRC Press, 1984.

Facchinetti, F., et al. "Oral Magnesium Successfully Relieves Premenstrual Mood Changes." *Obstetrics and Gynecology* 78 (August 1991): 177–181.

Fagala, G. E., and C. L. Wigg. "Psychiatric Manifestations of Mercury Poisoning." *Journal of the American Academy of Child and Adolescent Psychiatry* 31 (March 1992): 306–311.

Fava, G. A., et al. "Prevention of Recurrent Depression with Cognitive Behavioral Therapy: Preliminary Findings." *Archives of General Psychiatry* 55 (September 1998): 816–820.

Fava, G. A., et al. "Cognitive-Behavioral Management of Drug-Resistant Major Depressive Disorder." *Journal of Clinical Psychiatry* 58 (June 1997): 278–282.

Fava, M., et al. "The Thyrotropin Response to Thyrotropin-Releasing Hormone as a Predictor of Response to Treatment in Depressed Outpatients." *Acta Psychiatrica Scandinavica* 86 (July 1992): 42–45.

Field, T., et al. "Massage and Relaxation Therapies' Effects on Depressed Adolescent Mothers." *Adolescence* 31 (Winter 1996): 903–911.

Field, T., et al. "Massage Reduces Anxiety in Child and Adolescent Psychiatric Patients." *Journal of the American Academy of Child and Adolescent Psychiatry* 31 (January 1992): 125–131.

Fieve, Ronald. *Moodswing*, rev. ed. New York: Morrow, 1989.

Figiel, G. S., et al. "The Use of Rapid Rate Transcranial Magnetic Stimulation (rTMS) in Refractory Depressed Patients." *Journal of Neuropsychiatry and Clinical Neurosciences* 10 (Winter 1998): 20–25.

Fisch, R. Z., and A. Lahad. "Drug-Induced Suicidal Ideation." *Israeli Journal of Psychiatry and Related Sciences* 28, no. 1 (1991): 41–43.

Forsyth, L. M., et al. "Therapeutic Effects of Oral NADH on the Symptoms of Patients with Chronic Fatigue Syndrome." *Annals of Allergy, Asthma and Immunology* 82 (February 1999): 185–191.

Fox, Arnold, and Barry Fox. *DLPA to End Chronic Pain and Depression*. New York: Pocket Books, 1985.

Frankel, Paul, with Nancy Bruning. *The Methylation Miracle*. New York: St. Martin's, 1999.

Fraser, T. N., "Cerebral Manifestations of Addisonian Pernicious Anaemia." *Lancet* (August 27, 1960): 458–459.

Freeman, E. W., et al. "A Double-Blind Trial of Oral Progesterone, Alprazolam, and Placebo in Treatment of Severe Premenstrual Syndrome." *Journal of the American Medical Association* 274 (July 5, 1995): 51–57.

Freeman, E. W., et al. "Ineffectiveness of Progesterone Suppository Treatment for Premenstrual Syndrome." *Journal of the American Medical Association* 264 (July 18, 1990): 349–353.

Fremont, J., and L. W. Craighead. "Aerobic Exercise and Cognitive Therapy in the Treatment of Dysphoric Moods." *Cognitive Therapy and Research* 11, no. 2 (1987): 241–251.

Frenkel, E. P., et al. "Cerebrospinal Fluid Folate and Vitamin B_{12} in Anti-Convulsant-Induced Megaloblastosis." *Journal of Laboratory and Clinical Medicine* 81 (1973): 105–115.

Fujiwara R., et al. "Effects of a Long-Term Inhalation of Fragrances on the Stress-Induced Immunosuppression in Mice." *Neuroimmunomodulation* 5 (November–December 1998): 318–322.

Fulcher, K. Y., and P. B. White. "Randomised Controlled Trial of Graded Exercise in Patients with the Chronic Fatigue Syndrome." *British Medical Journal* 314 (June 7, 1997): 1647–1652.

Fulder, Stephen. *Ginseng: The Magical Herb of the East*. Wellingborough, Northamptonshire, England: Thorsons, 1988.

Galanter, M. "Zealous Self-Help Groups as Adjuncts to Psychiatric Treatment: A Study of Recovery, Inc." *American Journal of Psychiatry* 145 (October 1988): 1248–1253.

Gangadhar, B. N., et al. "Twice versus Thrice Weekly ECT in Melancholia: A Double-Blind Prospective Comparison." *Journal of Affective Disorders* 27 (April 1993): 273–278.

Gardos, G., et al. "The Acute Effects of a Loading Dose of Phenylalanine in Unipolar Depressed Patients with and Without Tardive Dyskinesia." *Neuropsychopharmacology* 6 (June 1992): 241–247.

Geagea, K., and J. Ananth. "Response of a Psychiatric Patient to Vitamin B_{12} Therapy." *Diseases of the Nervous System* 36 (June 1975): 343–344.

Gelenberg, A. J., et al. "Tyrosine for Depression: A Double-Blind Trial." *Journal of Affective Disorders* 19 (June 1990): 125–132.

Gelenberg, A. J., et al. "Tyrosine for Depression." *Journal of Psychiatric Research* 17, no. 2 (1982/83): 175–180.

Gelenberg, A. J., et al. "Neurotransmitter Precursors for the Treatment of Depression." *Psychopharmacology Bulletin* 18, no. 1 (1982): 7–18.

Gelenberg, A. J., et al. "Tyrosine for the Treatment of Depression." *American Journal of Psychiatry* 137 (1980): 622–623.

Gendlin, Eugene. *Focusing*. New York: Bantam, 1981.

George, M. S., et al. "Transcranial Magnetic Stimulation: Applications in Neuropsychiatry." *Archives of General Psychiatry* 56 (April 1999): 300–311.

George, M. S., et al. "Dr. George and Colleagues Reply" (letter). *American Journal of Psychiatry* 156 (April 1999): 669–670.

George, M. S., et al. "Daily Repetitive Transcranial Magnetic Stimulation (rTMS) Improves Mood in Depression." *Neuroreport* 6 (1995): 1853–1856.

George, M. S., et al. "CSF Neuroactive Steroids in Affective Disorders: Pregnenolone, Progesterone, and DBI." *Biological Psychiatry* 35 (May 15, 1994): 775–780.

George, M. S., et al. "CSF Magnesium in Affective Disorder: Lack of Correlation with Clinical Course of Treatment." *Psychiatry Research* 51 (February 1994): 139–146.

Ghadirian, A. M., et al. "Efficacy of Light Versus Tryptophan Therapy in Seasonal Affective Disorder." *Journal of Affective Disorders* 50 (July 1998): 23–27.

Gharote, M. L., and Maureen Lockhart, eds. *The Art of Survival: A Guide to Yoga Therapy*. London: Unwin Paperbacks, 1987.

Giannini, A. J., et al. "The Serotonin Irritation Syndrome—A New Clinical Entity." *Journal of Clinical Psychiatry* 47 (January 1986): 22–25.

Gittleman, Ann Louise, with J. Maxwell Desgrey. *Beyond Pritikin*. New York: Bantam, 1988.

Glueck, B. C., and C. F. Stroebel, "Biofeedback and Meditation in the Treatment of Psychiatric Illnesses." *Comprehensive Psychiatry* 16 (July/August 1975): 303–321.

Goggins, M., and D. Kelleher. "Celiac Disease and Other Nutrient-Related Injuries to the Gastrointestinal Tract." *American Journal of Gastroenterology* 89 (August—Supplement, 1994): S2–17.

Gold, Mark S., with Lois B. Morris. *The Good News About Depression*. New York: Bantam, 1987.

Gold, Mark S., et al., eds., *Advances in Psychopharmacology: Predicting and Improving Treatment Response*. Boca Raton, FL: CRC Press, 1984.

Gold, M. S., and J. S. Carman. "Thyroid Failure and Clinical Misdiagnosis." In *Advances in Psychopharmacology: Predicting and Improving Treatment Response*, edited by Mark S. Gold, et al., 67–81. Boca Raton, FL: CRC Press, 1984.

Gold, M. S., et al. "The Role of the Laboratory in Psychiatry." In *Advances in Psychopharmacology: Predicting and Improving Treatment Response*, edited by Mark S. Gold, et al., 307–317. Boca Raton, FL: CRC Press, 1984.

Gold, M. S., et al. "Hypothyroidism and Depression: Evidence from Complete Thyroid Function Evaluation." *Journal of the American Medical Association* 245 (May 15, 1981): 1919–1922.

Gold, M. S., et al. "Grades of Thyroid Failure in 100 Depressed and Anergic Psychiatric Inpatients." *American Journal of Psychiatry* 138 (February 1981): 253–255.

Goldberg, I. K. "L-Tyrosine in Depression." *Lancet* (August 16, 1980): 364–365.

Goldberg, M. "Dehydroepiandrosterone, Insulin-Like Growth Factor-I, and Prostate Cancer." *Annals of Internal Medicine* 129 (October 1, 1998): 587–588.

Goodyer, I. M., et al. "Adrenal Steroid Secretion and Major Depression in 8- to 16-Year-Olds, III: Influence of Cortisol/DHEA Ratio at Presentation on Subsequent Rates of Disappointing Life Events and Persistent Major Depression." *Psychological Medicine* 28 (March 1998): 265–273.

Gorman, Jack M. *The Essential Guide to Psychiatric Drugs.* New York: St. Martin's Press, 1990.

Gould, R. C., and V. E. Krynicki. "Comparative Effectiveness of Hypnotherapy on Different Psychological Symptoms." *American Journal of Clinical Hypnosis* 32 (October 1989): 110–117.

Greenberg, R. P., et al. "A Meta-Analysis of Antidepressant Outcome Under 'Blinder' Conditions." *Journal of Consulting and Clinical Psychology* 60 (October 1992): 664–669.

Gregoire A. J., et al. "Transdermal Oestrogen for Treatment of Severe Postnatal Depression." *Lancet* 347 (April 6, 1996): 930–933.

Grisaru, N., et al. "Transcranial Magnetic Stimulation in Mania: A Controlled Study." *American Journal of Psychiatry* 155 (November 1998): 1608–1610.

Hall, K., "Allergy of the Nervous System: A Review." *Annals of Allergy* 36 (January 1976): 49–64.

Hall, Richard C. W., ed. *Psychiatric Presentations of Medical Illness.* Jamaica, NY: Spectrum Publications, 1980.

Hall, R. C. W., et al. "Unrecognized Physical Illness Prompting Psychiatric Admission: A Prospective Study." *American Journal of Psychiatry* 138 (May 1981): 629–635.

Hall, R. C. W., et al. "Physical Illness Manifesting as Psychiatric Disease." *Archives of General Psychiatry* 37 (September 1980): 989–995.

Hall, R. C. W., et al. "Physical Illness Presenting as Psychiatric Disease." *Archives of General Psychiatry* 35 (November 1978): 1315–1320.

Hallert, C., et al. "Reversal of Psychopathology in Adult Coeliac Disease with the Aid of Pyridoxine (Vitamin B_6)." *Scandinavian Journal of Gastroenterology* 18 (March 1983): 299–304.

Han, J. S., "Electroacupuncture: An Alternative to Antidepressants for Treating Affective Diseases?" *International Journal of Neuroscience* 29 (1986): 79–92.

Hardaway, R. A. "Subliminally Activated Symbiotic Fantasies: Facts and Artifacts." *Psychological Bulletin* 107 (March 1990): 177–195.

Harrer, G., et al. "Comparison of Equivalence Between the St. John's Wort Extract LoHyp-57 and Fluoxetine." *Arzneimittelforschung* 49 (April 1999): 289–296.

Harrington, R., et al. "Systematic Review of Efficacy of Cognitive Behaviour Therapies in Childhood and Adolescent Depressive Disorder." *British Medical Journal* 316 (May 23, 1998): 1559–1563.

Harris, Steven B. "5-HTP + B6 = Trouble; Doc Harris Presents Green Banana Award." sci.med.nutrition (Internet newsgroup) (December 28, 1996).

Hasanah, C. I., et al. "Reduced Red-Cell Folate in Mania." *Journal of Affective Disorders* 46 (November 1997): 95–99.

Hathcock, John N., ed. *Nutritional Toxicology,* Vol. 1. New York: Academic Press, 1982.

Hawkes, W. C., and L. Hornbostel. "Effects of Dietary Selenium on Mood in Healthy Men Living in a Metabolic Research Unit." *Biological Psychiatry* 39 (January 15, 1996): 121–128.

Hawkins, D. R., et al. "Extended Sleep (Hypersomnia) in Young Depressed Patients." *American Journal of Psychiatry* 142 (August 1985): 905–910.

Hazell, P., et al. "Efficacy of Tricyclic Drugs in Treating Child and Adolescent Depression: A Meta-Analysis." *British Medical Journal* 310 (April 8, 1995): 897–901.

Heimlich, Jane. *What Your Doctor Won't Tell You.* New York: HarperCollins, 1990.

Hendler, Sheldon Saul. *The Oxygen Breakthrough.* New York: William Morrow, 1989.

Hendrick, V., et al. "Psychoneuroendocrinology of Mood Disorders: The Hypothalamic-Pituitary-Thyroid Axis." *Psychiatric Clinics of North America* 21 (June 1998): 277–292.

Heresco-Levy, Uriel, et al. "Efficacy of High-Dose Glycine in the Treatment of Enduring Negative Symptoms of Schizophrenia." *Archives of General Psychiatry* 56 (January 1999): 29–36.

Hibbeln, J. R. "Fish Consumption and Major Depression." *Lancet* 351 (April 18, 1998): 1213.

Hibbeln, J. R., and N. Salem, Jr. "Dietary Polyunsaturated Acids and Depression: When Cholesterol Does Not Satisfy." *American Journal of Clinical Nutrition* 62 (1995): 1–9.

Hibbeln, J. R., et al. "Essential Fatty Acids Predict Metabolites of Serotonin and Dopamine in Cerebrospinal Fluid Among Healthy Control Subjects, and Early- and Late-Onset Alcoholics." *Biological Psychiatry* 44 (1998): 235–242.

Hirschfeld, R. M. A., and F. K. Goodwin. "Mood Disorders." In *The American Psychiatric Press Textbok of Psychiatry*, edited by John Talbott, et al., 403–441. Washington DC: American Psychiatric Press, 1988.

Hoes, M. J. "L-Tryptophan in Depression and Strain." *Journal of Orthomolecular Psychiatry* 11, no. 4 (1982): 231–242.

Hofeldt, F. D. "Reactive Hypoglycemia." *Endocrinology and Metabolism Clinics of North America* 18 (March 1989): 185–201.

Hoffer, Abram. *Hoffer's Laws of Natural Nutrition*. Kingston, Ontario, Canada: Quarry Press, 1996.

———. *Common Questions on Schizophrenia and Their Answers*. Los Angeles: Keats Publishing, 1987.

———. "Allergy, Depression and Tricyclic Antidepressants." *Journal of Orthomolecular Psychiatry* 9, no. 3 (1980): 164–70.

Hoffer, Abram, and Morton Walker. *Putting It All Together: The New Orthomolecular Nutrition*. Los Angeles: Keats Publishing, 1996.

———. *Nutrients to Age Without Senility*. Los Angeles: Keats Publishing, 1980.

———. *Orthomolecular Nutrition*. Los Angeles: Keats Publishing, 1978.

Hoffman, R. S. "Diagnostic Errors in the Evaluation of Behavioral Disorders." *Journal of the American Medical Association* 248 (August 27, 1982): 964–967.

Horrobin, D. F. "The Role of Essential Fatty Acids and Prostaglandins in the Premenstrual Syndrome." *Journal of Reproductive Medicine* 28 (July 1983): 465–468.

Horrobin, D. F., and Y.-S. Huang. "Schizophrenia: The Role of Essential Fatty Acid and Prostaglandin Metabolism." *Medical Hypotheses* 10 (1983): 329–336.

Horrobin, D. F., and M. S. Manku. "Possible Role of Prostaglandin E_1 in the Affective Disorders and in Alcoholism." *British Medical Journal* 280 (June 17, 1980): 1363–1366.

Horsten, M., et al. "Depressive Symptoms, Social Support, and Lipid Profile in Healthy Middle-Aged Women." *Psychosomatic Medicine* 59 (September–October 1997): 521–528.

Huggins, Hal A. *It's All in Your Head: The Link Between Mercury Amalgams and Illness*. Garden City Park, NY: Avery, 1993.

Hughes, E. C., et al. "Migraine: A Diagnostic Test for Etiology of Food Sensitivity by a Nutritionally Supported Fast and Confirmed by Long-Term Report." *Annals of Allergy* 55 (1985): 28–32.

Hutchison, Michael. *The Book of Floating*. New York: William Morrow, 1984.

"idclub." "The l-phenylalanine WARNING continues. . . ." sci.med.psychobiology (Internet newsgroup) (October 17, 1997).

Ikeda, T., et al. "Treatment of Alzheimer-Type Dementia with Intravenous Mecobalamin." *Clinical Therapeutics* 14 (May–June 1992): 426–437.

International Society of Sport Psychology. "Physical Activity and Psychological Benefits: A Position Statement." *Sport Psychologist* 6 (June 1992): 199–203.

Iruela, L. M., et al. "Toxic Interaction of S-Adenosylmethionine and Clomipramine" (letter). *American Journal of Psychiatry* 150 (March 1993): 522.

Irving, G, et al. "Psychological Factors Associated with Recurrent Vaginal Candidiasis: A Preliminary Study." *Sexually Transmitted Infections* 74 (October 1998): 334–338.

Jacobsen, F. M. "Fluoxetine-Induced Sexual Dysfunction and an Open Trial of Yohimbine." *Journal of Clinical Psychiatry* 53 (April 1992): 119–122.

Jacobson, N. S., and S. D. Hollon. "Cognitive-Behavior Therapy versus Pharmacotherapy: Now That the Jury's Returned Its Verdict, It's Time to Present the Rest of the Evidence." *Journal of Consulting and Clinical Psychology* 64 (February 1996): 74–80.

Jacobson, N. S., et al. "Couple Therapy as a Treatment for Depression: II. The Effects of Relationship Quality and Therapy on Depressive Relapse." *Journal of Consulting and Clinical Psychology* 61 (June 1993): 516–519.

Jamison, Kay Redfield. *An Unquiet Mind*. New York: Knopf, 1995.

Jaret, Peter. "Move the Body, Heal the Mind." *Health* 13 (January/February 1999): 48.

Jarrett, R. B., et al. "Treatment of Atypical Depression with Cognitive Therapy or Phenelzine: A Double-Blind, Placebo-Controlled Trial." *Archives of General Psychiatry* 56 (May 1999): 431–437.

Jarrett, R. B., et al. "Is There a Role for Continuation Phase Cognitive Therapy for Depressed Outpatients?" *Journal of Consulting and Clinical Psychology* 66 (December 1998): 1036–1040.

Jaspan, J. B. "Hypoglycemia: Fact or Fiction?" *Hospital Practice—Office Edition* 24 (March 30, 1989): 11–12, 14.

Jewett, D. L., et al. "A Double-Blind Study of Symptom Provocation to Determine Food Sensitivity." *New England Journal of Medicine* 323 (August 16, 1990): 429–433.

Jin, P. "Efficacy of Tai Chi, Brisk Walking, Meditation, and Reading in Reducing Mental and Emotional Stress." *Journal of Psychosomatic Research* 36 (May 1992): 361–370.

Joffe, R., et al. "Change in Thyroid Hormone Levels Following Response to Cognitive Therapy for Major Depression." *American Journal of Psychiatry* 153 (March 1996): 411–413.

Joly, P., et al. "Development of Pseudobullous Morphea and Scleroderma-Like Illness During Therapy with L-5-Hydroxytryptophan and Carbidopa." *Journal of the American Academy of Dermatology* 25 (August 1991): 332–333.

Kabat-Zinn, Jon. *Full Catastrophe Living*. New York: Delta, 1991.

Kabat-Zinn, J., et al. "Effectiveness of a Meditation-Based Stress Reduction Program in the Treatment of Anxiety Disorders." *American Journal of Psychiatry* 149 (July 1992): 936–943.

Kagan, B. L., et al. "Oral S-Adenosylmethionine in Depression: A Randomized, Double-Blind, Placebo-Controlled Trial." *American Journal of Psychiatry* 147 (May 1990): 591–595.

Kakar, Sudhir. *Shamans, Mystics & Doctors*. New York: Knopf, 1982.

Kaminski, Patricia. "Flower Essence Therapy: Integrating Body and Soul Wellness." In Bassman, 1998, pp. 257–272.

Kaplan, Harold I., and Benjamin J. Sadock, eds. *Comprehensive Textbook of Psychiatry/VI*. Baltimore: Williams & Wilkins, 1995.

Kaplan, J. R., et al. "Demonstration of an Association Among Dietary Cholesterol, Central Serotonergic Activity, and Social Behavior in Monkeys." *Psychosomatic Medicine* 56 (November–December 1994): 479–484.

Karle, Hellmut W. A. *Hypnosis and Hypnotherapy: A Patient's Guide*. Wellingborough, Northamptonshire, England: Thorson's, 1988.

Kaslof, Leslie J., ed. *Wholistic Dimensions in Healing*. Garden City, NY: Doubleday, 1978.

Katerndahl, D. A. "Neuropsychiatric Disorders Associated with Depression." *Journal of Family Practice* 13 (1981): 619–24.

Kathol, R. C. "Patient Evaluation." In *Therapeutic Potential of Mood Disorder Clinics*, edited by R.A. Munoz, 71–82. San Francisco, CA: Jossey-Bass, 1984.

Katz, A. "Magnetic Depression—Scientists May Zap the Blues Away." *New Haven Register* (September 4, 1997).

Kaufman, Marc. "Fish Oil May Aid Against Manic Depression." *Washington Post* (April 27, 99): Z07.

Kay, D. S. G., et al. "The Therapeutic Effect of Ascorbic Acid and EDTA in Manic-Depressive Psychosis: Double-Blind Comparisons with Standard Treatments." *Psychological Medicine* 14 (August 1984): 533–539.

Kay, R. W. "Geomagnetic Storms: Association with Incidence of Depression as Measured by Hospital Admission." *British Journal of Psychiatry* 164 (March 1994): 403–409.

Kendler, K. S., and C. A. Prescott. "A Population-Based Twin Study of Lifetime Major Depression in Men and Women." *Archives of General Psychiatry* 56 (January 1999): 39–44.

Kendler, K. S., et al. "The Prediction of Major Depression in Women: Toward an Integrated Etiologic Model." *American Journal of Psychiatry* 150 (August 1993): 1139–1148.

King, D. S. "Can Allergic Exposure Provoke Psychological Symptoms? A Double-Blind Test." *Biological Psychiatry* 16 (January 1981): 3–19.

Kirov, G. K., and K. N. Tsachev. "Magnesium, Schizophrenia and Manic-Depressive Disease." *Neuropsychobiology* 23, no. 2 (1990): 79–81.

Kite, S. M., et al. "Development of an Aromatherapy Service at a Cancer Centre." *Palliative Medicine* 12 (May 1998): 171–180.

Klawansky, S., et al. "Meta-Analysis of Randomized Controlled Trials of Cranial Electrostimulation: Efficacy in Treating Selected Psychological and Physiological Conditions." *Journal of Nervous and Mental Diseases* 183, no. 7 (1995): 478–485.

Kleijnen, J., and P. Knipschild. "Ginkgo Biloba for Cerebral Insufficiency." *British Journal of Clinical Pharmacology* 34 (1992): 352–358.

Kleijnen, J., et al. "Clinical Trials of Homoeopathy." *British Medical Journal* 302 (February 9, 1991): 316–323.

Klein, E., et al. "Therapeutic Efficacy of Right Prefrontal Slow Repetitive Transcranial Magnetic Stimulation in Major Depression: A Double-Blind Controlled Study." *Archives of General Psychiatry* 56 (April 1999): 315–320.

Klerman, G. L., and M. M. Weissman. "Increasing Rates of Depression." *Journal of the American Medical Association* 261 (April 21, 1989): 2229–2235.

Klerman, Gerald L., et al. *Interpersonal Psychotherapy of Depression.* Northvale, NJ: Jason Aronson, 1994.

Koenig, H. G., et al. "Religious Coping and Health Status in Medically Ill Hospitalized Older Adults." *Journal of Nervous and Mental Diseases* 186 (September 1998): 513–521.

Koenig, H. G., et al. "Religiosity and Remission of Depression in Medically Ill Older Patients." *American Journal of Psychiatry* 155 (April 1998): 536–542.

Komori, T., et al. "Effects of Citrus Fragrance on Immune Function and Depressive States." *Neuroimmunomodulation* 2 (May–June 1995): 174–180.

Kopecky, G. "Have a Good Cry." *Redbook* 179 (May 1992): 106.

Koppen, A., et al. "Synergistic Effect of Nicotinamide and Choline Administration on Extracellular Choline Levels in the Brain." *Journal of Pharmacology and Experimental Therapeutics* 266 (August 1993): 720–725.

Koranyi, E. K. "Somatic Illness in Psychiatric Patients." *Psychosomatics* 21 (November 1980): 887–891.

———. "Morbidity and Rate of Undiagnosed Physical Illnesses in a Psychiatric Population." *Archives of General Psychiatry* 36 (April 1979): 414–419.

Korhonen, S., and S. Saarijarvi. "Oestradiol Treatment Helped a Depressed Postmenopausal Woman to Stop Her Psychotropic Medication: A Case Report." *Acta Psychiatrica Scandinavica* 94 (December 1996): 480–481.

Korn, Errol R. "Imagery." In *A Clinical Hypnosis Primer,* edited by George J. Pratt, et al., 73–89. New York: Wiley, 1988.

Kostrubala, Thaddeus. *The Joy of Running.* New York: Lippincott, 1976.

Kramer, Peter. *Listening to Prozac.* New York: Penguin, 1993.

Kraus, R. P., et al. "Exaggerated TSH Responses to TRH in Depressed Patients with 'Normal' Baseline TSH." *Journal of Clinical Psychiatry* 58 (June 1997): 266–270.

Krieger, Delores. *Accepting Your Power to Heal: The Personal Practice of Therapeutic Touch.* San Francisco: Bear and Co., 1993.

Kripke, D. F. "Light Treatment for Nonseasonal Depression: Speed, Efficacy, and Combined Treatment." *Journal of Affective Disorders* 49 (1998): 109–117.

Krupitsky, E. M., et al. "The Administration of Transcranial Electric Treatment for Affective Disturbances Therapy in Alcoholic Patients." *Drug and Alcohol Dependence* 27 (January 1991): 1–6.

Kunin, Richard A. *Mega-Nutrition.* New York: McGraw Hill, 1980.

Kurtz, L. F. "Mutual Aid for Affective Disorders: The Manic Depressive and Depressive Association." *American Journal of Orthopsychiatry* 58 (January 1988): 152–155.

Kusumi, I., et al. "Chronobiological Approach for Treatment-Resistant Rapid Cycling Affective Disorders." *Biological Psychiatry* 37 (April 15, 1995): 553–559.

Laidlaw, T. M., et al. "The Variability of Type I Hypersensitivity Reactions: The Importance of Mood." *Journal of Psychosomatic Research* 38 (January 1994): 51–61.

Langworth, S. "Experiences from the Amalgam Unit at Huddinge Hospital—Somatic and Psychosomatic Aspects." *Scandinavian Journal of Work, Environment and Health* 23 (Supplement 3, 1997): 65–67.

Lauritzen, C., et al. "Treatment of Premenstrual Tension Syndrome with Vitex Agnus Castus: Controlled, Double-Blind Study versus Pyridoxine." *Phytomedicine* 4, no. 3 (1997): 183–189.

Lawrence, Ron, et al. *Magnet Therapy: The Pain Cure Alternative.* Rocklin, CA: Prima Health, 1998.

Lazarus, A. A. "The Multimodal Approach to the Treatment of Minor Depression." *American Journal of Psychotherapy* 46 (January 1992): 50–57.

Lechin, F., et al. "Doxepin Therapy for Postprandial Symptomatic Hypoglycaemic Patients." *Clinical Science* 80 (April 1991): 373–384.

Ledochowski, M., et al. "Fructose Malabsorption Is Associated with Early Signs of Mental Depression." *European Journal of Medical Research* 3 (June 17, 1998): 295–298.

Ledochowski, M., et al. "Lactose Malabsorption Is Associated with Early Signs of Mental Depression in Females: A Preliminary Report." *Digestive Diseases and Sciences* 43 (November 1998): 2513–2517.

Leibenluft, E., and T. A. Wehr. "Is Sleep Deprivation Useful in the Treatment of Depression?" *American Journal of Psychiatry* 149 (February 1992): 159–168.

Leibenluft, E., et al. "Effects of Exogenous Melatonin Administration and Withdrawal in Five Patients with Rapid-Cycling Bipolar Disorder." *Journal of Clinical Psychiatry* 58 (September 1997): 383–388.

Leibowitz, Judith, and Bill Connington. *The Alexander Technique.* New York: Harper & Row, 1990.

Lesser, Michael. *Nutrition and Vitamin Therapy.* New York: Grove Press, 1980.

Letemendia, F. J., et al. "Therapeutic Advantage of Bifrontal Electrode Placement in ECT." *Psychological Medicine* 23 (May 1993): 349–360.

Levine, J., et al. "High Serum and Cerebrospinal Fluid Ca/Mg Ratio in Recently Hospitalized Acutely Depressed Patients." *Neuropsychobiology* 39, no. 2 (1999): 63–70.

Levine, J., et al. "Inositol-Induced Mania?" *American Journal of Psychiatry* 153 (June 1996): 839.

Levine, J., et al. "Double-Blind, Controlled Trial of Inositol Treatment of Depression." *American Journal of Psychiatry* 152 (May 1995): 792–794.

Lewinsohn, Peter, et al. *Control Your Depression.* New York: Simon & Schuster, 1992.

Lewy, A. J., et al. "Winter Depression and the Phase-Shift Hypothesis for Bright Light's Therapeutic Effects." In *Seasonal Affective Disorders and Phototherapy,* edited by Norman E. Rosenthal and Mary C. Blehar, 295–310. New York: Guilford Press, 1989.

Lewy, A. J., et al. "Phase Delay and Hypersomnia" (letter). *American Journal of Psychiatry* 143 (May 1986): 679–680.

Lieb, J., et al. "Elevated Levels of Prostaglandin E_2 and Thromboxane B_2 in Depression." *Prostaglandins, Leukotrienes and Medicine* 10 (1983): 361–367.

Liebowitz, Michael R. *The Chemistry of Love.* New York: Little, Brown, 1983.

Lingaerde, O., et al. "Can Winter Depression Be Prevented by Ginkgo Biloba Extract? A Placebo-Controlled Trial." *Acta Psychiatrica Scandinavica* 100 (July 1999): 62–66.

Linde, K., et al. "Are the Clinical Effects of Homoeopathy Placebo Effects? A Meta-Analysis of Placebo-Controlled Trials." *Lancet* 350 (September 20, 1997): 834–843.

Linde, K., et al. "St. John's Wort for Depression—An Overview and Meta-Analysis of Randomised Clinical Trials." *British Medical Journal* 313 (August 3, 1996): 253–258.

Linderman, Hal A. *The Healing Energies of Music.* Wheaton, IL: Theosophical Publishing House, 1983.

Linnoila, V. M., and M. Virkkunen. "Aggression, Suicidality, and Serotonin." *Journal of Clinical Psychiatry* 53 (Supplement, October 1992): 46–51.

Lis-Balchin, M. "Essential Oils and 'Aromatherapy': Their Modern Role in Healing." *Journal of the Royal Society of Health* 117 (October 1997): 324–329.

Little, K. Y., et al. "Altered Zinc Metabolism in Mood Disorder Patients." *Biological Psychiatry* 26 (October 1989): 646–648.

Lipton, M. A., and J. C. Wheless. "Diet as Therapy." In *Nutrition & Behavior*, edited by Sanford Miller, 213–233. Philadelphia: Franklin Institute Press, 1981.

Lipton, M. A., and G. Burnett. "Pharmacological Treatment of Schizophrenia." In *Disorders of the Schizophrenic Syndrome*, edited by Leopold Bellak, 320–352. New York: Basic Books, 1979.

Lockhart, M. "The Teacher's Role in the Therapeutic Process." In *The Art of Survival: A Guide to Yoga Therapy*, edited by M. L. Gharote and Maureen Lockhart, 37–65. London: Unwin Paperbacks, 1987.

Long, T. D., and R. G. Kathol. "Critical Review of Data Supporting Affective Disorder Caused by Nonpsychotropic Medication." *Annals of Clinical Psychiatry* 5 (December 1993): 259–270.

Lonsdale, D., and R. J. Shamberger. "Red Cell Transketolase as an Indicator of Nutritional Deficiency." *American Journal of Clinical Nutrition* 33 (February 1980): 205–211.

Loving, R. T., et al. "Bright Light Augmentation of Antidepressant Medication." *Society of Light Treatment and Biological Rhythms Abstracts* 11 (1999): 33.

Lowen, Alexander. *Depression and the Body*. Harmondsworth, Middlesex, England: Penguin Books, 1973.

Lowinger, P. "Prostaglandins and Organic Affective Syndrome" (letter). *American Journal of Psychiatry* 146 (December 1989): 1646–1647.

Lucini, V., et al. "Predictive Value of Tryptophan/Large Neutral Amino Acids Ratio to Antidepressant Response." *Journal of Affective Disorders* 36 (January 22, 1996): 129–133.

Lundberg, A. "Psychiatric Aspects of Air Pollution." *Otolaryngology and Head and Neck Surgery* 114 (February 1996): 227–231.

Luo, H., et al. "Clinical Research on the Therapeutic Effect of the Electro-Acupuncture Treatment in Patients with Depression." *Psychiatry and Clinical Neurosciences* 52 (Supplement, December 1998): S338–340.

McClain, C. J., et al. "Zinc Status Before and After Zinc Supplementation of Eating Disorder Patients." *Journal of the American College of Nutrition* 11 (December 1992): 694–700.

McLean, P. "Behavioral Therapy: Theory and Research." In *Short-Term Psychotherapists for Depression*, edited by John A. Rush, 19–49. New York: The Guilford Press, 1982.

McMahan, S., et al. "Depressive Symptomatology in Women and Residential Proximity to High-Voltage Transmission Lines." *American Journal of Epidemiology* 139 (January 1, 1994): 58–63.

Maes, M., et al. "Lower Serum High-Density Lipoprotein Cholesterol (HDL-C) in Major Depression and in Depressed Men with Serious Suicidal Attempts: Relationship with Immune-Inflammatory Markers." *Acta Psychiatrica Scandinavica* 95 (March 1997): 212–221.

Maes, M, et al. "Lower Serum Zinc in Major Depression Is a Sensitive Marker of Treatment Resistance and of the Immune/Inflammatory Response in That Illness." *Biological Psychiatry* 42 (September 1, 1997): 349–358.

Maes, M, et al. "Alterations in Iron Metabolism and the Erythron in Major Depression: Further Evidence for a Chronic Inflammatory Process." *Journal of Affective Disorders* 40 (September 9, 1996): 23–33.

Maes, M., et al. "Disturbances in Dexamethasone Suppression Test and Lower Availability of L-Tryptophan and Tyrosine in Early Puerperium and in Women Under Contraceptive Therapy." *Journal of Psychosomatic Research* 36 (February 1992): 191–197.

Maggioni, M., et al. "Effects of Phosphatidylserine Therapy in Geriatric Patients with Depressive Disorders." *Acta Psychiatrica Scandinavica* 81 (March 1990): 265–270.

Magill, P. J. "Investigation of the Efficacy of Progesterone Pessaries in the Relief of Symptoms of Premenstrual Syndrome: Progesterone Study Group." *British Journal of General Practice* 45 (November 1995): 589–593.

Maizlish, N. A., et al. "Neurobehavioural Evaluation of Venezuelan Workers Exposed to Inorganic Lead." *Occupational and Environmental Medicine* 52 (June 1995): 408–414.

Maleskey, G. "Find Your Food Foes and Discover Relief." *Prevention* 38 (April 1986): 97–112.

Maltz, Maxwell. *Psycho-Cybernetics*. New York: Pocket Books, 1966.

Mann, J. "D-Phenylalanine in Endogenous Depression." *American Journal of Psychiatry* 137 (December 1980): 1611.

Manning, Martha. *Undercurrents*. San Francisco: Harper San Francisco, 1996.

Mansfield, L. E. "The Role of Food Allergy in Migraine: A Review." *Annals of Allergy* 58 (May 1987): 313–317.

"Marketplace." CBC television (December 19, 1989).

Marshall, P. S. "Allergy and Depression: A Neurochemical Threshold Model of the Relation Between the Illnesses." *Psychological Bulletin* 113 (January 1993): 23–43.

Martinsen, E. M. et al. "Comparing Aerobic with Nonaerobic Forms of Exercise in the Treatment of Clinical Depression: A Randomized Trial." *Comprehensive Psychiatry* 4 (July/August 1989): 324–331.

Martinsen, E. W., et al. "Effects of Aerobic Exercise on Depression: A Controlled Study." *British Medical Journal* 291 (July 13, 1985): 109.

Martorano, J.T., et al. "Differentiating Between Natural Progesterone and Synthetic Progestins: Clinical Implications for Premenstrual Syndrome and Perimenopause Management." *Comprehensive Therapy* 24 (June–July 1998): 336–339.

Matthews, Dale A., with Connie Clark. *The Faith Factor: Proof of the Healing Power of Prayer*. New York: Viking, 1998.

Mayer, G., et al. "Effects of Vitamin B_{12} on Performance and Circadian Rhythm in Normal Subjects." *Neuropsychopharmacology* 15 (November 1996): 456–464.

Melchart, D, et al. "A Multicenter Survey of Amalgam Fillings and Subjective Complaints in Non-Selected Patients in the Dental Practice." *European Journal of Oral Sciences* 106 (June 1998): 770–777.

Menkes, D. L., et al. "Right Frontal Lobe Slow Frequency Repetitive Transcranial Magnetic Stimulation (SF r-TMS) Is an Effective Treatment for Depression: A Case-Control Pilot Study of Safety and Efficacy." *Journal of Neurology, Neurosurgery and Psychiatry* 67 (July 1999): 113–115.

Michelson, D., et al. "Bone Mineral Density in Women with Depression." *New England Journal of Medicine* 335 (October 17, 1996): 1176–1181.

Michelson, D., et al. "An Eosinophilia-Myalgia Syndrome Related Disorder Associated with Exposure to L-5-Hydroxytryptophan." *Journal of Rheumatology* 21 (December 1994): 2261–2265.

Miller, D. R., and K. C. Hayes. "Vitamin Excess and Toxicity." In *Nutritional Toxicology*, Vol. 1, edited by John N. Hathcock, 81–133. New York: Academic Press, 1982.

Miller, Emmett E. *Software for the Mind: How to Program Your Own Mind for Optimum Health & Performance*. Berkeley, CA: Celestial Arts, 1987.

Miller, I. W., et al. "Cognitive-Behavioral Treatment of Depressed Inpatients: Six- and Twelve-Month Follow-Up." *American Journal of Psychiatry* 146 (October 1989): 1274–1279.

Miller, L., et al. "Religiosity and Depression: Ten-Year Follow-Up of Depressed Mothers and Offspring." *Journal of the American Academy of Child and Adolescent Psychiatry* 36 (October 1997): 1416–1425.

Miller, Sanford, ed. *Nutrition & Behavior*. Philadelphia: Franklin Institute Press, 1981.

Mills, Simon Y. *The Dictionary of Modern Herbalism*. Rochester, VT: Healing Arts Press, 1988.

Mindell, Earl, and Carol Colman. *Earl Mindell's Secret Remedies*. New York: Fireside, 1997.

Misiaszek, J., et al. "The Calming Effect of Negative Air Ions on Manic Patients." *Biological Psychiatry* 22 (January 1986): 107–110.

Möhler, H., et al. "Nicotinamide Is a Brain Constituent with Benzodiazepine-Like Actions." *Nature* 278 (April 5, 1979): 563–565.

Moller, S. E., et al. "Relationship Between Plasma Ratio of Tryptophan to Competing Amino Acids and the Response to L-Tryptophan." *Journal of Affective Disorders* 2 (March 1980): 47–59.

Mouret, J., et al. "Treatment of Narcolepsy with L-Tyrosine." *Lancet* (December 24/31, 1988): 1458–1459.

Mudd, S. H. "Vitamin-Responsive Genetic Abnormalities." In *Advances in Nutritional Research,* Vol. 4, edited by Harold H. Draper, 1–34. New York: Plenum, 1982.

Mufson, L., et al. Efficacy of Interpersonal Psychotherapy for Depressed Adolescents." *Archives of General Psychiatry* 55 (June 1999): 573–579.

Muneyvirci-Delale, O., et al. "Sex Steroid Hormones Modulate Serum Ionized Magnesium and Calcium Levels Throughout the Menstrual Cycle in Women." *Fertility and Sterility* 69 (May 1998): 958–962.

Munoz, R. A., ed. *Therapeutic Potential of Mood Disorder Clinics.* San Francisco: Jossey-Bass, 1984.

Murphy, G. E., et al. "Cognitive Behavior Therapy, Relaxation Training, and Tricyclic Antidepressant Medication in the Treatment of Depression." *Psychological Reports* 77 (October 1995): 403–420.

Murray, Michael T. *5-HTP.* New York: Bantam, 1999.

———. *Natural Alternatives to Prozac.* New York: William Morrow, 1996.

Mynors-Wallis, L. M. "Problem-Solving Treatment: Evidence for Effectiveness and Feasibility in Primary Care." *International Journal of Psychiatry in Medicine* 26 , no. 3 (1996): 249–262.

Mynors-Wallis, L. M., et al. "Randomised Controlled Trial Comparing Problem-Solving Treatment with Amitriptyline and Placebo for Major Depression in Primary Care." *British Medical Journal* 310 (February 18, 1995): 441–445.

Naga Venkatesha Murthy, P. J., et al. "P300 Amplitude and Antidepressant Response to Sudarshan Kriya Yoga (SKY)." *Journal of Affective Disorders* 50 (1998): 45–48.

Nahas, Z., et al. "Safety and Feasibility of Repetitive Transcranial Magnetic Stimulation in the Treatment of Anxious Depression in Pregnancy: A Case Report." *Journal of Clinical Psychiatry* 60 (January 1999): 50–52.

Narang, R. L., et al. "Levels of Copper and Zinc in Depression." *Indian Journal of Physiology and Pharmacology* 35 (October 1991): 272–274.

Naylor, G. J., and A. H. W. Smith. "Vanadium: A Possible Aetiological Factor in Manic Depressive Illness." *Psychological Medicine* 11 (1981): 257–263.

Nazzaro, Ann, and Donald Lombard, with David Horrobin. *The PMS Solution: The Nutritional Approach.* Montreal: Eden Press, 1985.

Neumeister, A., et al. "Effects of Tryptophan Depletion vs. Catecholamine Depletion in Patients with Seasonal Affective Disorder in Remission with Light Therapy." *Archives of General Psychiatry* 55 (June 1998): 524–530.

Neumeister, A., et al. "Bright Light Therapy Stabilizes the Antidepressant Effect of Partial Sleep Deprivation." *Biological Psychiatry* 39 (January 1, 1996): 16–21.

Newbold, H. L. "Vitamin B_{12}: Placebo or Neglected Therapeutic Tool." *Medical Hypotheses* 28 (1989): 155–164.

———. *Mega-Nutrients for Your Nerves.* New York: Berkley Books, 1975.

Nezu, A. M. "Efficacy of a Social Problem-Solving Therapy Approach for Unipolar Depression." *Journal of Consulting and Clinical Psychology* 54, no. 4 (1986): 196–202.

Nezu, A. M., and M. G. Perri. "Social Problem-Solving Therapy for Unipolar Depression: An Initial Dismantling Investigation." *Journal of Consulting and Clinical Psychology* 57, no. 3 (1989): 408–413.

Nidecker, A. "Fish Oil Fatty Acids May Soothe Some Disorders." *Clinical Psychiatry News* 26 (November 1998): 10.

Nishino, S., et al. "Salivary Prostaglandin Concentrations: Possible State Indicators for Major Depression." *American Journal of Psychiatry* 146 (March 1989): 365–368.

Norden, Michael J. *Beyond Prozac.* New York: HarperCollins, 1995.

Nordfors, M., and P. Hartvig. "St John's Wort Against Depression in Favour Again" (in Swedish). *Lakartidningen* 94 (June 18, 1997): 2365–2367.

O'Connor, Richard. *Undoing Depression.* Boston: Little, Brown, 1997.

Ohta, T., et al. "Daily Activity and Persistent Sleep-Wake Schedule Disorders." *Progress in Neuropsychopharmacology and Biological Psychiatry* 16 (July 1992): 529–537.

Okawa, M., et al. "Vitamin B$_{12}$ Treatment for Delayed Sleep Phase Syndrome: A Multi-Center Double-Blind Study." *Psychiatry and Clinical Neurosciences* 51 (October 1997): 275–279.

Oren, D. A., and T. A. Wehr. "Hypernyctohemeral Syndrome After Chronotherapy for Delayed Sleep Phase Syndrome" (letter). *New England Journal of Medicine* 327 (December 10, 1992): 1762.

Orentreich, N., et al. "Low Methionine Ingestion by Rats Extends Lifespan." *Journal of Nutrition* 123 (February 1993): 269–274.

Osmond, H., and A. Hoffer. "Schizophrenia and Suicide." *Journal of Schizophrenia* 1 (1967): 54–64.

Palardy, J., et al. "Blood Glucose Measurements During Symptomatic Episodes in Patients with Suspected Postprandial Hypoglycemia." *New England Journal of Medicine* 321 (November 23, 1989): 1421–1425.

Papaioannou, R., and C. C. Pfeiffer. "Pure Water for Drinking." *Journal of Orthomolecular Medicine* 1, no. 3 (1986): 184–98.

Papassotiropoulos, A., et al. "The Risk of Acute Suicidality in Psychiatric Inpatients Increases with Low Plasma Cholesterol." *Pharmacopsychiatry* 32 (January 1999): 1–4.

Parikh, S. V., et al. "Psychosocial Interventions as an Adjunct to Pharmacotherapy in Bipolar Disorder." *Canadian Journal of Psychiatry* 42 (Supplement 2, August 1997): 74S–78S.

Parker, H. "Do You Have the Miracle Healer in You?" *Prevention* 50 (December 1998): 106.

Parry, B. L, et al. "Early versus Late Partial Sleep Deprivation in Patients with Premenstrual Dysphoric Disorder and Normal Comparison Subjects." *American Journal of Psychiatry* 152 (March 1995): 404–412.

Partonen, T., et al. "Randomized Trial of Physical Exercise Alone or Combined with Bright Light on Mood and Health-Related Quality of Life." *Psychological Medicine* 28 (November 1998): 1359–1364.

Pascual-Leone, A., et al. "Beneficial Effect of Rapid-Rate Transcranial Magnetic Stimulation of the Left Dorsolateral Prefrontal Cortex in Drug-Resistant Depression." *Lancet* 348 (1996): 233–237.

Pauling, Linus, *How to Live Longer and Feel Better*. New York: W. H. Freeman, 1986.

———. "Orthomolecular Psychiatry." *Science* 160 (April 19, 1968): 265–271.

Pavlinac, D., et al. "Magnesium in Affective Disorders." *Biological Psychiatry* 14, no. 4 (1979): 657–661.

Pearlstein, T., et al. "Mood Disorders and Menopause." *Endocrinology and Metabolism Clinics of North America* 26 (June 1997): 279–294.

Pennebaker, James W. *Opening Up: The Healing Power of Confiding in Others*. New York: William Morrow, 1990.

Perry, F. S., et al. "Environmental Power Frequency Magnetic Fields and Suicide." *Health Physics* 41 (1981): 267–277.

Perry, S., et al. "Power Frequency Magnetic Field; Depressive Illness and Myocardial Infarction." *Public Health* 103 (May 1989): 177–180.

Pfeiffer, Carl C. *Mental and Elemental Nutrients*. Los Angeles: Keats Publishing, 1975.

Pfeiffer, C. C., and R. Mailloux. "Excess Copper as a Factor in Human Diseases." *Journal of Orthomolecular Medicine* 2, no. 3 (1987): 171–182.

Philip, P., et al. "Efficiency of Transcranial Electrostimulation on Anxiety and Insomnia Symptoms During a Washout Period in Depressed Patients: A Double-Blind Study." *Biological Psychiatry* 29 (March 1, 1991): 451–456.

Philpott, William H., and Dwight K. Kalita. *Brain Allergies: The Psychonutrient Connection*. Los Angeles: Keats Publishing, 1980, 1987.

Placidi, G., et al. "Exploration of the Clinical Profile of Rubidium Chloride in Depression: A Systematic Open Trial." *Journal of Clinical Psychopharmacology* 8 (June 1988): 184–188.

Plioplys, A. V., and S. Plioplys. "Amantadine and L-Carnitine Treatment of Chronic Fatigue Syndrome." *Neuropsychobiology* 35, no. 1 (1997): 16–23.

Podell, Richard N. *Doctor, Why Am I So Tired?* New York: Pharos Books, 1987.

Pollack, M. H., and P. Hammerness. "Adjunctive Yohimbine for Treatment in Refractory Depression." *Biological Psychiatry* 33 (February 1, 1993): 220–221.

Poole, C., et al. "Depressive Symptoms and Headaches in Relation to Proximity of Residence to an Alternating-Current Transmission Line Right-of-Way." *American Journal of Epidemiology* 137 (February 1, 1993): 318–332.

Portier, C. J., and M. S. Wolfe, eds. *Assessment of Health Effects from Exposure to Power-Line Frequency Electric and Magnetic Fields: Working Group Report.* NIH Publication No. 98-3981 (August 1998). Available online at www.niehs.nih.gov/emfrapid/html/WGReport/WorkingGroup.html.

Posaci, C., et al. "Plasma Copper, Zinc and Magnesium Levels in Patients with Premenstrual Tension Syndrome." *Acta Obstetrica et Gynecologica Scandinavica* 73 (July 1994): 452–455.

Post, Robert M. "Mood Disorders: Somatic Treatment." In *Comprehensive Textbook of Psychiatry/VI,* edited by Harold I. Kaplan and Benjamin J. Sadock, 1152–1178. Baltimore: Williams & Wilkins, 1995.

Post, Robert M., and James C. Ballenger, eds. *Neurobiology of Mood Disorders.* Baltimore: Williams & Wilkins, 1984.

Praschak-Rieder, N., et al. "Suicidal Tendencies as a Complication of Light Therapy for Seasonal Affective Disorder: A Report of Three Cases." *Journal of Clinical Psychiatry* 58 (1997): 398–392.

Pratt, George J., et al., eds. *A Clinical Hypnosis Primer.* New York: Wiley, 1988.

Propst, L. R. "The Comparative Efficacy of Religious and Non-Religious Imagery for the Treatment of Mild Depression in Religious Individuals." *Cognitive Research and Therapy* 4 (1982): 167–178.

Radetsky, Peter. *Allergic to the Twentieth Century.* Boston: Little, Brown, 1997.

Rainer, Tristine. *The New Diary.* Los Angeles: Tarcher, 1978.

Rampes, H., and J. Davidson. "Images in Psychiatry: Samuel Hahnemann, 1755–1843." *American Journal of Psychiatry* 154 (October 1997): 1450.

Randolph, Theron G., and Ralph W. Moss. *An Alternative Approach to Allergies,* rev. ed. New York: Harper & Row, 1989.

Reading, C. M. "Relatively Speaking: Family Tree Way to Better Health: Orthomolecular Genetics." *Journal of Orthomolecular Medicine* 1, no. 2 (1986): 113–119.

Reddy, P. L., et al. "Erythrocyte Membrane Sodium-Potassium Adenosine Triphosphatase Activity in Affective Disorders." *Journal of Neural Transmission—General Section* 89, no. 3 (1992): 183–209.

Rees, B. L. "Effect of Relaxation with Guided Imagery on Anxiety, Depression, and Self-Esteem in Primiparas." *Journal of Holistic Nursing* 13 (September 1995): 255–267.

Rehm, L. P., et al. "Cognitive and Behavioral Targets in a Self-Control Therapy Program for Depression." *Journal of Consulting and Clinical Psychology* 55, no. 1 (1987): 60–67.

Reynolds, C. F., et al. "Nortriptyline and Interpersonal Psychotherapy as Maintenance Therapies for Recurrent Major Depression: A Randomized Controlled Trial in Patients Older Than 59 Years." *Journal of the American Medical Association* 281 (January 6, 1999): 39–45.

Rhyne, Janie. *The Gestalt Art Experience.* Monterey, CA: Brooks/Cole Publishing, 1973.

Richter, P., et al. "Imaginary versus Real Light for Winter Depression." *Biological Psychiatry* 31 (March 1992): 534–536.

Risch, S. C., and D. S. Janowsky. "Cholinergic-Adrenergic Balance in Affective Illness." In *Neurobiology of Mood Disorders,* edited by Robert M. Post and James C. Ballenger, 652–663. Baltimore: Williams & Wilkins, 1984.

Robertson, J. M., and P. E. Tanguay. "Case Study: The Use of Melatonin in a Boy with Refractory Bipolar Disorder." *Journal of the American Academy of Child and Adolescent Psychiatry* 36 (June 1997): 822–825.

Robins, C. J., and A. M. Hayes. "An Appraisal of Cognitive Therapy." *Journal of Consulting and Clinical Psychology* 61 (April 1993): 205–214.

Rosa, L., et al. "A Close Look at Therapeutic Touch." *Journal of the American Medical Association* 279 (April 1, 1998): 1005–1010.

Rose, J. D. R. "Disturbed Hypothalamic Control of Na,K-ATPase: A Cause of Somatic Symptoms of Depression." *Medical Hypotheses* 19 (1986): 179–183.

Rose, J., Ed. *Trace Elements in Health*. Stoneham, MA: Butterworths, 1983.

Rosenbaum, J. F., et al. "An Open-Label Pilot Study of Oral S-adenosyl-L-methionine in Major Depression: Interim Results." *Psychopharmacology Bulletin* 24, no. 1 (1988): 189–194.

Rosenfeld, Isadore. *The Complete Medical Exam*. New York: Simon & Schuster, 1978.

Rosenthal, N. E., and C. Cameron. "Exaggerated Sensitivity to an Organophosphate Pesticide" (letter). *American Journal of Psychiatry* 148 (February 1991): 270.

Rosenthal, N. E., et al. "Phase-Shifting Effects of Bright Morning Light as Treatment for Delayed Sleep Phase Syndrome." *Sleep* 13 (August 1990): 354–361.

Rosenthal, Norman E., and Mary C. Blehar, eds. *Seasonal Affective Disorders and Phototherapy*. New York: Guilford Press, 1989.

Rosenvold, Lloyd. *Can a Gluten-Free Diet Help? How?* Los Angeles: Keats Publishing, 1992.

Ross, Harvey M. *Fighting Depression*. Los Angeles: Keats Publishing, 1992.

Rossman, Martin L. *Healing Yourself: A Step-by-Step Program for Better Health Through Imagery*. New York: Walker, 1987.

Rouillon, F., and P. Gorwood. "The Use of Lithium to Augment Antidepressant Medication." *Journal of Clinical Psychiatry* 59 (Supplement 5, 1998): 32–39.

Rowe, K. S., and K. J. Rowe. "Synthetic Food Coloring and Behavior: A Dose Response Effect in a Double-Blind, Placebo-Controlled, Repeated-Measures Study." *Journal of Pediatrics* 125 (Part 1, November 1994): 691–698.

Rubinow, D. R. "Gonadal Steroids and Perimenopausal Depression" [91D]. *The American Psychiatric Association 152nd Annual Meeting*. Washington, DC, 1999.

Rudin, D. O. "The Major Psychoses and Neuroses as Omega-3 Essential Fatty Acid Deficiency Syndrome: Substrate Pellagra." *Biological Psychiatry* 16 (September 1981): 837–850.

Rudin, Donald O., and Clare Felix. *Omega 3 Oils: To Improve Mental Health, Fight Degenerative Diseases, and Extend Your Life*. Garden City Park, NY: Avery Publishing Group, 1996.

Ruhrmann, S., et al. "Effects of Fluoxetine versus Bright Light in the Treatment of Seasonal Affective Disorder." *Psychological Medicine* 28 (July 1998): 923–933.

Rush, John A., ed. *Short-Term Psychotherapies for Depression*. New York: The Guilford Press, 1982.

Sabelli, H. C. "Rapid Treatment of Depression with Selegiline-Phenylalanine Combination" (letter). *Journal of Clinical Psychiatry* 52 (March 1991): 137.

Sabelli, H. C., et al. "Sustained Antidepressant Effect of PEA Replacement." *Neuropsychiatry Clinics and Neuroscience* 8, no. 2 (1996): 168–171.

Sabelli, H. C., et al. "Clinical Studies on the Phenylalanine Hypothesis of Affective Disorder: Urine and Blood Phenylacetic Acid and Phenylalanine Dietary Supplements." *Journal of Clinical Psychiatry* 47 (February 1986): 66–70.

Sachs, G. S., et al. "Enhancement of ECT Benefit by Yohimbine." *Journal of Clinical Psychiatry* 47 (October 1986): 508–510.

Sachs, Michael L., and Gary W. Buffone, eds. *Running as Therapy*. Lincoln: University of Nebraska Press, 1984.

Sack, D. A., et al. "The Timing and Duration of Sleep in Partial Sleep Deprivation Therapy of Depression." *Acta Psychiatrica Scandinavica* 77 (February 1988): 219–224.

Sack, D. A., et al. "Potentiation of Antidepressant Medications by Phase Advance of the Sleep-Wake Cycle." *American Journal of Psychiatry* 142 (May 1985): 606–607.

Sahelian, Ray. *5-HTP: Nature's Serotonin Solution*. Garden City Park, NY: Avery Publishing Group, 1998.

———. *Pregnenolone: Nature's Feel Good Hormone*. Garden City Park, NY: Avery Publishing Group, 1997.

Sakamoto, T., et al. "Psychotropic Effects of Japanese Valerian Root Extract." *Chemical and Pharmaceutical Bulletin* 40 (March 1992): 758–761.

Salter, C. A. "Dietary Tyrosine as an Aid to Stress Resistance Among Troops." *Military Medicine* 154 (March 1989): 144–146.

Samuels, Mike, and Nancy Samuels. *Seeing with the Mind's Eye*. New York: Random, 1975.

Sandower, Martha. "Manic Depression: An Alternative Treatment." *Journal of Orthomolecular Medicine* 2, no. 3 (1987): 154–157.

Sartori, H. E. "Lithium Orotate in the Treatment of Alcoholism and Related Conditions." *Alcohol* 3 (March–April 1986): 97–100.

Savitz, D. A., et al. "Prevalence of Depression Among Electrical Workers." *American Journal of Industrial Medicine* 25 (February 1994): 165–176.

Schmauss, M., et al. "Effects of Alpha-2 Receptor Blockade in Addition to Tricyclic Antidepressants in Therapy-Resistant Depression." *Journal of Clinical Psychopharmacology* 8 (April 1988): 108–111.

Schottenfeld, R. S., and M. R. Cullen. "Organic Affective Illness Associated with Lead Intoxication." *American Journal of Psychiatry* 141 (November 1984): 1423–1426.

Schultz, K. D. "The Use of Imagery in Alleviating Depression." In *Imagination and Healing*, edited by Anees A. Sheikh, 129–158. Farmingdale, NY: Baywood Publishing, 1984.

Schweitzer, I., and V. Tuckwell. "Risk of Adverse Events with the Use of Augmentation Therapy for the Treatment of Resistant Depression." *Drug Safety* 19 (December 1998): 455–464.

Sealey, Robert C. *Orthomolecular Healthcare References*. North York, Ontario, Canada: SEAR Publications, 1999.

Seidman, S. N., and J. G. Rabkin. "Testosterone Replacement Therapy for Hypogonadal Men with SSRI-Refractory Depression." *Journal of Affective Disorders* 48 (1998): 157–161.

Seligman, Martin E. P. *Learned Optimism*. New York: Pocket Books, 1998.

Shapiro, D. H. "Adverse Effects of Meditation: A Preliminary Investigation of Long-Term Meditators." *International Journal of Psychosomatics* 39, no. 1–4 (1992): 62–67.

Shapiro, S. L., et al. "Effects of Mindfulness-Based Stress Reduction on Medical and Premedical Students." *Journal of Behavioral Medicine* 21 (December 1998): 581–599.

Shealy, C. N. "Self-Health: From Pain to Health Maintenance." In *Wholistic Dimensions in Healing*, edited by Leslie J. Kaslof, 176–178. Garden City, NY: Doubleday, 1978.

Sheikh, Anees A., ed. *Imagination and Healing*. Farmingdale, NY: Baywood Publishing, 1984.

Shelton, R. C., and P. T. Loosen. "Sleep Deprivation Accelerates the Response to Nortriptyline." *Progress in Neuropsychopharmacology and Biological Psychiatry* 17 (January 1993): 113–123.

Sherman, C. "Short-Term Modality Effective in Depressed Elderly." *Clinical Psychiatry News* 27, no. 5 (1999): 21.

———. "Acupuncture Can Improve Symptoms in Depression Patients." *Clinical Psychiatry News* 26, no. 8 (1998): 29.

———. "Eastern Anxiolytic Herbs Have Novel Mechanisms." *Clinical Psychiatry News* 26, no. 6 (1998): 23.

———. "Herbal Remedies May Be Useful Anxiolytics." *Clinical Psychiatry News* 26, no. 6 (1998B): 23.

Sherwin, B. B. "Affective Changes with Estrogen and Androgen Replacement Therapy in Surgically Menopausal Women." *Journal of Affective Disorders* 14 (1988): 177–187.

Siblerud, R. L. "A Comparison of Mental Health of Multiple Sclerosis Patients with Silver/Mercury Dental Fillings and Those with Fillings Removed." *Psychological Reports* 70 (June 1992): 1139–1151.

———. "The Relationship Between Mercury from Dental Amalgam and Mental Health." *American Journal of Psychotherapy* 43 (October 1989): 575–587.

Sichel, D. A., et al. "Prophylactic Estrogen in Recurrent Postpartum Affective Disorder." *Biological Psychiatry* 38 (December 15, 1995): 814–818.

Simons, A. D., et al. "Cognitive Therapy and Pharmacotherapy for Depression." *Archives of General Psychiatry* 43 (January 1986): 43–48.

Simonson, M. "L-Phenylalanine" (letter). *Journal of Clinical Psychiatry* 46 (August 1985): 355.

Sinclair, H. M. "Essential Fatty Acids in Perspective." *Human Nutrition: Clinical Nutrition* 38C (1984): 245–260.

Slagle, Priscilla. *The Way Up from Down*. New York: Random House, 1987.

Smith, D. F., and M. Schou. "Kidney Function and Lithium Concentrations of Rats Given an Injection of Lithium Orotate or Lithium Carbonate." *Journal of Pharmacy and Pharmacology* 31 (March 1979): 161–163.

Smith, Lendon. *Feed Yourself Right.* New York: McGraw-Hill, 1983.

Smith, R. N., et al. "A Randomised Comparison Over 8 Months of 100 Micrograms and 200 Micrograms Twice Weekly Doses of Transdermal Oestradiol in the Treatment of Severe Premenstrual Syndrome." *British Journal of Obstetrics and Gynaecology* 102 (June 1995): 475–484.

Smithies, J. R., et al. "Abnormalities of One-Carbon Metabolism in Psychiatric Disorders." *Biological Psychiatry* 21 (1986): 1391–1398.

Snow, R. F. "Letter from the Editor: Family Heroes." *American Heritage* 49 (November 1998): 9.

Song, C., et al. "The Inflammatory Response System and the Availability of Plasma Tryptophan in Patients with Primary Sleep Disorders and Major Depression." *Journal of Affective Disorders* 49 (June 1998): 211–219.

Sourkes, T. L. "Toxicology of Serotonin Precursors." *Advances in Biological Psychiatry* 10 (1983): 160–175.

South, James. "Controversy Erupts About Safety of 5-HTP." *Nutritional News* 11 (March 1997). Also published at www.vrp.com.

Southmayd, S. E., et al. "Therapeutic Sleep Deprivation in a Depressed Patient: Prolongation of Response with Concurrent Thyroxine." *Acta Psychiatrica Scandinavica* 86 (July 1992): 84–85.

Souza, F. G., and G. M. Goodwin. "Lithium Treatment and Prophylaxis in Unipolar Depression: A Meta-Analysis." *British Journal of Psychiatry* 158 (May 1991): 666–675.

Soyka, Fred, and Alan Edmunds. *The Ion Effect.* Toronto: Lester and Orpen, 1977.

Spector, R., et al. "Is Idiopathic Dementia a Regional Vitamin Deficiency State?" *Medical Hypotheses* 5 (1979): 763–767.

Spring, B., et al. "Psychobiological Effects of Carbohydrates." *Journal of Clinical Psychiatry* 50 (Supplement, May 1989): 27–34.

Stahl, S. M. "Why Settle for Silver When You Can Go for Gold? Response vs. Recovery as the Goal of Antidepressant Therapy." *Journal of Clinical Psychiatry* 60 (April 1999): 213–214.

———. "Basic Psychopharmacology of Antidepressants, Part 2: Estrogen as an Adjunct to Antidepressant Treatment." *Journal of Clinical Psychiatry* 59 (Supplement 4, 1998): 15–24.

Staufenberg, E. F., and D. Tantam. "Malignant Hyperpyrexia Syndrome in Combined Treatment" (letter), *British Journal of Psychiatry* 154 (April 1989): 577–578.

Stavrovskaia, I. G., et al. "Optimization of Energy-Dependent Processes in Mitochondria from Rat Liver and Brain After Inhalation of Negative Air Ions" (in Russian). *Biofizika* 43 (September–October 1998): 766–771.

Steinman, David. *Diet for a Poisoned Planet.* New York: Harmony Books, 1990.

Sternbach, H. "Age-Associated Testosterone Decline in Men: Clinical Issues for Psychiatry." *American Journal of Psychiatry* 155 (October 1998): 1310–1318.

Sternberg, D. E. "Testing for Physical Illness in Psychiatric Patients." *Journal of Clinical Psychiatry* 47 (Supplement, January 1986): 3–9.

Sternberg, E. M., et al. "Development of a Scleroderma-Like Illness During Therapy with L-5-Hydroxytryptophan and Carbidopa." *New England Journal of Medicine* 303 (October 2, 1980): 782–787.

Sterner, R. T., and W. R. Price. "Restricted Riboflavin: Within Subject Behavioral Effects in Humans." *American Journal of Clinical Nutrition* 26 (1973): 150–160.

Stewart, D. E. "Psychiatric Assessment of Patients with '20th Century Disease' ('Total Allergy Syndrome')." *Canadian Medical Association Journal* 133 (1985): 1001–1006.

Stewart, J. W., et al. "Low B_6 Levels in Depressed Outpatients." *Biological Psychiatry* 19, no. 4 (1984): 613–616.

Stoll, A. L., and L. B. Marangell. "In Reply." *Archives of General Psychiatry* 56 (May 1999): 415–416.

Stoll, A. L., et al. "Omega-3 Fatty Acids in Bipolar Disorder: A Preliminary Double-Blind, Placebo-Controlled Trial." *Archives of General Psychiatry* 56 (May 1999): 407–412.

Stoll, A. L., et al. "Choline in the Treatment of Rapid-Cycling Bipolar Disorder: Clinical and Neurochemical Findings in Lithium-Treated Patients." *Biological Psychiatry* 40 (September 1, 1996): 382–388.

Strong, G. A. "Health Risks Associated with Mercury from Dental Amalgams" (letter). *Nurse Practitioner* 18 (June 1993): 14–15, 21.

Strupp, H. H., and S. W. Hadley. "Specific vs. Nonspecific Factors in Psychotherapy: A Controlled Study of Outcome." *Archives of General Psychiatry* 36 (September 1979): 1125–1136.

Strupp, H. H., et al. "Psychodynamic Therapy: Theory and Research." In *Short-Term Psychotherapies for Depression,* edited by John A. Rush, 215–250. New York: The Guilford Press, 1982.

Studd, J. "Oestrogens and Depression in Women" (editorial). *British Journal of Hospital Medicine* 48 (September 2–15, 1992): 211–213.

Styron, William. *Darkness Visible: A Memoir of Madness.* New York: Vintage Books, 1992.

Suboticanec, K., et al. "Vitamin C Status in Chronic Schizophrenia." *Biological Psychiatry* 28 (1990): 959–956.

Suedfeld, P., et al. "Reduction of Post-ECT Memory Complaints Through Brief, Partial Restricted Environmental Stimulation (REST)." *Progress in Neuro-Psychopharmacology & Biological Psychiatry* 13 (1989): 693–700.

Sugerman, A. A., et al. "A Study of Antibody Levels in Alcoholic, Depressive and Schizophrenic Patients." *Annals of Allergy* 48 (March 1982): 166–171.

Sullivan, G. M., et al. "Low Levels of Transthyretin in the CSF of Depressed Patients." *American Journal of Psychiatry* 156 (May 1999): 710–715.

Sulman, Felix G. *Short and Long-Term Changes in Climate,* Vols. I and II. Boca Raton, FL: CRC Press, 1982.

Summers, W. K., et al. "The Psychiatric Physical Examination—Part II: Findings in 75 Unselected Psychiatric Patients." *Journal of Clinical Psychiatry* 42 (March 1981): 99–102.

Sussman, Aaron, and Ruth Goode. *The Magic of Walking.* New York: Simon & Schuster, 1967.

Swartz, C. M., and G. Guadagno. "Melancholia with Onset During Treatment with SSRIs." *Annals of Clinical Psychiatry* 10 (December 1998): 177–179.

Talbott, John, et al., eds. *The American Psychiatric Press Textbook of Psychiatry.* Washington, DC: American Psychiatric Press, 1988.

Tamborini, A., and R. Taurelle. "Value of Standardized Ginkgo Biloba Extract (EGb 761) in the Management of Congestive Symptoms of Premenstrual Syndrome" (in French). *Revue Francaise de Gynecologie et de Obstetrique* 88 (July–September 1993): 447–457.

Taylor, Joyal. *The Complete Guide to Mercury Toxicity from Dental Fillings.* San Diego: Scripps Publishing, 1988.

Taylor, L. A., and S. J. Rachman. "The Effects of Blood Sugar Level Changes on Cognitive Function, Affective State, and Somatic Symptoms." *Journal of Behavioral Medicine* 11, no. 3 (1988): 279–291.

Teasdale, J. D. et al. "How Does Cognitive Therapy Prevent Depressive Relapse and Why Should Attentional Control (Mindfulness) Training Help?" *Behaviour Research and Therapy* 33 (January 1995): 25–39.

Teicher, M. H., et al. "Antidepressant Drugs and the Emergence of Suicidal Tendencies." *Drug Safety* 8 (March 1993): 186–212.

Terman, M, et al. "A Controlled Trial of Timed Bright Light and Negative Air Ionization for Treatment of Winter Depression." *Archives of General Psychiatry* 55 (October 1998): 875–882.

Terman, M., and J. S. Terman. "Treatment of Seasonal Affective Disorder with a High-Output Negative Ionizer." *Journal of Alternative and Complementary Medicine* 1 (January 1995): 87–92.

Terr, A. I. "Clinical Ecology" (editorial). *Journal of Allergy and Clinical Immunology* 79 (March 1987): 423–426.

Thakar, J. H., et al. "Erythrocyte Membrane Sodium-Potassium and Magnesium ATPase in Primary Affective Disorder." *Biological Psychiatry* 20 (July 1985): 734–740.

Thase, M. E., and E. S. Friedman. "Is Psychotherapy an Effective Treatment for Melancholia and Other Severe Depressive States?" *Journal of Affective Disorders* 54 (July 1999): 1–19.

Thase, M. E., et al. "Treatment of Major Depression with Psychotherapy or Psychotherapy-Pharmacotherapy Combinations." *Archives of General Psychiatry* 54 (November 1997): 1009–1015.

Thase, M. E., et al. "Social Skills Training and Endogenous Depression." *Journal of Behavior Therapy and Experimental Psychiatry* 15 (June 1984): 101–108.

Thompson, Tracy. *The Beast: A Reckoning with Depression.* New York: Plume, 1996.

Thomson, J., et al. "The Treatment of Depression in General Practice: A Comparison of L-Tryptophan, Amitriptyline, and a Combination of L-Tryptophan and Amitriptyline with Placebo." *Psychological Medicine* 12 (November 1982): 741–751.

Thoreau, Henry David. "Walking." *Atlantic Monthly* (June 1862). Reprinted in *The Magic of Walking*, by Aaron Sussman and Ruth Goode. New York: Simon & Schuster, 1967.

Tierra, M. "Kava: Powerful Antistress Herb." No date. Published online at www.planetherbs.com.

Tierra, Michael. *Biomagnetic and Herbal Therapy.* Twin Lakes, WI: Lotus Press, 1997.

Tonge, W. L. "Nicotinic Acid in the Treatment of Depression." *Annals of Internal Medicine* 38 (1953): 551–553.

Torrey, E. Fuller. *Witchdoctors and Psychiatrists: The Common Roots of Psychotherapy and Its Future.* New York: Harper & Row, 1986.

Trowbridge, John Parks, and Morton Walker. *The Yeast Syndrome.* New York: Bantam, 1986.

Truss, C. O. "The Role of Candida Albicans in Human Illness." *Journal of Orthomolecular Psychiatry* 10, no. 4 (1981): 228–238.

Tu, J. B., et al. "Iron Deficiency in Two Adolescents with Conduct, Dysthymic and Movement Disorders." *Canadian Journal of Psychiatry* 39 (August 1994): 371–375.

Turner, J. G., et al. "The Effect of Therapeutic Touch on Pain and Anxiety in Burn Patients." *Journal of Advanced Nursing* 28 (July 1998): 10–20.

Uhde, T. W., et al. "Glucose Tolerance Testing in Panic Disorder." *American Journal of Psychiatry* 141 (November 1984): 1461–1463.

Ulett, G. "Food Allergy—Cytotoxic Testing and the Central Nervous System." *Psychiatric Journal of the University of Ottawa* 5, no. 2 (1980): 100–108.

Ulett, G. A., et al. "Electroacupuncture: Mechanisms and Clinical Application." *Biological Psychiatry* 44 (July 15, 1998): 129–138.

Ullman, Dana. *Homeopathy: Medicine for the 21st Century.* Berkeley, CA: North Atlantic Books, 1988.

Ullman, Robert, and Judyth Reichenberg-Ullman. *Prozac-Free: Homeopathic Medicine for Depression, Anxiety, and Other Mental and Emotional Problems.* Rocklin, CA: Prima Publishing, 1999.

Urban, M. J. "Auditory Subliminal Stimulation: A Reexamination." *Perceptual and Motor Skills* 74 (April 1992): 515–541.

Vallbona, C., et al. "Response of Pain to Static Magnetic Fields in Postpolio Patients: A Double-Blind Pilot Study." *Archives of Physical Medicine and Rehabilitation* 78 (November 1997): 1200–1203.

Van Hiele, L. J. "L-5-hydroxytryptophan in Depression: The First Substitution Therapy in Psychiatry?" *Neuropsychobiology* 6, no. 4 (1980): 230–240.

Van Praag, Herman M. "Studies in the Mechanism of Action of Serotonin Precursors in Depression." *Psychopharmacology Bulletin* 20 (Summer 1984): 599–602.

Van Praag, H. M. "Management of Depression with Serotonin Precursors." *Biological Psychiatry* 16, no. 3 (1981): 291–310.

Vanselow, W., et al. "Effect of Progesterone and Its 5 Alpha and 5 Beta Metabolites on Symptoms of Premenstrual Syndrome According to Route of Administration." *Journal of Psychosomatic Obstetrics and Gynaecology* 17 (March 1996): 29–38.

Van Tiggelen, C. J. M., et al. "Vitamin B_{12} Levels of Cerebrospinal Fluid in Patients with Organic Mental Disorder." *Journal of Orthomolecular Psychiatry* 12, no. 4 (1983): 305–311.

Van Wassenhoven, M. "Homeopathy" (in French). *Revue Medicale de Bruxelles* 19 (September 1998): A277–282.

Veleber, D. M., and D. I. Templer. "Effects of Caffeine on Anxiety and Depression." *Journal of Abnormal Psychology* 93 (February 1984): 120–122.

Venolia, Carol. *Healing Environments*. Berkeley, CA: Celestial Arts, 1988.

Vlissides, D. N., et al. "A Double-Blind Gluten-Free/Gluten-Load Controlled Trial in a Secure Ward Population." *British Journal of Psychiatry* 148 (April 1986): 447–451.

Vogel, W., et al. "A Comparison of the Antidepressant Effects of a Synthetic Androgen (Mesterolone) and Amitriptyline in Depressed Men." *Journal of Clinical Psychiatry* 46 (January 1985): 6–8.

Vollmann, J., and M. Berger. "Sleep Deprivation with Consecutive Sleep-Phase Advance Therapy in Patients with Major Depression: A Pilot Study." *Biological Psychiatry* 33 (1993): 54–57.

Vorbach, E. U., et al. "Efficacy and Tolerability of St. John's Wort Extract LI 160 Versus Imipramine in Patients with Severe Depressive Episodes According to ICD-10." *Pharmacopsychiatry* 30 (Supplement 2, September 1997): 81–85.

Wagner, G. J., and J. G. Rabkin. "Testosterone Therapy for Clinical Symptoms of Hypogonadism in Eugonadal Men with AIDS." *International Journal of STD and AIDS* 9 (January 1998): 41–44.

Wagner, G. J., et al. "Testosterone as a Treatment for Fatigue in HIV+ Men." *General Hospital Psychiatry* 20 (July 1998): 209–213.

Wagner, G. J., et al. "A Comparative Analysis of Standard and Alternative Antidepressants in the Treatment of Human Immunodeficiency Virus Patients." *Comprehensive Psychiatry* 37 (November–December 1996): 402–408.

Walker, A. F., et al. "Magnesium Supplementation Alleviates Premenstrual Symptoms of Fluid Retention." *Journal of Women's Health* 7 (November 1998): 1157–1165.

Warnecke, G. "Psychosomatic Dysfunctions in the Female Climacteric: Clinical Effectiveness and Tolerance of Kava Extract WS 1490" (in German). *Fortschritte Der Medizin* 109 (1991): 119–122.

Warner, R. L., et al. "Transcranial Electrostimulation Effects on Rat Opioid and Neurotransmitter Levels." *Life Sciences* 54, no. 7 (1994): 481–490.

Washburne, A. C. "Nicotinic Acid in the Treatment of Certain Depressed States: A Preliminary Report." *Annals of Internal Medicine* 32 (February 1950): 261–269.

Weeks, Nora. *The Medical Discoveries of Edward Bach, Physician*. Los Angeles: Keats Publishing, 1979.

Wehr, T. A., et al. "Treatment of Rapidly Cycling Bipolar Patient by Using Extended Bed Rest and Darkness to Stabilize the Timing and Duration of Sleep." *Biological Psychiatry* 43 (June 1, 1998): 822–828.

Wehr, T. A., et al. "Seasonal Affective Disorder with Summer Depression and Winter Hypomania." *American Journal of Psychiatry* 144 (December 1987): 1602–1603.

Wehr, T. A., et al. "Phase Advance of the Circadian Sleep-Wake Cycle as an Antidepressant." *Science* 206 (1979): 710–713.

Weil, Andrew. *Natural Health, Natural Medicine*, rev. ed. Boston: Houghton Mifflin, 1995.

Weintraub, P. "Scentimental Journeys." *Omni* (April 1986): 48–49, 52, 114, 116.

Weiss, B. "Intersections of Psychiatry and Toxicology." *International Journal of Mental Health* 14, no. 3 (1985): 7–25.

———. "Behavioral Toxicology and Environmental Health Science." *American Psychologist* (November 1983): 1174–1187.

Wells, A. S., et al. "Alterations in Mood After Changing to a Low-Fat Diet." *British Journal of Nutrition* 79 (January 1998): 23–30.

Wensel, Louise O. *Acupuncture in Medical Practice*. Reston, VA: Reston Publishing, 1980.

Wessel, K., et al. "Double-Blind Crossover Study with Levorotary Form of Hydroxytryptophan in Patients with Degenerative Cerebellar Diseases." *Archives of Neurology* 52, no. 5 (1995): 451–455.

Wheatley, D. "Hypericum in Seasonal Affective Disorder (SAD)." *Current Medical Research and Opinion* 15, no. 1 (1999): 33–37.

Williams, S. "Can Magnets Ease Severe Depression?" *Newsweek* 132 (September 21, 1998): 107.

Winter, Arthur, and Ruth Winter. *Eat Right, Be Bright.* New York: St. Martin's Press, 1988.

Wirz-Justice, A., et al. "An Open Trial of Light Therapy in Hospitalized Major Depression." *Journal of Affective Disorders* 52 (1999): 291–292.

Wirz-Justice, A., et al. "'Natural' Light Treatment of Seasonal Affective Disorder." *Journal of Affective Disorders* 37 (April 12, 1996): 109–120.

Wittenborn, J. R. "A Search for Responders to Niacin Supplementation." *Archives of General Psychiatry* 31 (1974): 547–552.

Wolkowitz, O. M., et al. "Double-Blind Treatment of Major Depression with Dehydroepiandrosterone." *American Journal of Psychiatry* 156 (April 1999): 646–649.

Wong, A. H. C., et al. "Herbal Remedies in Psychiatric Practice." *Archives of General Psychiatry* 55 (November 1998): 1033–1044.

Wood, N. C., et al. "Abnormal Intestinal Permeability: An Aetiological Factor in Chronic Psychiatric Disorders?" *British Journal of Psychiatry* 150 (1987): 853–856.

Wooten, P. "Humor: An Antidote for Stress." *Holistic Nursing Practice* 10 (January 1996): 49–56.

Worwood, Valerie Ann. *The Fragrant Mind.* Novato, CA: New World Library, 1996.

Wurtman, R. J., and J. J. Wurtman. "Carbohydrates and Depression." *Scientific American* (January 1989): 68–75.

Wyatt, K. M., et al. "Efficacy of Vitamin B$_6$ in the Treatment of Premenstrual Syndrome: Systematic Review." *British Medical Journal* 318 (May 22, 1999): 1375–1381.

Wynn, V., et al. "Tryptophan, Depression and Steroidal Contraception." *Journal of Steroid Biochemistry* 6 (1975): 965–970.

Yapko, Michael. *Breaking the Patterns of Depression.* New York: Doubleday, 1997.

Yaryura-Tobias, J. A., et al. "Phenylalanine for Endogenous Depression." *Journal of Orthomolecular Psychiatry* 3, no. 2 (1974): 80–81.

Young, S. N. "The Use of Diet and Dietary Components in the Study of Factors Controlling Affect in Humans: A Review." *Journal of Psychiatry and Neuroscience* 18 (November 1993): 235–244.

Zamm, A. V. "Candida Albicans Therapy." *Journal of Orthomolecular Medicine* 1, no. 4 (1986): 261–266.

Zmilacher, K., et al. "L-5-hydroxytryptophan Alone and in Combination with a Peripheral Decarboxylase Inhibitor in the Treatment of Depression." *Neuropsychobiology* 20 (1988): 28–35.

Zuess, Jonathan. *The Wisdom of Depression: A Guide to Understanding and Curing Depression Using Natural Medicine.* New York: Harmony Books, 1998.

Zwerling, M. H., et al. "'Think Yeast'—The Expanding Spectrum of Candidiasis." *Journal of the South Carolina Medical Association* 9 (September 1984): 454–456.

Index